The Financial System, Financial Regulation and Central Bank Policy

Traditional money and banking textbooks are long, expensive and full of so much institutional and technical modeling detail that students can't understand the big picture. Thomas F. Cargill presents a new alternative: a short, inexpensive book without the "bells and whistles" that teaches students the fundamentals in a clear, narrative form. In an engaging writing style, Cargill explains the three core components of money and banking, and their interactions: 1), the financial system; 2), government regulation and supervision; and, 3), central bank policy. Cargill focuses on the interaction between government financial policy and central bank policy and offers a critique of the central bank's role in the economy, the tools it uses, how these tools affect the economy and how effective these policies have been, providing a more balanced perspective of government policy failure versus market failure than traditional textbooks.

Professor Thomas F. Cargill has taught and conducted research on financial and monetary economics at the University of California, Davis; the University of Hawaii, at both Honolulu and Saigon (Ho Chi Minh City), Vietnam; California State University, Sacramento; Purdue University, at West Lafayette, Indiana; and, since 1973, the University of Nevada, Reno. He has written extensively as a single and joint author on U.S. financial and central banking issues and has also conducted similar research on China, South Korea, Japan and Vietnam. His work has been published in *The Journal of Economic History*, *Journal of Money, Credit and Banking*, *The Journal of Finance*, *Journal of Political Economy*, *Review of Economics and Statistics* and *International Finance*. His work has also been published by Cambridge University Press, Hoover Institution Press, the MIT Press and Oxford University Press.

The Financial System, Financial Regulation and Central Bank Policy

THOMAS F. CARGILL
University of Nevada, Reno

CAMBRIDGE
UNIVERSITY PRESS

CAMBRIDGE
UNIVERSITY PRESS

University Printing House, Cambridge CB2 8BS, United Kingdom

One Liberty Plaza, 20th Floor, New York, NY 10006, USA

477 Williamstown Road, Port Melbourne, VIC 3207, Australia

4843/24, 2nd Floor, Ansari Road, Daryaganj, Delhi - 110002, India

79 Anson Road, #06-04/06, Singapore 079906

Cambridge University Press is part of the University of Cambridge.

It furthers the University's mission by disseminating knowledge in the pursuit of education, learning and research at the highest international levels of excellence.

www.cambridge.org
Information on this title: www.cambridge.org/9781107035676
DOI: 10.1017/9781139565172

© Thomas F. Cargill 2017

First published 2017

Printed in the United States of America by Sheridan Books, Inc.

A catalogue record for this publication is available from the British Library

Library of Congress Cataloging-in-Publication data
Names: Cargill, Thomas F., author.
Title: The financial system, financial regulation and central bank policy /
Thomas F. Cargill.
Description: New York : Cambridge University Press, 2017. | Includes
bibliographical references and index.
Identifiers: LCCN 2017001521 | ISBN 9781107035676 (hardback) |
ISBN 9781107689763 (paperback)
Subjects: LCSH: Banks and banking, Central. | Finance–Government policy. |
Banking law. | BISAC: BUSINESS & ECONOMICS / International / Economics.
Classification: LCC HG1811 .C373 2017 | DDC 332.1/1–dc23
LC record available at https://lccn.loc.gov/2017001521
ISBN 978-1-107-03567-6 Hardback
ISBN 978-1-107-68976-3 Paperback

Contents

Figures

Tables

Preface

There are many excellent monetary economics textbooks in terms of coverage and pedagogical tools written by accomplished monetary economists. So why another textbook? This book differs from the traditional money and banking textbook in three significant ways: first, it offers a unifying framework; second, it approaches many topics from a different perspective from other textbooks; and, third, it offers a less encyclopedic approach than that presented in other textbooks.

Unifying Framework in This Book

The topics and the order of chapters are presented in the context of a unifying framework referred to as the nation's financial and monetary regime. The nation's financial and monetary regime consists of these three parts: 1) the financial system; 2) government regulation and supervision; and 3) central banks and central bank policy. Each component of the regime is addressed in a logical order so that the student can obtain a unified perspective of the most important topics covered in a monetary economics course.

Approach to Topics in This Book

In the context of the unifying framework of the nation's financial and monetary regime, this book offers different perspectives, both in terms of pedagogical presentation and issues.

First, discussion of central bank policy itself is organized around a five-step sequence to assist student understanding of the role of central banks and central bank policy: 1), the central bank; 2), the tools of monetary policy; 3), policy instruments; 4), the model; and, 5), the final policy targets. Like the unifying framework of the nation's financial and monetary regime, this five-step sequence provides a unifying framework for the student to organize the many elements of central banks and central bank policy.

Second, the book aims to incorporate history and policy along with the analytical concepts necessary to understand the nation's financial and monetary regime; that is, the subject is viewed more from a political economy perspective than from the analytical and detailed model perspective of most traditional textbooks. The analytical subjects are not central to the book and are developed only to the extent necessary to understand the nation's financial and monetary regime. The IS/LM model is not included. Instead, the "old" and "new" Phillips curves, along with a brief introduction to the AD/AS model, are used to illustrate the relationship between central bank policy and the economy. Rather than devote space to a detailed macroeconomic model, more attention is devoted to the three major periods of economic distress in the United States – 1), the Great Depression; 2), the Great Inflation; and, 3), the Great Recession – as well as two periods of a stable macroeconomic environment: 4), the Great Moderation; and, 5), financial liberalization.

Third, the book emphasizes the interaction between government financial policy and central bank policy as the source of much economic and financial distress and, unlike traditional textbooks, focuses on the problems of Federal Reserve policy. The majority of textbooks, in this writer's opinion, devote insufficient attention to the policy errors made by the Federal Reserve in the past. Some may regard this as normative, but the large body of research now available suggests that the Federal Reserve has importantly contributed to economic and financial distress far more often than is discussed in the majority of commonly used textbooks. This book attempts to present a more balanced perspective of government policy failure versus market failure. There is indeed much market failure, and there is indeed much necessity for government involvement in the financial and monetary regime to support economic growth, but, at the same time, there have been mistakes in monetary policy and financial regulation that have generated economic and financial distress, and this needs to be presented.

Fourth, this book presents a more realistic perspective of central bank independence. The treatment of central bank independence in traditional textbooks is often superficial and misleading; for example, ignoring the distinction between *de jure* and *de facto* independence; ignoring the documented close relationship between the Federal Reserve and the government during the period of the Great Inflation from 1965 to 1979; and failing to point out that formal independence has been a rather poor predictor of good monetary policy outcomes, as manifested by the experiences of the Federal Reserve and the Bank of Japan during the Great Inflation period. In contrast to most traditional textbooks, which downplay the political economy of monetary policy and the public choice perspective of central bank policy, this book emphasizes the overwhelming evidence that the policy of the Federal Reserve, despite its formal independence, has been strongly influenced by government. Central bank independence is more myth than reality.

Fifth, the book emphasizes how the structure of the financial system and monetary policy interact and, at times, generate economic and financial distress. The financial distress in the 1970s was not only due to inflation in the context of Regulation Q and other portfolio limitations but was also a well-documented failure of the Federal Reserve to even take into account the resource allocation effects of Regulation Q. The same error was made in the first few years of the new century, when the Federal Reserve failed to take into account how an unprecedented easy monetary policy combined with a financial structure designed to allocate credit to imprudent mortgage lending supported by government-sponsored enterprises distorted resources and generated a bubble, such as had happened in Japan 15 years earlier. The United States devotes significant resources to subsidizing the housing sector, with two suboptimal outcomes: first, in terms of homeownership, the United States ranks well below other countries that do not subsidize housing to the same degree as in the United States; and, second, the subsidization of housing has imposed a serious resource cost on the economy, especially in its contributing role in the Great Inflation and the Great Recession.

Sixth, there is no serious debate in the economic profession over the long-run neutrality of monetary policy, but considerable debate over the nonneutrality of monetary policy in the short run. While current textbooks do a good job explaining the difference between the short- and long-run effects of monetary policy, the detailed models presented in most traditional money and banking textbooks confuse students because the limits of monetary policy are not emphasized, implying that monetary policy is capable of short-run stabilization, whereas institutional, historical and theoretical developments over the last four decades suggest that this is not realistic. This book emphasizes the limits of central bank policy to a greater extent than the traditional money and banking textbooks.

The Structure of This Book Focuses on the Primary Elements of the Nation's Financial and Monetary Regime

The structure of typical money and banking textbooks shares several common features. They are encyclopedic in coverage. They are long. They are expensive, because of length, production characteristics and other attempts at product differentiation. In their effort to be encyclopedic in coverage, they lack a unifying framework that can be used to organize the various topics. This writer includes his own money and banking textbook, published by Prentice Hall in 1979, in this group. The book was reasonably successful; however, by the fourth edition, published in 1991, it had become encyclopedic, long and expensive. As a result, this writer ceased using his own textbook and resorted to a "yellow book" approach, consisting of a few chapters from the book, specifically prepared notes, data and figures, and articles organized around a unifying framework. The objective was to cover all of the relevant topics in a one-semester course, which is virtually impossible with any traditional textbook. The "yellow book" designation came from the color of the front and back covers. The yellow book, combined with lectures, presented a different perspective on the subject with a unifying structure that made it easier for the students to understand the various topics as part of one framework rather than a series of disconnected chapters. The students appreciated the cost (cheap compared to any textbook) and seemed to better understand the material because of the unifying framework. The majority of my money and banking students are business majors who need an overview of money and banking as part of their business program. I have used the approach presented in this book for a number of years in various monetary economic courses at both the undergraduate and MBA level at the University of Nevada, Reno, the University of Hawaii, Honolulu, and the University of Hawaii, Saigon (Ho Chi Minh City), Vietnam.

The yellow book approach attracted the attention of another academic publisher while I was working on a Japanese financial and monetary policy project, but as the project evolved I was increasingly encouraged to make the book more traditional, such as including the IS/LM macroeconomic model, at which point I lost interest and returned the publisher's advance. A decade later, while working with Cambridge University Press on another Japan project, I was encouraged to prepare a manuscript that would be an alternative in presentation and less expensive than the traditional money and banking textbooks that now dominate the market. This book is the outcome.

Organization of the Book

The book is divided into five parts, for a total of 17 chapters.

Part I – Introduction to the Financial and Monetary Regime: Chapters 1 and 2 present the basic elements of the nation's financial and monetary regime: the three components of the regime; the relationship between the regime and economic activity; case studies of how a malfunctioning regime generates economic and financial distress (Chapter 1); and basic concepts regarding the definition, measurement and value of money and the basic short-run and long-run relationship between money and economic activity (Chapter 2).

Part II – The Financial System Component of the Financial and Monetary Regime: Chapters 3 through 7 discuss the first component of the regime – the financial system – and present the structure of the financial system in flow of funds terms (Chapter 3), interest rate basics (Chapter 4), the level of the interest rate (Chapter 5), the structure of interest rates (Chapter 6) and exchange rates and other international dimensions of the financial system (Chapter 7).

Part III – The Role of Government in the Financial and Monetary Regime: Chapters 8 through 10 discuss the second component of the regime – the general argument for the role of government to prevent the "economic equivalent of counterfeiting" – in the context of the historical evolution of monetary systems (Chapter 8), asymmetric information and adverse selection and the various levels of government financial regulation and supervision (Chapter 9) and a short history of government financial regulation and central banking in the United States (Chapter 10).

Part IV – Five Steps to Understanding Central Banks and Central Bank Policy: Chapters 11 through 16 discuss the third component of the regime – central banks and central bank policy – in terms of a five-step sequence of central bank policy. These chapters discuss the institutional design of central banks (Chapter 11 – Step 1), the money supply process in the context of a modern monetary system (Chapter 12), the tools of monetary policy and monetary policy instruments (Chapter 13 – Steps 2 and 3), the central bank macroeconomic model (Chapter 14 – Step 4) and the final policy targets (Chapter 15 – Step 5). A separate discussion of the tactics and strategy of monetary policy involving all five steps is presented (Chapter 16), with a discussion of the Federal Reserve's evolution of a tactical and strategic framework, the Taylor rule, debate between the discretion and rules approaches to monetary policy, and the concepts of the Lucas critique and time inconsistency.

Part V – Performance of the U.S. Financial and Monetary Regime: Chapter 17 completes the book with a review of the performance of the U.S. financial regime, focusing on five periods in chronological order: 1), the Great Depression; 2), the Great Inflation; 3), financial liberalization; 4), the Great Moderation; and, 5), the Great Recession. Three are periods of economic and financial distress while two are periods of stability. The different views of the Great Recession are presented, along with a concluding discussion of the challenges facing the Federal Reserve as we close the second decade of the new century.

The chapters are designed for a one-semester course in money and banking. The length of the book is designed so that most, or even all, chapters can be assigned. Instructors who might use this book can eliminate any chapter they wish; however, the book is written as a unified presentation. Chapters 10 and 17 are the most historical of the book and thus would be candidates for omission without an adverse impact on presenting the topics as part of the unified framework of the nation's financial and monetary regime.

Note of Appreciation

In closing, I would like to thank Susanna Powers, a former MA student at the University of Nevada, Reno, for her careful review of two drafts of the manuscript and for preparing multiple choice/true–false questions for the book, which were reviewed and extended by the author; T. Steven Jackson, another former MA student, for reading the manuscript and using the manuscript in his MBA class on monetary and financial economics at the University of Nevada, Reno; and Jeffrey L. Stroup, a former undergraduate and graduate student at the University of Nevada, Reno, for reading the manuscript. Any remaining errors are the responsibility of the author. I would also like to thank the many undergraduate and graduate MBA students at the University of Nevada, Reno, the University of Hawaii, Honolulu, and the University of Hawaii, Ho Chi Minh City, Vietnam, who over the years have used the yellow book version of this manuscript. The manuscript for this book was used by this writer in Vietnam in June 2016 and at the University of Nevada, Reno, in fall 2016. I especially wish to thank University of Nevada, Reno, money and banking students Hannah Bass, Megan Boyden and Narae Wadsworth for providing a number of comments on many chapters.

It was these students and their need for a straightforward approach to monetary economics that served as the catalysts for this book. I thank Cambridge University Press for their confidence in me and willingness to offer a different alternative to the traditional money and banking textbook. Finally, I thank Mary Cargill, my wife of 53 years, for her support and encouragement.

Part I

Introduction to the Financial and Monetary Regime

Chapter 1

The Financial and Monetary Regime

1.1 Introduction

This book is about a country's financial and monetary regime and the interaction between the regime and the economy. The financial and monetary regime is an important element of the economic and political environment in which we live and work, and some basic knowledge of it is necessary if one wants to consider oneself educated. In fact, anyone not familiar with the basic elements of the financial and monetary regime and its relationship to economic activity should consider him-/herself less than well informed, both as an individual and as a member of society. Lacking knowledge about its basic elements is not only dangerous to your economic health but dangerous to your ability to participate in the political process.

Knowledge of the financial and monetary regime will not guarantee economic success, but it will help you avoid mistakes that will surely limit your lifetime wealth. On a broader level, lacking knowledge about the basic elements of the financial and monetary regime renders you a low-information voter, or "useful idiot", easily manipulated by politicians on either side of the aisle. The term gained new life in late 2014 when it became widely known that one of the major consultants to the 2010 Affordable Care Act claimed, to a group of economists at a conference, that the public's lack of economic understanding and their basic "stupidity" about economics played an important role in enacting a major overhaul of and expanded role of government in the U.S. health system (Bierman, 2014).

This was a dark day for the role of an economist in public policy, but it offers an important lesson. Irrespective of one's view of the Act, the mindset that subterfuge is acceptable for major expansions in government should give everyone pause about government activism. Government, whether to the right or left, does not always have the best interest of the individual in mind and often relies on uninformed voters to pass complex legislation and pursue policies that may not be in the best interests of the country. At a minimum, understanding the basic elements

3

of the financial and monetary regime will help you manage your wealth and render you a more informed observer of important public policy debates that greatly influence your life and reduce your reliance on "talking heads", who dominate the news media and who, unfortunately, haven't a clue about most of the contents of this book.

1.2 A Country's Financial and Monetary Regime

Every country has a financial and monetary regime consisting of diverse private and public institutions and markets, and in most cases the basic components of the financial and monetary regime and their responsibilities are country-invariant. That is, while the institutional details differ from country to country, determined by their political structure, industrial policy, culture and history, the differences pale in comparison to the similarities of their respective financial and monetary regimes.

In the most general sense, a country's financial and monetary regime consists of three components: the *financial system*; *government financial regulation and supervision*; and the *central bank and central bank policy*.

The *financial system* consists of financial institutions and markets. Banks and insurance companies are examples of financial institutions that obtain funds by offering deposits, insurance policies, retirement programs to the public, and then lend those funds. Financial markets deal in money and capital market instruments such as commercial paper, government bonds, corporate bonds and equities. The financial system has five basic functions in the economy: first, institutionalize the savings-investment process; second, provide for an efficient transfer of funds from lenders to borrowers; third, provide flexibility in response to the changing requirements of different stages of economic growth; fourth, provide stability in the transfer of funds from lenders to borrowers; and, fifth, provide a platform for the conduct of central bank policy that ensures a wide and effective distribution of the impact of central bank policy.

Government regulation and supervision of the financial system are designed to ensure the safety and soundness of the financial system, ensure that the financial system is transparent and ensure that the financial system provides a wide range of financial services to the public. Government regulation and supervision, however, often adopt additional objectives, such as using the financial system as an instrument of industrial policy to support specific sectors of the economy or as an instrument of social policy, ranging from policies to eliminate perceived discrimination based on race, gender, etc. to using the financial system to reduce income inequality by subsidizing credit to specific sectors of the economy, such as housing for low- to moderate-income households.

The *central bank* is a special government institution that conducts *central bank policy* designed to influence money, credit, interest rates and the overall level of economic activity. Central banks also provide a national payments system by establishing check-clearing facilities, wire transfer facilities and currency. It is one of the most powerful economic institutions in any country. Central banks can also play a role as a financial regulatory and supervisory authority; however, this varies from country to country. The Federal Reserve System, the U.S. central bank, plays a major role in financial regulation and supervision while other central banks, such as the Bank of Japan, play a much smaller role.

At this point, the discussion of the financial and monetary regime is general and meant only to introduce the reader to the concept of a country's financial and monetary regime. The detail will come later. However, the important point to grasp, at this introductory stage, is that every country has a financial and monetary regime; the financial and monetary regime plays an important role in the economy; and, while the institutional details differ from country to country, the basic design and responsibilities are more important than the differences that one might expect.

At this introductory stage, there are four topics to help understand the relationship between the financial and monetary regime and economic activity. First, the placement of the financial and monetary regime in overall economic activity; second, the measures of economic activity that are important indicators of economic welfare for the country; third, the channels through which the financial and monetary regime influences economic activity; and, fourth, the role of the financial and monetary regime in the most significant periods of economic and financial distress in the history of the United States, along with two examples drawn from world history.

1.3 The Real and Financial Sectors of the Economy

How does the financial and monetary regime in general fit into an economist's concept of the economy? Economists conceptualize the economy as consisting of two sectors: the real sector and the financial sector. The real sector focuses on the "real" aspects of economic activity, which manifest themselves in the form of domestic output of goods and services, foreign output of goods and services, consumption, saving, investment, government spending and taxes, employment, productivity, etc. In a general sense, the real sector focuses on a country's output of goods and services, resources that are used to produce the goods and services and the prices the goods and services sell for in the market. The price level at which the goods and services are sold and purchased is not a real variable but a variable that permits us to distinguish between the nominal and real values of many variables in the real sector; for example, we use the price level to distinguish between nominal or money wages and real wages, between nominal output and real output, etc.

In contrast, the financial sector focuses on financial assets and liabilities, lending and borrowing, credit, money and interest rates. The financial sector is no less "real" than the real sector but, in the most general sense, focuses on the financial aspect of real activity; that is, instead of focusing on saving and investment, the financial sector focuses on lending and borrowing. Instead of focusing on spending and employment, it focuses on the financial resources used to support spending and employment, such as credit and money. The price level plays a role in the financial sector, as it does in the real sector, by distinguishing between nominal and real values of financial variables; for example, nominal and real credit flows, nominal and real money supply, nominal and real interest rates, etc.

One cannot have one sector without the other. The two sectors are closely interrelated and changes in one sector influence the other, as illustrated by first considering how the real sector influences the financial sector:

$$\text{Real Sector} > \text{Financial Sector} \tag{1.1}$$

Assume a given interest rate determined in the financial sector. At this interest rate, the real sector determines the level of output, spending, employment, etc. As part of this process, the real sector determines saving, which, in turn, influences the supply of loanable funds in the financial sector, and spending influences the demand for loanable funds in the financial sector. The real sector thus influences the financial sector (Expression 1.1), but, in turn, the financial sector then feeds back onto the real sector:

$$\text{Financial Sector} > \text{Real Sector} \tag{1.2}$$

The supply of and demand for loanable funds influence the interest rate we started with in the real sector and change the interest rate. The changed interest rate feeds back onto the real sector by influencing output, spending, employment, prices, etc. in the real sector (Expression 1.2). The influence on the real sector then influences the supply of and demand for loanable funds in the financial sector, which in turn changes the interest rate and feeds back onto the real sector (Expression 1.2), which in turn influences the financial sector (Expression 1.1), which in turn influences the real sector (Expression 1.2), and so on.

The country's financial and monetary regime is thus part of the financial sector in the broad sense, which in turn influences the real sector, and so on; thus, the financial and monetary regime is an integral part of the overall economy.

1.4 Measuring Economic Performance

An important premise in this book is that a significant malfunction in the country's financial and monetary regime has an adverse impact on economic activity, and, as such, it is important to be familiar with how economic activity is measured. A country's economic performance can be measured in a variety of ways; however, five variables, most of which are drawn from the real sector, provide a good overview of how well an economy is performing over both the short and long run.

These are: actual real gross domestic product, or real GDP; potential real GDP; the unemployment rate; the natural unemployment rate; and the price level. The price level itself is not a real variable but is an important indicator of economic activity and permits us to distinguish between nominal and real values of economic variables where appropriate. Variables that measure the financial sector, such as interest rates, money, credit, etc., are also important, but ultimately it's the overall level of economic performance represented by these five variables that determines the wealth and growth of the nation.

Actual and potential real GDP: Real GDP is the final output of goods and services produced in the country over a period of time, holding prices constant. Real GDP is measured by the spending on final output measured by consumer spending (C), investment spending (I), government spending (G) and net foreign spending [exports of goods and services (X) minus imports of goods and services (M)]:

$$\text{Real GDP} = C + I + G + (X - M) \tag{1.3}$$

Nominal or market GDP is the final output of goods and services valued at current or market prices and related to real GDP by the following:

$$\text{Real GDP} = (\text{Nominal GDP/Price Index}) \tag{1.4}$$

where the price index is divided by 100 to convert it from a percent to a real number.

While real GDP is what the economy actually produced over a given period of time, the economy's potential real GDP is the level of real output an economy is capable of producing over a period of time utilizing its resources with its given structure and technology. Potential GDP is also referred to as the level of output the economy produces at "full employment"; however, full employment does not mean zero unemployment, because even at "full employment" there is a non-zero level of unemployment determined by the structure of the economy, referred to as natural unemployment.

There is nothing special or desirable about potential GDP in that it can be high or low depending on the country's structure, resource base and technology. Potential GDP is simply a base to measure actual economic performance against its potential, but there is nothing optimal about potential output. An economy might have inefficiencies that limit a country's potential output. Consider the former command economies of China and the Soviet Union that collapsed in the latter part of the twentieth century. Despite resources and access to technology, the inherent inefficiency of these command economies limited their potential levels compared to the West; that is, the government-controlled structure limited the country's potential output at a given level of resources and technology. This is a major reason why these economies collapsed and/or had so much "deadweight loss" they shifted to more open markets and less government planning.

The difference between real and potential GDP indicates whether the economy is operating above or below its potential or natural output path. The GDP gap is

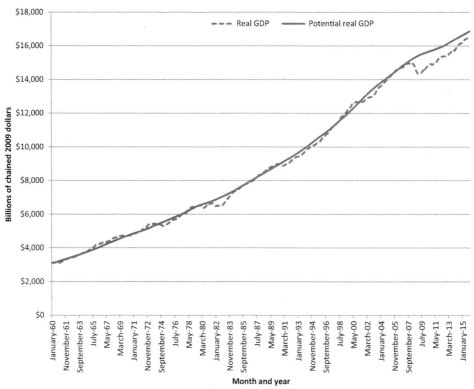

Figure 1.1. Quarterly Real GDP and Potential Real GDP, 1960:1 to 2016:1, in Chained 2009 Dollars. *Source:* FRED, Federal Reserve Bank of St. Louis (https://fred.stlouisfed.org).

the difference between actual real GDP and potential GDP expressed as a ratio of potential GDP:

$$\text{GDP Gap} = (\text{Real GDP} - \text{Potential GDP})/\text{Potential GDP} \qquad (1.5)$$

The GDP gap is often expressed in percentage terms by multiplying Expression 1.5 by 100.

Figure 1.1 illustrates U.S. quarterly real GDP and potential GDP from the first quarter of 1960 (1960:1) to the first quarter of 2016 (2016:1), and, while the U.S. economy has grown over time, actual GDP has moved above and below its potential. These swings in economic activity are more apparent in the GDP gap, illustrated in Figure 1.2. The GDP gap exhibits definite cyclical movements, which are called business fluctuations or cycles. To highlight the business cycle movements, Figure 1.2 highlights periods of recession and expansion established by the National Bureau of Economic Research (NBER). The shaded areas in Figure 1.2 are recessions and the non-shaded areas, by definition, are periods of expansion in the U.S. economy. Notice how the GDP gap is negative during recession periods and positive during expansion periods.

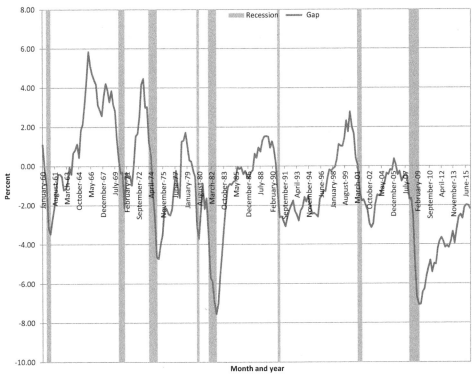

Figure 1.2. Real GDP Gap, 1960:1 to 2016:1. *Source:* FRED, Federal Reserve Bank of St. Louis.

Actual and natural unemployment rate: There are several measures of the unemployment rate. The most frequently used is the civilian unemployment rate, defined as

$$UR = ((LF - E)/LF)*100 = (NE/LF)*100 \tag{1.6}$$

where UR is the unemployment rate and LF is the labor force, defined as the sum of those employed (E) and not employed (NE). NE are those in the labor force not working but actively seeking employment. This measure of the unemployment rate is the most frequently cited in the news media; however, it does not accurately measure unemployment at any point in time. Some individuals become discouraged and cease looking for work during periods of labor market distress in an economic decline and, hence, are not included in LF; that is, a reduction in the LF and NE by the same amount lowers the measured unemployment rate and provides an inaccurate picture of the unemployment situation. Consider a case where there are 100 individuals in the labor force (LF = 100) and 90 are working (E = 90) and ten are not employed but actively looking for work (NE = 10). The unemployment rate, UR, is 10 percent; however, if five of the ten job seekers become discouraged and are no longer actively looking for work, NE = 5, E = 90 and LF = 95. The calculated unemployment rate is now 5.3 percent! The same phenomenon can occur in

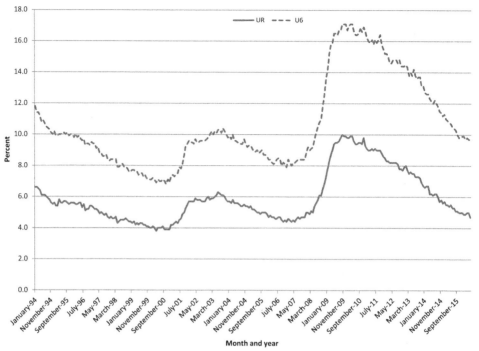

Figure 1.3. Standard Unemployment Rate and U6 Unemployment Rate (SA), January 1994 to May 2016. *Source:* FRED, Federal Reserve Bank of St. Louis.

the opposite direction during the early stages of an economic expansion, as individuals who had been on the sidelines start looking for work, increasing the size of LF so that, at a given E, UR increases.

Aside from discouraged workers, the UR does not accurately measure unemployment, because of the presence of marginal workers and those working part-time who desire to work full-time. Marginal workers are not included in the labor force but, unlike discouraged workers, have looked for a job in the past 12 months. There are workers working part-time who are defined as employed because they worked the threshold of 30 hours per week but would like to work full-time. During contractions the number of marginal and part-time workers who want to work more increases, and during expansions it decreases.

A measure of the broader and more accurate unemployment rate has been published since 1994 and is referred to as the U6 unemployment rate (the standard civilian unemployment rate is referred to as U3). The U6 unemployment rate incorporates discouraged workers, marginal workers and part-time workers who want to work more. Figure 1.3 illustrates the standard unemployment rate, UR, and the U6 unemployment rate from January 1994 through May 2016. On average, U6 exceeds UR by 4.7 percentage points.

Related to the unemployment rate, and similar in concept to potential real GDP, is the natural unemployment rate. The natural unemployment rate is the unemployment rate an economy will operate at when the GDP gap is zero or what amounts to

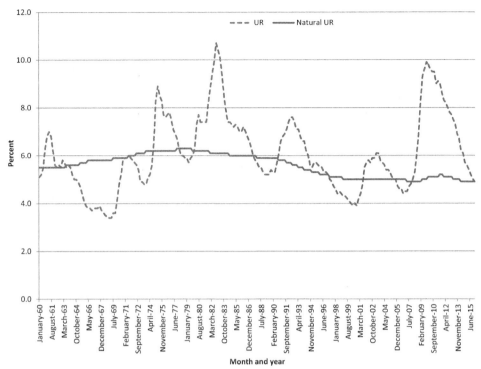

Figure 1.4. Actual Unemployment Rate and Natural Unemployment Rate, 1960:1 to 2016:1. *Source:* FRED, Federal Reserve Bank of St. Louis.

the same thing, when the economy is growing along its potential or natural growth path. Like potential output, the natural unemployment rate is determined by technology and the structure of the economy, and, like potential output, it is a base to determine relative employment. The more efficient the economy and the more technological progress the lower the natural unemployment rate, and the less efficient and the smaller the degree of technological progress the higher the natural unemployment rate.

Another way to think of the natural unemployment rate is to consider three types of unemployment: cyclical, frictional and structural. Cyclical unemployment is due to the swings in the economy and represented by the movement of the measured unemployment rate around the natural unemployment rate. Frictional unemployment is related to the time it takes to move from one position to another. The length of the job search process is influenced by the structure of the economy. Structural unemployment is determined by the structure of the economy, the economy's resource base and technology. The natural unemployment rate can be considered as the sum of frictional and structural unemployment. There are also other ways to define natural unemployment; however, the one used here is reasonable.

Figure 1.4 illustrates the relationship between the actual unemployment rate, UR, and the natural unemployment rate from 1960 to early 2016 on a quarterly basis.

Okun's law: There is an important relationship between actual/potential real GDP and actual/natural unemployment, since the differences with each represent departures from long-run or potential performance levels of the economy. Okun's law, named after an economic advisor to President Kennedy in the 1960s, is a useful expression of the relationship:

$$\text{GDP Gap} = -\beta(\text{Actual Unemployment Rate} - \text{Natural Unemployment Rate})$$
$$(1.7)$$

where β is a coefficient that defines the magnitude of the relationship between the two sides of Expression 1.7. The left-hand side of Expression 1.7 is the gap between actual and potential real GDP while the right-hand side is referred to as the employment gap between the actual and natural unemployment rate.

Economists have attempted to estimate the coefficient, and there is some debate as to whether the simple relationship in Expression 1.7 is even capable of estimation; however, these issues are not important for the purposes of this discussion. Okun's law is useful for understanding a country's economic performance in terms of the human cost measured by unemployment caused by departures of actual GDP from its potential; the importance of structural and technology aspects of the economy; the importance of the structure of the financial and monetary regime; and for understanding central bank policy.

Holding the coefficient β constant, there are three possible relationships between the four variables according to Okun's law:

Actual GDP	>	Potential GDP (Positive Gap), then Actual Unemployment Rate < Natural Unemployment Rate
Actual GDP	<	Potential GDP (Negative Gap), then Actual Unemployment Rate > Natural Unemployment Rate
Actual GDP	=	Potential GDP (Zero Gap), then Actual Unemployment Rate = Natural Unemployment Rate

The price level: There are four important measures of the price level. The consumer price index (CPI) represents prices paid for goods and services by the urban household. The producer price index (PPI) represents prices of commodities used in the production process. The GDP deflator is the price index used to convert nominal GDP to real GDP (Expression 1.4). The personal consumption expenditure price index (PCE) is similar to the CPI but a somewhat broader measure of consumer prices used by the Federal Reserve. Of the four measures of the price level, the PCE is the least utilized; however, since it is used by the Federal Reserve, the PCE needs to be included as a measure of the price level.

A price index is a method of measuring the average behavior of a number of prices of items weighted by the importance of the item over time with reference to a base period; that is, the base year is set to 100 and the index is calculated

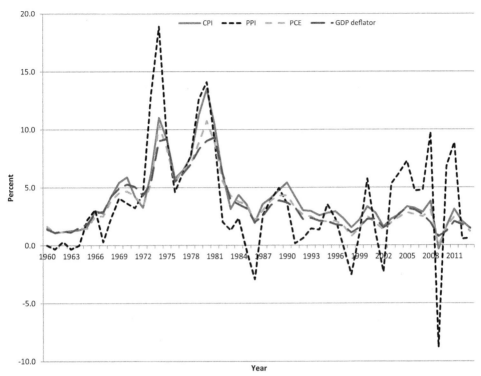

Figure 1.5. Percentage Change in the CPI, PPI, PCE and GDP Deflator Price Indexes, 1960 to 2013. *Source:* FRED, Federal Reserve Bank of St. Louis.

in reference to that base year. If the index is higher (lower) than 100, on average prices are higher (lower) than the base year. Annual percentage changes in each of the four measures of the price level are presented in Figure 1.5 from 1960 to 2013. All four measures of the price level on average are similar, but the PPI is more volatile than the other three. The average annual percentage change from 1960 to 2013 for the CPI, PPI, PCE and GDP deflator are 3.9 percent, 3.6 percent, 3.5 percent and 3.5 percent, respectively; that is, on average they are similar. However, the respective standard deviation for each is 2.8 (CPI), 4.7 (PPI), 2.4 (PCE) and 2.3 (GDP deflator), indicating that the PPI varies much more than the CPI, PCE or GDP deflator.

1.5 Data Sources and Components of a Time Series

Where to find measures of economic activity: The federal government collects an enormous amount of economic information for both the real and financial sectors from a domestic and an international perspective and makes this information readily available to the public. With regard to the five measures of economic performance discussed above, the U.S. Department of Commerce publishes quarterly estimates of real and nominal GDP and monthly estimates of the PCE index. The Department of Labor publishes monthly estimates of the CPI, PPI and unemployment rate. The Congressional Budget Office publishes estimates of potential GDP and the natural unemployment rate.

The data for these other real and financial indicators of the economy can be obtained through the Federal Reserve Economic Data (FRED) system maintained by the Federal Reserve Bank of St. Louis. It is "free" to anyone who accesses the Website, but there is "no free lunch". Revenue earned by the Federal Reserve on its assets, of which government securities are a major component, is used to support FRED. The Federal Reserve, like most central banks, transfers about 80 to 90 percent of its revenue to the Treasury each year as an intergovernmental transfer of funds. As a result of spending revenue on FRED, less revenue is transferred back to the U.S. Treasury, thus increasing the size of the deficit or reducing the size of the surplus. The magnitudes are not large in the case of FRED, but the reader needs to realize that, though FRED is a powerful data source free to those who use the Website, it's not free to everyone. There's no such thing as a "free lunch"!

Decomposing an economic time series: An economic variable such as GDP, the unemployment rate, etc. measured over time is called a time series because the observations of the variable are for discrete points in time, as opposed to a cross-section measure that holds time constant. For example, a cross-section of consumption spending would represent consumption at, say, January 1, 2016, for different households in the United States. Consumption spending for all households each quarter or year over time is a time series of consumption. Macroeconomics and monetary economics rely primarily on time series data and, as such, it is useful to understand how an economist characterizes the movements in a time series.

A time series of any economic variable consists of four components:

$$TS = T + BC + S + R \tag{1.8}$$

where TS is the time series of the economic variable; T is the trend component; BC is the business cycle component; S is the seasonal component; and R is the random component.

The *trend component* is the underlying long-term movement of the variable, which can be upward, downward or constant as well as shifting direction over time. Not all economic time series exhibit a clear trend over time. The trend is sometimes so strong that looking at the level of an economic variable provides little insight into how the variable changes over time; for example, Figure 1.6 illustrates the level of quarterly real GDP and annual percentage change in real GDP measured as the percentage change from the current quarter to the same quarter in the previous year from 1960:1 to 2016:1. The level of real GDP, because of its strong upward trend, masks the year-to-year movements in GDP. In fact, transforming the level of an economic variable into changes is a statistical method for removing the trend for a large number of economic variables measured over time to identify the other components of the time series, especially the business cycle component.

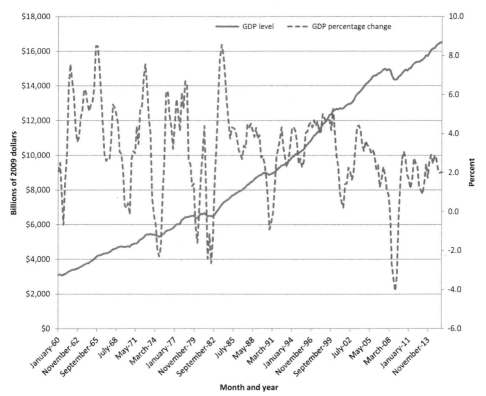

Figure 1.6. Level and Percentage Change in Quarterly GDP, 1960:1 to 2016:1. *Source:* FRED, Federal Reserve Bank of St. Louis.

The economy seldom grows along a steady trend over time; in fact, more often than not the economy is subject to ups and downs, which are a prominent feature of any market-oriented economic system but are masked by trends in the data. The *business fluctuation* or *cycle component* has occupied the attention of economists for well over 200 years. The business cycle exhibits four well-defined phases: expansion, peak, contraction and trough. The phrase "business fluctuation" is a more accurate description of these swings because the swings do not exhibit well-defined cycles, like sine or cosine waves; nonetheless, they are more often referred to as cycles than as fluctuations. The business cycle or fluctuation is a cumulative movement in economic activity in one direction that spreads throughout the economy and reaches a turning point, is then followed by a cumulative movement in economic activity in the other direction that spreads through the economy and reaches a turning point, and so on.

The NBER is a non-profit economic research institution established in 1925. The NBER has become the nation's business cycle time keeper. The NBER has estimated the turning points in the U.S. economy as far back as 1854 (Table 1.1), based on movements in real GDP, employment, real income, employment, industrial production and wholesale-retail prices. The NBER does not define a recession

Table 1.1. *NBER Business Cycle Turning Points, 1854 to 2014*

Peak month	Trough month	Duration, peak to trough	Duration, trough to peak	Duration, peak to peak	Duration, trough to trough
	December 1854				
June 1857	December 1858	18	30		48
October 1860	June 1861	8	22	40	30
April 1865	December 1867	32	46	54	78
June 1869	December 1870	18	18	50	36
October 1873	March 1879	65	34	52	99
March 1882	May 1885	38	36	101	74
March 1887	April 1888	13	22	60	35
July 1890	May 1891	10	27	40	37
January 1893	June 1894	17	20	30	37
December 1895	June 1897	18	18	35	36
June 1899	December 1900	18	24	42	42
September 1902	August 1904	23	21	39	44
May 1907	June 1908	13	33	56	46
January 1910	January 1912	24	19	32	43
January 1913	December 1914	23	12	36	35
August 1918	March 1919	7	44	67	51
January 1920	July 1921	18	10	17	28
May 1923	July 1924	14	22	40	36
October 1926	November 1927	13	27	41	40
August 1929	March 1933	43	21	34	64
May 1937	June 1938	13	50	93	63
February 1945	October 1945	8	80	93	88
November 1948	October 1949	11	37	45	48
July 1953	May 1954	10	45	56	55
August 1957	April 1958	8	39	49	47
April 1960	February 1961	10	24	32	34
December 1969	November 1970	11	106	116	117
November 1973	March 1975	16	36	47	52
January 1980	July 1980	6	58	74	64
July 1981	November 1982	16	12	18	28
July 1990	March 1991	8	92	108	100
March 2001	November 2001	8	120	128	128
December 2007	June 2009	18	73	81	91
1854–2009 (33 cycles)		17.5	38.7	56.4	56.2
1854–1919 (16 cycles)		21.6	26.6	48.9	48.2
1919–1945 (6 cycles)		18.2	35.0	53.0	53.2
1945–2009 (11 cycles)		11.1	58.4	68.5	69.5

Source: National Bureau of Economic Research (www.nber.org/cycles.html).

as two consecutive quarters of decline in real GDP, as often stated in the news media, but uses a much broader perspective.

A useful feature of FRED is that the U.S. data can be presented in a form that marks periods of recession (shaded) and expansion (not shaded). Figure 1.2, which presented the GDP gap since 1960, clearly shows the ups and downs of the economy as measured by the NBER, as do the percentage changes in real GDP in Figure 1.6.

Many economic variables measured on a monthly or quarterly basis contain a *seasonal component*. The *seasonal component* represents a movement in the variable that repeats itself more or less every year and is most often weather-related and/or holiday-related. There are some components of employment, for example, that are influenced by the seasons – agriculture, tourism, certain sports-activity-related employment. An annual sporting event such as the Super Bowl generates a seasonal movement in some economic data. The seasonal component is not as interesting from an economic perspective, because it is largely due to noneconomic forces that repeat themselves from year to year, and is fairly predictable from year to year. The seasonal component of an economic time series can be removed by various procedures, ranging from simple to complex; hence, a large number of time series reported for periods less than a year are seasonally adjusted and published in both seasonally adjusted (SA) and not seasonally adjusted (NSA) forms. In general, the SA form is preferable for those data that have a meaningful seasonal component.

The fourth component of a time series is a *random component* that remains after the trend, business cycle and seasonal components have been identified. The random component is not explainable and relatively small, as economic time series are dominated by the first two components – trend and business cycle – and, to a lesser degree, the seasonal component.

1.6 The Financial and Monetary Regime and Economic Performance

A properly functioning financial and monetary regime is necessary for stable, sustained and noninflationary economic growth at the economy's potential and provides a necessary foundation for increasing potential output over time. As a necessary condition, a country cannot expect to achieve stability, increased wealth and an increased standard of living without a well-functioning financial and monetary regime. At the same time, a well-functioning financial and monetary regime is not sufficient to achieve increases in wealth and the standard of living.

The overall level of economic performance is essentially the outcome of three forces: *demand and supply shocks*; the *structure of the economy*; and the *structure and operation of the financial and monetary regime*.

Demand and supply shocks: Demand shocks are autonomous or *exogenous* changes in spending, as opposed to induced or *endogenous* changes in spending.

To illustrate the difference between autonomous and induced spending consider the following consumption function:

$$C = \beta_0 + \beta_1 Y \qquad\qquad (1.9)$$

where C is real consumer spending; Y is real income; β_0 indicates the level of consumption independent of income; and β_1 indicates the relationship between consumption and income. The β_1 coefficient indicates how C will change in a predictable way when Y changes; that is, this part of C is induced or endogenously determined by the level of income. The constant term, β_0, indicates the level of consumption independent of the level of Y. A change in the β_0 coefficient term represents an autonomous or exogenous change in C unrelated to the Y. Any component of spending can change autonomously in either direction and thereby influence economic activity in either direction.

Supply shocks are autonomous or *exogenous* changes in the prices and supplies of commodities used in the production process, such as oil or any energy-related commodity. Since the early 1970s the most important supply shocks have come from the energy sector, especially the supply and price of oil. Supply shocks can also occur as a result of changes in technology or changes in labor productivity. Like demand shocks, supply shocks can occur in either direction, and either increase or decrease the level of economic activity; for example, there have been periods during the last four decades when real oil prices have increased and periods when they have decreased, with significant effects on economic activity.

Demand and supply shocks play a key role in the business cycle, both as causes of the business cycle and, in the case of demand shocks, as a reflection of government stabilization policy designed to change demand to reduce the swings in economic activity and stabilize the economy. Government stabilization policy can be thought of as "leaning or pushing against the wind" in an effort to generate changes in demand to offset other forces that are causing the economy to expand too rapidly or expand too slowly; hence, the phrase "countercyclical" stabilization policy is used to describe government stabilization policy.

Government stabilization policy consists of fiscal policy (government spending and taxation) and central bank or monetary policy (credit, interest rates and money supply) designed to reduce the amplitude of the business cycle over time and increase the length of the expansion phase and reduce the length of the contraction or recession phase.

Structure of the economy: The structure of the economy influences economic activity through two channels. First, the structure of the economy influences the potential and natural growth path of the economy measured by potential GDP and the natural unemployment rate. Second, the structure of the economy influences the amplitude of the business cycle and the relative lengths of the expansion and contraction phases; that is, the structural aspects of the economy influence not only the long-run growth path of the economy but also the economy's swings around that growth path over time. The following is a list of some of the more important structural aspects of the economy, though by no means an exhaustive list: the degree of competition permitted in the private markets, labor unions and government policy; the degree and type of relationships between government and businesses (crony capitalism) and public employee labor unions (crony unionism); the degree and type of government regulation and supervision in the private sector, including financial regulation and supervision policies; the degree of international openness; and demographic trends such as changes in population and changes in the age distribution of the population.

The financial and monetary regime: The financial and monetary regime is an important determinant of economic activity. A well-functioning financial and monetary regime is not sufficient to generate economic growth and reduce the swings in economic activity, but it is a necessary condition. Demand shocks, supply shocks and, especially, the structure of the economy play a key role in the ability of the financial and monetary regime to fulfill its basic role in the economy. That is, depending on the nature of the demand shocks, supply shocks and structural characteristics of the economy, a well-functioning financial and monetary regime can easily be transformed into a not so well-functioning financial and monetary regime. This may seem an obvious point, but it needs to be emphasized. Of course, a less than well-functioning financial and monetary regime, on its own account, can be the source of much economic and financial distress independent of other forces.

How does the financial and monetary regime influence economic performance? The answer to this question is straightforward in terms of the financial and monetary regime's positive influence on economic activity. If the financial and monetary regime is functioning well then it provides a stable financial and monetary environment for economic growth and contributes to reducing the amplitude of the business cycle, increasing the length of expansions and reducing the length of contractions and providing a foundation for an increase in the economy's potential over time. In particular, a well-functioning financial and monetary regime supports the saving/investment process; provides an efficient channel to transfer funds from lenders to borrowers; provides financial stability; provides adaptability to the changing needs of the economy; and stabilizes the value of the nation's money supply by achieving a low and steady inflation rate. Again, a well-functioning financial and monetary regime is only a necessary condition for economic stability and not a sufficient condition. Demand and supply shocks and structural aspects of the economy can offset the positive impact of a well-functioning financial and monetary regime on the economy.

In contrast, if the financial and monetary regime fails to fulfill any of these fundamental roles there's going to be "Trouble in River City" for the economy akin to the song in the old Broadway play and movie *Music Man* (check YouTube for some cultural education: www.youtube.com/watch?v=LI_Oe-jtgdI). There are many examples in U.S. history and world history to illustrate how a less than well-functioning financial and monetary regime significantly impacted economic performance, but at this stage of the discussion only a brief outline of five episodes is required to drive home the point that problems in the country's financial and monetary regime can have adverse impacts on the economy.

1.7 Periods of Major Economic and Financial Distress and the Financial and Monetary Regime

Five episodes of intense economic, financial and sometimes political distress illustrate the point that a malfunctioning financial and monetary regime can importantly contribute to economic instability. There have been other periods during which the regime functioned well and supported sustained and noninflationary growth, but these periods highlight the consequences of a malfunctioning financial and monetary regime. Three episodes are drawn from U.S. history, one from post-WWI Germany and the last from post-WWII Japan. In each case, problems in each country's financial and monetary regime combined with other factors generated great distress and, in the case of Germany, played an important role in the rise of Nazism there, and WWII. Each will be briefly discussed in turn.

We begin with the three U.S. episodes and then turn our attention to Germany and Japan.

1.8 The United States

There are three periods of intense economic instability that stand out in U.S. history: the Great Depression of the 1930s; the Great Inflation from 1965 to 1985; and the Great Recession, which started with the collapse of real estate prices in early 2006 and, as of 2016, still had not been fully resolved. In each of these three periods, poorly designed financial regulation and structural problems in the financial system combined with policy errors by the Federal Reserve imposed significant economic and financial distress on the U.S. economy.

The Great Depression, which lasted from 1929 to 1941, was once attributed to various degrees of market failure that indicated the need for an expansive and activist government to return the economy to stability and economic growth. The Great Depression rationalized an unprecedented expansion of government spending and policy under the New Deal of the Roosevelt administration. In fact, the edifice of government stabilization, regulation and supervision that characterizes the U.S. economy today started in the 1930s, and the then widely accepted interpretation of the causes of the Great Depression continues in many quarters to the present despite evidence to the contrary. Government blamed the private sector and private self-interest for the collapse of the financial system and economy, for high unemployment throughout the 1930s and for an economy that operated far below its potential. That is, the Great Depression was blamed on market failure, and only an expanded and activist government could offset market failure and return the economy to full employment. The pro-government, anti-market perspective of the Great Depression can be summed up in the following: the economy began to recover with the New Deal policies of increased government spending, increased regulation and supervision to rein in the "animal spirits" of capitalism; began to recover more strongly with the mobilization for WWII, starting with the Lend Lease Act of 1939; and fully recovered with America's entry into the war on December 7, 1941, when Japan attacked Pearl Harbor, and then Germany declared war on the United States on December 11, 1941.

This is a well-known story that continues to be taught in high school history textbooks and many university history courses, and is frequently used by modern-day politicians who emphasize market failure as the source of instability to rationalize the need for an activist government. Evidence, however, suggests that this pro-government anti-market interpretation of the Great Depression places too much emphasis on market failure and omits the policy errors made by government policy that importantly contributed to the depth and length of the Great Depression. An intellectually balanced view of the Great Depression needs to recognize the importance of policy errors by the government, especially Federal Reserve policy. Milton Friedman and Anna Jacobson Schwartz (1963) were among the first to challenge the then accepted view of the Great Depression. They argue in their *Monetary History of the United States: 1867 to 1960* that a series of policy errors by the Federal Reserve turned what would have been a normal recession that started in 1929 into a major economic catastrophe that lasted a decade. They identify other factors, but place the major cause of the Great Depression on policy errors by the Federal Reserve. It was not market failure but government failure, according to Friedman and Schwartz, that was responsible for the economic and financial distress of the 1930s. Monetary policy was not the sole cause but, as part of the financial and monetary regime, rendered the financial system incapable of fulfilling its basic responsibilities. There continues to be debate about how monetary policy errors impacted the economy, but there is no serious economist who does not recognize that Federal Reserve policy errors are an important part of understanding the causes of the Great Depression.

No other authority need be cited than former governor of the Federal Reserve Ben Bernanke (2006–2014). In a celebration of Friedman's 90th birthday at the University of Chicago, Bernanke (2002) closed his speech by focusing on the contributions of Friedman and Friedman and Schwartz to monetary economics in the following manner:

> The brilliance of Friedman and Schwartz's work on the Great Depression is not simply the texture of the discussion or the coherence of the point of view. Their work was among the first to use history to address seriously the issues of cause and effect in a complex economic system, the problem of identification ... For practical central bankers, among

which I now count myself, Friedman and Schwartz's analysis leaves many lessons. [One] is the idea that monetary forces, particularly if unleashed in a destabilizing direction, can be extremely powerful. The best thing that central bankers can do for the world is to avoid such crises by providing the economy with, in Milton Friedman's words, a "stable monetary background" – for example as reflected in low and stable inflation.

Let me end my talk by abusing slightly my status as an official representative of the Federal Reserve. I would like to say to Milton and Anna: Regarding the Great Depression. You're right, we did it. We're very sorry. But thanks to you, we won't do it again.

The Great Depression is now attributed to a significant degree to a malfunctioning financial and monetary regime and in particular to a series of policy errors made by the Federal Reserve. There were structural problems in the financial system that needed government reform and degrees of market failure, but the collapse of the financial system and its impact on the U.S. economy for the entire decade of the 1930s is largely due to Federal Reserve policy errors. In addition, economic research suggests that much of the New Deal policies, including government spending, did little to improve the economy after 1933. On the eve of WWII the U.S. economy was still operating with high unemployment (19.1 percent in 1938) that likely understated the degree of unemployed due to the discouraged and marginal worker effect and a large negative GDP gap (–24.1 percent).

The Great Inflation, 1965 to 1985, was characterized by high inflation and high unemployment (stagflation) due to a combination of structural problems in the financial system related to government policies to subsidize homeownership; flawed understanding of how central bank policy worked; and excessively easy monetary policy by the Federal Reserve. Disruptions in the flow of funds were a serious problem during the Great Inflation when the then existing structure of the financial system and government regulation encouraged depositors to shift funds from depository institutions (commercial banks, savings and loan associations [S&Ls], savings banks and credit unions) to direct money market whenever market interest rates rose significantly above the interest rate ceilings imposed on saving and time deposits (Regulation Q).

Regulation Q ceilings were a major part of the financial system from 1933, when they were first imposed, until the ceilings were phased out over the period from 1980 to 1986. The process of shifting funds from interest-rate-controlled deposits to money market instruments (Treasury bills, commercial paper, large certificates of deposit [CDs], etc. not subject to interest rate ceilings) was called "disinter-mediation". Disintermediation generated several "credit crunches" in the 1970s in which mortgage and consumer credit was not available at any depository institution almost at any interest rate. Disintermediation greatly threatened the viability of all depository institutions, but especially the S&L industry. In fact, the S&L industry collapsed in the 1980s partly because of disintermediation, interest rate ceilings and government efforts to protect them as specialized mortgage lenders who borrowed short and lent long. The taxpayer-financed bailout of the S&L industry from 1989 to 1999 cost $214 billion in 2014 dollars.

The high market interest rates were due to inflation caused by excessively easy monetary policy on the part of the Federal Reserve. As discussed in a later chapter, easy monetary policy can often be associated with high, not low, interest rates. The easy monetary policy was due to flawed models of how monetary policy influenced the economy: failures in policy by the Federal Reserve to understand the relationship between monetary policy and financial structure; and politicization of monetary policy. Like the Great Depression, failures in the country's financial and monetary regime, especially Federal Reserve policy errors combined with a flawed financial system designed to support homeownership, played a major role in economic and financial distress that lasted two decades and imposed a large cost on taxpayers. This is not meant to suggest there was no market failure that played a role. There was market failure, such as imprudent lending and fraud in the S&L industry, but these elements pale in importance compared to the Federal Reserve policy errors, combined with flawed financial regulation to maintain the S&L industry as specialized mortgage lenders.

The Great Recession, starting in early 2006 with the collapse of housing prices, has yet to be fully resolved as of 2016. The economy continued to operate below its potential through early 2016 (Figure 1.1) and, while the unemployment rate has declined to its natural level, the U6 unemployment rate remains high and the labor force participation rate has declined significantly. In fact, if one measured the standard unemployment rate with the labor force participation rate that existed prior to the Great Recession, the standard unemployment rate would be much higher by several percentage points. Hence, while the economy has recovered to a reasonable degree, the recovery is widely regarded as weak by historical standards at the time of this writing.

The Great Recession is importantly tied to the bubble in house prices that started around 2002, peaked in early 2006 and collapsed over the next seven years (Figure 1.7). Because the collapse of house prices took some time to permeate the rest of the economy, the recession did not officially begin until December 2007, according to the NBER, and the recession did not take on an international character and sense of panic until after the September 15, 2008, bankruptcy of Lehman Brothers.

Lehman Brothers' bankruptcy represented the largest bankruptcy of any private entity in U.S. history, with about $750 billion in assets. The collapse of Lehman Brothers had a significant impact on the flow of funds in both the United States and much of the world. One of the consequences of the bankruptcy was the threat to the stability of money market funds that are issued by investment companies. Money market funds held by the public are considered part of the nation's money supply and represent shares in a fund of money market or short-term financial instruments managed by the investment company. Many money market funds held Lehman-Brothers-issued commercial paper.

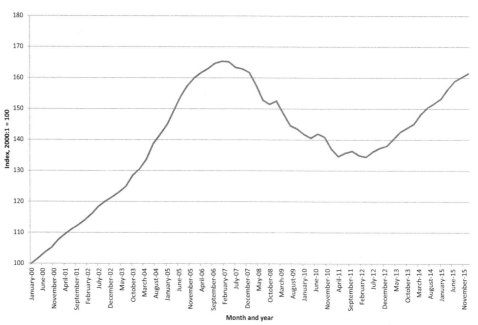

Figure 1.7. All-Transactions House Price Index, 2000:1 to 2016. *Source:* FRED, Federal Reserve Bank of St. Louis.

The sharp decline in the value of this commercial paper made it difficult for investment companies to honor their decades-long commitment not to "break the buck"; that is, the holder of a $1.00 share in money market funds would always be able to withdraw that share at $1.00. Receiving less than $1.00 is "breaking the buck", and several money market funds did break the buck in 2008 and 2009. There was fear that the collapse of Lehman Brothers' commercial paper would generate a run on money market funds as holders attempted to cash in their funds and collapse the financial system, as in the early 1930s. The U.S. Treasury took the unprecedented step of extending a government deposit guarantee up to $250,000 per account to all money market funds for one year other than those who held federal, state or local government securities.

The fundamental cause of the Great Recession is rooted in the cause of the bubble in house prices from 2002 to late 2005 and the collapse of the housing bubble after early 2006. To understand the bubble and its bursting is to understand the Great Recession. But, unlike the Great Depression and Great Inflation, there remains considerable debate as to the role of government policy. Many claim it was greed and fraud and other manifestations of market failure that were the cause of the housing bubble, while others – including this writer – attribute the bubble to the combined influence of a flawed financial structure and monetary policy errors. During the run-up of real estate prices from 2002 to early 2006 the cost and conditions of borrowing to purchase a house did not reflect the risk–return tradeoff embedded in mortgage lending. A good part of this was the direct result of government policy to support homeownership. The government through two government-sponsored agencies, Freddie Mac and Fannie Mae, provided incentives to expand real estate lending by lowering the loan standards, reducing the down payment and aggressively marketing subprime mortgages.

Subprime mortgages had a much higher degree of default risk than ordinary or prime mortgages. As long as house prices increased at 10 to 20 percent per year, a subprime mortgage appeared economically reasonable; but all bubbles burst. The Federal Reserve conducted an aggressively easy monetary policy from 2001 to 2005 that lowered interest rates, especially on mortgage credit, to levels that had not been seen in half a century. The low interest rates understated the risk of mortgage lending/borrowing and, as a result, mortgage credit expanded significantly from 2002 to late 2005 and supported the bubble in house prices. When the Federal Reserve shifted policy in mid-2004 the damage had already been done, since monetary policy impacts the economy with a substantial lag. House prices were by then determined by the "bigger fool theory", based on the unconditioned expectation that house prices next period would be higher than the current period. In essence: "I know I am a fool for paying $500,000 for a track home in some urban area, but in one year a bigger fool will pay me $1,000,000 next year for the home." All bubbles are based on the bigger fool theory and all bubbles collapse when the market recognizes that the unconditioned expectation of increasing house prices lacks economic reality.

Hence, it was the combined policy of the Federal Reserve and the structure of the financial system to support homeownership that played a major role in the Great Recession. This is not to deny any role to market failure; in fact, there was market failure, in the transparency of complex financial derivatives that were based on low-quality mortgages; however, again in this writer's opinion and many others, these pale in comparison to the government policy failures. Ironically, Bernanke was willing to accept Federal Reserve responsibility for being a causative agent of the Great Depression, but has denied any such causative role for the Federal Reserve in the Great Recession (Bernanke, 2013). This is debatable. The last chapter revisits the Great Recession, providing more detail on both perspectives.

In sum, the three periods represent economic and financial distress caused by a dysfunctional financial and monetary regime. Government policy errors played an important role, and, while debate continues over the relative roles of government failure versus market failure, any balanced interpretation of these three periods requires that government failure be assigned at least as much responsibility as market failure.

1.9 Germany and Japan

Germany and Japan are important international case studies because, in the case of Germany, the malfunctioning financial and monetary regime changed world history and, in the case of Japan, foreshadowed events in the United States a decade later that continue through 2016.

Germany: Germany is a case study of how a malfunctioning financial and monetary regime can generate extreme economic, financial and political distress in a country that ends up adversely impacting the world. Germany signed the instrument of surrender bringing an end to WWI on November 11, 1918. The Allies (Britain, France, Italy and the United States primarily) forced Germany to sign the Treaty of Versailles on June 28, 1919. The treaty imposed harsh reparations on Germany and required Germany to make large payments to various countries. The French and Belgian military actually occupied part of Germany in 1923 to ensure that Germany honored the terms of the treaty. Germany was unable to meet the reparation requirements and other conditions without imposing hardships on the population and, like many governments in times of economic and political turmoil, resorted to printing money.

The Bundesbank, Germany's central bank, began to print money at an ever-increasing rate, starting in 1921, which led to one of the most famous periods of hyperinflation in world history. Hyperinflation is a process in which the price level increases so greatly and rapidly that no one wants to hold money; instead, people spend money as fast as they can to hold goods because they expect the price of those goods to accelerate. The hyperinflation started August 1922 and ended November 1923, and during this period prices increased several hundred percent every month.

The hyperinflation was brought to an end by reducing the nominal value of all debt contracts and introducing a new currency. Germany quickly stabilized and generated impressive economic growth for the remainder of the 1920s, but the hyperinflation had done much damage. The hyperinflation and its aftermath had two major impacts and one minor impact that were to change world history: first, it destroyed much of the wealth of the middle class; second, it destroyed the faith in the new democratic institutions established by the Weimar Republic after WWI; and, third, the economic turbulence provided a platform for the Nazi Party to gain a small foothold in the German legislature in 1923, providing the Nazis over the coming years a foundation from which to assume complete control of the German government in 1933.

It is sometimes claimed that Germany's hyperinflation provided the basis for the rise of Nazi Germany. This is incorrect, because it wasn't until the end of the 1920s that the Nazi Party became a serious contender for the control of Germany. However, the hyperinflation did provide a conducive environment for the rise of the Nazis, and rendered a group of revolutionaries a platform that they would not have had in the absence of the major malfunctioning of Germany's financial and monetary regime.

It was the Great Depression in the early 1930s that generated much of the economic and financial distress in Germany and provided Adolf Hitler the foundation to assume complete control in 1933. After the return to stability in 1924, German industry and Germany's recovery depended greatly on U.S. credit, but this flow of credit and money ceased when the U.S. economy and financial system began to unravel in 1930. Deflation and unemployment in Germany in the early 1930s, following the hyperinflation less than a decade earlier, provided the perfect storm for Hitler and the Nazis to assume control over the government in 1933. The rest is history.

The important point here, however, is that a malfunctioning of Germany's financial and monetary regime – hyperinflation in the early 1920s and deflation and bank failures in the early 1930s – set the stage for one of history's great cataclysms.

Japan: Japan's episode of a malfunctioning financial and monetary regime is important for three reasons. First, the malfunction is similar to that of the United States during the Great Recession; that is, the financial and monetary problems in Japan were the same combination of monetary policy errors and a flawed financial structure as in the United States a decade later. Second, the malfunction generated one of the world's largest recorded asset bubbles, and one of the world's largest bursts of an asset bubble. Third, the government's response to the aftermath of the burst of the bubble was to introduce extraordinarily easy monetary policy and government deficit spending, much like the United States a decade later in response to the Great Recession. It is not an exaggeration to claim that Federal Reserve policy in the past decade has been much in the shadow of Bank of Japan policy.

Japan's impressive economic progress in the post-WWII period began to unravel in the second half of the 1980s as real estate prices (Figure 1.8) and stock prices (Figure 1.9) began to increase rapidly. At the start, higher asset prices were supported by economic fundamentals such as high real GDP growth, low interest rates, high profits in the export sector and increased demand for office space in Tokyo as a result of permitting greater foreign participation in Japan's financial system. By 1987, however, asset prices were increasing at rates that could not be justified by economic fundamentals, and price increases became dominated by the unconditioned expectation that prices in each period would be higher than in the preceding period. The equity bubble burst at the beginning of 1990 and the burst of the real estate bubble occurred about a year later.

The asset bubble in Japan was the combined result of easy monetary policy and a flawed financial structure and policy as well as various degrees of market failure, but, again, market failure pales in importance to the series of government policy errors (Cargill and Sakamoto, 2008). Despite rapid real GDP growth in the second half of the 1980s the Bank of Japan had lowered the discount rate to historical lows by early 1989. The Bank of Japan's easy monetary policy was largely dictated by external considerations designed to limit yen appreciation, and, because the rate of inflation was low, the Bank believed it could pursue other objectives. However, the Bank of Japan, like the Federal Reserve, failed to consider the impact of easy monetary policy on a flawed financial structure. The flawed financial system and policies were the result of an incomplete financial liberalization process started in

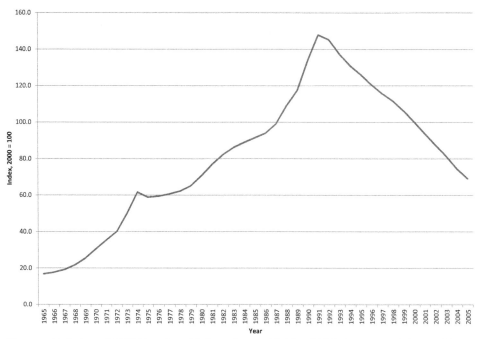

Figure 1.8. Index of All Urban Land Prices, Japan, 1965 to 2005. *Source:* Ministry of Internal Affairs and Communications, Statistics Bureau (www.stat.go.jp/english).

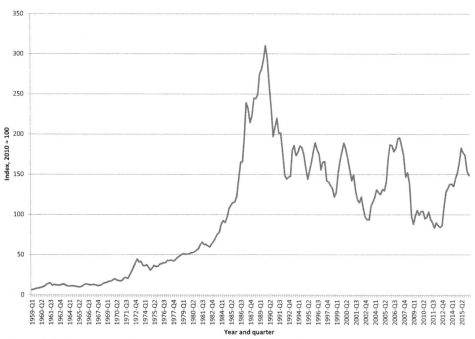

Figure 1.9. Index of Stock Prices, Japan, 1959:1 to 2016:2. *Source:* Organisation for Economic Co-operation and Development (https://data.oecd.org/price/share-prices.htm).

1976. Despite significant institutional redesign of the domestic and external flow of funds in Japan, the fundamental characteristic of the old financial regime remained in place, making Japan's financial and monetary regime an accident waiting to happen. At the time of this writing, Japan is now in the middle of its third lost decade of economic and financial development.

References

Bernanke, Ben S. (2002). "On Milton Friedman's Ninetieth Birthday". Remarks at Chicago University, Chicago, November 8, www.federalreserve.gov/boarddocs/ Speeches/2002/20021108/default.htm.

Bernanke, Ben S. (2013). *The Federal Reserve and the Financial Crisis*. Princeton: Princeton University Press.

Bierman, Noah (2014). "MIT Professor Apologizes for Remark on Voters". *Boston Globe*, December 9, www.bostonglobe.com/news/nation/2014/12/09/mit-professor-jonathan-gruber-apologizes-congress-for-remarks-about-stupidity-american-voter/ AlrfLb2yWKWNTL9OvSaPFJ/story.html.

Cargill, Thomas F., and Takayuki Sakamoto (2008). *Japan since 1980*. New York: Cambridge University Press.

Friedman, Milton, and Anna Jacobson Schwartz (1963). *A Monetary History of the United States: 1867 to 1960*. Princeton: Princeton University Press.

Chapter 2
Basic Concepts Regarding Money

2.1 Introduction

In the introductory chapter, we established that a financial and monetary regime consists of three components:

1) the financial system, consisting of financial institutions and markets;
2) financial regulation and supervision, established by the government and enforced by government regulatory agencies; and
3) the central bank and central bank policy.

The introductory chapter outlined the basic structure and responsibilities of each of the three components; discussed various measures of economic activity that are influenced by the nation's financial and monetary regime; and identified several notable periods of U.S. and world history in which the financial and monetary regime did not satisfactorily meet its responsibilities. These periods generated much economic and financial distress, reduced the standard of living for many, reduced the quality of life for many and on some occasions, as in Germany in the 1920s and early 1930s, contributed to geopolitical distress with grave consequences for world history.

The three components will be discussed in more detail in the coming chapters, but before we turn to that discussion there are four basic definitions and concepts needed to understand a country's financial and monetary regime: first, the *concept and measurement of money*; second, the *concept and measurement of the value of money*; third, the *evolution of monetary standards*; and, fourth, the *relationship between money and economic activity*.

2.2 The Concept and Measurement of Money

The following considerations provide the basis for understanding the U.S. money supply, as well as the money supply for any nation: the concept of money;

measuring the money supply; the M1 and M2 measures of money; the "best" measure of money; and what is not money.

The general concept of money: The concept of money can be approached from two perspectives. The first considers money in the most general sense and the second considers money in terms of the important functions it performs in the economy.

The general concept of money views money as any item a society decides to use to make payments for debt, goods or services. History records many different items that have been accepted by society to function as money. Shells, precious stones, pearls, sharks' teeth, gold, silver and even cigarettes in POW camps during past wars have served as money. Note that the general concept focuses on what society decided to use as money and not what government determined to be money. This is an important point, as money is a market innovation, not a government innovation; that is, money emerged in the private sector to overcome the inefficiencies inherent in a barter economy when goods were exchanged for goods. In a money economy, goods are exchanged for money, and money, in turn, is exchanged for other goods. Government over time increased its role in the money supply, but it wasn't until the twentieth century that government began to play the major role in a nation's money supply.

The functional concept of money: The general concept of money is correct and important, but the functional concept and measurement of money is more detailed and provides a specific set of functions money performs in an economy that better help understand how to measure the nation's money supply. There are three specific functions performed by money in any economy.

First, money serves as a *unit of account* and allows us to compare the value of dissimilar things in an easy and convenient manner. The dollar is the unit of account in the United States, the yen in the unit of account in Japan, the euro is the unit of account in many European countries, and so on. To understand the importance of the unit of account function, image walking into Macy's without the dollar as the unit of account. You now need to carry in your mind thousands upon thousands of ratios to compare the value of any one commodity with other items in the store. One shirt of a given quality and style is worth three pairs of socks of a given style and quality, worth two belts of a given style and quality, worth one-half of a pair of pants of a given style and quality, and so on. In fact, if there were n commodities in Macy's for sale, we need $n(n-1)/2$ ratios to represent all the relative values. If Macy's had 5,000 items in the store, you would need 12,497,500 ratios! Now, if one of the commodities, say the shirt, is selected to serve as the unit of account, we could greatly simplify the relative value calculation. In this case, only 4,999 price ratios are required, because the value of every item is now expressed in terms of the shirt, which would have a price of unity. Money is like the shirt. It is the common denominator used to value dissimilar commodities and services. Continuing with the Macy's example, the 5,000 items are valued in terms of the dollar, and therefore we can easily compare the relative value of any one item with all the other items. Money as a unit of account actually makes it possible to compare apples and oranges in the marketplace!

Second, money functions as a *medium of exchange*. As a medium of exchange, or generalized purchasing power, money is a vast improvement over barter. In a barter economy, commodities exchange for commodities, and, for exchange to occur, there has to be a coincidence of wants between the two sides of the transaction. That is, each trader must desire the other trader's commodity or else trade will not take place. In a money economy, commodities exchange for money, which, in turn, can be exchanged for commodities. In this way we eliminate the need for a coincidence of wants. If you desire the commodity held by another person, you merely offer money to purchase the commodity, and the money received by the other person can then be used to purchase whatever the other person wishes. Another way to conceptualize money as eliminating the need for a coincidence of wants before trade can take place is to think of money as a medium of exchange separating the decision to buy and the decision to sell.

Third, money functions as a *store of wealth*. Wealth consists of the assets on the balance sheet, and net wealth is equal to assets less the liabilities on the balance sheet. Wealth or assets can be held either in the form of real or financial assets. Financial assets represent a claim on someone else's wealth or income while real assets represent tangible assets owned by you, such as a car, house, etc. Financial assets and real assets together represent what you own, and subtracting liabilities determines your net wealth.

All assets on your balance sheet have some degree of liquidity. The liquidity of any asset is the ability of that asset to be immediately accepted in the marketplace as payment for commodities, services or debt. This can be represented by the ability of any asset to be transformed into the one asset that has 100 percent liquidity – money. Money is a special type of financial asset that is 100 percent liquid since it has immediate command over resources in the market. Money talks! Two dollars talk twice as loud as one dollar and market participants stand up and listen when money comes into the marketplace. Other financial assets and real assets on the balance sheet have varying degrees of liquidity in their ability to be transformed into money but, most often, will require transactions cost to be sold and will experience a capital loss if sold for less than the original purchase price.

In general, financial assets possess more liquidity than real assets, but, even here, many financial assets have considerably less liquidity than money. Consider a share of IBM stock. If you wish to tap its liquidity and use that liquidity to purchase a commodity or service or pay off a debt, you will need to sell it in the market, incur a transactions cost and perhaps incur a capital loss. Or consider a one-year time deposit account held at a bank. If you wish to tap its liquidity before the time deposit matures you will need to withdraw the funds by visiting the bank, and will likely incur an interest penalty since you agreed to leave the funds on deposit for one year.

Real assets possess, in general, less liquidity than financial assets. Consider your car. It has some degree of liquidity in the sense that you can convert it into money; however, you will have to incur transactions costs in selling the car, you may have to sell the car at discount or it may take time to sell the car; hence, the car is not a very liquid asset.

It is beneficial to hold your financial wealth in a diversified form across different types of financial assets; that is, it is best not to put all your eggs in one basket. A diversified financial portfolio provides more services, lower risk and more flexibility than non-diversified portfolios. Money provides flexibility in managing wealth since it allows us to hold part of our wealth in a form that is 100 percent liquid, which, in turn, gives us instant command over resources.

The fact that money serves as a store of wealth because of its 100 percent degree of liquidity does not mean money is an optimal way to hold wealth or that a large part of wealth should be held in the form of money. There is no "free lunch"; that is, there is a price for liquidity. The more liquid the financial wealth, the less interest income earned. The less liquid the financial wealth, the more interest income earned. The interest on any financial asset partly depends on the liquidity of that asset. Some forms of money today pay no interest while other forms pay a very small rate of interest.

An optimal distribution of assets on the balance sheet would involve some being held in the form of money (100 percent liquid), but it would also include a wide range of financial and real assets. Money provides a cushion and helps stabilize the value of your wealth in response to market changes. In a sense, money as a store of wealth plays the same role as shock absorbers on your car. Imagine driving a car without shock absorbers. Every bump will be felt, even on good roads, but with shock absorbers the ride is relatively smooth, even on bad roads. Like the shock absorber on the car, money as the most liquid asset on the balance sheet provides flexibility as one travels through the ups and downs of the economy.

The above discussion of the store of wealth function of money focuses on liquidity as the foundation for this function. There is another perspective on why holding money in your portfolio is desirable even though it pays either a zero or small interest rate. Money is less risky than other financial assets. Holding risk and other things constant for financial assets, higher interest rates on financial assets provide incentives to hold less money, while lower interest rates provide incentives to hold more money in the balance sheet.

The measurement of money: Armed with either the general or the functional concept of money, one might think it would be easy to measure the nation's money supply. One would need only to add up those financial assets that satisfy the general and functional definition of money. Unfortunately, the measurement of money is complicated, for two reasons.

First, from a static perspective, setting aside the fact that the financial system and financial assets evolve and change over time, there are many financial assets with less than 100 percent liquidity but not that far away from 100 percent liquidity, and, as such, they might be considered money. The problem is: where does one draw the line? That is, do we consider any financial asset with 95 percent or higher liquidity as part of the measured money supply? What about expanding the charmed circle to include any financial asset with 90 percent or higher liquidity? Hence, we lack a specific degree of liquidity that separates money confined to only those items with 100 percent liquidity with other financial assets with high but less than 100 percent liquidity.

Second, even if we can decide on which financial assets can reasonably be regarded as money, the changing nature of the financial system raises another problem for measuring money. That is, from a dynamic perspective, the financial system is an evolving entity, introducing financial assets that might be considered money. The past four decades have witnessed major changes in the financial system and the financial assets traded in the financial system. This is part of a process, referred to as deregulation or financial liberalization, that has permitted market forces to play a more important role in the flow of funds than previously. Financial liberalization, combined with advances in computer technology, has changed the financial system and is likely to continue to change the financial system in the foreseeable future. That is, the set of financial assets today that can be considered money is likely to change as new forms of financial assets and services are made available. In 1980, for example, the official measures of the money supply were changed significantly because new forms of money had emerged in the 1970s. While the pace of financial liberalization has slowed in the last two decades, the continuing evolution of the financial system along with advances in computer technology suggest that some forms of money in use today will become less important over time and new forms of money will emerge in the future.

Hence, measuring the money supply is not straightforward. It is difficult to decide which financial assets have sufficient liquidity to be included in the charmed circle called money, and the set of financial assets that serve as money changes over time.

The M1 and M2 measures of the money supply: Central banks are responsible for measuring the nation's money supply. The Federal Reserve System publishes two official measures of the money supply: M1 and M2. Collectively, money supply measures are referred to as the *monetary aggregates*. The Federal Reserve releases estimates of the money supply on Thursday of each week as Statistical Release H.6.

Table 2.1 presents the M1 and M2 measure of the money supply and their respective components for September 2014. The two measures of the money supply satisfy the unit of account function; however, the two measures differ in terms of the relative weight given to the medium of exchange and store of wealth functions. M1 focuses on those financial assets that clearly satisfy the medium of exchange function of 100 percent liquidity. At the same time, M1 is not a very good store of

Table 2.1. *The M1 and M2 Measures of the Money Supply, SA, September 2014*

	Amount (billions of dollars)	Percent
M1		
Currency Held by the Public	$1,227	42.3
Checking Accounts or Checkable Deposits	$1,673	57.7
Demand Deposits at Commercial Banks	$1,148	
Other Checkable Deposits (NOW and AST Accounts)		
Commercial Banks	$262	
Thrifts (S&Ls, Savings Banks and Credit Unions)	$217	
Total	**$2,900**	**100.0**
M2		
M1 Money Supply	$2,900	25.2
Savings Deposits	$7,463	64.8
Commercial Banks	$6,388	
Thrifts	$1,075	
Small-Denomination Time Deposits	$529	4.6
Commercial Banks	$394	
Thrifts	$135	
Retail Money Market Funds	$627	5.4
Total	**$11,518**	**100.0**

Source: Federal Reserve Statistical Release, Money Stock Measures, November 6, 2014.

wealth because the components of M1 pay either no interest or only a low interest rate compared to other financial assets. M2, on the other hand, includes financial assets that focus more on the store of wealth function and less on the medium of exchange function; that is, while the additional components of M2 over M1 are not 100 percent liquid, they are preferable forms of holding financial wealth compared to M1 because they pay higher interest. But, because they are close to 100 percent liquid, they also serve as a medium of exchange, though not as easily as the components of M1.

The M1 measure is the base measure of the money supply and, by any reasonable standard, is 100 percent liquid. M1 consists of currency (including coin) held by the public, traveler's checks issued by depository institutions and checking accounts or checkable deposits held at depository institutions. Coin and currency are issued by the U.S. Treasury and the Federal Reserve, respectively, and earn no interest. Coin and currency are mainly used for small transactions. Traveler's checks are used as a substitute for currency, especially when traveling, because, if lost, they can be replaced. Traveler's checks represent less than 1 percent of M1 and are included as a component of demand deposits in Table 2.1.

Checking accounts are extensively used throughout the economy for everyday transactions and issued by depository institutions. Depository institutions are divided into two categories: commercial banks and thrifts. Thrifts consist of savings and loan associations, savings banks and credit unions. Checkable deposits can be accessed by the deposit holder either by a written order or electronically for the purpose of making a payment to another person or entity.

There are four types of checking accounts or checkable deposits: demand deposits, NOW (negotiable order of withdrawal) accounts, ATS (automatic transfer service) accounts and credit union share drafts. Demand deposits are subject to transfer by check or electronically on demand, and, for all practical purposes, commercial banks have a monopoly on issuing demand deposits, partly because of tradition but mainly because government regulation limits the ability of for-profit businesses to hold other forms of deposits. NOW accounts in general can be held only by individuals, government agencies and non-profit entities. ATS accounts can be held only by individuals. Only individuals can be a member of a credit union, and thus only individuals can hold share draft deposits.

NOW accounts are savings deposits subject to transfer by check or electronically, and, while they have been treated as payable on demand since they were introduced in the early 1970s, a depository institution technically can require the depositor to wait seven days before the funds are transferred. NOW accounts are issued by commercial banks, S&Ls and savings banks and are permitted to pay interest.

ATS accounts are not standalone accounts but linked to a demand deposit, NOW or credit union share draft account. ATS accounts are set up to permit transfers of funds from savings deposits to checkable deposit accounts. ATS accounts are permitted to pay interest.

Credit union share drafts are essentially NOW accounts, but, because credit unions are organized as cooperatives and exempt from income taxes, unlike commercial banks, S&Ls and savings banks, credit union checking accounts are officially labeled credit union share draft accounts.

Depository institutions: There are four classes of depository institutions that issue checkable deposits. They are referred to as depository institutions because they obtain their funds primarily by issuing deposits. These deposits in turn support lending and investment operations of the depository institutions. In the past the four classes of depository institutions were more notable for their differences in the types of loans they made and the types of deposits they offered; however, as a result of deregulation and financial liberalization, the similarities between the four classes are now more notable than the differences. In fact, you can walk into any one of these institutions and in many respects have trouble figuring out which type of depository institution you are visiting. It is best to consider all four classes as different variations of the same type of institution; however, a few of the differences should be noted.

Commercial banks are the largest and most diversified of the depository institutions. Banks issue demand deposits, NOW accounts and ATS accounts. S&Ls and savings banks issue NOW and ATS accounts, and, while they can issue demand deposits on a limited basis, banks dominate the demand deposit market for all practical purposes. S&Ls and savings banks differ from banks in that they tend to specialize in consumer and real estate lending and much less on lending to businesses. Credit unions issue credit union share drafts (life NOW accounts) and ATS accounts but are specialized tax-exempt financial institutions organized around a common bond of membership, usually occupation; for example, credit unions can be organized around government employees, employees working for a large private corporation, etc. Credit unions focus on consumer lending, though some larger credit unions have more diversified loan portfolios, including real estate lending.

There is one final point about M1 worth making. All components of M1 are guaranteed by the government. Currency and coin issued by the government are guaranteed by the full faith and credit of the government. All checking deposits, as well as other deposits, issued by depository institutions are federally insured by the Federal Deposit Insurance Corporation up to $250,000 per account, or, in the case of credit unions, the National Credit Unions Administration.

M2 broadens the M1 measure by including items that have less medium of exchange characteristics than M1 but possess better store of wealth characteristics than M1, because they are still high in liquidity and offer a higher interest rate. M2 is defined as M1 plus savings deposits, small-denomination time deposits and retail money market funds. Savings deposits and small-denomination time deposits are issued by all four depository institutions; however, money market funds are issued by security companies. All deposits issued by depository institutions are federally insured up to $250,000 per account; however, money market funds are not insured by the government.

Savings deposits are not subject to transfer by check; however, there is a subclass of savings deposits called money market deposit accounts that have limited transactions features, such as being able to write three checks per month. The wide distribution of ATMs (automatic teller machines), however, has increased the liquidity of savings deposits because they can more easily be withdrawn in the form of cash, though depository institutions frequently limit the number of withdrawals from a savings deposit or charge a fee for withdrawals.

Small-denomination time deposits are time deposits of less than $100,000 and not legally negotiable; that is, small-denomination time deposits cannot be sold to another entity before they mature. A time deposit is essentially a savings deposit with a maturity date, and, while the funds can be withdrawn before maturity, the depository institution can impose a penalty for early withdrawal. In contrast, large-denomination time deposits or certificates of deposit are issued primarily by large depository institutions in denominations of $100,000 or more and are legally negotiable; that is, they can be sold in the secondary market before maturity. Large banks issue most of the large CDs and account for about 80 percent of all large CDs issued by depository institutions.

Money market funds represent shares in a fund of money market instruments (Treasury bills, commercial paper, large CDs, etc.) with maturities up to one year and managed by a securities company. There are two types of money market funds:

retail and institutional. Retail money market funds are held by individuals, and institutional funds are held by institutional investors such as banks, insurance companies, securities companies, pension funds and even money market mutual fund companies. About 30 percent of outstanding market funds are held by individuals, and these are included in the M2 measure of the money supply, while funds held by institutions are not included in M2.

Retail funds can be used like checking accounts to some degree, and, even though securities companies attempt to convince the public that they are as safe as insured deposits at depository institutions, money market funds are subject to default risk and liquidity risk. Money market funds emerged in the early 1970s and have become an important part of the money supply and financial system, and, while they are not as secure as deposits at depository institutions, because they are not federally insured, there have been few problems in the past four decades, with the exception of the financial crisis in 2008. Since then there has been growing concern the securities industry has overstated the safety of money market funds, especially retail funds held by individuals. The practice has been to keep $1.00 of a money market fund share always available at $1.00, when in fact the value of the underlying securities can fluctuate significantly and, as in 2008/2009, they can decline in value, so that $1.00 of a money market fund is available at less than $1.00. When this occurs the fund is "breaking the buck".

In contrast, savings and time deposits (including CDs) are insured up to $250,000 by the Federal Deposit Insurance Corporation or the National Credit Union Administration, and this guarantee is backed by the full faith and credit of the government. The securities industry does not have the resources to provide the same guarantee. In fact, three events have adversely impacted the public's confidence in money market funds: a stock market bubble that started around 1995 and collapsed in 2000; a series of financial scandals in the first few years of the new century; and, finally, the financial collapse of 2008/2009 and the Great Recession. Figure 2.1 shows that, from 1980 through the end of the 1990s, retail money market funds increased their role in M2, but since the late 1990s the percentage of retail money market funds in M2 has declined.

Other measures of the money supply – M3: For decades the Federal Reserve published an even broader measure of money called M3, defined as M2 plus institutional money market funds, CDs and other short-term money market instruments. As of March 9, 2006, however, the Federal Reserve no longer publishes estimates of M3, for three reasons: first, M3 did not appear to contain any additional information not already revealed by M2; second, M3 has not played any meaningful role in Federal Reserve policy; and, third, the large banks objected to the cost of collecting data and providing it to the Federal Reserve. At the same time, not all central banks have ceased publishing estimates of an M3 money supply. Some central banks continue to use and publish estimates of an M3-type money supply.

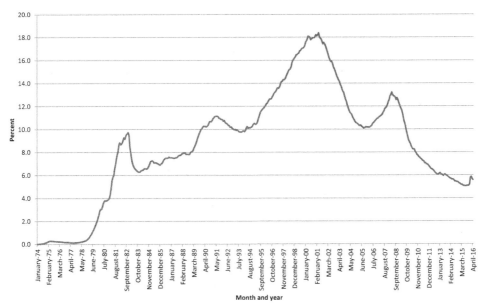

Figure 2.1. Retail Money Market Funds as a Percentage of M2 Money, SA, January 1974 to April 2016. *Source:* FRED, Federal Reserve Bank of St. Louis.

The best measure of the money supply? To monitor the nation's financial and monetary regime, especially in the conduct of central bank policy, a reasonable measure of the money supply is required. What is the best measure of money? Figure 2.2 illustrates annual growth rates of monthly M1 and M2 from January 1960 to April 2016, and, while both exhibit similar patterns, there are significant differences in their behavior over time. The average annual percentage changes in M1 and M2 are not greatly different (M1 = 5.7% and M2 = 6.9%); however, the standard deviation of M1 is 4.6, compared to 2.9 for M2. Not only is M1 more volatile but the empirical evidence indicates that M1 has a less reliable relationship to economic activity than M2.

Economists know money is an important determinate of economic activity and often decide which measure is the most appropriate based on how well a given money measure predicts economic activity. M2 has proved to be a more reliable predictor of economic activity than M1 and a more reliable indicator of the direction of Federal Reserve policy, but even here the correlation is not high on a year-to-year basis. The more erratic behavior of M1 is due to its narrow perspective of money only as financial assets with 100 percent liquidity, but the growing role of savings deposits, small-denomination time deposits and money market funds in influencing spending and economic performance suggest M2 is a more appropriate measure of money. M2 is the basic money measure in the United States and most other countries, though the European Central Bank continues to use a type of M3 measure as well. No central bank seriously regards M1 as a good measure of the

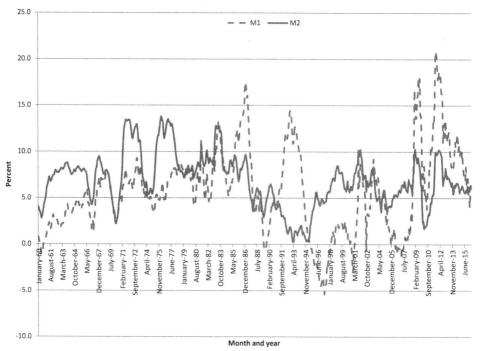

Figure 2.2. Annual Percentage Change of Monthly Values of M1 and M2 (SA), January 1960 to April 2016. *Source:* FRED, Federal Reserve Bank of St. Louis.

money supply; however, one needs to understand M1 in order to understand M2. Hence, M2 is a reasonable measure of the nation's money supply and the official measure of the U.S. money supply.

What is not money: We need to eliminate from any measure of money some items the public mistakenly regard as money because they are used to make purchases of goods and services. In particular, some regard debit cards and new forms of purchasing goods and services on the Internet, such as eChecks and e-cash, as money. At one level, they appear to be money because they are used to make purchases. None of these items, however, are regarded as money, though they ultimately involve a transfer of money at some point. But the important point is that, when these items are used, they are not money themselves but represent a transfer of money either immediately or sometime in the future.

Some also regard credit cards as money, but credit cards are fundamentally different from money. When you use your credit card you are using a portion of a prearranged line of credit and, hence, you are increasing your liabilities. Money is a financial asset, not a liability, in your portfolio. At some point, when you pay your credit card bill, money comes into the picture, because you will use the funds in your checking account to pay the bill. The credit card represents credit and not money, and, while credit and money are closely related, they are not the same. They show up on opposite sides of the balance sheet.

2.3 The Value of Money

The value of any form of money is determined by the power of money to command resources in the marketplace, and that power is measured by the price level of those resources. The value of a $100 bill, $100 checking account, $100 savings or time deposit and $100 money market fund is determined by the price level; for example, if a Burger King Whopper costs $1.00, then $100 will purchase 100 Whoppers, but if the price of Whoppers increases or decreases, the $100 of money will purchase fewer or more than 100 Whoppers, respectively.

There is an inverse relationship between the value of a given stock of money and the price level; that is, increases in the price level (inflation) lower the value of money while decreases in the price level (deflation) increase the value of money. In fact, this is nothing more than a general relationship between the nominal value of any economic variable and its real value; for example, the real value of one's nominal salary is determined by the price level – the higher (lower) the price level, the lower (higher) the real value of your salary. In general, the relationship between the nominal and real value of any economic variable is expressed by the following:

$$\text{Real Value} = \text{Nominal Value}/\text{Price Level} \qquad (2.1)$$

where the price level is measured by an index divided by 100.

Movements in the price level are expressed by the percentage change in the price level. In Chapter 1, Figure 1.5 illustrated the percentage changes of the four important measures of the price level since 1960. In general, the CPI, PCE and GDP deflator exhibit similar trends and exhibit similar movements over time. Not only does the PPI exhibit a more erratic movement, the PPI is not a measure of the prices of the final output of goods and services, since it measures the prices of commodities that are used in the production process. Of the three measures of the price level of those commodities and services purchased as final output, the CPI is the most frequently cited and institutionalized in the form of cost of living adjustments in wage contracts, government entitlements, etc.

How good are the measures of the price level and, especially, the CPI? Like any measure of an economic variable, each is subject to measurement error. There are two types of measurement error: random errors, which are not correlated over time, and nonrandom errors, which are correlated over time. Both are important, but nonrandom errors bias the measure in one direction and present more serious problems for using that variable given any existing random measurement error. There are important nonrandom errors in any price index that cause the price measure to be biased and reduce the reliability of the price level as a reasonable measure of the price level and, hence, reduce its reliability in Expression 2.1.

This is not a trivial statistical issue, because measures of the price level, especially the CPI, play an important role in judging the performance of the economy, influencing how wages are set, influencing government spending and taxation and influencing the formulation, execution and policy objectives of monetary policy. In this regard, there are important nonrandom errors in estimating any price level that generate a bias that needs to be taken into consideration. To understand the inherent bias in measuring the price level we focus on the CPI, because it plays such an important role in the economy; however, any measure of the price level will be subject to the type of nonrandom errors identified for the CPI. Price indexes like the CPI tend to have an upward bias.

2.4 The Upward Bias in the CPI and the Boskin "1.1% Bias"

In the 1950s economists became aware of an upward bias in the CPI and other measures of the price level, but because inflation was steady and low in the 1950s and into the early 1960s the issue was not considered important. Even during the Great Inflation period, from 1965 to 1985, the upward bias was not considered important because, as the inflation rate was so high for so many years, it was difficult to get excited over whether the inflation rate was 10 percent or 8 percent. In the 1990s, however, attention began to be directed to the bias in the CPI, not because it led to an overstatement of inflation but because the upward bias increased government spending and reduced government tax revenue. Correcting the bias was seen as a method to reduce the growth in government spending on entitlements and employee compensation and increase tax revenue.

In 1995 President Clinton established the Advisory Commission to Study the Consumer Price Index. The Commission came to be known as the Boskin Commission, after Michael Boskin of Stanford University, who served as chair. In 1996 the Boskin Commission report was published and concluded that, as of 1996, the CPI overstated the inflation rate by 1.1 percentage points; that is, if the measured inflation rate is 3.0 percent, the "real" inflation rate is 1.9 percent, corrected for the upward bias. The "Boskin 1.1%" was widely discussed, influenced the way the Bureau of Labor Statistics measures consumer prices and continues to be a subject of debate among economists and, especially, politicians because of the political implications of the Commission's findings. But, first, we need to review the sources of the bias before turning to the public policy issues. There are four sources of bias in the computation of the CPI that generate an overstatement of the inflation rate.

Substitution bias: The CPI is based on the prices of each item in a market basket of goods and services, each weighted to represent its importance in the consumer budget. The weights are necessary to assign more importance in the CPI to those items that are a large part of one's budget compared to other items that are less important; for example, a 10 percent increase in the price of pencils is far less important for computing the CPI than a 10 percent increase in the price of food. It is time-consuming and expensive to change the weights, and hence the weights remain constant for lengthy periods of time. This generates a substitution bias when relative prices change that bias the CPI upward.

Consider what happens when the price of fish increases relative to meat, either because a new medical study claims eating fish instead of meat increases life expectancy or because of some event that limits the supply of fish. The higher price of fish induces a shift from fish to meat consumption as consumers substitute the less expensive meat for the more expensive fish; that is, the relative price change has changed the actual weights of fish and meat in the household budget. If the CPI statistical weights for fish and meat remain unchanged, however, the CPI will overstate the increase in average prices because the higher-priced commodity (fish) is given too much weight and the lower-priced commodity (meat) is given too little weight.

Quality bias: An increase in the price of a good or service can be interpreted as an increase in the price only if the characteristics of the good or service remain the same between the time the price is measured. However, technology advances have increased the quality of many services and goods over time. Visiting a doctor in 1960 cost $10 while a typical MD visit today is $100. At first glance, this appears to represent a 1,000 percent increase in the price of the MD visit; however, this would be correct only if the quality of the visit remained constant. It has not remained constant. The MD visit today, even though about the same in terms of time, is of a much higher quality than in 1960. Today's MD visit involves a more knowledgeable medical provider with access to medications and diagnostic equipment that could only be dreamed of in 1960. Hence, a good part of the increase in the price of the MD visit represents a quality improvement in the MD visit rather than an increase in price for the same service. Or consider car tires. In 1960 tire quality was considerably less than today. Today's tires are safer and last longer so, if a tire cost $25 in 1960 and today costs $200, the 800 percent increase in price is importantly due to paying a higher price for a better product.

New product bias: Many new products, especially electronic products, come into the market at high prices, but are not immediately included in the market basket until they became part of the typical household budget. They are included only when they become commonplace, but, as a result, the CPI fails to take into account the price declines that usually follow the introduction of a new product. Consider the flat-screen TV. When first introduced in the 1990s, a Sony flat-screen TV might have sold for $10,000, but today a Sony flat-screen TV can be purchased for $1,000 or less. The new product bias is especially important for new technology products and services that have become increasingly important in the past decades with the advancement of computer and telecommunications technology.

Outlet bias: The CPI has difficulty keeping up with the growth in new forms of places to purchase goods and services that offer these goods and services at a lower price; for example, big-box stores and the Internet are becoming more and more important compared to traditional retail outlet stores for purchasing consumer goods and services. The prices of the goods and services purchased from big-box stores and the Internet are generally lower than those for goods and services purchased from traditional outlets. To the extent that the CPI under-represents purchases from big-box stores and the Internet, it over-represents retail outlets with higher prices compared to outlets with lower prices and, hence, biases the CPI upwards. It should be kept in mind, however, that some of the higher prices relative to big-box stores and the Internet include a service component that is often not provided by the nontraditional retail outlets. But, even taking this into account, the outlet bias is real and important.

Response to the Boskin Commission: The Boskin Commission generated much technical and political discussion, which continues to the present.

First, at the technical level, there is little debate about the sources of the bias, but much debate over the size of the bias. The degree of the bias is not a trivial issue even if the bias is less than the Boskin 1.1 percentage point bias estimate. To illustrate, consider a CPI of 100 in 2016. If the measured inflation rate is 3 percent, the CPI will increase to 116 in five years; that is, prices will be 16 percent higher. If the measured inflation rate has a bias of 0.5 percentage points, the "real" inflation rate is 2.5 percent and the CPI in five years will increase only to 113. This means that, if your wages, disability entitlement, social security entitlement, Medicare compensation, etc. were subject to a cost of living adjustment (COLA), you would be overcompensated in year five by 2.7 percent. If the bias is 1.0 percentage points, the overcompensation is increased to 5 percent. Hence, even with a small bias the impact on the CPI is not trivial over time.

Second, at the political level the debate became very heated, because of the importance of the CPI for adjusting government spending, especially entitlements, labor union wage contracts and collecting tax revenue. If the CPI has a 1.0 percentage point upward bias then entitlement recipients and workers covered by union contracts are being overcompensated for inflation as a result of standard COLA alteration. If social security payments are adjusted upward by the measured CPI inflation rate, say 3 percent, social security recipients are being overcompensated because the "real" inflation rate is 2 percent. If public employees are given a COLA based on the measured CPI then they are being overcompensated for inflation. Hence, using a less biased measure of the CPI would reduce government spending by a significant amount and thereby lower the government deficit and outstanding debt.

The CPI also plays a role in tax revenue. Since 1986 income tax rates have been adjusted for last year's change in the CPI; that is, if the measured CPI increased 3 percent, the tax brackets are adjusted upward by 3 percent so that an increase in earnings to compensate for inflation of 3 percent does not increase one's real tax burden. However, if the "real" inflation rate is 2 percent, the tax brackets are adjusted upward too much and, as a result, the biased CPI generates less tax revenue for the government.

Using a measure of the CPI that corrects to some degree for the upward bias will lower government spending and increase tax revenue, but special interest groups ranging from entitlement recipients to businesses oppose such an adjustment. In recent years there have been several suggestions to correct for the bias; for example, one proposal was to simply subtract 0.5 percentage points from the measured inflation to calculate the COLA alteration for social security payments. Obviously, this did not sit well with those on social security and the activist groups that support those on social security. Nonetheless, the issue is not likely to disappear, and, despite the obvious political aspects of the bias, no country is well served by using a biased measured of the price level.

2.5 The Evolution of Monetary Standards

In primitive economies barter was the primary method of exchanging goods, but barter is inefficient since it requires a coincidence of wants in order for exchange to take place. The introduction of money as a medium of exchange was a major improvement over barter in the exchange for goods and services and represented a market financial innovation that increased the country's potential output. A financial innovation is the introduction of a new financial asset or service that circumvents restrictions on economic activity and profit. Money, as a market innovation, was established by market participants in order to circumvent the restrictions of economic activity imposed by the barter system.

There are three reasons why we should be familiar with the development of monetary standards: first, to highlight the role of financial innovation by the market, as opposed to government innovation; second, to understand the basic operation of the modern monetary system, which forms the basis of all modern financial and monetary regimes in the world; and, third, to understand the rationale as to why government has come to play an important role in money and the financial and monetary regime. The third reason will be discussed in Chapter 8.

The development of money and monetary standards in virtually every country has gone through three stages: *commodity money*, *representative commodity money* and the *modern money system*, characterized as the fiat, fiduciary, fractional reserve and credit-based system. Each monetary standard has had a long history both in the United States and in other countries.

Commodity money: In a *commodity money system*, a commodity becomes widely used as money. The commodity needs to be scarce, easy to identify and divisible. This is why silver and gold have been the commodities of choice throughout history. Commodity money satisfies the three functions of money and is an immense improvement over a barter system; however, a commodity standard has three basic problems.

First, the commodity selected to be used as money has an opportunity cost, since it has nonmonetary uses in the economy and to the degree it is used as money, production that uses the commodity will be adversely impacted. Gold or silver, for example, have nonmonetary uses, such as jewelry, art and religious artifacts, as well as industrial uses. Withdrawing the commodity from general use to money use will reduce the economy's potential. Second, the commodity selected as money must be scarce or else commodity money would have no value because it would be so common. As a result, significant amounts of human and non-human resources are devoted to finding the commodity used for money. These resources have an opportunity cost and hence reduce the potential output of the economy because they are used in obtaining the commodity money. One needs only to consider the tremendous human efforts expended in the past trying to locate gold or silver. Third, the supply of commodity money is not responsive to the needs of trade, as the supply of the commodity is uncertain. Gold and silver discoveries do not occur smoothly over time, but come at discrete points in time often separated by many years. As an economy grows over time, it requires increasing amounts of money on a continuous basis to support trade. The commodity money standard has difficulty matching the supply of the commodity with the needs of the economy.

Representative commodity money: Monetary systems next evolved to *representative commodity standard*, in which individuals found it advantageous to store their commodity money with specialized warehouse institutions. The receipts or promises to pay issued by these institutions were backed 100 percent by the commodity money. As the public began to regard the promises to pay as redeemable at any time into commodity money, the public found it more advantageous to use the promises to pay rather than the actual commodity as money. The promises to pay required less effort to use than the actual commodity and were not subject to the same wear and tear from exchange as the commodity money. Let's consider gold is being used as the commodity money and illustrate how the gold commodity standard shifts into a representative gold standard.

Hickenlupper, an entrepreneur, searches for a way to make a profit and recognizes an inefficiency in the commodity standard that can be resolved by establishing Hickenlupper's Gold Warehouse. The problem is that using gold is cumbersome, especially for large purchases, and gold is not easy to conceal. "Paper gold" or paper backed 100 percent by gold would be easier to use and easier to conceal. Hickenlupper's Gold Warehouse is represented by the following balance sheet:

Hickenlupper's Gold Warehouse

Assets		Liabilities	
Gold	1 million	Promises to pay (gold certificates)	$1 million

Hickenlupper accepts deposits of gold and issues promises to pay or gold certificates as a receipt. The promises to pay can be issued in any denomination.

Hickenlupper earns income chiefly by providing safe storage services for the gold. The more Hickenlupper's promises to pay circulate as money, the more likely Hickenlupper will receive additional deposits of commodity money for safe keeping. The more Hickenlupper redeems any promise to pay for gold without difficulty, the more the public will have confidence in Hickenlupper's Gold Warehouse and be willing to use Hickenlupper's promises to pay as money.

The representative standard offered some advantages over the commodity standard; however, it was essentially a commodity standard with the three problems of the commodity standard. That is, the representative system did not economize on gold as the same amount of gold was required. The gold had nonmonetary uses; the gold required resources to acquire; and the supply of gold was not always responsive to the needs of trade.

Modern money: At this point in the evolution of money, a fundamental innovation occurred. The longer the gold warehouse remained in business, an important fact became clear to Hickenlupper. If the public saw that Hickenlupper's Gold Warehouse always redeemed any promise to pay without difficulty, the public continued to use Hickenlupper's promises to pay as money, and only a small percentage of the promises to pay were actually presented for redemption into gold. The Hickenlupper Gold Warehouse at this point embarked on an innovation that would have profound implications for the monetary and financial systems of the world.

Based on experience and the willingness of the public to use the Hickenlupper promises to pay as money, Hickenlupper realized that a fractional reserve of gold would be sufficient to meet requests for any future conversion of the outstanding promises to pay into gold. Hickenlupper could then issue additional promises to pay and distribute these by making loans to the public. In this manner, Hickenlupper would earn more profit by providing a financial service to the community, since there were always other entrepreneurs with good ideas but no or little money. The borrowers would then use these new promises to pay, called Hickenlupper Bank Notes, as money. There might be a period of time before the public accepted the new promises to pay as money, but, as long as Hickenlupper's Gold Warehouse always redeemed the promises to pay, the two types of promises to pay – gold certificates and bank notes – would circulate as money. Hickenlupper's Gold Warehouse now becomes Hickenlupper's Bank, with the following balance sheet:

Hickenlupper's Bank

Assets		Liabilities	
Commodity money	$1 million	Promises to pay	$10 million
		Gold certificates	$1 million
		Bank notes	$9 million
Loans	$9 million		

The balance sheet assumes Hickenlupper can safely operate with a 10 percent gold reserve against all its promises to pay; that is, the $1 million in gold represents 10 percent of all the outstanding promises to pay.

In this case, $1 million in commodity money (reserve) supports the original $1 million in promises to pay (gold certificates) as well as an additional $9 million in promises to pay in the form of bank notes. In order for this modern money system to work, Hickenlupper had to redeem any promises to pay without difficulty in order to gain and retain public confidence that the promises to pay were always redeemable; had to operate the bank in a transparent manner to gain and retain public confidence that the promises to pay were redeemable; and had to make only loans with a low default risk so as to ensure repayment of the loan assets that backed the new promises to pay. If Hickenlupper failed to meet any of these three conditions, the whole system would collapse and Hickenlupper's promises to pay would no longer be accepted as money.

The new modern system is characterized by four elements. First, it is a *fractional reserve system*, in that only a fraction of the promises to pay are held as a reserve; that is, Hickenlupper's Bank operated with only a 10 percent reserve requirement against promises to pay. Second, it is a *fiat system*, in that the promises to pay issued as the proceeds of the loan are simply defined to have value by the institution. That is, when Hickenlupper makes a $10,000 loan and provides the borrower with $10,000 in bank notes, Hickenlupper is by fiat defining the $10,000 in bank notes as being worth $10,000 in the marketplace. There is only a 10 percent reserve behind all the promises to pay, with the remainder dependent on Hickenlupper's promise to pay. Third, it is a *credit-based system*, since the majority of promises to pay are directly linked to credit. Fourth, it is a *fiduciary-based system*, since it places a fiduciary responsibility on Hickenlupper to operate the firm in a transparent and honest manner and to make only loans that have a high probability of being serviced per the loan contract.

This fractional reserve, fiat, credit and fiduciary system is far more efficient than either of the two commodity-based systems. The new system eliminates many of the problems with any commodity-based system. It is less resource-using because a given amount of commodity money now supports a much larger amount of money in the form of promises to pay. It is more responsive to the needs of trade since economic growth would be matched by increased demand for credit, which would be translated into increased supply of promises to pay as banks expanded credit. During periods of slower economic growth the demand for credit would decline, as would the promises to pay. Thus, the promises to pay were better able to meet the needs of trade than the strict commodity standard.

The modern system began to emerge around the seventeenth century throughout much of the world. It was tied to a commodity such as gold for many years, but by the first part of the twentieth century neither gold nor any commodity played a meaningful role in the nation's money supply any longer. Instead, the reserve itself

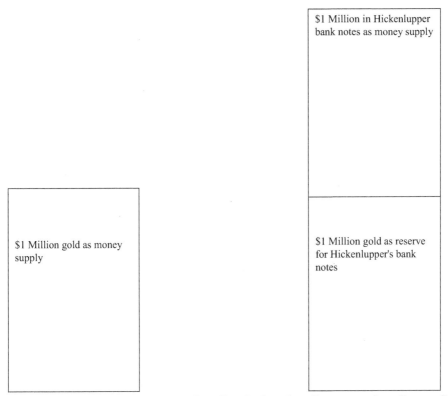

Figure 2.3. Illustration of a Commodity Standard and a Representative Commodity Standard.

became fiat money supplied by central banks, and, instead of bank notes, banks and other depository institutions issued checking accounts. Today Hickenlupper's Bank is now Hickenlupper's Depository Institution, with the following balance sheet:

Hickenlupper's Depository Institution

Assets		Liabilities	
Reserves	$1 million	Promises to pay – checking accounts	$10 million
Loans	$9 million		

The modern system as an inverted pyramid: Comparing the first two stages of Hickenlupper's enterprise to the last stage reveals an important insight into a modern financial and monetary regime. The commodity and representative commodity systems can be represented as an upright box, as in Figure 2.3. The commodity standard is illustrated as an upward-standing box indicating that the money supply consists of $1 million gold. The representative commodity standard is illustrated as

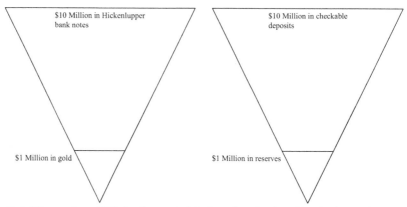

Figure 2.4. Illustration of Hickenlupper's Modern Standard and Today's Modern Standard.

a box twice as high but divided into two equal parts: the bottom or base represents the amount of the commodity ($1 million), which does not circulate as money, and the upper part represents the promises to pay ($1 million), which do circulate as money. In both cases the commodity base of $1 million generates a money supply of $1 million. The representative commodity standard is merely a more efficient way to use the same amount of gold.

Figure 2.4 illustrates the modern system as an inverted pyramid to represent Hickenlupper's modern system and today's modern system. In the case of Hickenlupper, the bottom of the inverted pyramid is the base, consisting of $1 million in gold that, because of fractional reserves, supports a total money supply of $10 million in promises to pay. The ratio of the top part of the inverted pyramid to the bottom is determined by the reserve ratio. The lower (higher) the reserve ratio, the larger (smaller) the top part of the inverted pyramid. Today gold no longer plays a meaningful role in the financial and monetary regime. Instead of gold or any commodity as the base, reserves provided by the central bank represent the base, now referred to as "base money" or "high-powered money". Base money supports all the components of M2 money, some of which have no reserve requirements, such as saving deposits, time deposits and money market funds and checking accounts subject to a fractional reserve. The modern monetary system is well illustrated by the right side of Figure 2.4; however, the actual relationship between base money and money varies over time and is far more complex than illustrated in Figure 2.4. The inverted pyramid will be discussed in more detail in a later chapter, but to gain an appreciation of how this works consider Figure 2.5, which indicates the ratio of M2 money to a measure of the base in the inverted pyramid. Notice that the ratio, while still greater than one, has declined in recent years.

There is a certain irony in the evolution of monetary standards. The introduction of commodity money, followed by the innovation of representative commodity money and, finally, modern money, were largely market innovations. Government

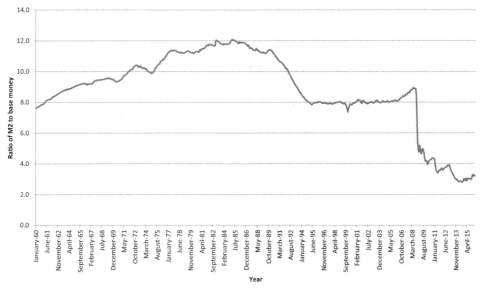

Figure 2.5. Ratio of the Top Part of the Inverted Pyramid, Defined as M2 Money, to the Bottom Part of the Inverted Pyramid, Defined as the Monetary Base, Estimated by the Federal Reserve Bank of St. Louis (SA), January 1960 to April 2016. *Source:* FRED, Federal Reserve Bank of St. Louis.

did not introduce these innovations, though government played a minor role in minting gold and silver coins. As the monetary system evolved to the modern system, certain fragilities in the system began to emerge and required an expanded role on the part of government. Ironically, government was now needed to ensure the system was stable and provided a money supply that supported economic growth. We return to this subject in Chapter 8, when we discuss the detailed role of government in the financial and monetary regime.

2.6 The Relationship between Money and Economic Activity

The previous chapter indicated the importance of a nation's financial and monetary regime for economic performance. A well-functioning financial and monetary regime is a necessary foundation for sustained noninflationary economic growth and an increased standard of living. The concluding section of this chapter focuses more narrowly on how the nation's money supply, which under a modern monetary system is under the control of the central bank, influences economic activity. A useful framework to understand the relationship between money and economic activity at this introductory stage is the quantity theory of money (QTM), which has a long history in the development of economic thinking.

The quantity theory of money: The QTM can be traced to Nicolaus Copernicus in 1517. It was an important part of the Classical School of economics, from 1776 to 1936, when it was criticized by John Maynard Keynes and rejected. The theory reemerged in the 1960s as part of the monetarist–Keynesian debate, and can be used to illustrate the relationship between money and economic performance.

According to the QTM, the price level (and the nominal wage rate) depends on the level of the money supply, other things held constant. In terms of levels of the variables, the QTM can be expressed by

$$MV = PY \qquad (2.2)$$

where M is the nation's money supply; V is the velocity of money, indicating how fast money is exchanged for goods and services; Y is real GDP; and P is the price level. PY is nominal GDP and represents all the final goods purchased and sold at current or market prices. MV is the money supply times the number of transactions used to purchase the GDP. Hence, PY is total spending and MV is how fast the money turned over to support total spending, and, by definition, MV = PY. V is equal to PY/M.

Expression 2.2 can be transformed into changes over time by first expressing the variables as natural logs:

$$\ln M + \ln V = \ln Y + \ln P \qquad (2.3)$$

and then taking the total differential of 2.3 with respect to time to express each variable in terms of a rate of change:

$$m + v = y + p \qquad (2.4)$$

where lower-case characters represent the rate of growth of the upper-case variables.

There are two perspectives of the QTM in Expressions 2.2 and 2.4. First, these are mere definitions without any causative relationship between the variables, much as a balance sheet (assets = liabilities + net worth) is a definition. Balance sheets always balance because they are defined to balance, and the same holds true of M, V, Y and P. To illustrate, in 2000 Y = \$9,817 billion; P = 100, setting the price index base as 2000; M2 = \$4,789. If we define V = \$9,817/\$4,789 = 2.05 then, by definition, MV = YP (\$4,789*2.05 = \$9,817*1.00). In this perspective, Expressions 2.2 and 2.4 are tautologies – true by definition. The second perspective, however, is what economists call the QTM, in that Expressions 2.2 and 2.4 are equilibrium conditions that hold only in equilibrium once the underlying macroeconomic model relationships are balanced. There is a substantial macroeconomic model implied by the equilibrium Expressions 2.2 and 2.4. In the following discussion, this is the perspective of the QTM that is being utilized.

In the long-run version of the QTM, the growth of the money supply does not affect the growth of real output. The growth of real output will be the same as the growth of the economy's potential real output because any significant departure from potential output will generate self-correcting adjustments in wages, prices and interest rates that, in the long run, will return the economy to its natural growth

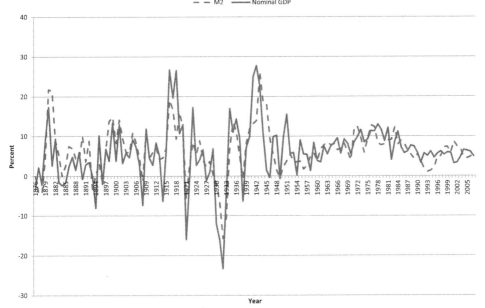

Figure 2.6. Annual Percentage Changes in Nominal GDP (YP) and M2 Money (M), 1876 to 2007. *Source:* Based on data provided by Robert J. Gordon.

path. In the long run, natural and actual unemployment are also equal. In the long-run version of the QTM, the growth of velocity is constant and, as a result, there is a direct relationship between money and prices in the long run.

In the long-run QTM, y is determined by the resource base and structure of the economy, and y equals the growth of potential output; that is, the GDP gap is zero. In the long run, v is constant. Thus, there is a proportional relationship between the growth of money and the growth of prices. Double the growth rate of money and, in the long run, the rate of growth of the price level will also double. In the long-run version of the QTM, money is neutral in the sense that it does not influence real variables, only nominal variables. Consider the game of Monopoly to illustrate this point. Double the amount of money in a game of Monopoly and prices will double if there is no change in the amount of real estate or number of houses and apartments (real variables) and if individuals don't change the rate at which they spend money, because one can spend money only when one has the dice.

Hence, there is a long-run relationship between money and the price level, and, in the long run, money does not change the real performance of the economy. In the long run, inflation and deflation are essentially monetary phenomena. The long-run version of the QTM is widely accepted; however, there is disagreement about how money affects economic performance in the short run. In the short run, changes in the money supply can impact both real output and the price level, and the impact of money on output and prices is not easy to predict because velocity is not stable.

How close is the relationship between money and nominal GDP as suggested by the QTM? Figure 2.6 presents the annual percentage changes in nominal GDP

(YP) and the M2 money supply (M) from 1876 to 2007 for the United States. There is a reasonably close relationship between the two series over time, but there are periods when the relationship is less than others. The simple correlation coefficient between the two series is 0.69, suggesting a long-run relationship.

Considerable research and debate have taken place over the relationship between money and economic activity as summarized by the QTM; however, modern macroeconomic models tend to agree on two results. First, changes in money (M) in the short run influence both real output (Y) and the price level (P). Second, changes in money (M) in the long run have no impact on real output (Y) and influence only the price level (P). In the long run, real output is determined by the resource base and the structure and the technology of the economy. In technical terms, changes in the money supply in the short run are nonneutral, in that money influences the real performance of the economy as well as prices in the short run. In the long run, however, money is neutral, in that money has no influence on the real performance of the economy but only influences prices.

Part II

The Financial System Component of the Financial
and Monetary Regime

Chapter 3

The Financial System and the Country's Flow of Funds

3.1 Introduction

The financial system is a component of the country's financial and monetary regime. The financial system consists of markets and institutions designed to transfer funds from lenders to borrowers through two channels: *direct finance* and *indirect finance*.

Funds transferred through markets constitute direct finance and account for about 30 percent of the flow of funds in the United States. There are two types of financial markets: money markets, which deal in financial instruments with a maturity up to one year, and capital markets, which deal in financial instruments with a maturity greater than one year. Despite the fact that the financial markets represent only about 30 percent of the flow of funds, they are the foundation of the entire financial system. Interest rates are determined in the financial markets directly between lenders and borrowers; financial markets provide liquidity to the rest of the financial system and economy; and some financial markets come about as close to the model of perfect competition as one can find in any economy, because they consist of large numbers of well-informed participants purchasing and selling a well-defined product.

The majority of funds in the United States and in most countries, however, are transferred through financial institutions and referred to as indirect finance, and sometimes *intermediation finance*. Examples of financial institutions are banks, S&Ls, credit unions, insurance companies, pension funds and finance companies. Financial institutions provide not only the majority of financial needs of the economy but also financial services to a larger number of smaller lenders and borrowers than cannot be accommodated in direct financial markets. Direct financial markets support the borrowing needs of large businesses and government, while indirect finance supports the borrowing needs of large and small businesses alike as well as virtually all consumer and mortgage credit needs.

Financial markets and institutions both transfer funds but are considered separately because they represent two distinctly different channels of finance, even though they have important interactions between each other. These interactions have increased dramatically since the 1970s, when deregulation and liberalization of the financial system became an ongoing process.

Financial markets are, essentially, electronic meeting places for lenders and borrowers rather than the usual "bricks and mortar" financial institutions most people think of as the financial system. Financial markets have no ongoing balance sheet. Even though an agent or broker assists in bringing the lender and borrow together and charges a fee for that service, the lending and borrowing transaction does not appear on the agent's or broker's balance sheet. The agent or broker is merely an intermediary who takes no position in the promise to pay that is purchased by the lender and sold by the borrower. In contrast, financial institutions are ongoing financial businesses, are frequently identified as "bricks and mortar" businesses and have an ongoing balance sheet that reflects the lending and borrowing transaction.

The financial system, consisting of both markets and institutions, is complex and continuously evolving over time, as a result of market and regulatory innovations; the increasing economic and financial integration of the world economy; and advances in computer and telecommunications technology. The U.S. financial system and the financial systems of a large number of countries today are much different from how they were even a few decades ago. In addition, the relationship between government and financial systems has also changed significantly. These changes will be discussed in subsequent chapters.

This chapter focuses on developing a general framework to understand the financial system in any given country. Understanding the general framework then makes it easier to understand financial regulation and supervision, changes in the financial system in the past several decades and the financial system of any country. In regard to the latter point, despite the complexity, the basic nature of a financial system is straightforward and can be understood in the context of a *flow of funds framework*. Once a general framework is established the institutional details can be added.

3.2 The Financial System from the Perspective of the Country's Flow of Funds

The flow of funds approach is based on the notion that any economic entity (individual, business, government, financial institution) or an aggregation of economic entities (households, businesses, governments, financial institutions) can be viewed in terms of the sources and uses of the funds that support their economic activity.

There are four steps to understanding the financial system from a flow of funds perspective.

First, the economy is divided into sectors; each sector's real and financial decisions, as reflected by the income and balance sheet statements, can be summarized by the *fundamental flow of funds equation*. In terms of the financial system, each sector is either a surplus, deficit or balanced unit.

Second, three perspectives, or what it means for a sector to be a surplus, deficit or balanced unit, are developed, each of which permits us to define the financial system as bringing the three units together to transfer funds.

Third, there are two channels through which funds can be transferred between surplus, deficit and balanced units: direct and indirect finance.

Fourth, a flow of funds matrix for the entire economy can be constructed to bring all the elements of the financial system together.

3.3 Sector Budgets, Income and Balance Sheets and the Fundamental Flow of Funds Equation

The economy is divided into five sectors: *household sector*, *nonfinancial business sector*, *government sector*, *financial institutions sector* and *international sector*. There is no sector for financial markets because financial markets themselves do not have a balance sheet with assets representing lending and with liabilities representing borrowing. Again, financial markets are merely meeting places for lenders and borrowers, facilitated by an agent or broker who takes no position in the transaction. Once a transaction is completed, the changes in assets and liabilities show up only on the lender's and borrower's respective balance sheets.

Sectors and their budgets: The following discussion presents a simplified version of the official flow of funds accounts maintained by the Federal Reserve to highlight the essential nature of the financial system. Each of the five sectors can be characterized in terms of a budget of receipts as sources of funds and expenditures as uses of funds.

The household sector obtains receipts by supplying labor services in exchange for wages and spends the receipts on goods and services. Expenditures on goods are divided into nondurable and durable categories. Nondurable expenditures consist of spending on goods that last no longer than a year, such as food or services. Durable expenditures consist of spending on goods that last longer than a year, such as a car or house. Every year, however, a portion of durable goods becomes nondurable goods because of depreciation.

The nonfinancial business sector consists of corporations, unincorporated businesses and small businesses, which obtain their receipts by selling goods and services and use those receipts to pay ongoing expenses of doing business, investing in plant and equipment and earning a profit. Nonfinancial business sector spending is divided into nondurable and durable expenditures, like the household sector, in terms of how long the item purchases lasts.

The government sector obtains its receipts from taxes and fees and uses its receipts to support government spending, which consists mainly of wages paid to government workers and transfers or entitlements to specific groups in the economy.

The international sector is also part of the U.S. flow of funds system, since the rest of the world lends to the United States – referred to as a financial inflow from the perspective of the United States – and borrows from the United States – referred to as a financial outflow. The international sector has been a net lender to the U.S. financial system because of trade and current account imbalances with the rest of the world for the past several decades.

The financial institutions sector obtains its receipts in the form of deposits and other financial sources of funds and uses its receipts to make loans and financial investments.

The budget of any sector has only three outcomes:

1 balanced budget (receipts equal expenditures);
2 surplus budget (receipts exceed expenditures); or,
3 deficit budget (expenditures exceed receipts).

Historically, the household sector is a surplus budget sector because most of the households in the sector in a given period do not make large expenditures on durable goods such as cars and houses that greatly exceed their receipts. This has not been the case, however, in recent years, as the household sector often operates as a deficit sector. The business sector is historically a deficit sector because much of its uses of funds are for investment in plant, equipment and development that cannot be covered by receipts. The government sector is supposed to be a balanced sector but governments have many incentives to spend more than they receive in tax revenue and, hence, operate as a deficit sector frequently. The international sector can be either a surplus or deficit sector depending on the real and financial relationship between the United States and the rest of the world. In the past several decades the international sector has been a surplus sector. Finally, the financial institutions sector by definition is a balanced sector since the uses of funds (lending) are the same as the sources of funds (borrowing); that is, in terms of a budget, receipts and expenditures are identical.

To understand how each sector can be represented in a flow of funds framework, we consider the income statement and balance sheet of a general nonfinancial sector to derive the fundamental flow of funds equation. The general nonfinancial sector is represented by an individual household in the household sector. Aggregating the fundamental flow of funds equations for each household then provides the fundamental flow of funds equation for the household sector. It is then straightforward to apply the framework to any sector, including the financial institutions sector.

Sector income statement and balance sheet: Table 3.1 illustrates the income statement of an individual household. The sources of funds (receipts) are placed on the right side of the T account while the uses of funds are placed on the left side. Uses of funds are bifurcated into current expenditures and saving. Current

Table 3.1. *Income Statement for the Hickenlupper Household*

Uses of funds		Sources of funds	
Current expenditures	$30,000	Receipts	$50,000
Saving	$20,000		
Total	$50,000		$50,000

expenditures are expenditures on goods that last no longer than a year and services. Saving is a balancing item that balances the two sides of the T account. Saving is the difference between current expenditures and receipts and can be zero (receipts equal current expenditures), positive (receipts exceed current expenditures) or negative (current expenditures exceed receipts). That is, saving is the balancing item to ensure that uses and sources of funds balance.

In Table 3.1 saving is a positive $20,000 because receipts of $50,000 exceed current expenditures of $30,000 by the amount of $20,000. There is no reason why saving should be positive; for example, if current expenditures and receipts are equal, saving is zero, and, if current expenditures exceed receipts, saving is negative.

Where does saving show up in this household's activity? Saving shows up in the balance sheet; however, the balance sheet in the flow of funds perspective needs to be considered as a flow rather than a stock statement. The balance sheet is normally presented as a measure of the level of assets, liabilities and net worth at a point in time and is thus regarded as a stock statement because it records the stock of assets, liabilities and net worth at a specific point in time. In contrast, the income statement records receipts, current expenditures and saving over a specific period of time and, hence, is a flow statement. The balance sheet can be transformed from a stock to a flow statement by expressing assets, liabilities and net worth in terms of changes or flows from one period to another. That is, instead of examining the balance sheet as of December 31, 2015, we examine the change in balance sheet components from December 31, 2014, to December 31, 2015.

Table 3.2 illustrates the household's balance sheet based on a specific set of assumptions about how the household uses its saving. Assets are divided into real and financial assets. Real assets are items that last longer than a year and financial assets are claims on someone else's income or wealth. The change in net worth is

Table 3.2. *Balance Sheet in Flow Terms for the Hickenlupper Household*

Uses of funds		Sources of funds	
Δ Assets			
Δ Real assets	+$5,000	Δ Liabilities	−$5,000
Δ Financial assets	+$10,000	Δ Net worth	$20,000

$20,000 in Table 3.2 and equals the amount of saving in Table 3.1. Saving from the income statement and net worth from the balance sheet tie the two statements together. This is not a coincidence; in fact, whatever the value of saving from the income statement, saving equals the change in net worth in the balance sheet. The transactions in assets and liabilities generate the change in net worth, which must be equal to the saving from the income statement.

Consider the $20,000 saving in Table 3.1. What does the household do with the $20,000 value of saving? There are many ways to dispense with the $20,000 in saving, all of which will change assets, liabilities or both in such a manner that the resulting change in net worth will equal saving. In Table 3.2, the household purchases a real asset, such as a home theater system, for $5,000. Real assets thus increase by $5,000. The household increases holding of M2 money by $2,000, purchases life insurance for $2,000 and purchases corporate and government securities of $6,000. Financial assets in total thus increase by $10,000. The household uses the remainder of saving to reduce outstanding debt by $5,000. The combined effect of the change in real assets, financial assets and liabilities is an increase in net worth by $20,000, which is exactly the same as saving in the income statement. In fact, no matter what combination of changes on the balance sheet, the change in net worth will equal the saving from the income statement.

It is also easy to see from Tables 3.1 and 3.2 how a household can operate with negative saving; that is, the excess of current expenditures over receipts is accommodated by a decline in net worth. The decline in net worth can be accommodated by selling a real asset, such as a car, which reduces real assets; selling corporate and government bonds, which reduces financial assets; or by increased borrowing, which increases liabilities.

To construct an income statement and balance sheet statement for the entire household sector we simply aggregate the receipts, current expenditures, saving, change in real and financial assets, change in liabilities and change in net worth. In the case of the other sectors, we merely change the description of receipts and current expenditures.

Fundamental flow of funds equation: The income statement and balance sheet can be used to determine the fundamental flow of funds equation for each sector derived in the following two steps.

First, expand the basic balance sheet to distinguish between real and financial assets:

$$\Delta A = \Delta LIAB + \Delta NW$$
$$\Delta A = \Delta RA + \Delta FA$$
$$\Delta RA + \Delta FA = \Delta LIAB + \Delta NW \qquad (3.1)$$

where A, LIAB and NW represent assets, liabilities and net worth, respectively; RA and FA represent real and financial assets, respectively; and Δ represents the change of each from one period to another.

Second, change the terminology of the expanded balance sheet in the following ways. Substitute investment, I, for the change in RA; substitute lending, L, for the change in FA; substitute borrowing, B, for the change in LIAB; and substitute saving, S, for the change in net worth. Rewrite the expanded balance sheet with the new terminology as

$$I + L = B + S \tag{3.2}$$

and rearrange Expression 3.2 to derive the fundamental flow of funds equation:

$$I = S + (B - L) \tag{3.3}$$

Expression 3.3 is derived from a sector's income and balance sheet statement and reflects real economic activity (I and S) and financial activity (B and L). This fundamental flow of funds equation provides the foundation for understanding the nation's financial system.

3.4 The Financial System in Terms of Surplus, Deficit and Balanced Sectors

The financial system can be viewed as a collection of institutions and markets that transfer funds from entities with surplus budgets to entities with deficit budgets. The surplus unit has more liquidity than needed and is willing to provide funds to the financial system by holding financial assets or promises to pay depending on the interest rate. The higher the interest rate, the more willing the surplus unit to hold interest-earning financial assets instead of money or real assets. The deficit unit is in need of liquidity and willing to pay interest to obtain that liquidity by issuing promises to pay, which become the financial assets held by the surplus unit.

That is, the financial system is illustrated by surplus units on one side and deficit units on the other side, but, as we will see, the balanced sector plays a role in the financial system even though it is neither a net demander nor a net supplier of funds. There are three different ways to define surplus, deficit (and balanced) sectors.

First, they can be defined in terms of the relationship between total receipts, TR, and total expenditures, TE, keeping in mind that $TE = CE + I$:

Surplus Unit
   $TR > TE$;
Deficit Unit
   $TR < TE$; and
Balanced Unit
   $TR = TE$

Second, they can be defined in terms of saving and investment in the follow manner, keeping in mind that $S = TR - CE$:

Table 3.3. *Definitions of Surplus, Deficit and Balanced Unit*

Surplus unit	Deficit unit	Balanced unit
TR > TE	TR < TE	TR = TE
TR > CE + I	TR < CE + I	TR = CE + I
TR − CE > I	TR − CE < I	TR − CE = I
S > I	S < I	S = I
L > B	L < B	L = B

Third, combining the relationship between S and I for each unit and the fundamental flow of funds equation, we can define surplus, deficit and balanced units in terms of lending and borrowing as illustrated in Table 3.3. Based on Expression 3.3, if S > I, then lending > borrowing, and, if S < I, then borrowing > lending. If S = I and L = B, the balanced sector provides funds to and obtains funds from the financial system. The advantage of the third perspective is that it emphasizes that balanced units play a role in the financial system even though they are not net lenders or borrowers.

Table 3.3 indicates the three different ways to define a surplus, deficit and balanced unit. The financial system can then be thought of as a collection of markets and institutions that bring surplus, deficit and balanced units together, though on a net basis the financial system places the surplus unit on the supply side and the deficit unit on the demand side. Of the three perspectives of the surplus, deficit and balanced unit, the third, based on lending and borrowing, is the most useful.

Surplus units are net lenders to the financial system, deficit units are net borrowers from the financial system and balanced units lend and borrow in equal amounts, but nonetheless are serviced by the financial system. The net lender/net borrower perspective is important for constructing a flow of funds matrix of the economy; however, the financial system can also be illustrated as lenders on one side supplying funds and borrowers on the other side demanding funds.

Table 3.4 illustrates the financial system in terms of lenders on the side supplying funds and borrowers on the other side demanding funds. Note that each sector shows up on both sides of the financial system. Based on the fundamental flow of funds equation in Expression 3.3, a lender may be a surplus unit (S > I and L > B), a deficit unit (S < I and L < B) or a balanced unit (S = I and L = B). In all three cases, lending takes place. Likewise, a borrower may be a surplus unit (S > I and L > B), a deficit unit (S < I and L < B) or a balanced unit (S = I and L = B). In all three cases, borrowing takes place. Table 3.4 also illustrates the two channels of finance discussed in the next section.

3.5 Two Channels of Finance: Direct and Indirect Finance

Irrespective of how we characterize the financial system, any financial transaction involves an act of supplying funds and an act of demanding funds. Funds can be

Table 3.4. *Financial System in Terms of Lenders and Borrowers*

Nonfinancial lenders	Nonfinancial borrowers
Households	Households
Businesses	Businesses
Federal government	Federal government
Local and state governments	Local and state governments
Foreign	Foreign

Direct finance

Lenders supply funds directly to borrowers through money and capital markets. The lender purchases a promise to pay instrument issued by the borrower. The promise to pay instrument becomes an asset held by the lender and a liability of the borrower to the lender.

Indirect finance

Lenders supply funds to a financial institution by purchasing promises to pay issued by the financial institution (deposits, insurance policies, pension policies), which become an asset held by the lender and a liability of the financial institution. The financial institution then lends the funds received from the lender by purchasing promises to pay issued by the borrower. The borrower's promise to pay becomes an asset held by the financial institution and a liability of the borrower to the financial institution.

supplied and demanded through financial markets or financial institutions. We can think of the supply of funds as purchasing a financial asset or promise to pay and the demand for funds as selling a financial asset or promise to pay.

Direct finance: Direct finance occurs when the lender deals directly with the borrower on an "eye-to-eye" basis or through an agent or broker. The key element of direct finance is that the lender accepts the borrower's promise to pay and assumes whatever risk and other conditions are embedded in the promise to pay. Direct finance takes place through financial markets in which promises to pay or financial instruments are purchased by lenders and sold by borrowers. The purchased financial instrument becomes an asset to the lender and the sold financial instrument becomes a liability to the borrower; for example, when the U.S. government sells a bond in the bond market, the government is the borrower and the bond becomes a liability on the government's balance sheet, while the purchaser of the bond is the lender and the bond becomes a financial asset on the lender's balance sheet. Financial markets in the United States are the broadest, deepest and most diversified in the world.

Table 3.5 lists the most important financial instruments used in direct U.S. financial markets bifurcated by maturity. Financial instruments up to one year in maturity are *money market instruments* and those longer than one year in maturity are *capital market instruments*. Table 3.4 also indicates whether the instrument has default risk and a secondary market. Default risk is the probability that the issuer of the financial instrument will not service the debt by not paying the interest, the

Table 3.5. *Money and Capital Market Instruments Used in Direct Finance*

Financial instrument	Description	Degree of default risk	Secondary market
Money market instruments			
Treasury bills (T-bills)	Issued by the federal government in maturities up to one year; they pay no interest coupon and, hence, are sold at a discount – sold at a price lower than the face value of the Treasury bill.	None	Active
Large certificates of deposits (CDs)	Issued by large banks in denominations of $100,000 or larger and are legally negotiable; that is, they can be sold to another entity before maturity and issued in a range of maturities.	Amounts above $250,000	Modest
Commercial paper	Short-term debt issued by banks and nonfinancial business entities with maturities up to nine months.	Yes	Modest
Repurchase agreements (repos)	Banks, nonfinancial entities or any entity that holds securities used as collateral for the repo. The issuer uses securities such as T-bills for collateral. The issuer sells the repo with a promise to repurchase it in a short period of time, usually "overnight" or less than two weeks.	Determined by default risk of securities	None
Federal funds	"Overnight" loans of reserve balances held by a bank at the Federal Reserve to another bank with a deposit account at the Federal Reserve. Federal funds are not loans by the federal government or Federal Reserve. The name comes from the fact that funds are transferred from the lending bank to the borrowing bank via the Federal Reserve's wire transfer facility. The interest rate on federal funds, called the federal funds rate, is a key variable in the conduct of monetary policy.	Depends on default risk of bank	None
Capital market instruments			
Equities or stock	Issued by financial and nonfinancial corporations without any maturity.	Yes	Active
Corporate bonds	Issued by financial and nonfinancial corporations in a wide range of maturities up to 20 and 30 years.	Yes	Active
Treasury notes (T-notes)	Issued by the federal government in maturities up to ten years.	No	Active

Table 3.5 (*continued*)

Financial instrument	Description	Degree of default risk	Secondary market
Treasury bonds (T-bonds)	Issued by the federal government in maturities greater than ten years and up to 30 years.	No	Active
Municipals	Bonds issued by local, regional and state governments of up to 30 years in maturity.	Yes	Moderate
U.S. government agency securities or U.S. government-sponsored enterprise (GSE) securities	Issued by agencies supported by government, but not guaranteed by government. Prominent agencies are: Student Loan Marketing Association (Sallie Mae); Federal National Mortgage Association (Fannie Mae); Federal Home Loan Mortgage Corporation (Freddie Mac); Government National Mortgage Association (Ginnie Mae); the 11 Federal Home Loan banks; Federal Farm Credit banks. GSEs issue bonds of up to 30 years in maturity to obtain funds and then loan the funds to selected sectors of the economy.	Technically, yes; but have built in an implicit government guarantee	Active
Mortgages and mortgage-backed bonds	Mortgages are long-term loans issued by banks, S&Ls, savings banks, credit unions and mortgage brokers. The mortgages are then sold, in many cases to mortgage-related GSEs, which hold the mortgages or bundle them into a mortgage-backed bond to sell in the capital market.	Yes	Active

principal or both. Federal government debt is regarded as default-free because the central government has the ability to issue more debt to service or pay off maturing debt; increase tax revenue; or increase the money supply through the central bank. History shows, however, this may not always be the case.

In August 2011 Standard & Poor made a slight downward credit rating of U.S. government debt, from AAA to AA+; however, the other rating agencies, Moody's Investor Service and Fitch Ratings, did not follow suit. Despite this rating change, U.S. government debt, including currency and coin, has zero default risk. At the same time, governments have defaulted on their debt, and the slight downgrade of U.S. debt is a reminder of that fact. In contrast to federal debt, debt instruments issued by local, regional or state governments possess some degree of default risk because the issuers of these instruments do not have the same ability as the federal government to issue new debt to service old debt; nor do they have the same degree of power to raise taxes. All private financial instruments in Table 3.4, with the exception of that portion of large CDs issued by banks up to $250,000, possess some degree of default risk.

Limitations of direct financial markets: Financial markets in the United States represent about 30 percent of the flow of funds at any time. They are national and international in scope. However, direct finance presents limitations for small lenders and borrowers.

First, financial instruments are issued with a fixed face value and, hence, require a coincidence of denomination; second, financial instruments with the exception of stocks are issued with fixed maturity and, hence, require a coincidence of maturity; third, financial instruments require some degree of technical knowledge to sell and purchase, which is not a common denominator among smaller lenders and borrowers; fourth, small lenders lack the ability to evaluate and monitor the creditworthiness of borrowers; fifth, small lenders are not able to diversify because of insufficient funds; and, sixth, small lenders and borrowers lack the resources and the ability to obtain and provide information to evaluate credit risk and monitor credit.

These restrictions create a fundamental problem for small lenders and borrowers in direct markets. The small borrower has difficulty borrowing in direct markets because the minimum denomination of instruments is large and the small borrower lacks the resources to provide financial disclosure to the potential lenders in the direct market so that they can evaluate risk. Small lenders have a different problem, in that the risk–return tradeoff of the small lender is likely incompatible with any borrower, small or large. This can be illustrated with the risk–return tradeoff curves illustrated in Figure 3.1.

The risk–return tradeoff is an upward-sloping curve for a given level of utility for different portfolios of expected return and risk. The lender's utility is a positive function of the expected return of the portfolio and an inverse function of the risk of the portfolio. A risk–return curve closer to the vertical axis implies a more risk-averse lender and, for any given curve, the steeper the curve, the more risk-averse the lender. In Figure 3.1 the risk–return curve RR1 is the base curve for a large lender, indicating the lender's tradeoff between return and risk. RR1 indicates that the lender will incur risk only if compensated by a higher expected return. There are special exceptions to the tradeoff illustrated by RR1, but they are not important for the normal operation of the financial system.

RR2 is closer to the origin and steeper and represents the risk–return tradeoff of a small lender relative to the base lender. Since RR2 is closer to the vertical axis, the lender will demand a higher expected return for the same level of risk as illustrated with RR1. RR2 is not only closer to the vertical axis but steeper than RR1, because, for this lender, an increase in risk must be compensated with a larger increase in expected return than for the base lender.

Expected return

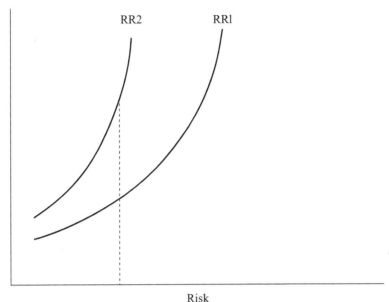

Risk

Figure 3.1. Risk–Return Tradeoff for Small Lender versus Base Lender Shows Small Lender Will Require Higher Expected Return for a Given Level of Risk.

What accounts for the difference? The small lender is unable to diversify and thus forced to put more eggs in one basket than the base lender. The small lender is unable to spend the same resources as the base lender to evaluate and monitor credit. The small lender lacks the detailed knowledge of the technicalities of direct finance of the base lender. As a result, the small lender in direct finance will have a tradeoff curve closer to the vertical axis and steeper than that of the base lender.

To illustrate how small lenders are at a disadvantage in direct finance, assume that a lender is contemplating making a loan for $50,000 to a borrower for five years; thus, there is no problem with a coincidence of denomination and maturity. But, given the lender's degree of risk aversion, the lender requires an expected rate of return of 20 percent. Assume the borrower is a business that wants to use the $50,000 over the five-year period to expand plant and equipment to generate more revenue. The borrower analyzes the cost and revenue flow of the expansion, then computes an internal rate of return that equalizes the present value of the revenue and cost stream to determine how much interest he/she can afford to render the expansion profitable. Assume the internal rate of return is 10 percent; that is, the investment is profitable if the borrower can borrow $50,000 at less than 10 percent. The lender, however, is unwilling to lend the $50,000 at any rate less than 10 percent. As a result, there is an incompatibility between the risk–return tradeoff of the lender and the default risk of the borrower, and no lending and borrowing will take place.

The risk–return tradeoff of the small lender is incompatible with the requirements of the borrower. No financial transaction will take place. The small borrower also is restricted in the direct markets because of a lack of resources to provide information for the lender to evaluate risk. In contrast, large lenders and borrowers, because of the amount of funds they are willing to loan and borrow, respectively, have the resources and knowledge to evaluate and monitor credit, in the case of the lender, and to provide financial disclosure, in the case of the borrower. Most importantly, the large lender can diversify the loan portfolio and reduce systemic risk. Thus, small lenders and borrowers are not welcomed in the direct financial markets.

Indirect or intermediation finance provides increased access to the financial system: The problems of direct finance for small lenders and borrowers are resolved by indirect or intermediation finance. In indirect finance a financial institutions is placed between the lender and borrower and fundamentally changes the relationship between them. In direct finance, the lender assumes all of the risk and other characteristics of the promise to pay offered by the borrower, and for many small lenders and small borrowers this excludes them from the market. Indirect finance eliminates this problem, as well as other restrictions, such as the need for a coincidence of maturity and denomination.

The role of the financial institution in the financial system can be illustrated with the fundamental flow of funds equation (Expression 3.3) for the financial institutions sector. There are two major differences between Expression 3.3 for a financial institution and the other sectors of the economy. First, a financial institution, by definition, is a firm primarily focused on collecting funds and distributing those funds in the form of loans and investments, and, as a result, I and S are relatively small parts of Expression 3.3 compared to B and L. Second, financial institutions, by definition, largely distribute what they collect since they are required to pay interest or offer other services to obtain funds to lend, and, as a result, financial institutions are essentially balanced budget entities. Not only are I and S relatively small compared to B and L, but I = S and B = L.

Take the example of a depository financial institution. The institution borrows by offering deposits, which are insured up to \$250,000; deposits are offered in small to large denominations and deposits are offered in short to long maturities. The lenders to a depository institution thus in most cases have zero default risk, retain flexibility in the denomination and maturity of their lending to the depository intuition and still earn an interest rate. In addition, the promise to pay can be used as money. The depository institution uses the accumulated funds to lend. Because the depository institution specializes in credit evaluation and credit monitoring, it can evaluate default risk better than any small lender. Because the depository institution can make loans to many borrowers and thus put its eggs in many baskets, the overall risk of the loan portfolio is far less than for any small lender. As a result, the depository institution can lend to riskier borrowers than could any small lender.

Table 3.6. *Important Financial Institutions that Constitute Indirect Finance*

	Borrowing (sources of funds)	Lending (uses of funds)
Depository financial institutions		
Commercial banks	Checking, saving and time deposits, and large CDs	Consumer and business loans; mortgages; Treasury securities; and municipal securities
S&Ls	Checking, saving and time deposits	Mostly mortgage loans, but also consumer loans
Savings banks	Checking, saving and time deposits	Mostly mortgage loans, but also consumer loans
Credit unions	Checking, saving and time deposits	Mostly consumer loans, but also mortgage loans
Nondepository financial institutions		
Contractual savings institutions		
Life insurance companies	Life insurance policies	Corporate bonds, equity and mortgages
Casualty insurance companies	Casualty insurance policies	Corporate bonds, equity and mortgages
Pension funds	Retirement policies – employer and employee contributions	Corporate bonds and equity
Investment institutions		
Finance companies	Finance paper, bonds and equities	Consumer and business loans
Money market funds	Shares	Money market instruments
Mutual funds	Shares	Bonds and equities

Financial institutions are divided into two types depending primarily on their borrowing or sources of funds: depository and nondepository financial institutions. Nondepository institutions are further divided into contractual saving and investment institutions. The most important financial institutions are described in Table 3.6.

Depository institutions consist of banks, S&Ls, savings banks and credit unions. S&Ls, savings banks and credit unions are collectively referred to as *thrifts*. The term "thrift" evolved decades ago, when these nonbank depository institutions did not offer checking accounts, only saving and time deposits; however, they now function much like banks in many respects, but the term "thrift" is still used even though not accurate.

Depository institutions offer a promise to pay in the form of checking deposits, and saving and time deposits. Of the three, banks are the largest in number and size. There are about 6,500 banks, compared to about 800 S&Ls and savings banks and 7,500 credit unions. Banks are the most diversified of all financial institutions, deal with the largest number of lenders and borrowers and are at the center of the nation's financial and monetary regime. While S&Ls, savings banks and credit unions play a smaller role in the financial system, they have become more similar to banks during the past few decades but still tend to specialize to a greater extent than banks.

Nondepository financial institutions are fundamentally the same as depository institutions in terms of their role in the flow of funds; however, their promises to pay (borrowing in Expression 3.3) are less liquid and, as a result, not part of the money supply, with the exception of retail money market funds. However, their promises to pay offer important financial services and, because their sources of funds are less liquid, they can make a wider range of loans with longer maturity than depository institutions. Life insurance companies illustrate this point. Life insurance companies offer life insurance policies as a means of obtaining funds (B in Expression 3.3), which, even though not very liquid, provide important services to the insured. Likewise, because their sources of funds are long-term in nature, life insurance companies can make long-term loans.

Nondepository financial institutions are usually divided into two groups: contractual savings institutions (life insurance companies, casualty insurance companies, and private and government pension funds) and investment institutions (finance companies, money market funds that invest in money market instruments, and mutual funds that invest in capital market instruments).

Interaction between direct and indirect finance: The two channels of finance are analytically different, but they are closely interrelated as a result of extensive innovations in the financial system over the past several decades. Many loans, especially mortgage loans, generated in indirect finance are bundled into a security that is then sold in the direct markets. Treasury securities and municipal securities are held by financial institutions, as are commercial paper, corporate bonds and even equities to varying degrees. Hence, the distinction between the two channels is real, but in many ways the two channels overlap.

3.6 Bringing It Together: A Flow of Funds Matrix of the Economy

The financial system can now be summarized by a simple flow of funds matrix of the economy based on the actual matrix published by the Federal Reserve; in fact, most central banks of the world compute and publish detailed flow of funds statistics that highlight the role of the financial system in the economy, indicate who is lending and who is borrowing, indicate who the net suppliers and demanders of funds are and indicate the amounts of finance that go through direct and indirect channels.

Table 3.7 is based on dividing the economy into three real sectors and a financial institutions sector. Again, there is no sector for direct finance, since direct finance exists only for the time it takes to exchange funds for a promise to pay. A fundamental flow of funds equation is constructed for each sector. The top two rows of Table 3.7 indicate S and I for each sector. The household sector is a surplus sector, with S exceeding I by $110,000; that is, the household sector is a net lender to the financial system. How did the household sector distribute the surplus or be a net

Table 3.7. *Flow of Funds Matrix of the Financial System*

Fundamental flow of funds equation	Household	Business	Government	Financial institutions	Total
Investment	$20,000	$100,000		$5,000	$125,000
Saving	$130,000	$50,000	−$60,000	$5,000	$125,000
Surplus (+), deficit (−) or balance (0)	$110,000	−$50,000	−$60,000	$0	$0
Borrowing (net change in liabilities)	−$10,000	$60,000	$60,000	$60,000	$170,000
Checking deposits				$40,000	$40,000
Saving and time deposits				$20,000	$20,000
Loans	−$10,000	$20,000			$10,000
Treasury securities			$60,000		$60,000
Corporate securities		$40,000			$40,000
Lending (net change in financial assets)	$100,000	$10,000	$0	$60,000	$170,000
Checking deposits	$30,000	$10,000			$40,000
Saving and time deposits	$20,000				$20,000
Loans	$0			$10,000	$10,000
Treasury securities	$30,000			$30,000	$60,000
Corporate securities	$20,000			$20,000	$40,000
Net lender	$110,000				
Net borrower		$50,000	$60,000		
Balanced entity				$0	$0

lender? The household sector reduced its borrowing by $10,000 by paying off a loan owed to the financial institutions sector. The household sector increased its lending by increasing its holdings of promises to pay in four ways: increased checking deposits ($30,000); increased saving and time deposits ($20,000); increased Treasury securities ($30,000); and increased corporate securities ($20,000).

The nonfinancial business sector is a deficit unit, with I exceeding S by $50,000, and thus has a net demand of funds from the financial system. How did the business sector finance its deficit of $50,000? The business sector borrowed $60,000 by selling $40,000 in corporate securities and taking a loan of $20,000 from the financial institutions sector. The business sector sold $20,000 of securities to the household sector and $20,000 of securities to the financial institutions sector. The business sector also was a lender because it increased its checking deposits by $10,000. Hence, the business sector is a net demander of funds of $50,000.

All government expenditures are considered current expenditures, so that any deficit, surplus or balance in the budget is indicated by negative, positive or zero S. In Table 3.7 the government sector is operating with a deficit of $60,000, which is financed by selling $60,000 of Treasury securities. The household and financial institutions sectors each purchased $30,000.

The financial institutions sector is a balanced entity, since S = I, and a financial entity, since its real transactions – represented by S and I – are small compared to its borrowing and lending. The funds or borrowing come from issuing checking deposits to the household sector ($30,000) and business sector ($10,000) and issuing saving and time deposits to the household sector ($20,000). In addition, the financial sector received a payment of $10,000 for an outstanding loan to the household sector, which is netted against lending of $20,000 to the business sector. The financial sector loaned a net of $10,000 – a $20,000 loan to the business sector and a –$10,000 loan to the household sector.

Table 3.7 indicates five important aspects of the financial system.

First, the financial system is a collection of deficit, surplus and balanced units engaged in lending and borrowing to support their real transactions, represented by saving and investment.

Second, lending and borrowing take place through direct and indirect finance. Direct finance occurs when the household and financial institutions sectors purchase government securities in the open market and when the household sector purchases corporate securities in the open market. The securities are purchased in a market with the assistance of an agent or broker; that is, they show up on the balance sheets of the household, business, government and financial institutions sectors only since the broker facilitates the transfer for a fee. Indirect finance, however, does manifest itself on the balance sheet of financial institutions.

Third, while direct and indirect finance are fundamentally different, they are interrelated; for example, the financial institutions sector not only provides loans to households and businesses but is also a participant in the direct financial markets. In Table 3.7 the financial institutions sector purchased directly from the business and government sectors promises to pay with funds obtained from deposits held by the household and business sectors.

Fourth, lending and borrowing are not necessarily equal for each sector, but, when all sectors are combined, lending equals borrowing because every act of lending is an act of borrowing. Lending equals borrowing and saving equals investment for the entire economy even though they can be unequal for individual sectors.

Fifth, financial institutions are fundamentally different from the three real sectors because their real transactions pale in comparison to their lending and borrowing and, by and large, their lending and borrowing are equal because that is their nature – they are an institutional conduit to transfer funds from one group to another.

Chapter 4

Interest Rates in the Financial System

4.1 Introduction

Interest rates are key variables in the nation's economy and determined by the inter-action of lenders and borrowers in the financial system. Interest rates and changes in interest rates impact virtually every type of private and public spending, the finan-cial health of private and public enterprises, the value of wealth of individuals and the nation, and the economic and financial relationship a country has with the rest of the world. Not only are interest rates a key variable in every lending and borrow-ing transaction, they are the focal point of monetary policy. Virtually every central bank conducts policy by setting an interest rate target and then uses its tools of monetary policy to achieve that target. The interest rate target indicates the direc-tion of monetary policy. Lacking basic knowledge about interest rates is clearly dangerous to your own economic health, aside from the more general problem of being clueless about monetary policy and the financial system in general.

This and the next two chapters discuss interest rates from three perspectives. In this chapter, the following basic concepts needed to understand interest rates are discussed: the essential nature of the interest rate; the distinction between interest rates in indirect and direct finance; efforts by government to regulate interest rates; and basic technical aspects of interest rates. In the next chapter, the determinants of the level of interest rates in terms of the flow of funds framework are outlined. This framework can then explain why interest rates change over time. In that discussion, we lump all interest rates together into just one interest rate to focus on the basic determinants of the *level of the interest rate*, which can then be applied to any one of the many interest rates in the financial system. In the chapter after next, the assumption of one interest rate is dropped to focus on the *structure of interest rates*. The structure of interest rates explains how different interest rates are related to each other and how key elements of the relationship are used to measure risk in the financial system; indicate changes in the public's expected inflation; and indicate the probability the economy will expand in the future or the probability the economy will contract in the future.

4.2 Interest Rates Connect the Present to the Future, and Vice Versa

The interest rate is a key element of the transfer of funds from lender to borrower in any financial transaction, whether lending funds indirectly to borrowers through indirect finance (financial institutions) or directly through direct finance (money and capital markets). The interest rate is the return to the lender for providing the funds and the cost of the funds to the borrower. Interest rates relate the present to the future; that is, the interest rate ties the present to the future and the future to the present. This is illustrated by the concept of future and present value. The future value of A dollars loaned at the start of the first period earning r percent per period for m periods is

$$A_m = A_1(1 + r)^m \qquad (4.1)$$

where A_1 is the amount of dollars loaned at the start of the first period; r is the interest rate expressed as a fraction – that is, r is the interest rate in percentage terms divided by 100 (5.0% is expressed as 0.05); and A_m is the future amount of the A_1 dollars invested at the start of the first period for m periods. Expression 4.1 indicates the future or appreciated amount of A dollars earning r for any period. Assume $A_1 = \$100$ and $r = 0.10$; then A_m is \$110 for $m = 1$ [\$100 $(1 + .10)^1$]; \$161.05 for $m = 5$ [\$100 $(1 + .10)^5$]; and \$259.37 for $m = 10$ [\$100 $(1 + .10)^{10}$]. Because interest rates are positive, the future value of A dollars is always larger than the value of A dollars at the start of the first period.

The present value of A future dollars at the end of m periods is equal to the amount of dollars invested at the start of the first period earning r percent. Expression 4.1 can be reversed to illustrate the value of any future amount in terms of today's value or the present value of the future amount

$$A_1 = A_m / (1 + r)^m \qquad (4.2)$$

where A_1 represents today's value at the start of the first period or present value of the future value of A_m dollars at the end of period m. In terms of the above example, the present value of \$110 received at the end of the first period ($m = 1$) is \$100 if the interest rate is 0.10; the present value of \$161.05 received at the end of the fifth period ($m = 5$) is \$100 if the interest rate is 0.10; and the present value of \$259.37 received at the end of the tenth period ($m = 10$) is \$100 if the interest rate is 0.10. Hence, the interest rate ties the present to the future, and vice versa.

In a lending–borrowing relationship, the lender is willing to give up liquidity for a return that satisfies their risk–return tradeoff; that is, lenders will not lend funds they could use today for some purpose unless they are paid for giving up that liquidity. The borrower needs liquidity today and is willing to pay a return on the borrowed funds. The interest rate is the market's balance between the wants of the lender and the borrower; that is, if the interest rate is r percent, the lender is willing to lend A_1 dollars today for m periods in exchange for A_m dollars at the end of the mth period and the borrower is willing to pay A_m dollars at the end of the mth period for A_1 dollars today.

Interest rates as connecting the present and future are the same in all markets, but market forces play a different role in the determination of interest rates whether we are considering interest rates in indirect finance or direct finance.

4.3 Interest Rates in Indirect and Direct Finance

Interest rates in the indirect markets are *administered but market-sensitive* interest rates. That is, the interest rate on deposits and loans is set by some administrative process that adjusts the interest rate from time to time depending on market conditions or ties the interest rate via a formula to another interest rate, usually a market-determined interest rate. Deposit rates on checkable accounts, saving and regular time deposits are usually constant for some period of time, such as a week or longer, until the depository institutions initiate a change in response to changes in market conditions. The same is true for loan rates.

The commercial bank prime interest rate and the adjustable-rate mortgage (ARM) illustrate the two types of administered rates on loans.

The prime interest rate is the rate charged by banks to their most creditworthy customers and is set through a consensus process among major banks. When conditions warrant a change in the prime rate, one or more banks will change its prime and, if the others agree the change is warranted by the market, other banks will set their prime rate to the new level. If not, the initiating bank(s) will return their prime to the consensus prime. The prime rate remains constant for a period that sometimes can be long; for example, the prime rate since the financial crisis of 2008/2009 through 2015 was unchanged (Figure 4.1). The interest rate for an ARM is another example of an administered interest rate, but, instead of being determined by an administrative process, the ARM interest rate is tied by a formula to a base rate, such as the five-year Treasury security rate, but remains constant for, say, a six-month period and then is automatically adjusted to the current five-year Treasury security rate according to the formula.

The behavior of an administered rate versus a market rate is illustrated in Figure 4.1, which presents the weekly prime rate and five-year constant maturity Treasury security rate from January 2000 to May 2016. Notice that the prime rate is constant for periods of time, especially starting late 2009, while the Treasury security rate fluctuates. The Treasury security rate is market-determined, rather than administered. The administered rate follows the market rate, but, while the market rate varies from week to week, the prime rate remains constant for periods of time. Administered interest rates, whether set by an administrator of some type

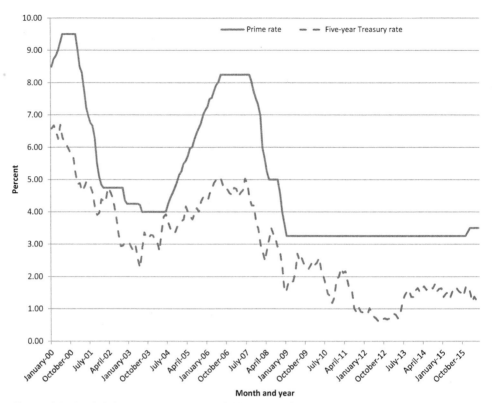

Figure 4.1. Bank Prime Interest Rate and Five-Year Constant Maturity Treasury Security Interest Rate, January 2000 to May 2016. *Source:* FRED, Federal Reserve Bank of St. Louis.

of formula, are market-sensitive to the extent that they are adjusted with a lag to the supply and demand conditions in the financial system. Administrated interest rates do not reflect market conditions on a day-by-day basis but, with a lag, reflect market conditions when they are adjusted.

In contrast, interest rates in the direct financial markets, such as the Treasury security rate in Figure 4.1, are *market-determined*, in that they are determined day by day, and even minute by minute, by large numbers of suppliers of direct market instruments and demanders of direct market instruments making their decisions on a wide range of information. The interest rates in the direct financial markets fully incorporate all of the forces that determine the interest rate without any significant lag.

The remainder of this chapter discusses two topics: first, attempts by government to regulate interest rates; and, second, several technical aspects of interest rates that the reader needs to understand before moving on to a detailed explanation of how interest rates are determined and how they are used in the conduct of monetary policy.

4.4 Government Interest Rate Regulation

Interest rates have a long and controversial history in the world. Interest rates have often been characterized as *usury*, to indicate that sometimes charging any interest for a loan is "unfair", but most of the time to indicate that only "excessive" or "unfair" interest rates are "unfair". There is much confusion over the concept of usury.

First, there is nothing improper about charging interest for the loan of funds. If someone is willing to reduce their liquidity and assume risk they may not be repaid, the interest rate is an appropriate price to compensate one for reduced liquidity and increased risk. The interest rate is likewise an appropriate price for the borrower to pay to obtain liquidity. This is a simple economic truth illustrated by the time value of money: future amounts of money are discounted to the present; that is, a lender of $100 is willing to lend that amount for a period only if they will receive a larger amount at a later time and the borrower is willing to accept $100 now and repay the loan with a larger amount at a later time. The time value of money or interest rate reflects the time preferences of the lender and the borrower.

Second, regarding interest rates themselves as an improper price is economic nonsense; however, much of the concern over interest rates, especially with regard to loans to small and uninformed borrowers, is that they are set in an unbalanced environment. Any noncompetitive market results in a high price, and financial markets are no exception; hence, when the small borrower has few choices and must deal with only one or a small number of lenders, the interest rate can indeed be excessive. But excessive in this sense does not mean the interest rate is an improper price, only that the interest rate is set in a noncompetitive environment and is excessive only in the sense it exceeds a competitively determined interest rate.

As a result of this long-time anti-interest-rate history, governments have at times attempted to prohibit interest, but more frequently they have attempted to regulate interest rates to prevent "excessive" interest rates. Interest rate regulations, however, have also been used for other purposes, such as subsidizing some politically favored activity or industrial objective. In the United States, from the 1930s until the start of the deregulation of the financial system in the 1970s, the government attempted to limit interest rates in the indirect part of the financial system. Command-type economies of that period, such as the former Soviet Union and China, set all interest rates, and even more market-oriented economies, such as Japan and South Korea, controlled the majority of interest rates. Until Japan began to liberalize its domestic and international financial system in the late 1970s, virtually every interest rate was regulated and administered by the government through the Bank of Japan, Ministry of Finance or some other government agency.

There are three issues one needs to keep in mind regarding government efforts to regulate interest rates.

First, any regulation of interest rates based on the view that interest rates are an inappropriate price is economic nonsense. Interest rates play an important role in allocating resources. The interest rate is a variable that connects the present to the future, and vice versa, and as such is required to allocate resources over time in an efficient manner. One of the reasons why command economies such as the Soviet Union and China failed in the latter part of the twentieth century is because they attempted to ignore economic forces such as interest rates. That is, interest rates are an important variable to balance the different time preferences of those who make up the economy.

Second, interest rate regulation substitutes the government for the market in setting interest rates and, as such, always ends up misallocating resources and having unintended impacts on the economy. Despite the claims often made by government that it can do a better job than the market in setting interest rates, history suggests otherwise. In virtually every case when governments attempted to regulate interest rates, for whatever reason, and they were significantly different from those determined by market forces, inefficiency and real unfairness resulted.

Third, rather than interest rate regulation, it is more beneficial to society to direct government efforts toward permitting more competition in the financial system, requiring greater transparency and ensuring that lenders (or borrowers) don't have unbalanced economic power in the flow of funds. This is a far more productive activity in terms of government regulation and supervision than setting interest rates to achieve "fairness".

4.5 A Short History of Interest Rate Regulation

Interest rates became legally permitted in Western civilization about 400 years ago but it wasn't until the twentieth century that governments seriously attempted to regulate interest rates to varying degrees and for various reasons. In the command-type economies of the former Soviet Union and China, interest rates were simply another price set by the central planning authority. In more market-oriented economies, such as Japan and the United States, interest rates were regulated to varying degrees for different reasons.

In the 1970s deregulation and liberalization of the flow of funds occurred throughout much of the world, and, as part of this process, governments gradually removed virtually all interest rate controls. Interest rate regulations in the United States went through three periods. Until the Great Depression interest rates in general were not subject to government regulation; however, starting in the 1930s, the government at both the federal and state levels imposed a wide range of interest rate controls and usury laws that limited the amount of interest that could be charged for a loan or paid on a deposit. These regulations were based on two foundations: first, in the case of loans, they were designed to limit excessive interest rates on loans, especially to consumers and small businesses; and, second, interest rate

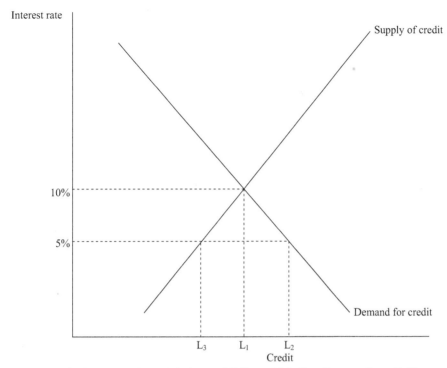

Figure 4.2. Consumer Loan Market and Effect of Binding Interest Rate Ceiling.

ceilings on deposits were designed to limit competition for deposits, and thus to limit incentives to adopt risky loan portfolios. Ceilings on deposits were also intended to reduce loan interest rates and keep loan rates below the usury limits.

In the 1960s and 1970s, however, interest rate ceilings generated much economic and financial distress, were often circumvented by financial innovation and often hurt the very groups they were designed to protect. Regulation Q generated disintermediation and contributed to the collapse of the S&L industry in the 1980s. Market innovations circumvented interest rate regulations; for example, the money market fund was an innovation designed to offer the public a market return on funds far above the ceilings placed on saving and time deposits. Thrifts in the 1970s introduced NOW accounts or savings accounts subject to transfer by check to offer the public an interest-paying checking account to compete with demand deposits offered by banks that were prohibited from paying interest (zero-interest-rate ceiling). Even banks were forced to innovate around the zero-interest-rate ceiling on demand deposits by offering special accounts and services to large depositors, which essentially permitted them to earn a market rate of interest on their checking and time accounts.

Interest rate ceilings on loans illustrate the unintended consequences of the ceilings in that they end up hurting the very group they are designed to protect from "excessive" interest rates. Figure 4.2 illustrates the market for consumer loans.

The demand for consumer loans is an inverse function of the interest rate, and the supply of consumer loans is a positive function of the interest rate. The market interest rate of 10 percent is at the intersection of the two functions. Assume that an advocacy group convinces the government that 10 percent is "unfair" and discriminates against low-income households, etc., and as a result the government imposes a usury limit of 5 percent to make sure everyone receives a "fair" interest on their consumer borrowing. A 5 percent ceiling on consumer loan interest, however, is below the market. As such, the ceiling will generate an excess demand for consumer loans. At 5 percent, lenders will supply a lesser amount of credit (L_3) then they would at the market rate of 10 percent (L_1); but borrowers will demand a greater amount of credit (L_2) then they would at the market rate of 10 percent (L_1).

How does the market close the excess demand for credit? Lenders will take one of two actions. First, they will simply ration consumer loans and make consumer loans only to their low-risk borrowers, who are generally higher-income and longer-employed borrowers; that is, the very group of lower-income and less employed borrowers that the usury ceiling is designed to protect will now be eliminated from obtaining consumer credit. Second, lenders will find ways to circumvent the interest rate limit by imposing application fees or requiring compensating deposits in the case of a bank that are inefficient and involve transactions costs to both the lender and the borrower.

The 1970s were a period of high inflation, which increased interest rates in some parts of the financial system that were not regulated, such as money and capital market interest rates, while other interest rates, such as loan and deposit rates, were subject to varying degrees of controls. The larger the gap between unregulated and regulated interest rates, the greater the economic and financial distress. In the 1980s and 1990s interest rate ceilings on loans and deposits were gradually removed or raised to high levels by a series of legislative acts and administrative decisions at both the federal and state levels. There was one exception: the zero-interest-rate ceiling applicable to demand deposits remained in force until 2010, when the 2010 Dodd–Frank Act ended the zero-interest-rate ceiling on demand deposits. Today interest rates on loans and deposits are either directly determined by or sensitive to market forces.

4.6 Basic Technical Aspects of Interest Rates

The next two chapters focus on the level and structure of interest rates, respectively; however, before we can turn to that discussion, there are several technical aspects of interest rates that need to be reviewed as they apply to interest rates in the financial system. They are:

1 yield to maturity;
2 yield on a simple loan, deposit account and fixed-payment loan;

3 yield on a debt without coupon payment feature;
4 yield on debt with coupon payment feature;
5 yield on equity;
6 interest rate risk; and
7 yield and total return.

Yield to maturity: This can be viewed from several perspectives. The yield to maturity of any financial asset is the interest return earned by holding the financial asset until it matures. The yield to maturity is also the interest rate that equates the present value of the cash flow generated by the financial asset to the present value cost of the asset, which is the price at which the asset is purchased. The yield to maturity from this perspective can also be considered an internal rate of return in determining the profitability of an investment in plant or equity. Interest rates in general are calculated and published on a yield to maturity basis; however, there are some exceptions – one of which will be discussed below. In general, the yield to maturity is the proper foundation for calculating and interpreting interest rates. The yield to maturity concept can be understood by considering yields on the most common financial assets used in the financial system.

Yield on a simple loan, deposit account and fixed-payment loan: A simple loan is a loan that will be paid at maturity in a lump sum; that is, there are no multiple payments over the maturity of the loan. The simple loan transaction involves a promise to pay. The promise to pay is a liability of the borrower and a financial asset to the lender and indicates the parameters of the loan: maturity, interest and the lump sum payment at maturity. To illustrate a simple loan, consider the following example: a loan of $100 for one year at 10 percent is repaid at the end of the year with a payment of $110 ($100 principal and $10 interest) and the same loan for two years is repaid at the end of the second year with a payment of $121 ($100 principal, $10 interest for the first year, and $11 interest on the balance of $110 for the second year).

In both cases, the interest rate of 10 percent is the yield to maturity. In the case of the one-year loan of $100, the present value of the loan is the cost of the financial asset, which is the loan amount or the amount paid to purchase the borrower's promise to pay ($100). The present value of the revenue generated by the financial asset ($110) is $100 using the interest rate of 10 percent [$100 = $110/(1.10)^1]. In the case of the two-year loan, the present value cost of the promise to pay is $100 and the present value of the revenue generated by the financial asset ($121) is $100 [$100 = $121/(1.10)^2].

This same calculation for a simple loan can be used to illustrate the interest rate on a deposit as the yield to maturity. If you leave $100 on deposit at a depository institution paying 10 percent per annum, you can withdraw $110 at the end of the first year, $121 at the end of the second year, and so on. The present value of each of these future amounts at 10 percent is the original deposit of $100.

The most common form of loan in indirect finance, however, is the fixed-payment loan; that is, the loan is paid over time with fixed payments over the maturity of the loan. Each payment consists of a partial payment for the loan and an interest payment. Over time the partial payment for the loan increases and the interest payment decreases; that is, the first payments consist mostly of interest and little principal while the later payments consist mostly of principal and little interest.

The present value equation for a fixed yearly payment loan for a maturity of m years is

$$L = P_1/(1+r)^1 + P_2/(1+r)^2 + P_3/(1+r)^3 + P_4/(1+r)^4 + \cdots + P_m/(1+r)^m$$
$$(4.3)$$

where L is the amount of the loan, P is the yearly payment, m is the maturity of the loan and r is the yield to maturity or interest rate.

This equation is nonlinear and can be solved for only one unknown variable; that is, for a given loan amount, L, and maturity, m, the equation can be solved to determine the fixed payment, P, only if we assume a given interest rate, r. Or, if we assume a given payment, we can solve for the interest rate. To illustrate, assume you borrow $20,000 to purchase a car today with a five-year loan at 4 percent per annum and, for simplicity, the loan has annual payments instead of monthly payments. What is the yearly payment? In this case, L = $20,000; m = 5; and r = 0.04. Solving the equation for these variables is not straightforward and requires a calculator with finance functions or spreadsheet program with finance functions. Using XLS and the PMT function, insert into a cell PMT(0.04,5,$20,000) to calculate the yearly payment, which is $4,495.54. These payments are assumed to be made at the end of each year, and the balance of the loan amount after the last payment is zero.

The yield or interest rate in Expression 4.3 is the rate that equates the present value of the cost of the financial asset (the loan amount, in this case) with the present value of the revenue flow, which consists of a fixed number of equal payments. In the case of the illustration, the present value of the five payments of $4,495.54 at 4 percent over the maturity of the loan is $20,000.

Zero-coupon, coupon and equity instruments: The promise to pay instrument used in the direct markets is either a money market debt instrument with a maturity up to one year, a capital market debt instrument with a maturity greater than one year or an equity instrument without a maturity date. A money or capital market debt instrument provides no ownership claim by the lender on the borrower but, instead, is a legal obligation of the borrower to pay interest and principal. In contrast, an equity instrument represents a residual claim on profits after all legal obligations have been satisfied. The equity carries no legal obligation to pay dividends or principal, but is contingent on the issuer earning a profit.

Yields on instruments used in direct financial markets can be viewed in terms of the institutional way in which interest is earned and paid.

Yields on money and capital market instruments – zero-coupon and coupon instruments: A zero-coupon debt instrument does not pay a periodic coupon interest payment over the maturity of the instrument and, at the time of maturity, pays only the face or par value of the instrument. Money market debt instruments with a maturity of one year or less do not pay a coupon interest payment; however, capital market instruments with maturities greater than one year are sold with and without a coupon interest payment feature.

The coupon interest payment, expressed as a percentage of the face value of the instrument, is fixed over time. The adjective "coupon" is based on the long-gone practice of issuing a long-term debt instrument with perforated coupons, which could be detached and either sent to the issuer of the bond for the coupon interest payment or presented to the bank that serviced the bond for payment. Today debt instruments do not have actual coupons, but the term continues to be used.

In the following, we illustrate the zero-coupon and coupon debt instrument for debt obligations issued by the U.S. government. Government securities are issued in three forms – Treasury bills, or TBs; Treasury notes, or TNotes; and Treasury bonds, or TBonds – with maturities of one year or less; greater than one year and up to ten years; and greater than ten years, respectively.

The TB is a zero-coupon instrument and is sold at a discount; that is, since it does not pay a coupon rate over the maturity of the TB, the return to the purchaser is determined by the relationship between the discount (face value minus market price) and the market price adjusted for maturity. The yield to maturity of a TB up to one year in maturity is determined by the following:

$$r = [(FV - MP)/MP](365/m) \qquad (4.4)$$

where r is the yield, FV is the face or par value of the TB, MP is the market price and m is the maturity in days with a 365-day year. The only cash flow generated by holding the TB is the face value paid at the maturity of the TB. In Expression 4.4, a $1,000 TB with a maturity of one year (m = 365) purchased for $950 generates a yield to maturity of 5.26 percent if it is held to maturity. The larger the discount, the greater the yield to maturity.

Expression 4.4 is based on the yield to maturity perspective; however, TBs are also expressed on a discount yield basis according to the following:

$$dr = [(FV - MP)/FV](360/m) \qquad (4.5)$$

where dr is the discount yield. The discount yield uses a 360-day year as opposed to a 365-day year and expresses the discount as a percentage of the face value rather than the market price of the instrument. As a result, the discount yield is always lower than the yield to maturity, because the discount is expressed as a percentage of a larger base (face value instead of market price) and a lower maturity factor (360 instead of 365 days). To illustrate, the discount yield for the $1,000 TB above is 5.0 percent compared to 5.26 percent, the yield to maturity. Yields on TBs such

Table 4.1. *Yield and Bond Price for a $100 Bond Paying a Coupon Payment of $10.00 per Year or a Coupon Rate of 10 Percent*

	Bond price			
Yield (%)	m = 5 years	m = 10 years	m = 15 years	m = 20 years
5.0	$121.65	$138.61	$151.90	$162.31
6.0	$116.85	$129.44	$138.85	$145.88
7.0	$112.30	$121.07	$127.32	$131.78
8.0	$107.99	$113.42	$117.12	$119.64
9.0	$103.89	$106.42	$108.06	$109.13
10.0	$100.00	$100.00	$100.00	$100.00
11.0	$96.30	$94.11	$92.81	$92.04
12.0	$92.79	$88.70	$86.38	$85.06
13.0	$89.45	$83.72	$80.61	$78.93
14.0	$86.27	$79.14	$75.43	$73.51
15.0	$83.24	$74.91	$70.76	$68.70
16.0	$80.35	$71.00	$66.55	$64.43
17.0	$77.60	$67.39	$62.73	$60.61
18.0	$74.98	$64.05	$59.27	$57.18
19.0	$72.48	$60.95	$56.12	$54.09
20.0	$70.09	$58.08	$53.25	$51.30

as provided by *The Wall Street Journal* or *The New York Times* are stated in both the yield to maturity and discount yield basis, though from an economic point of view the yield to maturity is the more appropriate measure of the interest rate.

TNotes and TBonds, in contrast to TBs, are offered on a zero-coupon and coupon basis. The yield to maturity on a coupon TNote or TBond is based on the following:

$$MP = CP_1/(1 + r)^1 + CP_2/(1 + r)^2 + CP_3/(1 + r)^3 + \cdots + CP_m/(1 + r)^m$$
$$+ FV_m/(1 + r)^m \tag{4.6}$$

where MP is the market price of the bond, CP is the coupon payment made each year, m is the maturity in years, FV is the face value of the Treasury security paid at maturity and r is the yield to maturity. The yield to maturity, r, is the interest rate that equates the present value of the earnings stream consisting of coupon payments each year and principal in the last year to the present value of the cost of the instrument, which is the market price paid to obtain the revenue flow. The same expression applies to any bond with a coupon feature.

Expression 4.6 consists of five parameters – three of which are known (CP, FV and m) and two of which are unknown (MP and r); hence, holding MP constant, r can be calculated and, holding r constant, P can be calculated. Table 4.1 presents various combinations of MP and r for a $100 bond issued at the start of the first year, with a maturity of five, ten, 15 and 20 years and a coupon payment of $10.00 paid at the end of each year. There are three aspects of the illustration in Table 4.1 worth noting: first, if the market rate is the same as the coupon rate (10 percent), the bond's market price is at par (no discount or premium); second, if the market rate is higher than the coupon rate, the bond's market price is below par (sells at a discount); and, third, if the market rate is lower than the coupon rate, the bond's market price is above par (sells at a premium).

TNotes and TBonds are also offered on a zero-coupon basis, or STRIPS (Separate Trading of Registered Interest and Principal of Securities). These were first offered in the early 1980s as stripped Treasury securities, in which the coupon payments are removed from the coupon bond and each payment is treated as a separate zero-coupon bond. This renders the stripped bond a zero-coupon bond. To illustrate, a 20-year TBond with a face value of $100,000 and a coupon payment of $10,000 per year can be stripped into 21 zero-coupon instruments – 20 coupon interest strips of $10,000 for each year and one principal strip payable at maturity.

Yield on equities: Equities differ from money market or capital market debt instruments in three ways: first, they are issued without maturity ($m = \infty$); second, they are a residual claim on profits determined by the issuer of equity; and, third, the return paid to the holder of the equity is referred to as a dividend rather than a coupon or interest payment. Nonetheless, equities have a yield and price like any debt instrument.

This can be illustrated by first considering a special type of capital market instrument that is actually not traded in the United States. A consol is a perpetual bond that has no maturity but promises to pay a coupon, like an annuity issued by government. Introduced in the United Kingdom in 1751, they continue to circulate primarily in the United Kingdom. Despite the fact that consols are not widely used as a debt instrument, they are widely used in financial and monetary economics because the relationship between price and yield is easy to illustrate with a much simpler formula than the above.

The market price of a consol is expressed by extending the coupon payments in Expression 4.6 to infinity and dropping the last term for the present value of the face amount of the bond:

$$MP = CP_1/(1+r)^1 + CP_2/(1+r)^2 + CP_3/(1+r)^3 + \cdots + CP_\infty/(1+r)^\infty$$
(4.7)

Expression 4.7 can be simplified in the following steps.

First, the CP in each year is the same; thus we can drop the time subscript. Define the variable $d = 1/(1+r)$ and insert into Expression 4.7:

$$MP = CPd^1 + CPd^2 + CPd^3 + \cdots + CPd^\infty$$
$$= CPd(1 + d^2 + d^3 + \cdots + d^\infty)$$
(4.8)

Second, since $d < 1$, the sequence $1 + d^2 + d^3 + \cdots + d^\infty$ in Expression 4.8 is an infinite geometric declining progression that can be approximated as $1/(1-d)$.

Substitute $1/(1 - d)$ for the infinite sequence and substitute $1/(1 + r)$ for d:

$$MP = CDd/(1 - d)$$
$$= [CD/(1 - r)]/[(1 + r - 1)/(1 + r)]$$
$$= CP/r \tag{4.9}$$

Hence, the MP of the consol is the CP divided by r. The market price of a $100 consol that pays a $5 per year coupon is determined by the current interest rate. If the market interest rate is 5 percent, the price of the consol is $100; that is, it trades at par. If the market interest rate is 6 percent, the price of the consol is $83.33; that is, it trades at a discount. And, if the market interest rate is 4 percent, the price of the consol is $125.00; that is, the consol trades at a premium.

Expression 4.9 is much simpler than the expression for the market price of a coupon bond and can be used to illustrate the yield on equities. Instead of a coupon payment, equities pay dividends; hence, the market price of an equity assuming the current level of dividends are paid into infinity is

$$MP = D/r \tag{4.10}$$

$$r = D/MP \tag{4.11}$$

where MP is now the market price of an equity and D is the current annual dividend assumed to be paid into infinity. The dividend-price ratio of any equity is an approximation of its current yield. More complex expressions allowing for changes in dividends over time can be developed, but Expressions 4.10 and 4.11 are sufficient to illustrate that the yield on an equity is fundamentally the same as the yield on any debt instrument.

Are the expressions mere mathematics with nothing to do with the market? Do these expressions work in the marketplace? Yes, and, in fact, if the lender who purchases any financial instrument ignores the fundamental relationships between price and yield in the above expressions, it would be like ignoring the winds and tides. If you ignore the wind and tides you do so at your own peril, and if you ignore the above expressions you will likely lose wealth.

A simple illustration will demonstrate this point. In Table 4.1, the price of a ten-year bond at a market interest rate of 8 percent is $113.42; that is, the bond pays a $10.00 coupon and, since the market rate is lower than the coupon rate (10 percent), the bond will trade at a premium. Assume a borrower tries to sell a ten-year bond at $121.07, which implies a 7 percent yield. He/she will be disappointed, as no one will purchase the bond at that price because the implied yield is 7 percent, which is below the going interest rate of 8 percent on $100 bonds with a ten-year maturity. The seller will be forced to drop the price. Assume the price is dropped to $106.42, but now the implied market rate is 9 percent, and the seller will have people lined up to purchase the bond and will raise the price. The price of the bond will very quickly settle at $113.42, the price that will generate a yield of 8 percent – the going market interest rate.

Interest rate risk: There are various types of risk associated with any instrument traded in the money and capital markets. Default risk and interest rate risk are the two major types of risk for dollar-denominated instruments. Instruments issued by private entities and local or state governments have both default and interest rate risk, but U.S. government debt is subject to only interest rate risk. The central government has much greater power to issue more debt than any state/local government or private entity; or increase taxes than any state/local government; or increase the money supply, which is a move unavailable to any state/local government or private entity.

Interest rate risk is an important risk that needs to be considered by any participant in the financial system. Interest rate risk is the risk of a change in the value of the instrument after it has been purchased due to changes in the interest rate for the remainder of the maturity of the bond. The following four points are important for understanding the concept of interest rate risk.

First, when a financial instrument is purchased the price and yield are known; however, from that point onward there is uncertainty as to what the market interest rate will be, and, hence, there is uncertainty as to what the price of the instrument will be in the future market. This is because the price of the bond is related to the market interest rate; whenever the interest rate changes, the price of the bond will change even though the coupon payment and face value remain constant. The maturity of the bond, however, will decrease with each passing day.

Second, the yield and price of any financial instrument vary inversely with each other. Why? Review each of the above expressions for the price of any debt or equity instrument traded in the money and capital markets. In each case, the expression indicates that when the yield increases the price of the instrument declines. If this is not sufficient, consider a more intuitive reason. If you purchase a $1,000 TB with a one-year maturity for $950, the yield is 5.26 percent. Any change in interest rates will change the price of the bond. If the market price increased $25 immediately after the TB was purchased – that is, the same TB now sells for $975 instead of $950 – the yield decreases from 5.26 percent to 2.56 percent. That is, since you now pay more for the revenue flow ($1,000 at the end of the year), the return on your purchase is less because of the higher price. Conversely, if the price decreased from $950 to $925, the yield increases from 5.26 percent to 8.11 percent. That is, since you now pay less for the revenue flow ($1,000 at the end of the year), the return on your purchase is higher because of the lower price.

Third, the change in the price of the bond due to a given change in the interest rate is directly related to maturity. The longer the maturity, the greater the degree of interest rate risk; that is, the greater the risk of a change in the value of the bond to a given change in the interest rate. This can be illustrated with the information in Table 4.1. Consider the value of two bonds if the market interest rate is 10.00 percent – a five-year bond and a 20-year bond. Both bonds will sell for par at $100 because the coupon interest rate is the same as the market rate. Assume interest rates increase from 10 percent to 15 percent. The five-year bond price declines from $100 to $83.24 for a price decline of 16.8 percent. The 20-year bond price declines from $100 to $68.70 for a price decline of 31.3 percent. The same result would occur if the interest rate declined from 10 percent to 5 percent; that is, the price of the 20-year bond would increase more in percentage terms than the price of the five-year bond.

Thus, the longer the maturity of the bond, the greater the degree of interest rate risk, because the longer the maturity, the greater the response of the price of the bond to a given change in the interest rate.

Fourth, the holding period is the period of time one expects to hold the bond. If the holding period is the same as the maturity of the bond there is no interest rate risk. At one time, those who purchased coupon bonds for earnings and held the bonds until they matured were referred to as "widows and orphans", as they were concerned only with earnings and planned to hold the bonds until maturity.

Yield and total return: The total return of any financial asset – or, in fact, any asset – is defined by the following:

$$\text{Total Return} = \text{Yield} + \text{Capital Gain} \qquad (4.12)$$

In the context of debt or equity instruments, Expression 4.12 can be illustrated by considering a long-term bond. The bond yield is known since it is established the moment the bond is purchased. Capital gain – the difference between the future price of the bond and the price paid for the bond – is unknown, however, because the interest rate changes over time. Capital gain can be calculated at any point in time up to the maturity of the bond by comparing the current market price of the bond with the purchased price of the bond and determining whether the capital gain is positive (current price exceeds what was paid for the bond), negative (current prices is lower than what was paid for the bond) or zero (current market price is the same as what was paid for the bond). If this is done without actually selling the bond in the secondary market, one has established the "paper capital gain", the capital gain that would be realized if the bond were sold. If the bond is actually sold, then the "paper capital gain" becomes the "realized capital gain".

In either case, the "paper total return" or "realized total return" is equal to the yield, which is determined when the bond was purchased, plus the "paper capital gain" or the "realized capital gain". There's a real lesson here for anyone managing a portfolio. One may experience a declining total return on a paper basis, as is the case when interest rates are increasing and asset prices are falling. But this becomes a realized decline in total return only if the asset is sold. So, be careful in managing your portfolio in a declining market. Living with a paper capital loss is easier than realizing the capital loss and perhaps ending up with a negative realized total return.

The difference between total return and yield can be illustrated with an example using Table 4.1. Assume a 20-year bond is purchased today but considered for sale at the end of five years. The bond now becomes a 15-year bond. Assume the market interest rate is 10 percent when the 20-year bond was purchased; hence, the bond was purchased for $100. If the interest rate increases from 10 percent to 15 percent at the end of five years, the price of a 15-year bond will be $70.76. The "paper" or "real" total return is –19.24 percent (10.0% + –29.24%). If the interest rate instead declines from 10 percent to 5 percent at the end of five years, the price of a 15-year bond will be $151.90 and the "paper" or "real" total return is 61.90 percent (10.0% + 51.90%). If the interest rate is 10 percent at the end of the five years, the "paper" or "real" total return is 10 percent (10.0% + 0.00%).

There are only two situations in which total return and yield are identical. First, if the bond is sold in the secondary market at the same price it was purchased, the total return is the yield. Second, if the bond is held to maturity, there is no capital gain. This is the "widows and orphans" case mentioned above.

Chapter 5

The Level of Interest Rates

5.1 Introduction

The previous chapter laid out the basic concepts needed to understand the determinants of the *level of the interest rate*. This chapter focuses on what determines the level of interest rates at any point in time, why interest rates increase and decrease over time, how interest rates respond to changes in monetary policy and whether interest rates are a reliable indicator of the intentions of the central bank. The next chapter focuses on the structure of interest rates.

In this chapter, we focus on the determinants of interest rates in direct financial markets, such as interest rates on Treasury securities, commercial paper, corporate bonds and municipal bonds, as opposed to interest rates in intermediation finance. There are three reasons for focusing only on interest rates in the direct financial markets.

First, interest rates in the money and capital markets are market-determined; that is, they are determined by market forces, respond quickly to market forces and are not subject to any administrative decision. Second, interest rates in the money and capital markets are the foundation for interest rates in the intermediation financial markets because they reflect all of the important market forces that determine interest rates; that is, when loan and deposit rates are administratively adjusted, the adjustment is in response to changes in the money and capital market interest rates. Third, interest rates in the money and capital markets reflect the cost of borrowing and return from lending without considering intermediation costs; that is, there is little difference between the ask and bid price or interest rate of a bond. In contrast, there is considerable difference between the rate of interest charged by a depository institution for a loan and the interest rate paid on deposits that represent the costs of intermediation. Another way to make the same point is to consider interest rates in money and capital markets as representing the equilibrium cost of funds determined by the coming together of a large number of well-informed borrowers and lenders in a competitive environment that comes very close to the model of perfect competition presented in introductory microeconomics. The only intermediary is a broker or agent, who assists in bringing together the lender and the borrower but who takes no risk position; that is, the broker or agent collects a fee and disappears.

To make the following discussion straightforward, we make the following assumptions:

1 all of the many interest rates in the direct money and capital markets are represented by only one interest rate, r;
2 the interest rate, r, is the yield on a medium-term bond with some degree of default risk;
3 the market price of the bond, MP, and the interest rate, r, vary inversely with each other through a mathematical and economic relationship;
4 borrowers sell bonds to obtain funds and lenders lend by buying bonds; and
5 lenders and borrowers assume that the general price level remains constant over the maturity of the bond.

The last assumption is unrealistic, especially for long-terms bonds, and will be dropped as the discussion proceeds, but for now we make the unrealistic assumption that market participants anticipate no change in the price level over the maturity of the bond in order to focus on the fundamental determinants of r and MP. Once this is accomplished, the assumption of a constant price level is dropped.

5.2 The Level of the Interest Rate: Loanable Funds and Liquidity Preference

There are two approaches to understanding how the interest rate and hence bond price are determined: the loanable funds approach and the liquidity preference approach. The loanable funds approach is the older of the two approaches, dating as far back as the eighteenth century, whereas the liquidity preference approach was introduced by Keynes in his 1936 book *The General Theory of Employment, Interest and Money*.

The loanable funds approach focuses on the supply of and demand for funds as the determinants of the interest rate whereas the liquidity preference approach focuses on the demand for and supply of money as the determinants of the interest rate. There are technical differences between the two approaches, in that loanable funds focuses on the *flow* of lending and borrowing whereas liquidity preference focuses on the *stock* of money demanded and supplied. At one time there was considerable debate about which was correct; however, there is no longer any debate, because it can be shown that each approach generates the same interest rate and bond price in a general model of the economy.

The following discussion utilizes the loanable funds approach, for three reasons. First, it is an extension of the flow of funds perspective of the financial system (emphasized in this book) that considers a wide range of financial assets

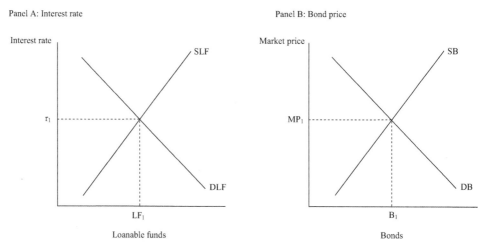

Figure 5.1. Equilibrium Interest Rate and Bond Price.

and promises to pay used to transfer funds from lenders to borrowers. On this level, it is institutionally intuitive for understanding the determinants of the interest rate, whereas the interest rate as the outcome of the supply of and demand for money is simply less intuitive. Second, the loanable funds approach is technically straightforward, and, while the supply of money is technically straightforward and will be discussed in a later chapter, the concept and measurement of the demand for money is technically more complex and not worth the effort. Third, the supply of, and especially the demand for, money have become more unstable and more difficult to estimate since the 1970s because of deregulation and financial liberalization. This further reduces the practicality of the liquidity preference approach.

5.3 The Loanable Funds Approach to Understanding the Interest Rate

The loanable funds approach views the interest rate as determined by the interaction between the supply of and demand for loanable funds or lending and borrowing, respectively, and, conversely, views the bond price as determined by the demand for bonds (supply of loanable funds or lending) and the supply of bonds (demand for loanable funds or borrowing). Let's first focus on the interest rate.

Figure 5.1 (panel A) indicates that the equilibrium interest rate, r_1, and equilibrium amount of lending and borrowing of loanable funds, LF_1, are determined at the intersection of the supply and demand functions for loanable funds. The supply of loanable funds (SLF) is positively related to the interest rate "other things held constant". The demand for loanable funds (DLF) is inversely related to the interest rate "other things held constant". An interest rate other than r_1 will generate either an excess supply of funds over demand for funds (interest rate higher than r_1) or an excess demand for funds over the supply of funds (interest rate lower than r_1). In this case, market forces will either decrease or increase the interest rate until it settles at r_1.

Figure 5.1 (panel B) illustrates the same lending–borrowing transaction in terms of the demand for and supply of bonds. The demand for funds function can be expressed as a supply function for bonds (SB), which is a positive function of the market price of bonds; that is, the higher the market price of bonds the greater the quantity of bonds supplied. The supply of funds can be expressed as a demand function for bonds (DB), which is an inverse function of the market price of bonds; that is, the higher the market price of bonds the smaller the quantity of bonds demanded. The equilibrium market price, MP_1, equates the quantity of bonds demanded and supplied, B_1. In dollar terms, B_1 and LF_1 are the same. The interest rate and market price of bonds are mathematically and economically interrelated.

In the previous chapter the inverse relationship between the interest rate and bond price was emphasized. Even though we have not yet discussed why the functions in Figure 5.1 shift, it is important to understanding that the supply of and demand for loanable functions and the demand for and supply of bonds are related. A rightward shift in the supply of loanable funds will decrease the interest rate in panel A, but will also be reflected in a rightward shift in the demand for bonds in panel B, thus increasing the bond price; that is, interest and bond price move inversely to each other. Likewise, a rightward shift in the demand for loanable funds will be accompanied by a rightward shift in the supply of bonds, and the interest rate will increase from the perspective of panel A and the bond price will decrease from the perspective of panel B.

In the following discussion we focus on the interest rate; however, keep in mind that the bond price is a mirror image of the interest rate. Whatever the interest rate, the bond price is determined by that interest rate, and vice versa, and whenever the interest rate changes because of a change in the demand for and supply of loanable funds, the demand and supply of bonds will change the market price of the bond.

Focusing on panel A of Figure 5.1, there are two aspects of each function one needs to understand. First, why does the supply function have an upward slope and the demand function a downward slope? Second, what determines the position of the supply and demand function and what causes each function to shift to the right or left?

5.4 The Supply of Loanable Funds Function or Lending

The supply function – why upward-sloping? The supply function in Figure 5.1 (panel A) is upward-sloping because, "holding other things constant", the lender is willing to lend more funds at higher interest rates and fewer funds at lower interest rates. The lender needs an incentive to reduce liquidity by lending today, and that incentive is the interest rate because it ties the present to the future. The greater (lesser) the future value of the funds lent today, the greater (lesser) the incentive to lend. This is nothing more than the general law of supply, in that, as the price of any good or service increases, holding other things constant, the market has an incentive to supply a greater quantity of the good or service, and vice versa.

Position and shifts in the supply function: The supply function in Figure 5.1 (panel A) is drawn in a given position, indicating that the quantity of loanable funds supplied is a positive function of the interest "other things held constant". There are a large number of variables "held constant" for the given supply function. A change in any variable held constant will shift the supply function to the right or left. If the function shifts to the right (left), the quantity of funds offered for loans is higher (lower) at any interest rate.

The following four fundamentals are considered important for shifts in the supply function for loanable funds:

1 changes in income, wealth or the stage of the business cycle;
2 technological or institutional changes;
3 changes in risk and uncertainty; and
4 changes in monetary policy.

Changes in income, wealth or the stage of the business cycle: Increasing income, increasing wealth or an expanding economy provides both incentives and ability to spend on goods and services and financial assets. To the extent that economic entities purchase more financial assets, such as bonds, they are increasing their willingness to lend at any interest rate and, hence, the supply of funds will shift to the right. That is, at any interest rate, the quantity of funds supplied to the financial system increases. Decreasing income, decreasing wealth or a contracting economy reduces spending on goods and services and financial assets and thus shifts the supply of funds to the left, so that, at any interest rate, the supply of loanable funds decreases.

Technological or institutional changes: The Internet has made it easier to purchase financial assets and lend in general. One of the more interesting developments in this regard is a financial innovation referred to as "peer-to-peer" lending, in which individuals make usually small loans (microloans) to entrepreneurs. Other types of institutional changes, such as changes in tax regulations, influence the willingness to purchase financial assets; for example, increased tax benefits obtained from funding medical, educational and retirement accounts increase the demand for financial assets and, hence, lending. To illustrate, if the government increases the limit on contributions to medical, educational or retirement accounts, the demand for financial assets and lending will increase and be reflected by a rightward shift in the supply function. If the government lowers the limit on contributions to these accounts or imposes other restrictions, the supply function will shift to the left at any interest rate.

Changes in risk and uncertainty: Any economic or political event that significantly influences risk and uncertainty in the economy will shift the supply function for loanable funds. A terrorist attack such as 9/11, financial scandals or political distress will shift the supply of loanable funds to the left at any interest rate, while a more stable and confident outlook that lowers risk and uncertainty will shift the supply of loanable funds to the right at any interest rate.

Changes in monetary policy: Central bank policy influences the supply of loanable funds. Easy monetary policy injects liquidity into the financial sector and shifts the supply of loanable funds to the right at any interest rate. Tight monetary policy reduces the liquidity in the financial sector and shifts the supply of loanable funds to the right at any interest rate.

In sum, there are four important fundamentals that influence the position of the supply for loanable funds, and changes in any fundamental will change the willingness of lenders to provide funds to the financial system at any interest rate. To this point we are only considering the proximate or first effects of a change in the underlying fundamentals and ignoring the secondary effects, which can be complex. Changes in an underlying fundamental can have secondary effects on the supply function as well as secondary effects on the demand for loanable funds.

5.5 The Demand for Loanable Funds Function or Borrowing

The demand function – why downward-sloping? The demand function in Figure 5.1 (panel A) is downward-sloping because, "holding other things constant", the borrower is willing to borrow more funds at lower interest rates and fewer funds at higher interest rates. The borrower is willing to return to the lender a larger amount of funds in the future in order to obtain liquidity today, and the lower the amount needed to be repaid (lower interest rate), the more willing the borrower is to borrow, and vice versa. The lesser (greater) the future value of the funds to be repaid, the greater (lesser) the incentive to borrow. This is nothing more than the general law of demand, in that, as the price of any good or service decreases, holding other things constant, the market has an incentive to demand a greater quantity of the good or service, and vice versa.

Position and shifts in the demand function: The demand function in Figure 5.1 (panel A) is drawn in a given position indicating that the quantity of loanable funds demanded is an inverse function of the interest "other things held constant". There are a large number of variables "held constant" for the given demand function. A change in any variable held constant will shift the demand function to the right or left. If the function shifts to the right (left), the quantity of funds demanded for loans is higher (lower) at any interest rate.

The following four fundamentals are considered important for shifts in the demand function for loanable funds:

1 changes in income, wealth or the stage of the business cycle;
2 technological or institutional changes;
3 changes in expected return and risk on borrowing; and
4 changes in government deficits.

Changes in income, wealth or the business cycle: Increasing income, increasing wealth or an expanding economy shifts the demand for loanable funds to the right. A growing economy is accompanied by increased consumer and business spending, which in turn is accompanied by increased demand for funds to support higher spending. Increasing income, increasing wealth or an expanding economy also shifts the supply of funds to the right, as discussed above, and as a result one might conclude that increasing income, increasing wealth or an expanding economy has no impact on the interest rate, since the rightward shift in the demand function (increased demand for funds) is offset by the rightward shift in the supply function (increased supply of funds). This is possible, but not likely.

The impact on the demand for funds of a change in these factors tends to be larger than on the supply of funds so that, on balance, increasing income, increasing wealth or an expanding economy leads to a higher interest rate. This is borne out by decades of the movement of interest rates with the business cycle. Over time interest rates vary with the business cycle, so that, during expansions, interest rates increase while, during contractions, interest rates decline.

Decreasing income, decreasing wealth or a contracting economy shifts the demand function to the left as reduced spending reduces the public's willingness to borrow. Again, the supply function will also shift to the left, but, because the effect on the demand function is greater than on the supply function, the interest rate will decrease on balance.

Technological and institutional changes: The expanding utilization of the Internet to access the financial system makes it easier for both households and businesses to borrow, causing the demand function to shift to the right. Permitting households to borrow on the equity of their home increases the willingness to borrow and shifts the demand function to the right. Government policies that subsidize homeownership, such as the mortgage interest deduction on income, or policies that permit less restrictive loan standards shift the demand for loanable funds to the right. Government policies that provide incentives to expand plant and equipment in the business sector shift the demand function to the right; for example, tax credits, lowered capital gains taxes, higher depreciation rates, etc. will shift the demand function to the right. New products and new markets change the institutional environment for both households and business and tend to shift the demand for funds to the right. An opposite change in any one of these fundamentals would shift the demand for funds to the left so there would be less borrowing at any interest rate.

Changes in expected return and risk on borrowing: Any event that increases expected return and/or reduces risk will shift the demand function to the right; for example, lower oil prices and an expected expanding economy will shift the demand for funds to the right. Lower capital gains taxes or lower business taxes will shift the demand for loanable funds to the right, as will a more pro-business government, both of which are also institutional changes. Higher oil prices, a contracting economy, higher capital gains taxes or higher business taxes in general and a more anti-business government will shift the demand function to the left. Any economic or political event that decreases (increases) business risk will shift the demand function to the right (left) at any interest rate.

Changes in government deficit spending: In the flow of funds matrix used to illustrate the financial system in Chapter 3 (Table 3.7), the government's budget position was indicated by whether saving was positive (surplus budget), negative (deficit budget) or zero (balanced budget) because of the convention to regard government spending as current consumption. The influence of the government's fiscal program on the interest rate can be considered from either the supply of loanable funds or the demand for loanable funds. In this discussion the influence of the government's fiscal program is reflected by shifts in the demand for loanable funds. Hence, if the government runs a surplus (not a frequent event), this would result in a leftward shift in the demand of funds, but in the more likely deficit situation an increase in the government deficit will shift the demand for funds to the right. Government surpluses decrease the interest rate and deficits increase the interest rate.

In sum, there are four important fundamentals that influence the position of the demand for loanable funds, and changes in any of the fundamentals will change the willingness of borrowers to demand funds from the financial system at any interest rate. To this point we are only considering the proximate or first effects of a change in the underlying fundamentals and ignoring the secondary effects, which can be complex; for example, changes in an underlying fundamental can have secondary effects on the demand function as well as secondary effects on the supply of loanable funds.

5.6 Bringing Supply and Demand Together: Examples

The interest rate is thus determined by the intersection of the demand for and supply of loanable funds. Any change in any one of the eight fundamentals (four for the supply of loanable funds and four for the demand for loanable funds) shifts the supply and demand function and thus changes the equilibrium interest rate. Keep in mind, however, that this is only the first step in understanding how the interest rate is determined, since we have assumed both lender and borrower assume the price level remains constant for the maturity of the loan, and once we drop this assumption we will add a fifth fundamental to account for the position of the supply and demand function for loanable funds. But, at this stage, let's continue with the constant price assumption.

To illustrate how the loanable funds framework helps us understand the level of the interest rate and why the level changes, consider the following changes and how they impact the interest rate:

1 increased subsidization of homeownership;
2 business cycle expansion;
3 lower capital gains tax rate;
4 higher oil prices;
5 increased money supply; and
6 increased government deficit.

Figure 5.1 (panel A) is the reference point, starting with r_1 and LF_1 as the equilibrium interest rate and amount of loanable funds supplied and demanded, respectively.

Increased subsidization of homeownership: Government policies designed to increase homeownership expanded greatly in the 1990s. Financial institutions were encouraged and incentivized to expand mortgage credit, especially to moderate- to low-income households. The overwhelming volume of mortgages ended up being financed in the direct markets even though they were originated in the indirect part of the financial system. Individual mortgages were bundled into one bond – a collateralized mortgage bond – and these bonds were then sold in the direct capital markets. Hence, the expanded support for homeownership starting in the 1990s shifted the demand for funds to the right (DLF_1 to DLF_2), increased the interest rate (r_1 to r_2) and increased the amount of borrowing and lending (LF_1 to LF_2), as illustrated in Figure 5.2. Reduced support for homeownership will shift the demand for funds to the left, decrease the interest rate and decrease the amount of borrowing and lending.

Business cycle expansion: The expanding economy will shift both the supply of and demand for funds to the right; however, it will have a greater effect on the demand function than the supply function, so that, on balance, an expanding economy will increase the interest rate other things held constant and increase the amount of borrowing and lending. In Figure 5.3 the supply function shifts from SLF_1 to SLF_2, but the demand function shifts further to the right from DLF_1 to DLF_2. As a result the interest rate increases from r_1 to r_2 and the amount of borrowing and lending increases from LF_1 to LF_2. A recession will do the opposite and decrease the interest rate and reduce the amount of borrowing and lending.

Lower capital gains tax rate: A reduced capital gains tax rate will increase expected return from any investment in real assets, since capital gains are already taxed at a lower rate than ordinary income. As a result, the demand for funds will shift to the right (DLF_1 to DLF_2), increase the interest rate (r_1 to r_2) and increase the amount of borrowing and lending (LF_1 to LF_2), as illustrated in Figure 5.4. An

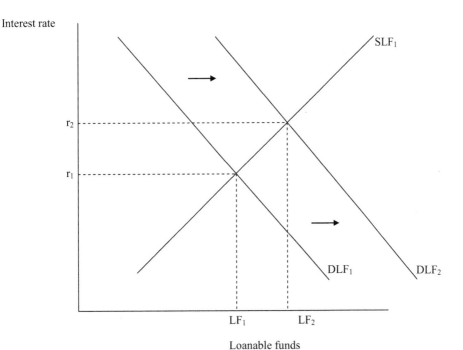

Figure 5.2. Expanded Support for Homeownership Shifts Demand for Loanable Funds to the Right and Increases the Interest Rate.

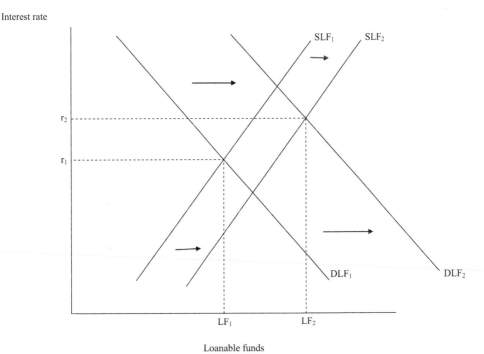

Figure 5.3. Business Cycle Expansion Shifts the Demand for Loanable Funds to the Right and the Supply of Loanable Funds to the Right and, on Balance, Increases the Interest Rate.

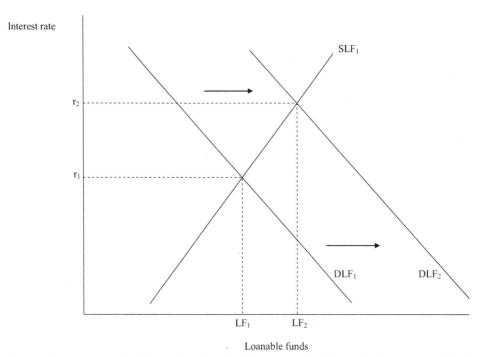

Figure 5.4. Lower Capital Gains Tax Rate Shifts Demand for Loanable Funds to the Right and Increases the Interest Rate.

increase in the capital gains tax will do the opposite and reduce the interest rate and amount of borrowing and lending.

Higher oil prices: Higher oil prices increase the cost of energy across the board. Energy is a major cost factor for many businesses, so higher energy prices decrease expected returns for existing and future investments in plant and equipment. The demand for funds shifts to the left from DLF_1 to DLF_2, decreases the interest rate from r_1 to r_2 and decreases the amount of borrowing and lending from LF_1 to LF_2, as illustrated in Figure 5.5. Lower oil prices will have the opposite impact.

Increase in the money supply: An increase in the money supply shifts the supply of funds to the right from SLF_1 to SLF_2, decreases the interest rate from r_1 to r_2 and increases the amount of borrowing and lending from LF_1 to LF_2, as illustrated in Figure 5.6. A decrease in the money supply does the opposite.

Increase in the government deficit: Increasing government deficits shift the demand for loanable funds to the right (DLF_1 to DLF_2), increase the interest rate (r_1 to r_2) and increase the amount of borrowing and lending (LF_1 to LF_2), as illustrated in Figure 5.7. A decrease in government deficits does the opposite.

5.7 Policy Implications: Government versus the Central Bank

The latter two examples highlight the potential conflict between the government's fiscal program and central bank policy. Government spending has an inherent

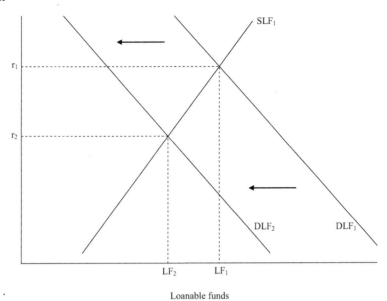

Figure 5.5. Higher Oil Prices Shift the Demand for Loanable Funds to the Left and Decrease the Interest Rate.

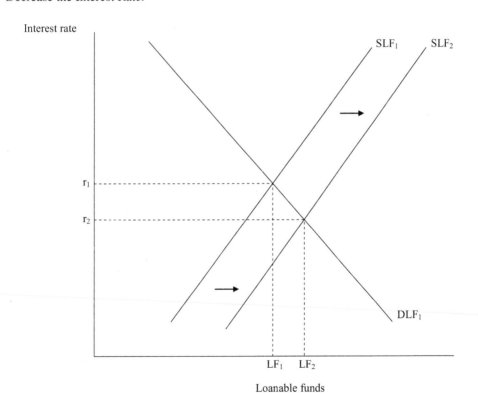

Figure 5.6. Increase in the Money Supply Shifts the Supply of Loanable Funds to the Right and Decreases the Interest Rate.

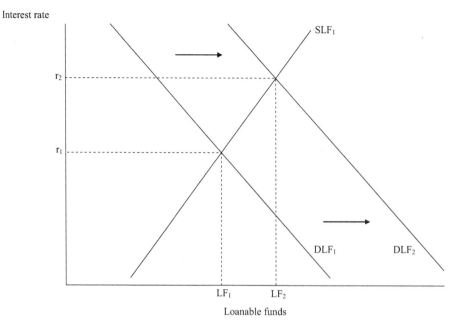

Figure 5.7. Increase in the Government Deficit Shifts the Demand for Loanable Funds to the Right and Increases the Interest Rate.

tendency to increase over time as politicians respond to special interest groups and use government spending as a way to remain in power. Government spending can be financed in only three ways: first, increasing taxes; second, increasing borrowing; and, third, increasing the money supply.

Governments know that relying on increased taxes to finance government spending is politically risky, though governments to the left are more inclined to raise taxes than governments to the right. But even governments to the left are careful in advocating higher taxes. Thus, relying on taxes to finance government spending is difficult and, as a result, borrowing is viewed as politically more feasible. But there's a downside to borrowing, because it shifts the demand for funds to the right and increases the interest rate (Figure 5.7). The higher interest rate draws attention to the economic impact of government spending, and the higher interest rate will reduce non-government spending; that is, increased government spending "crowds out" private spending. Nonetheless, borrowing is politically more feasible than increasing taxes, but a problem because government deficit spending increases interest rates.

Governments then find it politically convenient to directly or indirect encourage the central bank to increase the money supply to reduce the impact of the deficit on interest rates; that is, the central bank monetizes the new government debt issued to finance increased deficit spending (Figure 5.8), so that all or most of

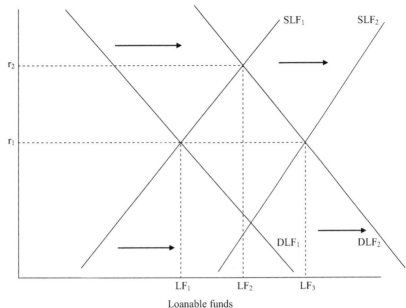

Figure 5.8. Increased Government Deficit Spending and Increase in the Money Supply and, on Balance, No Change in the Interest Rate.

the increase in the interest rate caused by increased government deficit spending is offset.

In this way, the deficits shift the demand function to the right (Figure 5.8: DLF_1 to DLF_2) and increase the interest rate from r_1 to r_2. The increase in the money supply, however, shifts the supply function to the right, from SLF_1 to SLF_2, and reduces the interest rate from r_2 back to r_1. In addition, borrowing and lending are even higher. The government deficit increases borrowing and lending from LF_1 to LF_2; however, the increase in the money supply not only brings the interest rate back to the original level but further increases the amount of borrowing and lending, from LF_2 to LF_3. This does not work in the long run, as will be explained later in the chapter, but in the short run the illustration in Figure 5.8 is realistic and suggests why central banks are targets of opportunity for politicians and the government.

Hence, there is a basic conflict between the government's fiscal program and central bank policy, and, as a result, much attention is directed toward establishing an "independent" central bank to reduce the ability of the government to pressure, directly or indirectly, central bank policy to monetize government deficit spending. In the past few decades central banks have been redesigned to provide greater independence from government. Much of this redesign was based on the view that an independent central bank is less susceptible to the conflict illustrated by

Figures 5.6, 5.7 and 5.8. We will return to this subject when we discuss the third component of the nation's financial and monetary regime: central banking and central bank policy.

5.8 The Nominal Interest Rate and the Real Interest Rate

It is time to drop the assumption that both lender and borrower anticipate no change in the price level over the maturity of the debt. This is accomplished by distinguishing between the nominal interest rate and the real interest rate. The nominal or market interest rate is the rate determined in the market while the real interest rate is the interest rate adjusted for expected inflation over the maturity of the loan. The nominal rate is observable while the real rate is unobservable. In the above discussion, the price level was assumed constant, and thus the expected inflation rate was zero. In this case, the nominal and real interest rates are equal, so that in all of the previous figures the demand for and supply of loanable funds determined the real (which was equal to the nominal) rate since expected inflation was zero.

The distinction between the nominal interest rate and the real interest rate is important, and, although it was known as far back as the eighteenth century, Irving Fisher over 100 years ago formalized the relationship by the following:

$$nr = rr + p_e \tag{5.1}$$

where nr is the nominal or market rate, rr is the real rate and p_e is the expected inflation rate. The maturity of the expected inflation rate matches the maturity of the interest rate; that is, if we are considering a one-year bond interest rate, the expected inflation rate is for the rate of inflation over the year. Expression 5.1 indicates that there is a one-to-one relationship between expected inflation and the nominal rate assuming a constant real interest rate. The nominal rate is 5 percent if expected inflation is zero assuming the real rate is 5 percent. If expected inflation increases by five percentage points, from 0 percent to 5 percent, the nominal rate will increase by the same amount – from 5 percent to 10 percent. Expression 5.1 is referred to as the *Fisher relationship*, and the effect of expected inflation on the nominal interest rate is referred to as the *Fisher effect*.

One can think of the real interest rate as the real return to lending and the real cost to borrowing determined by the loanable funds framework, assuming lenders and borrowers expect the price level to remain constant over the maturity of the loan. That is, the real interest rate is the equilibrium rate determined by the eight fundamentals as illustrated above. The nominal rate in general will not equal the real interest rate when the market anticipates a change in the price level over the maturity of the bond. As such, the nominal interest equals the real interest rate plus the expected inflation rate, p_e.

To fully understand the Fisher relationship, we need to deal with the following four questions. First, why is the nominal interest rate equal to the sum of the real interest rate and expected inflation? Second, is the magnitude of the relationship between the nominal interest rate and expected inflation equal to 1.0, as indicated by Expression 5.1? Third, how is expected inflation measured? Fourth, what are the bounds to Expression 5.1 (that is, will the nominal interest rate incorporate any expected inflation rate)?

Why the Fisher relationship makes sense: Consider a simple lending–borrowing transaction in which both lender and borrower anticipate no change in the price level; that is, $p_e = 0$. The lender is willing to loan the borrower $1,000 for one year at 10 percent. In real terms the lender expects to receive a real return of 10 percent at the end of the year when the principal and interest of $1,100 are paid; that is, the lender expects to not only have the principal repaid but to have that amount increased to represent a 10 percent increase in real purchasing power. The borrower is willing to incur a real cost of 10 percent or $100 plus the principal at the end of the year in order to receive $1,000 at the beginning of the year.

Now assume both lender and borrower anticipate a 5 percent increase in the price level over the year. If the lender accepted 10 percent for the loan, the real return at the end of the year would be 5 percent and not the equilibrium real return of 10 percent. That is, everything the lender wants to purchase at the end of the year has increased by 5 percent. The lender will now demand an inflation premium of five percentage points and, hence, ask for a 15 percent nominal interest rate to ensure a 10 percent real interest rate on the loaned funds. The borrower would like to obtain the funds without paying any interest, but the reality of the market is that the borrower will be willing to pay the 5 percent inflation premium for a total nominal interest rate of 15 percent. In real terms, the borrower is still paying a real interest rate of 10 percent, because the borrower anticipates his/her nominal earnings will increase by 5 percent.

Expected inflation now becomes a fifth fundamental that determines the interest rate. Figure 5.9 illustrates how expected inflation influences the interest rate in terms of the loanable funds approach. We start with the equilibrium nominal interest rate of 10 percent and borrowing and lending of $1,000, determined at the intersection of SLF_1 and DLF_1, which are based on the assumption the borrower and lender anticipate no change in the price level over the maturity of the bond – that is, $p_e = 0\%$. In this case, the 10 percent nominal interest rate is the real interest rate. The bracket next to the 10 percent equilibrium interest rate indicates the values of the three components of the Fisher relationship.

Assume now that the lender and borrower both anticipate a 5 percent inflation rate – that is, $p_e = 5\%$ – but none of the other underlying fundamentals embedded in SLF_1 and DLF_1 have changed, so that the real interest rate, rr, is still 10 percent. What happens next?

The demand for loanable funds will shift to the right from DLF_1 to DLF_2, because the expected inflation rate increased from 0 percent to 5 percent. Why? This is because, at any given nominal interest rate, the real cost of borrowing declines

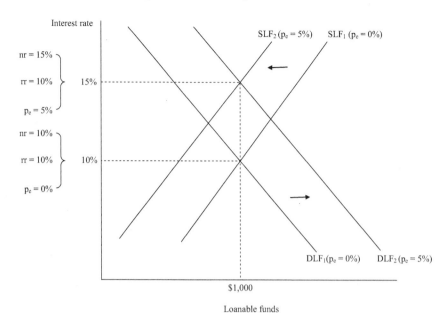

Figure 5.9. Expected Inflation Shifts the Demand for Loanable Funds to the Right and the Supply of Loanable Funds to the Left in Equal Amounts, So the Nominal Interest Rate Adjusts One to One to the Change in Expected Inflation.

with a 5 percent expected inflation rate. The borrower is always willing to borrow more at any nominal interest rate when higher inflation is expected since he/she can repay the loan with depreciated dollars. The demand function will shift to the right until the vertical distance between the new and old demand function is five percentage points. Why? If the borrower is willing to borrow \$1,000 at a nominal and real interest rate of 10 percent when $p_e = 0\%$, then the borrower should be willing to borrow \$1,000 at a nominal rate of 15 percent when $p_e = 5\%$. At a nominal rate of 15 percent the real rate to the borrower is 10 percent when $p_e = 5\%$, and at a nominal rate of 10 percent the real rate is 10 percent when $p_e = 0\%$.

The supply of loanable funds will shift to the left from SLF_1 to SLF_2 because expected inflation increases from 0 percent to 5 percent. Why? This is because, for any given nominal interest rate, the real return from lending declines with expected inflation; that is, the lender is always willing to lend less at any nominal interest rate if he/she expected higher inflation since he/she will be repaid with depreciated dollars. The supply function will shift to the left until the vertical distance between the new and old supply function is five percentage points. Why? If the lender is willing to lend \$1,000 at a nominal rate of 10 percent when $p_e = 0\%$, then the lender should be willing to lend \$1,000 at a nominal rate of 15 percent when $p_e = 5\%$. At a nominal rate of 15 percent the real rate to the lender is 10 percent when $p_e = 5\%$, and at a nominal rate of 10 percent the real rate is 10 percent when $p_e = 0\%$.

Hence, changes in expected inflation shift the demand for loanable funds to the right and the supply of loanable funds to the left in equal amounts, so that the nominal interest rate changes by the change in expected inflation. The real interest rate remains unchanged once the adjustment is complete since no other fundamental has changed. Economic research demonstrates that nominal interest rates not only rapidly adjust to changes in expected inflation but that much of the variation in nominal interest rates over time is due more to changes in expected inflation than to the real rate of interest.

Magnitude of the Fisher effect: Expression 5.1 and Figure 5.9 indicate that there is a one-to-one relationship between the nominal interest rate and expected inflation; that is, if the real interest rate is 10 percent and the expected inflation rate increases from 0 percent to 5 percent, the nominal interest rate will increase from 10 percent to 15 percent; and, likewise, if the expected inflation rate declines from 5 percent to 0 percent, the nominal interest rate will decline from 15 percent to 10 percent. There are times, however, when the relationship might be different from one to one; for example, the progressive income tax on interest earnings accounts for a greater than one-to-one relationship. In the above examples, the lender will require more than a 15 percent nominal interest rate if the high nominal interest rate pushes the lender into a higher tax bracket. The borrower will be willing to pay more than a 15 percent nominal interest rate since the interest deduction is higher. While the progressive income tax generates a Fisher effect greater than 1.0 percentage points, other factors generate a Fisher effect less than 1.0. The bottom line is that the Fisher relationship is about one to one, and economic research has found it to range from 0.8 to 1.2 percentage points over long periods of time.

Measuring expected inflation: The expected inflation rate is an important economic variable in macro- and monetary economics, and measures of the expected inflation rate are the only way to determine the real component of the nominal interest rate. There are three basic approaches to measuring expected inflation: first, to survey specific groups of individuals as to their expected inflation; second, to generate expected inflation based on econometric modeling; and, third, to use Treasury Inflation-Protected Securities (TIPS), introduced in 1997, to measure expected inflation.

The most well-known survey measure of expected inflation is based on the Livingston Survey of expected economic variables. Joseph Livingston, a financial columnist for *The Philadelphia Inquirer*, in 1946 started publishing the results of a survey conducted in June and December of each year of 40 to 60 "informed" individuals about their anticipations of several important economic variables, including their expected level of the CPI for the next year. Comparing the expected price index a year from the survey with the actual price index at the time of the survey generated an estimate of expected inflation for the next year. The Livingston Survey of expected inflation is the longest and most well-known measure of expected inflation

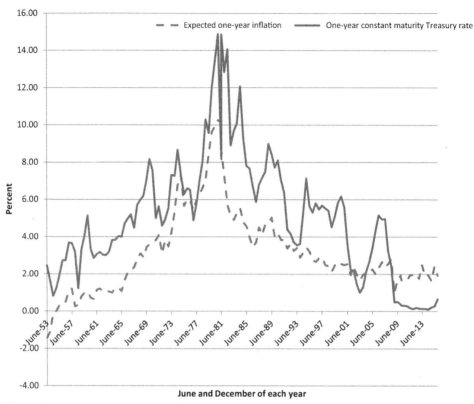

Figure 5.10. Livingston Survey of One-Year Expected Inflation and the One-Year Constant Maturity Treasury Security Interest Rate, June 1953 to December 2015. *Sources:* Federal Reserve Bank of Philadelphia (Livingston Survey expected inflation) and FRED, Federal Reserve Bank of St. Louis (constant maturity Treasury rate).

and has been frequently used in the economic literature to determine the relationship between economic variables, especially interest rates and expected inflation.

Figure 5.10 presents the Livingston Survey of expected inflation for one year on a biannual basis from June 1953 to December 2015 (dashed line). The one-year Treasury security interest rate is also presented (solid line) to show the close relationship between the nominal interest rate and expected inflation (correlation coefficient of 0.8), with the difference between the nominal interest rate and expected inflation representing an approximation of the real interest rate. The Livingston data and survey methods have been maintained by the Federal Reserve Bank of Philadelphia since 1990, representing the longest continuous series of expected inflation rates in the United States. Another widely used survey of expected inflation based on a different sample methodology is the University of Michigan Social Research Center survey of household expected inflation. All survey methods, however, are subject to sampling errors.

Econometric modeling based on combining a number of factors important in forming inflation expectations can also be used to estimate expected inflation; for example, the Federal Reserve Bank of Cleveland publishes estimates of expected inflation for different maturities based on a sophisticated time-series model. The problem with econometric modeling is the challenge of determining the correct set of factors that influence expected inflation and taking into account how those factors vary over time.

In January 1997 the U.S. Treasury began to issue bonds whose coupon payments and principal were indexed to the inflation rate, and, as a result, the TIPS interest rate is a direct estimate of the real interest rate. Comparing the interest rate on a non-indexed government security with the interest rate on a TIPS of the same maturity provides an estimate of the expected inflation rate over that maturity. The problem with this approach, however, is that the TIPS market is far less liquid than the market for government securities in general, and, as a result, the difference in yield between non-indexed government securities and TIPS is due to other factors than expected inflation. Also, TIPS interest rates have been available only since 1997.

In sum, all three approaches to measuring expected inflation have problems, but the survey-based methods, despite their sampling issues, are probably the best estimates of expected inflation because they are direct measures of what specific groups think the future price level will be at a specific point in time. The Livingston Survey continues to be used in academic research, and the results of the Survey are now published by the Federal Reserve Bank of Philadelphia.

Is the Fisher relationship bounded? The Fisher relationship is not bounded from above; that is, any expected inflation rate influences the nominal interest rate no matter how high the expected inflation. Nominal interest can incorporate very high inflation rates, even hyperinflation rates, though once the inflation rate reaches a certain point the financial and monetary regime of a country collapses, as money loses value literally by the hour, as it did in German hyperinflation after WWI.

However, the Fisher relationship is bounded from below, since the nominal interest rate cannot be lower than zero in normal times. A negative nominal interest rate implies the lender is willing to pay the borrower or the borrower returns an amount smaller than the loan in the future. This is economic nonsense; hence, the lower bound of the nominal interest rate is zero. But there have been several times in the past when some nominal interest rates have been negative in periods of uncertainty and high risk. These are special circumstances, each with its own story, but do not reject the argument that the Fisher relationship in Expression 5.1 is bounded from below by zero since the nominal interest rate cannot be zero, as the lender always has the option of not lending.

5.9 A Note on Negative Interest Rates

The issue of negative interest rates needs a little more attention, since in 2015 and 2016 several central banks announced negative interest rates on reserves of depository institutions, several countries experienced negative interest rates on government bonds and some private banks are starting to impose a negative interest rate on deposits.

In mid-2016 the European Central Bank and the central banks of Japan, Switzerland and Sweden were paying a negative interest rate on deposits, ranging from –0.40 percent for the European Central Bank to –0.10 percent for the Bank of Japan. These extraordinary rates are designed to discourage banks from holding reserves and, instead, lend those reserves to stimulate the economy. The intended effect, however, has not occurred, and these economies continue to experience distress.

Private banks in some cases are charging deposit customers a negative interest rate on liquid deposits; however, this is due to the generally very low interest rates they are receiving on loans and government bonds. In order to maintain a profitable interest rate spread some banks for some customers are finding it necessary to charge for holding the deposits in the form of a negative deposit rate.

Government bonds in Germany, Japan and Switzerland have paid a negative yield, which is most unusual. This means that bond holders are willing to pay the government for the privilege of holding bonds and are guaranteed a negative total return. The yield is negative and the capital gain will most likely be negative, because, if interest rates move up and into positive territory in the near future, the bond prices will decline. Many reasons have been offered for this remarkable development, and the loanable funds model of interest rates can technically generate a negative interest on government bonds. If the demand for bonds shifts sufficiently to the right, and the supply of funds thereby shifts sufficiently to the left, bond prices will increase and interest rates will decline toward zero and, under certain conditions, go below zero.

The issue of negative interest rates remains unresolved at this point, but two observations can be offered. First, they represent a much broader and unusual set of circumstances that indicate the limits of monetary policy to influence the economy. Second, these negative interest rates represent an exception to the lower bound condition on the Fisher equation, but they are not sustainable. They generate a wide range of distortions in the financial system and economy.

5.10 Interest Rates and Monetary Policy

The response of the interest rate to changes in monetary policy is important because many view interest rates as an indicator of the direction of monetary policy: easy monetary policy is identified with lower interest rates and tight monetary policy is identified with higher interest rates. This seems intuitive and consistent with the fact that most central banks conduct policy by targeting a very short-term interest rate, such as the federal funds rate, which is essentially an overnight interest rate in the federal funds market. At the same time, most interest rates are longer term

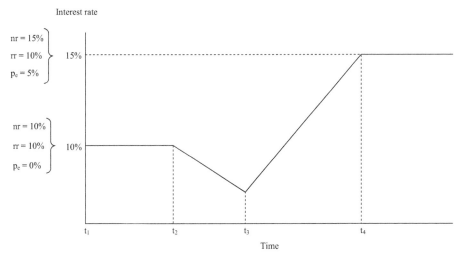

Figure 5.11. Response of the Interest Rate to an Increase in the Money Supply.

and subject to many influences beyond monetary policy, and generally are poor indicators of monetary policy.

This point can be illustrated by considering how the nominal and real interest rates respond to a change in monetary policy over time using the framework developed in this chapter. In Figure 5.11 the starting point is time t_1, when the nominal interest rate is 10 percent, the real interest rate is 10 percent and expected inflation is 0 percent. At time t_2, assume the Federal Reserve increases the growth of the money supply from 0 percent to 5 percent. The real interest rate declines as the supply of funds shifts to the right with a given demand for funds, and, since expected inflation has not changed, the decline in the nominal rate at t_2 is due entirely to a decline in the real rate. The lower real interest rate stimulates spending and increases income, which, in turn, shifts the demand for funds to the right and at first slows down the decline in the nominal and real interest rate and then increases the real interest rate starting at time t_3. At time t_3 expected inflation begins to increase as market participants begin to revise their expected inflation rate from 0 percent to a positive value in response to higher spending and income and resulting higher prices. The nominal interest rate will begin to increase further as expected inflation increases. How far will expected inflation be adjusted? According to the quantity theory of money, if the Federal Reserve increases the growth rate of money from 0 percent to 5 percent, the longer-term effect will be to increase inflation from 0 percent to 5 percent without changing the level of income, velocity and other variables from their pre-t_2 time. Let's assume this occurs at time t_4. At this point the real interest rate returns to its original level of 10 percent, because the nominal interest rate increases from 10 percent to 15 percent to incorporate the expected inflation rate of 5 percent.

Chapter 5. The Level of Interest Rates

The response of the interest rate to an increase in the money supply illustrated in Figure 5.11 can be divided into two parts. First, the *liquidity effect* from t_2 to t_3, during which the money supply increase reduces the real and nominal interest rate and begins to stimulate spending and income. Second, the *income effect* and *price expectations effect* from t_3 to t_4, during which spending, income, prices and expected inflation increase, increasing both the real and the nominal interest rate. Eventually the economy ends up with the same real rate, but a higher nominal rate to incorporate the higher expected inflation rate.

The time-phased response of the interest rate to an increase in the money supply illustrated in Figure 5.11 is not that far from what empirical research has demonstrated over the decades, and suggests three considerations. First, a simple illustration of how changes in money influence the interest rate holding inflationary anticipations constant (Figure 5.6) is just that – simple and often misleading. Part of the response to the increase in the money supply is a lower the real, and hence nominal, interest rate; however, eventually income, spending, prices and expected inflation increase. Second, the pressure placed on central banks to monetize government deficits works only in the shorter term, and, more likely than not, nominal interest rates will end up higher. Thus the monetization of debt is not a reliable policy in the longer term. The central bank cannot keep interest rates permanently low. Third, the interest rate is a poor indicator of the stance of monetary policy. In the liquidity phase, lower interest rates are the result of increased money supply; however, after the liquidity phase, increasing and higher interest rates are the result of increased money supply. Thus you get different perspectives on the stance of monetary policy depending on the time you consider the interest rate in response to the increase in the money supply.

Chapter 6

The Structure of Interest Rates

6.1 Introduction

The structure of interest rates is defined as the relationship between different interest rates at a point in time and how the relationship between various interest rates changes over time. Figure 6.1 illustrates this concept by presenting the one-year Treasury constant maturity rate, the five-year Treasury constant maturity rate, Moody's Seasoned Baa Corporate Bond Yield and the Bond Buyer 20 Municipal Bond Index from January 1998 to May 2016. It is clear that interest rates at points in time differ significantly from each other and that the relationship changes over time.

This chapter identifies the four basic determinants of the *structure of interest rates*: *default risk*, *liquidity*, *tax treatment* and *maturity*. The first three are straightforward while maturity is a subtly more complex influence on the structure of interest rates. While the influence of maturity on the structure of interest rates is complex, it provides important insights into the market's expectations of future inflation and economic activity. To emphasize the importance of maturity, the relationship between maturity and the structure of interest rates is referred to as the *term structure of interest rates*, as opposed to the more general concept of the structure of interest rates.

In the basic approach to understand how each of the four determinants of the structure of interest rates influences any interest rate and its relationship with other interest rates, one compares the interest rates on two securities, holding constant the other three factors. That is, to determine how default risk influences interest rates at a point in time and over time, compare the interest rate on securities with varying degrees of default risk with the interest rate on securities that have no default risk, holding constant liquidity, tax treatment and maturity for both securities. To determine how liquidity influences interest rates at a point in time and over time, compare the interest rates on securities with varying degrees of liquidity with the

115

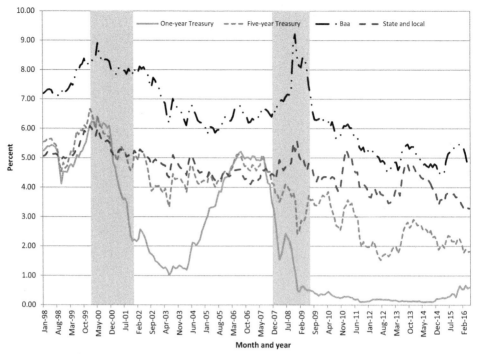

Figure 6.1. One-Year Treasury Constant Maturity Rate, Five-Year Treasury Constant Maturity Rate, Baa Corporate Bond Rate and State and Local Municipal Rate, January 1998 to May 2016. *Source:* FRED, Federal Reserve Bank of St. Louis.

interest rate on securities that have the highest degree of liquidity, holding default risk, tax treatment and maturity constant on both securities. To determine how maturity influences interest rates at a point in time and over time, compare the interest rate on securities with different maturities, holding constant default risk, liquidity and tax treatment on both securities.

Treasury securities (Treasury bills, Treasury notes and Treasury bonds) are usually the foundation or base interest rates to determine how default risk, liquidity, tax treatment and maturity influence other interest rates. Treasury securities have no default risk for all practical purposes; Treasury securities have a very high degree of liquidity; Treasury securities have the same tax treatment, with few exceptions; and interest rates on Treasury securities are available for a much wider range of maturities than other securities. There is extensive data on Treasury security interest rates in the form of interest rates for "constant maturities" of one, five, ten, etc. years; however, these interest rates are not for new Treasury securities with one-, five-, ten-, etc. year maturities, but are interest rates on existing Treasury securities with varying stated maturities but, at that point in time, have one, five, ten, etc. years of maturity remaining. That is, the ten-year Treasury constant maturity interest rate might include interest rates of 20- and 30-year bonds that have ten years of maturity remaining as well as ten-year bonds.

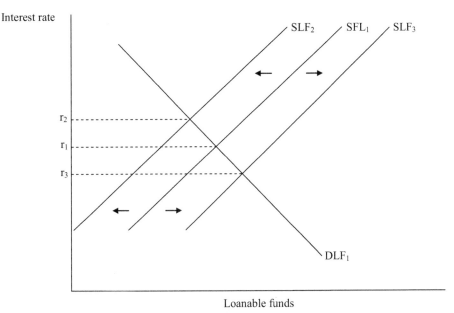

Figure 6.2. Effect of Default Risk on the Interest Rate.

In the following, we consider how each of the four determinants of the structure of interest rates influences any given interest rate and the structure of interest rates at a point in time and over time.

6.2 Default Risk

Default risk is the risk the issuer of the security will not pay the coupon interest and/or the principal of the security when it matures. Treasury securities as well as currency issued by the Federal Reserve and deposits at depository institutions (up to \$250,000) have no default risk for all practical purposes since the full faith and credit of the U.S. government stand behind these promises to pay. The federal government is able to deliver on this commitment more than any other issuer of a promise to pay. Government has far more ability to issue more securities to service existing securities than any state or local government; has the ability to increase taxes more than any state or local government; and, alone, has the ability to print money. Hence, debt issued by the federal government – coin, currency and securities – has no default risk, and nor do promises to pay issued by depository institutions up to the federal deposit insurance limit. All other promises to pay, unless guaranteed by the federal government, possess some degree of default risk. At the same time, the default-free status of government debt is not absolute.

The higher the degree of default risk for any given security, the higher the interest rate, other things held constant. This can readily be illustrated with the loanable funds approach in Figure 6.2. An increase in default risk shifts the supply of

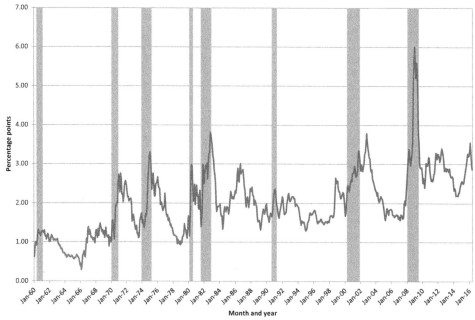

Figure 6.3. Moody's Seasoned Baa Corporate Bond Yield Relative to Yield on Ten-Year Treasury Constant Maturity, January 1960 to May 2016. *Source:* FRED, Federal Reserve Bank of St. Louis.

loanable funds to the left from SLF_1 to SLF_2 because, at any interest rate, the higher risk of the promise to pay reduces the willingness to lend. As a result, the interest rate increases from r_1 to r_2. A decrease in default risk shifts the supply of loanable funds to the right from SLF_1 to SLF_3 and the interest rate decreases from r_1 to r_3.

The degree of default risk embedded in an interest rate can be measured by comparing that interest rate to an interest rate with no default risk but with the same or close to the same degree of liquidity, tax treatment and maturity. To illustrate, the difference between the high-risk Baa corporate bond and the ten-year Treasury constant maturity interest rate in Figure 6.1 approximates the default risk on the corporate bond (Figure 6.3).

> Default Risk on Long-Term Baa Corporate Bond Interest Rate = Long-Term
> Baa Corporate Bond Interest Rate – Ten-Year Treasury Constant
> Maturity Interest Rate   (6.1)

The default risk effect varies over time, tending to decline during business cycle expansions and increase during contractions. Notice the sharp increase in the default risk component of the corporate bond rate during the financial crisis of 2008/2009. The interest rate spread in Figure 6.3, however, is not entirely due to differences in default risk, because corporate bonds are less liquid than Treasury securities and there exist differences in maturity, since the Baa rate includes various maturities whereas the Treasury rate is for a ten-year maturity.

In Chapter 5 the Fisher relationship was introduced to explain the difference between nominal and real interest rates:

$$nr = rr + p_e \qquad (6.2)$$

The Fisher relationship can be used as a foundation to illustrate how default risk, and the other determinants of the structure of interest rates, influence any given interest rate and the relationship between that interest rate and other interest rates. Expression 6.2 can be expanded to include a default risk premium by the following:

$$nr = rr + p_e + df \qquad (6.3)$$

where df is the default premium. In the case of Treasury securities, df = 0, but, in the case of all other securities, df > 0.

6.3 Liquidity or Marketability Effect

The liquidity of any real or financial asset is the ability to turn that asset into money by selling the asset on a secondary market. In the case of a security, there are two related determinants of the liquidity of the security: first, the existence, depth and extent of a secondary market for that security; and, second, the transactions cost of selling that security. Liquidity becomes an issue only if there is a non-zero probability the security will be sold before maturity.

The relationship between the liquidity and the interest rate can be illustrated with Figure 6.2, except now the shifts in the supply of loanable funds is due to changes in the liquidity of the promise to pay rather than default risk. A decrease in the liquidity of a security shifts the supply of loanable funds for that security to the left and thus increases the interest rate, while an increase in the liquidity of a security shifts the supply of loanable funds for that security to the right and thus decreases the interest rate. The change in the interest rate due to a change in liquidity is referred to as the liquidity premium effect.

The liquidity premium can be represented by the difference between a security with a low degree of liquidity and a security with a high degree of liquidity; for example, the spread between the corporate Baa interest rate and Treasury security rate illustrated in Figure 6.2 is partly the result of the liquidity premium, because corporate bonds possess less liquidity than Treasury securities. Not only do Treasury securities have a default risk effect of zero (df = 0), they are the most liquid financial assets in the money and capital markets. Treasury securities have lower selling transactions costs and a deeper and broader secondary market, with many participants, compared to any other security, but, unfortunately, the interest rate spread between Treasury securities and any other security reflects both the default risk and liquidity effect and there is no straightforward method to bifurcate the two effects.

The expanded Fisher relationship in Expression 6.3 can be extended to include the liquidity premium effect:

$$nr = rr + p_e + df + lp \qquad (6.4)$$

where lp is the liquidity premium that is added to an interest rate. In the case of Treasury securities, $lp = 0$, but, in the case of all other securities, $lp > 0$, since they possess less liquidity in terms of being able to be sold on the secondary market compared to Treasury securities.

6.4 Tax Treatment

The interest and capital gains received on securities are subject to federal income taxes as well as state income taxes in those states that have an income tax. The interest on municipal securities, however, is not subject to federal taxation nor state taxation for residents of a state holding that state's municipal securities. Municipal securities are subject to taxation on capital gains if sold before maturity, however. The exemption of interest on municipals from income taxes is a subsidy financed by the general taxpayer, rationalized by the fact that state, regional and local governments do not have the same resources as the federal government to provide basic infrastructure (roads, bridges, schools, hospitals, etc.), which has a large public good component that extends far beyond those living in the political boundaries of the issuing authority. The tax subsidy significantly reduces the cost of financing local infrastructure projects; however, in the past several decades most state, regional and local governments have abused the tax exemption by issuing municipals to finance sports stadiums, industrial parks and entertainment centers, which fall far outside the traditional rationale for the tax exemption.

To understand how the exemption of interest from income taxes influences the interest rate we need to consider the difference between before- and after-tax interest. The interest received on any security other than a municipal is the before-tax interest rate and, applying the appropriate tax rate, it is converted to an after-tax interest rate. Expression 6.5 illustrates this relationship between after-tax and before-tax interest:

$$nr_{aft} = nr_{bft}*(1 - tr) \qquad (6.5)$$

where nr_{aft} is the after-tax interest rate, nr_{bft} is the before-tax rate and tr is the marginal tax rate. Consider a Treasury security interest rate of 10 percent. The 10 percent interest rate is the before-tax interest rate, which, at a 40 percent marginal tax rate, becomes a 6 percent after-tax interest rate. In the case of municipal securities, $tr = 0$, so that the after-tax interest rate and the before-tax interest rate are the same.

The interest rate differential between municipal securities and high-grade corporate bond interest rates, assuming that default risk, liquidity and maturity are the same, is thus an implicit measure of the marginal tax rate. If the corporate before-tax interest rate is 10 percent and the municipal interest rate is 6 percent, this implies that the marginal tax rate on interest is 40 percent. Or another perspective is to assume the 40 percent marginal tax rate is the applicable tax rate for participants in the financial market; then the market will ensure that the interest rate on a municipal is 6 percent if the before-tax interest rate on an equivalent corporate security is 10 percent. If a state government attempted to sell a municipal at a higher-than-market price that generated a 5 percent interest rate, there would be no buyers, since the after-tax interest rate on the corporate security (6 percent) exceeds the municipal rate. If the state government lowered the municipal price to such a level that it generated a 7 percent interest rate, the market would bid up the price and lower the interest rate to 6 percent. The balance point of a before-tax interest rate of 10 percent on the corporate security and the 6 percent municipal rate is defined by Expression 6.5 assuming the marginal tax rate is 40 percent.

The extended Fisher relationship can be extended to incorporate a tax effect:

$$nr_{bft} = rr + p_a + df + lp$$
$$nr_{afr} = (rr + p_a + df + l\,p)^*(1 - tr) \tag{6.6}$$

In the case of municipal securities, $tr = 0$. As a result, municipal interest rates are consistently lower than interest rates on other securities with similar default risk, liquidity and maturity. It is difficult to illustrate the tax rate effect by comparing municipal rates with corporate or Treasury security rates even if one can match maturities because differences in default risk and liquidity risk also play a major role in determining the interest rate spread between municipal interest rates and other interest rates.

6.5 Maturity: The Term Structure of Interest Rates and the Yield Curve

Of the four determinants of the structure of interest rates, maturity is more complex and sometimes goes against intuition as to the relationship between interest rates and maturity. The term structure of interest rates is the relationship between interest rates and maturity, holding default risk, liquidity and tax treatment constant. Treasury securities provide the best set of interest rates to measure this relationship.

The term structure of interest rates is measured by the yield curve, which expresses yield as a function of maturity. The yield curve is usually presented in three forms on the same diagram: the yield curve as of today, the yield curve one week earlier, say, and the yield curve one year ago, say. Comparisons between the current yield curve and the previous yield curve provide information about the market's expectations regarding inflation and the direction of economic activity.

The yield curve exhibits one of three patterns (Figure 6.4): first, the ascending yield curve, in which interest rates are positively associated with maturity; second, the flat yield curve, in which interest rates are invariant to maturity; and, third, the

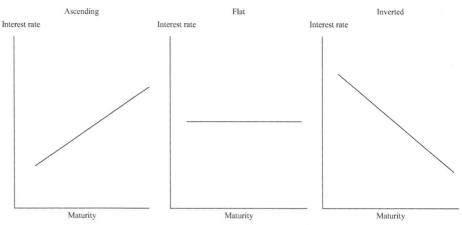

Figure 6.4. Three Common Shapes of the Yield Curve.

descending or *inverted* yield curve, in which interest rates are negatively associated with maturity. The ascending yield curve is intuitive to most readers, as they would expect to pay a higher rate for a longer-term loan; however, the flat and descending yield curve are not intuitive. All three yield curves have been observed, and even at one time in the 1970s, during the Great Inflation, the yield curve exhibited a "humped" shape; however, the upward-sloping or ascending yield curve is the most common shape.

There are two issues to be addressed with respect to the yield curves illustrated in Figure 6.4: first, what determines the shape of the yield curve; and, second, what can shifts in the yield curve reveal about market expectations of inflation and economic activity?

6.6 What Explains the Shape of the Yield Curve?

Any explanation of the yield curve needs to explain two empirical regularities about interest rates. First, interest rates tend to increase and decrease together, and as a result are highly correlated over time, as illustrated in Figure 6.1. Second, while all three shapes of the yield curve have been observed, including the humped shape that occurred in the late 1970s, the ascending or upward-sloping yield curve is the most frequently observed.

There are three explanations of the yield curve: the *unbiased expectations hypothesis*; the *liquidity premium or biased expectations hypothesis*; and the *segmented market* or *preferred habitat hypothesis*.

Unbiased expectations hypothesis: This view is based on the assumption that market participants over a given planning horizon are interested only in maximizing wealth and are indifferent to whether they hold a series of short-term securities over that planning horizon or one long-term security. Ignoring transactions cost, the interest rate on a bond of any maturity is equal to the average of the current short-term interest rate and the expected short-term interest rates over the maturity of the bond. A straightforward example illustrates the basic elements of the expectations hypothesis.

Consider a market participant with a planning horizon of two years who can choose a portfolio of one two-year bond or two one-year bonds. The transactions cost of the two portfolios are different, since transactions costs are lower for the portfolio with one two-year bond; however, we ignore transactions costs in this example. Transactions cost can be included in more detailed presentations of the expectations hypothesis without altering the basic premise that long-term interest rates are equal to the current short-term interest rate and the expected short-term interest rates over the maturity of the bond.

Assume the current interest rate on the one-year bond at the start of the first year is 5 percent and assume the market anticipates the short-term interest rate will be 10 percent at the start of the second year. It's not important as to how the market determines the expected short-term interest rate, but what is important is that the market makes portfolio decisions based on that expectation of the short-term interest rate at the start of the second year. Based on this expectation, the expected return of the portfolio of two one-year bonds is 7.5 percent – the average of the known short-term rate at the start of the first year and the expected short-term rate at the start of the second year.

What, then, must the interest rate at the start of the first year be on the two-year bond? It will equal 7.5 percent – the average of the current short rate and the expected short rate. Why? If the two-year bond rate were 8 percent, the market would realize that the portfolio of one two-year bond generated a higher expected return than a portfolio of two one-year bonds, which we determined is 7.5 percent. The demand for two-year bonds would increase, increasing price and reducing yield, until it was lowered to 7.5 percent. If the two-year bond rate were 6 percent, the market would decrease demand for two-year bonds, since the expected return on two one-year bonds is 7.5 percent. As a result, the price of two-year bonds would decrease and yield would increase to 7.5 percent.

In general, the interest rate on a bond with maturity of m periods at the beginning of the first period is

$$r_t^m = \text{Average}[r_t^1 + E(r^1_{t+1}) + E(r^1_{t+2}) \ldots E(r^1_{t+m})] \tag{6.7}$$

where the subscript t is time, the superscript is maturity in terms of periods, r_t^1 is the known rate of interest at the start of the first period for a bond with maturity of one period and E represents the market's expected interest rate on the one-period bond for each period starting at t+1 and ending at t+m.

Table 6.1 illustrates how Expression 6.7 works and how it can generate different shapes of the yield curve depending on the market's expected path of one-period bond interest rates over the maturity of the longer-maturity bond. Table 6.1 is based

Table 6.1. *Illustrating the Expectations Hypothesis and How It Generates Different Yield Curve Shapes*

Current year: 2015	One-year rate	Two-year rate	Three-year rate	Four-year rate	Five-year rate
Panel A					
Upward-sloping or ascending yield curve					
Current period, t (2015), one- to five-year market rates	**5.00**	**5.50**	**6.00**	**6.50**	**7.00**
Expected one-year market rate in t+1 (2016)	6.00				
Expected one-year market rate in t+2 (2017)	7.00				
Expected one-year market rate in t+3 (2018)	8.00				
Expected one-year market rate in t+4 (2019)	9.00				
Panel B					
Flat yield curve					
Current period, t (2015), one- to five-year market rates	**5.00**	**5.00**	**5.00**	**5.00**	**5.00**
Expected one-year market rate in t+1 (2016)	5.00				
Expected one-year market rate in t+2 (2017)	5.00				
Expected one-year market rate in t+3 (2018)	5.00				
Expected one-year market rate in t+4 (2019)	5.00				
Panel C					
Descending yield curve					
Current period, t (2015), one- to five-year market rates	**5.00**	**4.50**	**4.00**	**3.50**	**3.00**
Expected one-year market rate in t+1 (2016)	4.00				
Expected one-year market rate in t+2 (2017)	3.00				
Expected one-year market rate in t+3 (2018)	2.00				
Expected one-year market rate in t+4 (2019)	1.00				

on a five-period planning horizon. The current interest rates at time t (2015) are marked in bold. The other interest rates are expected interest rates. What needs to be explained is how the period 2, period 3, period 4 and period 5 one-period interest rates are determined at time t. The period 1 rate at time t is the base rate, with all other interest rates based on the known period 1 interest rate and the market's expectation of the one-period bond rate in each of the four remaining periods, t+1, t+2, t+3 and t+4.

The three panels of Table 6.1 illustrate how the expectations hypothesis generates the three yield curves. The shape of the yield curve is determined by the current one-period rate at time t and the expected one-period rate in periods t+1, t+2, t+3 and t+4 at time t.

In panel A the market expects one-period rates to increase each period through t+4 (2019) and, hence, the yield curve at time t is ascending. The period 2 bond rate is the average of the current one-period rate and the expected one-period rate in period t+1, or (5.00 + 6.00)/2 = 5.50; the period 3 bond rate is the average of the current one-period rate and the expected one-period rates in t+1 and t+2, or (5.00 + 6.00 + 7.00)/3 = 6.00; the period 4 bond rate is the average of the current one-period rate and the expected one-period rates in t+1, t+2 and t+3, or (5.00 + 6.00 + 7.00 + 8.00)/4 = 6.50; and, lastly, the period 5 rate is the average of the current one-period rate and the expected one-period rates in t+1, t+2, t+3 and t+4, or (5.00 + 6.00 + 7.00 + 8.00 + 9.00)/5 = 7.00.

In panel B the market expects one-period interest rates to remain constant at the current rate and, hence, the yield curve at time t is flat. In panel C the market expects one-period rates to decline and, hence, the yield curve at time t is inverted or descending.

Technically, Expression 6.7 is unbiased, because the interest rate on any long-term bond is the unbiased average of the current and expected short-term rates over the maturity of the bond, and hence it is sometimes referred to as the pure expectations hypothesis, to distinguish it from the liquidity premium hypothesis (below).

The expectations hypothesis can explain any shape of the yield curve, but does it incorporate the two empirical regularities of the term structure of interest rates? That is, can it explain the fact that interest rates move together over time, and can it explain why upward-sloping yield curves are more common than flat and inverted yield curves? The expectations hypothesis can easily explain why interest rates of different maturities move together, because the interest rate for every period 2, 3, 4 ... m bond at time t is an average of the current one-period bond rate and the expected interest rates on one-period bonds for periods 2, 3, 4 ... m. The expectations hypothesis, however, cannot explain why the upward-sloping yield curve is the most common, because it provides no insight into why markets expect any particular pattern of future interest rates on one-period bonds.

Liquidity premium hypothesis or biased expectations hypothesis: The liquidity premium hypothesis builds on the expectations hypothesis but, instead of assuming that market participants are indifferent between a portfolio of short- and long-term bonds, assumes market participants prefer to be short rather than long because of interest rate risk. The longer-term interest rate thus must be adjusted upward to include a liquidity premium to compensate for liquidity risk.

Expression 6.7 is modified to incorporate liquidity premiums:

$$r_t^m = \text{Average}[(r_t^1 + E(r_{t+1}^1) + E(r_{t+2}^1) + \ldots + E(r_{t+m}^1)] + lp_t^m \quad (6.8)$$

where lp_t^m is the liquidity premium at time t for a period m bond. The liquidity premium, lp_t, is a positive function of m; that is, the larger m is, the larger the lp factor that is added to the interest rate.

Table 6.2 illustrates the liquidity premium hypothesis. A liquidity premium at time t has been added to each panel used in Table 6.1. Notice that the liquidity premium at time t increases with maturity, as would be expected.

Table 6.2. *Illustrating the Liquidity Premium Hypothesis and How It Generates Different Yield Curve Shapes*

Current year: 2015	One-year rate	Two-year rate	Three-year rate	Four-year rate	Five-year rate
Panel A					
Upward-sloping or ascending yield curve					
Current period, t (2015), one- to five-year market rates	**5.00**	**5.55**	**6.06**	**6.57**	**7.08**
Expected one-year market rate in t+1 (2016)	6.00				
Expected one-year market rate in t+2 (2017)	7.00				
Expected one-year market rate in t+3 (2018)	8.00				
Expected one-year market rate in t+4 (2019)	9.00				
Liquidity premium (2015)		0.05	0.06	0.07	0.08
Panel B					
Flat yield curve					
Current period, t (2015), one- to five-year market rates	**5.00**	**5.05**	**5.06**	**5.07**	**5.08**
Expected one-year market rate in t+1 (2016)	5.00				
Expected one-year market rate in t+2 (2017)	5.00				
Expected one-year market rate in t+3 (2018)	5.00				
Expected one-year market rate in t+4 (2019)	5.00				
Liquidity premium (2015)		0.05	0.06	0.07	0.08
Panel C					
Descending yield curve					
Current period, t (2015), one- to five-year market rates	**5.00**	**4.55**	**4.06**	**3.57**	**3.08**
Expected one-year market rate in t+1 (2016)	4.00				
Expected one-year market rate in t+2 (2017)	3.00				
Expected one-year market rate in t+3 (2018)	2.00				
Expected one-year market rate in t+4 (2019)	1.00				
Liquidity premium (2015)		0.05	0.06	0.07	0.08

Considering panel A, the period 2 bond rate is the average of the current one-period rate and the expected one-period rate in period t+1 plus the liquidity premium at time t, or $(5.00 + 6.00)/2 + 0.05 = 5.55$; the period 3 bond rate is the average of the current one-period rate and the expected one-period rates in t+1 and t+2 plus the liquidity premium at time t, or $(5.00 + 6.00 + 7.00)/3 + 0.06 = 6.06$; the period 4 bond rate is the average of the current one-period rate and the expected one-period rates in t+1, t+2 and t+3 plus the liquidity premium at time t, or $(5.00 + 6.00 + 7.00 + 8.00)/4 + 0.07 = 6.57$; and, lastly, the period 5 bond rate is the average of the current one-period rate and the expected one-period rates in t+1, t+2, t+3 and t+4, or $(5.00 + 6.00 + 7.00 + 8.00 + 9.00)/5 + 0.08 = 7.08$. Notice that the yield curve in Table 6.2 compared to Table 6.1, for the same set of current and expected period 1 rates, has been shifted upward by the amount of the liquidity premium at each maturity; that is, the yield curve with the liquidity premium is now more upward-sloping than the upward-sloping yield curve without the liquidity premium (compare panel A in Table 6.2 with Table 6.1). The yield curve with the liquidity premium is now upward-sloping compared to the flat yield curve without the liquidity premium (compare panel B in Table 6.2 with Table 6.1). To obtain a flat yield curve the market's expected one-period interest rates must decline by the increase in the liquidity premiums so that the two influences offset each other. The yield curve with the liquidity premium is less downward-sloping than the downward-sloping yield curve without the liquidity premium (compare panel C in Table 6.2 with Table 6.1).

The liquidity hypothesis is also referred to as the biased expectations hypothesis, because the longer interest rate is a biased average of the current and expected short-term interest rates because it incorporates a positive liquidity premium that is directly related to maturity.

Like the expectations hypothesis, the liquidity premium hypothesis can explain the tendency for interest rates of different maturities to move together over time, because the liquidity premium is based on the same model in which each longer rate is an average of the current one-period bond rate and the expected one-period bond rate over the maturity of the longer-term bond. The liquidity premium, however, can account for the more frequent occurrence of upward-sloping yield curves. It biases each longer interest rate upward because each longer rate now includes a liquidity premium, which increases at a given time with maturity.

Segmented market or preferred habitat hypothesis: This view of the yield curve is much different from either the expectations or liquidity premium hypothesis in that it views short- and long-term bonds as separate markets, because participants have specific planning horizons and have specific asset–liability configurations or tax issues that provide incentives to operate in only one maturity range. The yield curve shape can then be explained by the relative interest rate and bond price determined in each segment of the market and, hence, can generate any shape of the yield curve. Most of the time, however, the segmented market hypothesis generates an upward-sloping yield curve because market participants are risk-averse and demand high liquidity premiums the longer the maturity of the bond. In contrast, the segmented market hypothesis has a little more difficulty explaining why interest rates of different maturities move together over time because each market, by definition, is separate. Also, financial liberalization and institutional change in the financial system over the past several decades make it hard to accept a view that emphasizes restraints on the substitutability of different maturity bonds.

In sum, of the three explanations of the shape of the yield curve, the expectations and liquidity premium hypotheses are preferable, and, of the two, the liquidity premium is probably the most reasonable explanation, because it can account for the more frequent occurrence of upward-sloping yield curves.

Table 6.3. *The Yield Curve as a Leading Indicator of Inflation*

Current year: 2015 Panel A: base case	One-year bond			Three-year bond
Period (t = 2015, t+1 = 2016, t+2 = 2017)	t	t+1	t+2	t
Real interest rate	3.00	3.00	3.00	3.00
Expected inflation	3.00	3.00	3.00	3.00
Nominal interest rate	6.00	6.00	6.00	6.00
Panel B: increased expected inflation	One-period bond			Three-period bond
Period (t = 2015, t+1 = 2016, t+2 = 2017)	t	t+1	t+2	t
Real interest rate	3.00	3.00	3.00	3.00
Expected inflation	3.00	4.00	5.00	4.00
Nominal interest rate	6.00	7.00	8.00	7.00

6.7 The Yield Curve as a Rorschach Inkblot Test of Expected Inflation

The yield curve and changes in the yield curve are considered leading indicators of future inflation because the yield curve is based on averages of expected nominal interest rates, which in turn consist of a real interest rate and expected inflation. Holding constant the real interest rate makes it possible to determine how the yield curve changes when expected inflation changes. There is evidence that the yield curve provides insight into what the market expects to happen to the inflation rate; however, while the evidence is suggestive and the underlying theory is sound, the yield curve cannot be mechanically used to predict future inflation because too many factors need to be held constant. In other words, use the yield curve as an indicator of future inflation with caution. We will first explain how the yield curve is an indicator of future inflation and then explain why the relationship needs to be considered in a broader context.

To accomplish this we need to decompose the variable r for the nominal interest rate in Expressions 6.7 and 6.8 into their two components: the real interest rate and expected inflation.

Table 6.3 provides an illustration of how the yield curve can be used as an indicator of future changes in the price level. Panel A is the base case. The base case consists of a three-period planning horizon and three different bond maturities: one-period, two-period and three-period bonds. The real interest rate, rr, on a one-period bond at the start of the first period, t, is 3 percent and expected to remain at 3 percent in periods t+2 and t+3; hence, the real rate on a three-year bond at the start of the first period is 3 percent based on the expectations hypothesis. The actual inflation rate and expected inflation rate at the start of the first period, t, are equal and set to 3 percent; however, the market expects no change in the inflation rate, so the expected inflation rate over the three periods is $(3.0 + 3.0 + 3.0)/3 = 3.0\%$.

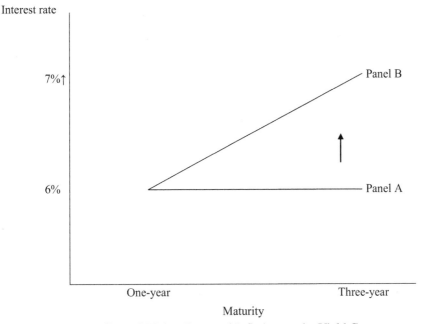

Figure 6.5. Effect of Higher Expected Inflation on the Yield Curve.

Using the Fisher relationship, the nominal interest rate on one-period bonds in t, t+1 and t+2 is 6.00 percent and the nominal interest rate at time t on three-period bonds is 6.00 percent. The yield curve at time t measured as the difference between the one- and three-period bond rates is zero or flat (Figure 6.5).

In panel B the market's expected real interest rate remains unchanged, but the expected inflation rate increases in t+1 to 4.0 percent and in t+2 to 5.0 percent. The three-period expected inflation is now 4.00 percent and the nominal interest rate on one-period bonds incorporates the higher expected inflation rate, so that in t+1 the expected interest rate increases from 6.00 to 7.00 percent and in t+2 the expected interest rate increases from 6.00 to 8.00 percent. The nominal interest rate at time t on three-period bonds increases from 6.00 to 7.00 percent. The yield curve at time t, measured as the difference between the one- and three-period bond rates, is +1.00 or upward-sloping (Figure 6.5).

Hence, other things held constant, increased expected inflation increases the slope of the yield curve, and, likewise, decreases in expected inflation reduce the slope of the yield curve. The problem is holding other things constant. There are at least two other factors that could cause the yield curve in this example to increase or decrease. Increases (decreases) in the liquidity premium could shift the yield curve up (down) holding expected inflation and the real interest rate constant. More important, increases (decreases) in real economic activity can change the shape of the yield curve in the same way, operating through changes in the expected one-period real interest rate rather than expected inflation.

Table 6.4. *The Yield Curve as a Leading Indicator of the Business Cycle*

Current year: 2015 Panel A: base case	One-period bond			Three-period bond
Period (t = 2015, t+1 = 2016, t+2 = 2017)	t	t+1	t+2	t
Real interest rate	3.00	3.00	3.00	3.00
Expected inflation	3.00	3.00	3.00	3.00
Nominal interest rate	6.00	6.00	6.00	6.00
Panel B: increased real economic activity	One-period bond			Three-period bond
Period (t = 2015, t+1 = 2016, t+2 = 2017)	t	t+1	t+2	t
Real interest rate	3.00	4.00	5.00	4.00
Expected inflation	3.00	3.00	3.00	3.00
Nominal interest rate	6.00	7.00	8.00	7.00

6.8 The Yield Curve as a Rorschach Inkblot Test of the Business Cycle

Shifts in the yield curve occur when the expected short-term interest rates change; however, the expected short-term nominal interest rate consists of the real interest rate and expected inflation. In Table 6.3 the real rate was held constant and we focused on changes in expected inflation to see how the yield curve can be used as an indicator of the market's expected inflation rate. Now we hold expected inflation constant and see how changes in the expected real interest rate can be used as an indicator of the future business cycle. An expansion in economic activity will increase the real interest rate, as discussed in Chapter 5; hence, an increase in expected real interest rates is consistent with an expected expansion in the economy. Likewise, a contraction in economic activity will decrease the real interest rate; hence, a decrease in expected real interest rates is consistent with an expected contraction in the economy.

Panel A in Table 6.4 is the same base case used in panel A of Table 6.3. Panel B illustrates how the market's expectation of increasing real economic activity influences the yield curve. The market expects a business cycle expansion, which in turn means that the market expects real interest rates to increase because it expects the demand for funds to shift further to the right than the supply of funds. The real interest rate at time t is still 3.00 percent, but the market expects the real interest rate in t+1 to increase from 3.00 percent to 4.00 percent and in t+2 from 3.00 percent to 5.00 percent. The yield curve shifts from 0.0 to +1.0, as illustrated in Figure 6.6. If the market expects a decline in the economy, reflected by the expected decline in the one-period real interest rate in period t+1 and t+2, the yield curve will shift from flat to descending or become inverted.

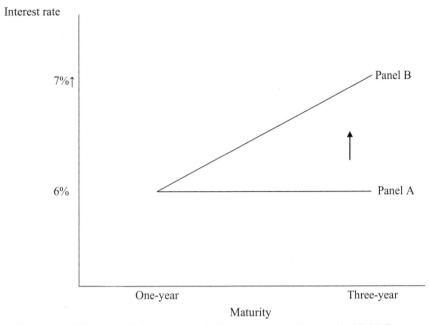

Figure 6.6. Effect of Higher Expected Economic Activity on the Yield Curve.

6.9 The Yield Curve as a Rorschach Inkblot Test of Both Inflation and the Business Cycle

Setting aside changes in the liquidity premium, an upward-shifting yield curve is consistent with both an increase in expected inflation and expected expansion of the economy. However, it is difficult to distinguish between the two causes of the upward-shifting yield curve, because expected inflation and expected increased economic activity are correlated. Likewise, a downward-shifting yield curve is consistent with both a decrease in expected inflation and expected contraction of the economy. However, they are correlated with each other, and thus it is difficult to separate their effect on the yield curve.

What this means, however, is that increasing yield curves are leading indicators of increased economic activity and/or inflation. Determining the degree to which each influences the yield curve is difficult, to say the least, and, taking into account changes in liquidity premiums, one should not attempt to use the yield curve as a mechanical indicator of future economic activity.

Chapter 7

International Dimensions of the Financial System

7.1 Introduction

The discussion up to this point has focused on domestic lending and borrowing and largely ignored the international dimensions of the financial system. This chapter reviews the international dimensions from several perspectives to complete the discussion of the nation's financial system. Aside from understanding the basics of international finance, international financial considerations are important for understanding central bank policy. Central banks often intervene in the international financial market and are often influenced by developments in the international financial market. This chapter focuses on the following dimensions of the international financial system considered the most important.

First, we consider how the balance of payments or international transactions accounts measure the real and financial relationship between the nation and the rest of the world, and, for simplicity, we refer to these accounts as the statement of international transactions (SIT). Second, the SIT is then used as a framework to explain the determination of exchange rates, the relationship between domestic interest rates and world interest rates and how central banks intervene in the foreign exchange market. Third, the two foreign exchange rate regimes – fixed and flexible exchange rates – are discussed in terms of how each functions and why fixed exchange rate regimes seldom work over long periods of time. This discussion includes a brief history of exchange rate regimes, focusing on the period since the end of WWII. Fourth, and finally, we consider the basic economics of trade imbalances between the nation and the rest of the world.

7.2 U.S. Statement of International Transactions

The SIT is a flow of funds statement of receipts from and payments to the rest of the world from the perspective of the United States. The receipts and payments

Table 7.1. *Statement of International Transactions, 2010 to 2013*

	2010	2011	2012	2013
Current account (millions of dollars)				
Exports of goods and services and income receipts (credits)	**$2,630,799**	**$2,987,571**	**$3,085,260**	**$3,178,744**
Goods	$1,290,273	$1,499,240	$1,561,689	$1,592,784
Services	$563,333	$627,781	$654,850	$687,410
Income receipts	$777,193	$759,727	$762,885	$780,120
Imports of goods and services and income payments (debits)	**$3,074,729**	**$3,446,914**	**$3,546,009**	**$3,578,998**
Goods	$1,938,950	$2,239,886	$2,303,785	$2,294,453
Services	$409,313	$435,761	$450,360	$462,134
Income payments	$726,466	$538,766	$559,892	$580,466
Balance on current account	**−$443,930**	**−$459,344**	**−$460,749**	**−$400,254**
Balance on goods and services	−$494,658	−$548,625	−$537,605	−$476,392
Balance on goods	−$648,678	−$740,646	−$742,095	−$701,669
Balance on services	$154,020	$192,020	$204,490	$225,276
Financial account (millions of dollars)				
Net U.S. acquisition of financial assets (net increase in assets/ financial outflow (+))	$963,606	$497,506	$179,246	$647,423
Net U.S. incurrence of liabilities (net increase in liabilities/ financial inflow (+))	$1,400,421	$1,012,079	$609,641	$1,017,669
Balance on financial account	**$436,815**	**$514,573**	**$430,395**	**$370,246**
Statistical discrepancy	$7,116	−$55,229	$30,353	$30,008
Balance on financial account adjusted for statistical discrepancy	**$443,931**	**$459,344**	**$460,748**	**$400,254**

Note: Transfers included in income category in current account.
Source: Bureau of Economic Analysis.

represent both real and financial transactions between the United States and the rest of the world. Receipts occur whenever the United States sells goods to, sells services to, receives income payments from or sells financial assets to the rest of the world. Receipts are sources of funds to the United States and recorded as a credit. Payments occur whenever the United States purchases goods from, purchases services from, makes income payments to or purchases financial assets from the rest of the world. Payments are uses of funds by the United States and recorded as a debit.

The SIT is a flow of funds statement and, as such, total receipts (sources of funds) equal total payments (uses of funds). Thus, any reference to an imbalance, such as a trade deficit or trade surplus, refers to an imbalance between receipts and payments for a specific subdivision of the total statement. Table 7.1 presents a condensed version of the actual U.S. SIT for the years from 2010 to 2013 to illustrate how the SIT is constructed and interpreted.

The SIT is divided into two parts: the *current account (CA)* and the *financial account (FA)*. The current account represents flows of goods, services, income payments and transfers while the financial account represents flows of financial assets. The FA is a mirror image of the CA, as is illustrated by the following expression:

Receipts in the CA + Receipts in the FA = Payments in the CA + Payments in the FA

Receipts in the CA – Payments in the CA = Payments in the FA – Receipts in the FA

Balance in the CA (Receipts – Payments) Offset by Balance in the FA (Receipts – Payments)   (7.1)

The current account: Receipts in the CA represent receipts received by the United States from the rest of the world when the United States exports goods (e.g., sells a car to Japan), exports services (e.g., Japan purchases U.S. transportation or financial services to get the car to Japan), receives income (Japan pays interest and dividend payments on U.S.-held Japanese financial instruments to the United States) or receives a transfer (Japan sends funds to someone living in the United States). Exports of goods, services, etc. to the rest of the world are thus a source of funds to the United States.

Payments in the CA represent payments made to the rest of the world when the United States imports goods (e.g., purchases a car from Japan), imports services (e.g., the United States purchases Japan transportation or financial services to get the car to the United States), makes income payments (the United States pays interest and dividend payments on U.S. financial instruments held by Japan) or makes a transfer (the United States sends funds to someone living in Japan). Imports of goods, services, etc. from the rest of the world are thus a use of funds by the United States.

Flows of goods, services, etc. in the CA are reflected by flows of financial assets in the FA; that is, they are mirror images of each other.

The financial account: Receipts in the FA represent funds received by the United States when it sells financial assets to the rest of the world. Receipts in the FA are referred to as *financial inflows* or borrowing. Payments in the FA represent payments made by the United States when it purchases financial assets from the rest of the world. Payments in the FA are referred to as *financial outflows* or lending.

Since the SIT is a sources and uses statement in which total sources and uses are equal, the balance in the CA must be offset by the balance in the FA, as illustrated by Expression 7.1. If the CA is in surplus (receipts > payments) then the FA is in deficit (receipts < payments). If the CA is in deficit (receipts < payments) then the FA is in surplus (receipts > payments), and if the CA is in balance (receipts = payments) then the FA is in balance (receipts = payments). This is obvious from the accounting identity that total sources must equal total uses, but there is an intuitive perspective to understand the relationship between the two parts of the SIT.

A CA deficit country is one that imports more than it exports and, as a result, the country must finance the difference by net borrowing from the rest of the world. In terms of the flow of funds framework, the country is a deficit unit and thus a net borrower. A CA surplus country is one that exports more than it imports and, as a result, the country must finance the difference by lending to the rest of the world. In terms of the flow of funds framework, the country is a surplus unit and thus a net lender.

The current and financial accounts in 2013: The 2013 SIT in Table 7.1 can be used to illustrate Expression 7.1. In 2013 the United States sold goods and services and received income from the rest of the world totaling $3,179 billion. The United States purchased goods and services and paid income to the rest of the world totaling $3,579 billion. As a result, in 2013, the United States had a CA deficit of $400 billion (indicated as –$400 billion); that is, in 2013 the United States made more payments to the rest of the world than it received from the rest of the world from the perspective of the CA.

The CA balance is the best overall measure of the relationship between the United States and the rest of the world in terms of flows of goods, services and income; however, one can compute various sub-balances within the CA listed in Table 7.1. There is the balance on goods and services (–$476 billion), the balance on goods (–$702 billion) and the balance on services ($225 billion). The balance on goods or trade balance is frequently cited in the news media far more than the current account balance; however, the current account balance is the most important, because it reflects how much the United States is a net borrower or net lender to the rest of the world. In addition, the sub-balance can provide a misleading view of the competitiveness of the United States in the world economy. Note that, while the goods or trade balance was in deficit in 2013, the service balance was in surplus. The United States is a major provider of services, especially financial services, to the rest of the world.

The overall SIT must balance because it is based on double-entry bookkeeping; that is, total receipts must equal total payments. A deficit in the CA is offset by net borrowing from the rest of the world and a surplus in the CA is offset by net lending to the rest of the world. In Table 7.1 the United States in 2013 increased its claims on the rest of the world (purchasing financial assets or lending) by $647 billion while, at the same time, it increased its liabilities to the rest of the world (selling financial assets or borrowing) by $1,018 billion. Hence, the FA is in surplus, since receipts ($1,018 billion) exceed payments ($647 billion) by $370 billion. The FA surplus of $370 billion, however, is not equal to the CA deficit of $400 billion, seeming to contradict Expression 7.1. The difference represents the difficulty of measuring the components of the SIT, especially financial flows. The SIT must balance, according to Expression 7.1; hence, a "statistical discrepancy" factor of

$30 billion is added to the FA balance to generate an adjusted FA balance of $400 billion, which is the same value as the CA balance except for rounding.

Therefore, Expression 7.1 can be restated in terms of the SIT for 2013 incorporating the value for statistical discrepancy, which in 2013 is a receipt in the FA. Totals are equal except due to rounding:

Receipts in the CA + Receipts in the FA = Payments in the CA + Payments in the FA

$3,179 + ($1,018 + $30) = $3,579 + $647

Receipts in the CA – Payments in the CA = Payments in the FA – Receipts in the FA

$3,179 – $3,579 = $647 – ($1,018 + $30)

Balance in the CA (Receipts – Payments) Offset by Balance in the FA (Receipts – Payments)

–$400 = $401   (7.2)

In 2013 the CA imbalance of –$400 billion was offset by net financial flows of $400, which represented an increase in foreign claims on the United States. The foreign claims on the United States occur in a variety of ways; for example, foreign financial inflows are used to purchase U.S. financial assets such as stocks, bonds and government securities; make direct investments in the United States, such as building factories; and purchase international reserves held by the United States.

7.3 Foreign Exchange Rates and the Foreign Exchange Market

The foreign exchange rate expresses the amount of one country's currency (the home country) needed to purchase another country's currency (the foreign currency). An exchange rate between the Japanese yen and the dollar of ¥100 to $1.00 indicates that $1.00 will purchase 100 yen or 1 yen will purchase $0.01. Before discussing the foreign exchange market and the exchange rate determined in that market, two questions need to be answered. Why are exchange rates important? How does one actually engage in a foreign exchange transaction?

Foreign exchange rates are important because the world conducts real and financial transactions in different currencies and the foreign exchange market facilitates international trade and finance with these different currencies. To illustrate, when you purchase a Japanese-made product in the United States, you pay dollars for the product. The Japanese exporter, however, wants to be ultimately paid in yen, so there has to be some mechanism for exchanging dollars into yen. Likewise, when Japan purchases a U.S. product in Japan, the purchase is made in yen, but ultimately the U.S. exporter wants to be paid in dollars. Not only does the foreign exchange market facilitate international economic activity in a world full of different currencies, but the exchange rate determined in these markets influences economic activity and central bank policy.

The foreign exchange rate influences a country's exports and imports, and, as the world becomes more economically integrated, exports and imports become a larger part of the domestic economy in every country. If a country's currency depreciates (the foreign currency appreciates) so that it buys less foreign exchange, the country's exports increase and imports decrease.

A depreciation of the dollar, for example, occurs when the yen/dollar exchange rate decreases from ¥100 to ¥50 per dollar. At the lower exchange rate, U.S.-produced goods and services become less expensive to the Japanese; for example, a $1,000 U.S.-produced good now costs the Japanese ¥50,000, instead of ¥100,000, at the lower rate with an appreciated yen. Thus, U.S. exports to Japan will increase. The lower exchange rate also increases the cost of Japanese-produced goods and services. A ¥100,000 Japanese-produced good now costs $2,000, instead of $1,000, at the lower rate with a depreciated dollar. Thus, U.S. imports from Japan will decrease. Changes in exports and imports are important determinants of domestic economic activity in any country.

Most readers are familiar with a small part of the foreign exchange market. Most have visited another country and purchased that country's currency with their own currency at the airport and, upon leaving the country, exchanged any remaining currency back into the home currency at the airport. This, however, is only part of a complex interrelationship between several hundred banks and other dealers that are willing to buy and sell deposits denominated in different currencies. These dealers don't buy or sell actual dollars, yen or euros but, instead, buy and sell deposits denominated in dollars, yen or euros. These transactions are in large denominations, usually well over a million dollars per transaction, and in any given day the volume of the transactions in deposits denominated in different currencies is enormous – several trillion dollars per day. The net foreign exchange transactions, however, are much less. If a U.S. bank owes $10 million in dollar deposits to a British bank that owes the U.S. bank $9 million in dollar deposits, the net transaction is $1 million.

The foreign exchange market consists of both a spot market and a futures or forward market. The spot market consists of buying and selling foreign exchange for immediate delivery, usually a two-day period. The forward market consists of buying and selling foreign exchange for delivery at some specific time in the future. The spot or current foreign exchange rate is today's price of one currency relative to another, whereas the forward foreign exchange rate is the market's expectation of the spot foreign exchange rate that will exist at some specific time in the future.

7.4 The Exchange Rate

The determinants of the exchange rate can be explained by considering only two countries – Japan and the United States. The exchange rate between the Japanese yen and the U.S. dollar can be understood either from the perspective of the supply

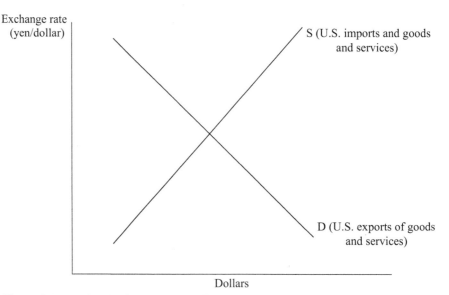

Figure 7.1. Foreign Exchange Market from the Perspective of the Current Account.

and demand for dollars or the supply and demand for yen. In the former case, the yen/dollar rate is the price variable, and, in the latter case, the dollar/yen rate is the price variable. In the following, the focus is on the demand and supply for dollars and the yen/dollar exchange rate.

The determinants of the exchange rate can be best understood by first considering how the exchange rate is determined from the perspective of the CA and then from the perspective of the FA. There is only one exchange rate, but the different factors that influence the exchange rate and the interrelationship between the CA and FA can best be understood by using this two-step approach.

The exchange rate from the perspective of the CA: Figure 7.1 illustrates the yen/dollar exchange rate determined by the demand and supply for dollars from the perspective of the CA.

Demand for dollars: Let's first consider the demand function for dollars by answering the following three questions. What does the demand for dollars represent? Why is the demand function downward-sloping? What are the fundamental factors that shift the demand for dollars?

The quantity of dollars demanded at any exchange rate represents U.S. exports of goods and services to Japan. Japanese purchasers of U.S.-produced goods and services pay in yen, but the yen is then supplied to the foreign exchange market to demand dollars to pay U.S. exporters. U.S. exporters ultimately want to be paid in dollars.

The demand for dollars is downward-sloping because, as the exchange rate declines, the yen price of U.S.-produced goods and services declines because it requires fewer yen to purchase dollars. In the above example, a $1,000 U.S.-produced good costs Japan ¥100,000 at the exchange rate of ¥100/$1.00, but at ¥50/$1.00 the same item costs Japan ¥50,000. Hence, as the exchange rate declines, the dollar depreciates and the yen appreciates, and the quantity of dollars demanded increases, and vice versa.

The demand function in Figure 7.1 is drawn holding "other things constant." Any change in these variables held constant will shift the demand function so that the quantity of dollars demanded at any exchange rate will either be higher (increase in demand – rightward shift in demand for dollars) or lower (decrease in demand – leftward shift in demand for dollars). The following six factors are considered important.

1 An increase in Japan's GDP will increase Japanese spending on both domestic and U.S.-produced goods and services and shift the demand function to the right. Likewise, a decrease in Japan's GDP will shift the demand function to the left.
2 An increase in Japan's preferences for U.S. goods and services will increase demand for U.S.-produced goods and services and shift the demand function to the right. A decrease in Japanese preferences for U.S. goods and services will shift the demand function to the left.
3 An increase in U.S. productivity will permit U.S. exporters to reduce prices and maintain profit margins; hence, lower prices of U.S.-produced goods and services will shift the demand function to the right. A decrease in U.S. productivity will shift the demand function to the left.
4 Increased government subsidies to U.S. exporters, such as tax credits or lower-interest-rate loans, will permit exporters to lower prices and, as a result, the demand function will shift to the right. Reduced U.S. government subsidies will shift the demand function to the left.
5 Decreased Japanese tariffs, quotas or other trade restrictions on U.S.-produced goods and services imported into Japan will shift the demand function to the right. Increased Japanese tariffs, quotas or other trade restrictions will shift the demand function to the left.
6 Lower U.S. prices on U.S.-produced goods and services exported to Japan will shift the demand function to the right. Higher domestic prices will shift the demand function to the left.

Supply of dollars: Let's now consider the supply function of dollars by answering the following same three questions. What does the supply of dollars represent? Why is the supply function upward-sloping? What are the fundamental factors that shift the supply of dollars?

The quantity of dollars supplied at any exchange rate represents U.S. imports of goods and services from Japan. U.S. purchasers of Japanese-produced goods and services pay in dollars, but the dollars are then supplied to the foreign exchange market to demand yen to pay Japanese exporters. Japanese exporters ultimately want to be paid in yen.

The supply of dollars is upward-sloping because, as the exchange rate declines, the dollar price of Japanese-produced goods and services increases because it now requires more dollars to purchase yen. In the above example, a ¥100,000 Japanese-produced good costs the United States $1,000 at the exchange rate of ¥100/$1.00, but at ¥50/$1.00 the same item costs the United States $2,000. Hence, as the exchange rate declines, the dollar depreciates and the yen appreciates, and the quantity of dollars supplied decreases, and vice versa.

The supply function in Figure 7.1 is drawn holding "other things constant." Any change in these variables held constant will shift the supply function so that the quantity of dollars supplied at any exchange rate will either be higher (increase in supply – rightward shift in supply) or lower (decrease in supply – leftward shift in supply). The following six factors are considered important.

1 An increase in U.S. GDP will increase U.S. spending on both domestic and Japanese-produced goods and services and shift the supply function to the right. Likewise, a decrease in U.S. GDP will shift the supply function to the left.

2 An increase in U.S. preferences for Japanese goods and services will increase demand for Japanese-produced goods and services and shift the supply function to the right. A decrease in U.S. preferences for Japan goods and services will shift the supply function to the left.

3 An increase in Japanese productivity will permit Japanese exporters to reduce prices and maintain profit margins; hence, lower prices for Japanese-produced goods and services will shift the supply function to the right. A decrease in Japanese productivity will shift the supply function to the left.

4 Increased government subsidies to Japanese exporters, such as tax credits or lower-interest-rate loans, will permit exporters to lower prices and shift the supply function to the right. Reduced Japanese government subsidies will shift the supply function to the left.

5 Decreased U.S. tariffs, quotas or other trade restrictions on Japanese-produced goods and services imported into the United States will shift the supply function to the right. Increased U.S. tariffs, quotas or other trade restrictions will shift the supply function to the left.

6 Lower Japanese prices will reduce prices on Japanese-produced goods and services exported to the United States and shift the supply function to the right. Higher domestic prices will shift the supply function to the left.

The fundamentals that determine the position of the demand and supply functions from the CA perspective are summarized in Table 7.2.

The exchange rate from the perspective of the FA: The financial account consists of flows of financial assets evaluated in dollars and can be understood using the same framework of demand and supply for dollars as used above, with the exception that the quantity variable is now dollar-denominated financial assets instead of the quantity of dollars to export and import goods and services. However, there are three differences between the FA and CA.

Table 7.2. *Fundamentals and the Exchange Rate from the U.S. Perspective,*
Demand for and Supply of Dollars

Change in fundamental impacting demand for dollars	Demand function shifts	Effect on exchange rate
Increase in Japan GDP	→	Dollar appreciates, yen depreciates
Decrease in Japan GDP	←	Dollar depreciates, yen appreciates
Increase in Japan's preference for U.S. goods & services	→	Dollar appreciates, yen depreciates
Decrease in Japan's preference for U.S. goods & services	←	Dollar depreciates, yen appreciates
Increase in U.S. productivity	→	Dollar appreciates, yen depreciates
Decrease in U.S. productivity	←	Dollar depreciates, yen appreciates
Increase in U.S. subsidies to exporters	→	Dollar appreciates, yen depreciates
Decrease in U.S. subsidies to exporters	←	Dollar depreciates, yen appreciates
Decrease in Japanese trade restrictions	→	Dollar appreciates, yen depreciates
Increase in Japanese trade restrictions	←	Dollar depreciates, yen appreciates
Decrease in U.S. domestic prices	→	Dollar appreciates, yen depreciates
Increase in U.S. domestic prices	←	Dollar depreciates, yen appreciates

Change in fundamental impacting supply of dollars	Supply function shifts	Effect on exchange rate
Increase in U.S. GDP	→	Dollar depreciates, yen appreciates
Decrease in U.S. GDP	←	Dollar appreciates, yen depreciates
Increase in U.S. preference for Japanese goods & services	→	Dollar depreciates, yen appreciates
Decrease in U.S. preference for Japanese goods & services	←	Dollar appreciates, yen depreciates
Increase in Japanese productivity	→	Dollar depreciates, yen appreciates
Decrease in Japanese productivity	←	Dollar appreciates, yen depreciates
Increase in Japanese subsidies to exporters	→	Dollar depreciates, yen appreciates
Decrease in Japanese subsidies to exporters	←	Dollar appreciates, yen depreciates
Decrease in U.S. trade restrictions	→	Dollar depreciates, yen appreciates
Increase in U.S. trade restrictions	←	Dollar appreciates, yen depreciates
Decrease in Japanese domestic prices	→	Dollar depreciates, yen appreciates
Increase in Japanese domestic prices	←	Dollar appreciates, yen depreciates

First, the day-to-day volume of flows in the FA far exceeds those in the CA, even though from Table 7.1 it appears that the flows in the FA are less than those in the CA. In fact, the gross financial flows far exceed those in the CA account; for example, if a U.S. bank has a $10 million claim on a British bank and the British bank has a $9 million claim on the U.S. bank, the net flow will only be a $1 million transfer from the British to the U.S. bank. Second, the FA flows are far more sensitive to short-run developments than the CA flows of goods and services, since financial transactions respond rapidly to any change in the fundamental determinants of the exchange rate. In fact, the day-to-day movements in the exchange rate are essentially determined by financial flows, while the longer-term movements in the exchange rate are essentially determined by flows of goods, services, etc. in the

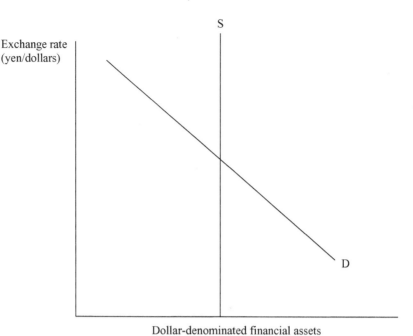

Figure 7.2. Foreign Exchange Market from the Perspective of the Financial Account.

CA. Third, while demand and supply are important for understanding the exchange rate from the perspective of the CA, the majority of exchange rate movements are dominated by changes in the demand for dollar-denominated financial assets, since the existing stock of financial assets is large relative to any changes in the supply of financial assets due to changes in the exchange rate. That is, for the purposes of understanding the exchange rate from the FA perspective, the supply of dollars is given; that is, the supply function is vertical, indicating that changes in the exchange rate have no effect on the quantity of the supply of dollar-denominated financial assets.

Figure 7.2 illustrates how the exchange rate is determined from the perspective of the FA. The supply function for dollar-denominated domestic financial assets is vertical at the existing stock of financial assets; that is, the supply of dollar-denominated financial assets is assumed fixed and does not change with the exchange rate. The demand function indicates the quantity of domestic financial assets demanded and is shown to be sensitive to the exchange rate. Why is the demand function downward-sloping and what are the underlying fundamentals that shift the demand function?

The demand for domestic financial assets is downward-sloping for the same reason the demand for dollars to purchase U.S.-produced goods, services, etc. is downward-sloping. As the exchange rate falls, the dollar depreciates and reduces the price of any domestic financial asset. That is, a $100,000 Treasury bill will cost less in terms of foreign exchange as the exchange rate falls.

There are two fundamentals that influence the position of the demand for dollar-denominated financial assets: the domestic real interest rate and the expected future exchange rate between the yen and the dollar.

Domestic real interest rates: In the following discussion, inflation expectations are held constant so that changes in the nominal rate represent changes in the real interest rate. An increase in the domestic interest rate increases the return on holding domestic financial assets relative to Japanese financial assets and shifts the demand function to the right. A decrease in the domestic interest rate lowers the return on holding domestic financial assets and shifts the demand function to the left.

Expected future exchange rate: The expected exchange rate connects the exchange rate from the FA perspective to the CA perspective because the expected future exchange rate is dependent on expected changes in the fundamentals summarized in Table 7.2. Two steps are needed to understand the relationship. First, how does the expected future exchange rate influence the demand for dollar assets? Second, what determines the expected future exchange rate?

Domestic financial assets pay interest and principal in dollars; hence, if the market expects the dollar to depreciate in the future, the demand for dollar-denominated financial assets will shift to the left. Fewer domestic financial assets will be demanded at any exchange rate because the market expects the interest payments and principal payments to decline in value because they will be made with a depreciated currency relative to the time the expectation is being formed. If the market expects the dollar to appreciate, the demand for dollar-denominated financial assets will shift to the right, because the value of interest and principal is expected to increase in terms of foreign exchange.

What determines the expected future exchange rate? Expected changes in the fundamentals listed in Table 7.2 determine the expected exchange rate. If the market expects U.S. GDP to increase in the future, it then expects the supply of dollars to shift to the right as U.S. imports from Japan increase and, thus, expects the dollar to depreciate. This would shift the demand for dollar-denominated financial assets to the left and decrease the exchange rate. At the same time, if the market expects Japanese GDP to increase in the future, it then expects the demand for dollars to shift to the right as U.S. exports to Japan increase and, thus, expects the dollar to appreciate. This would shift the demand for dollar-denominated financial assets to the right and increase the exchange rate.

As one can see, introducing expectations as a fundamental factor determining the exchange rate from the FA perspective ties the CA and FA together and also explains why exchange rates fluctuate from day to day. Expectations of future exchange rates are dependent on the expectations of a large number of fundamentals that influence the exchange rate.

Real and nominal interest rate effects on the exchange rate: In the above we did not distinguish between the real and nominal interest rates but, rather, assumed that changes in the exchange rate were due to changes in the real interest rate. More detail is now needed to fully understand the relationship between interest rates and the exchange rate.

The nominal interest rate is the sum of the real interest rate and expected inflation, as explained in Chapter 5. Any change in the real interest rate will have the above predicted effects on the demand for dollar-denominated financial assets and exchange rate; that is, an increase (decrease) in domestic real interest rates will shift the demand for dollar-denominated financial assets to the right (left) and appreciate (depreciate) the value of the dollar.

Now consider a change in the interest rates due to a change in expected inflation. The impact on the demand for financial assets is just the opposite of a change in the interest rate due to a change in the real interest rate.

An increase in the expected domestic inflation rate does not change the real interest rate and, hence, a change in expected inflation will not change the real return from holding domestic financial assets. However, an increase in the expected inflation rate will cause the expected future exchange rate to fall and then shift the demand for domestic assets to the left. Here's how it works. The higher expected inflation rate leads to an expected leftward shift in the demand for dollars from the CA perspective and, hence, an expected decline in the exchange rate, which in turn generates a leftward shift in the demand for domestic financial assets. Thus, an increase in interest rates due to an increase in the real interest rate appreciates the dollar, while an increase in interest rates due to an increase in expected inflation depreciates the dollar.

Two final notes: First, a change in any fundamental is always in the context of holding "other things constant," and, in the context of the foreign exchange market, this includes the fundaments in the other country. Thus, a change in U.S. interest rates, GDP, productivity, etc. is always considered as relative to the other country.

Second, in the above discussion, we have focused only on the primary effect of a change in any fundamental factor. In fact, a change in any fundamental factor has a series of effects on the exchange rate that are reinforcing. To illustrate, consider the impact of higher U.S. inflation on the exchange rate. The primary impact is to shift the demand for dollars in the CA to the left as U.S. goods and services are now more expensive than Japanese-produced goods and services. Japan now imports less from the United States. At the same time, the supply of dollars will shift to the right as U.S. residents substitute Japanese-produced goods and services for the higher-priced domestic goods and services. U.S. imports from Japan increase. The initial shift in demand depreciates the dollar, and the secondary effect of the shift in supply further depreciates the dollar. This type of secondary effect can be identified for virtually any change in a given fundamental.

7.5 Foreign Exchange Intervention by the Central Bank

The discussion to this point has emphasized the exchange rate as the outcome of market decisions about the demand for and supply of dollars from the perspective of the CA and FA; however, governments through their central banks frequently influence the exchange rate. There are two general ways the central bank can influence the exchange rate.

First, the central bank through general monetary policy actions designed to influence interest rates can indirectly shift the demand for dollars to the right or left. Expanding the money supply, for example, will lower the interest rate relative to foreign interest rates and thereby shift the demand function for dollar-denominated financial assets to the left and depreciate the dollar. Decreasing the money supply will increase interest rates and shift the demand for dollar assets to the right and appreciate the dollar.

Second, and in the context of the current discussion, central banks directly intervene in the foreign exchange market to influence the demand for their currency and other currencies to achieve specific exchange rate objectives. Central banks hold certain assets called international reserves (gold, key foreign exchange such as yen, euros or the British pound and other assets that serve as international reserve and investment assets) to purchase foreign currencies as well as use their own currencies (which the central bank can create) to purchase international reserve assets. If the central bank purchases other currencies, that currency appreciates relative to the home currency, whereas, if the central bank sells other currencies, those currencies depreciate relative to the home currency.

There is no evidence that the central bank can establish an exchange rate over a long period different from what market forces dictate, but central banks can influence the exchange rate over short periods of time. Central banks intervene in the foreign exchange market to smooth out exchange rate fluctuations and/or to achieve an exchange rate objective; for example, central banks often depreciate their own currencies to stimulate exports and increase domestic GDP. Asian central banks, for example, are particularity noted for depreciating or at least limiting the appreciation of their currency because of their reliance on an export-based development strategy. They do this by using their international reserve assets to purchase dollar assets (shift the demand for dollar assets to the right), and thereby appreciate the dollar and depreciate their own currency to encourage exports and discourage imports. China and Japan frequently intervene in the foreign exchange market for this purpose. Decisions to intervene in the foreign exchange market are usually the responsibility of the country's Treasury, but the actual operations are carried out by the central bank.

Central bank foreign exchange intervention is a rather complex process, and there is considerable debate as to whether central banks are able to influence the exchange rate directly even in the short run under all conditions. In any event, the Federal Reserve does conduct foreign exchange interventions to influence exchange rates, but for all practical purposes the exchange rate plays a rather minor role in the formulation and execution of monetary policy in the United States. In China and Japan, however, influencing the exchange rate is a far more important policy objective.

7.6 Exchange Rate Regimes

Historically there are two basic exchange rate regimes designed to convert one currency into another: fixed and flexible exchange rates. The claimed advantage of fixed rates is that they eliminate exchange rate risk in international trade and finance and, hence, encourage the growth of international trade and finance; however, the fixed rate system works only if countries play by the "rules" of the fixed exchange rate system. The claimed advantage of flexible rates is that they permit markets to determine exchange rates rather than governments and don't require politically difficult policies on the part of governments to maintain the fixed exchange rate system.

7.7 Fixed Exchange Rates: Basics, History and Demise

The gold standard is the traditional fixed exchange rate system. Only two conditions are required: first, each country establishes an official price of gold in terms of its currency; and, second, each country agrees to purchase any of its currency for gold at the official price. To illustrate, if the United States sets the price of gold at $25 per ounce and Japan sets the price of gold at ¥5,000, the exchange rate is ¥200 to $1.00. To maintain this exchange rate, Japan agrees to purchase yen with gold at the rate of 1 ounce of gold for ¥5,000, and the United States agrees to purchase dollars with gold at the rate of 1 ounce of gold for $25.

The gold standard and fixed exchange rates were a feature of international trade and finance before WWI; however, the low world production of gold after 1870 relative to the pace of world economic growth led to deflation in many countries, especially in the United States. After 1885 the world supply of gold increased and drove up prices until WWI. Countries returned to the gold standard after WWI, but the United Kingdom in particular overvalued its currency, making it difficult to adjust to the peacetime economy. The Great Depression disrupted international trade and finance, and countries abandoned the gold standard. Even before WWII had ended a new fixed exchange rate system for the peacetime world had been established, in July 1944, by the Allies at Bretton Woods, New Hampshire, and known as the Bretton Woods system of fixed exchange rates. WWII would continue in Europe until May 1945 and in Asia until August 1945; however, there was great confidence by mid-1944 that Germany and Japan would soon surrender (Italy had surrendered in September 1943).

The goals of the Bretton Woods system were to establish fixed exchange rates to encourage international trade and finance, establish an institutional mechanism to permit changes in the exchange rate under certain and controlled circumstances and establish institutions to maintain orderly balance of payments adjustments and changes in exchange rates and encourage international trade and finance.

The International Monetary Fund (IMF), originally consisting of 30 member countries and now with over 180 members, was designed to maintain the new fixed exchange rate standard and assist countries with current account deficits. The World Bank was established to provide loans to developing countries for infrastructure projects. The General Agreement on Tariffs and Trade (GATT) was set up in 1947 to monitor trade restrictions and encourage more open international trade. GATT evolved into the World Trade Organization in 1994. The roles of both the IMF and World Bank have changed since the 1970s, because of the collapse of the fixed exchange rate system in 1973 and financial liberalization in the 1980s and 1990s; however, they both, along with the WTO, form an important part of the institutional design of the present international financial system.

How was the Bretton Woods system designed to achieve a fixed exchange rate system and why did it collapse in 1973?

The United States emerged from WWII as the most powerful industrial and military nation in the world. It was the only major country untouched by war, with the exception of the Japanese attack on Pearl Harbor on Oahu (Hawaii), though Hawaii was only a U.S. territory at the time and would not become an official part of the United States until 1960. The United States had much of the world's manufacturing capacity and held most of the world's supply of gold. The Bretton Woods system thus established the dollar as the key or reserve currency; established a dollar price of gold at $35 per ounce; required convertibility of dollars into gold only for foreign governments; and established exchange rates between foreign currencies and the dollar. The special role of the dollar did not come without its problems. The United States was required to conduct its domestic policies to ensure that the dollar was convertible into gold at the rate of $35 per ounce. By the 1960s this would prove difficult.

The Bretton Woods system had good intentions, but it began to unravel in the 1960s and collapsed in 1973 when the world shifted to flexible exchange rates. There were many problems inherent in the Bretton Woods system, ranging from economic to political, but the fundamental reasons for failure was that countries did not adhere to the "rules" of the fixed exchange rate system.

Figure 7.3 highlights the basic flaw of any fixed exchange rate system. The official (fixed) exchange rate is indicated by OER. In panel A, the country operates with a CA balance so that the demand for and supply of dollars are equal at the official exchange rate. In this case the OER and the market-determined exchange rate are the same and no financial flow adjustment is required. In panel B, the country operates with a CA deficit at the OER; that is, the official exchange rate overvalues the

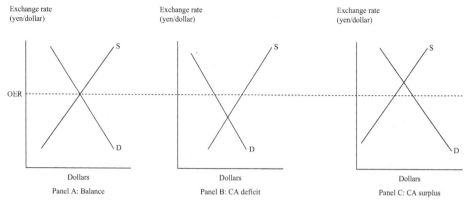

Figure 7.3. Current Account Balance and Imbalances in the Fixed Exchange Rate System.

currency. In panel C, the country operates with a CA surplus at the OER; that is, the office exchange rate undervalues the currency and financial flows are needed to offset the surplus.

The deficit country adjusts to the imbalance in the CA in two ways. First, in the short run, the deficit country deals with the excess supply of its currency at the OER by using its holdings of international reserves to purchase back the excess supply of currency. International reserves both under the Bretton Woods system and today consist of the following: gold; financial assets denominated in key or reserve currencies; and special drawing rights (SDRs), created by the IMF in 1969 to expand international reserves. Second, in the short run, the deficit country can borrow from other countries by selling those countries debt denominated in its currency. Essentially, borrowing is the equivalent of the deficit country asking other countries to hold onto the excess supply of its currency in the form of the deficit country's currency.

The deficit country's situation can be illustrated in the context of the SIT as follows:

CA: Receipts (Exports and Income Receipts) < Payments (Imports and Income Payments)

FA: Payments (Buying International Reserves and Lending) < Receipts (Selling International Reserves and Borrowing)

The problems with the two short-run responses to a CA deficit are that the supply of a country's international reserves is limited and the willingness of other countries to lend to the deficit country is limited. As long as the demand and supply functions for dollars (panel B) remain unchanged, the deficit will persist and eventually the short-run response will not resolve the CA deficit.

The persistent deficit requires a third response. To maintain the fixed exchange rate the deficit country needs to shift the demand for and supply of dollars to eliminate the CA deficit. This can be accomplished by slowing economic growth with monetary and fiscal policy and increasing interest rates. Slower economic growth will shift the supply function to the left and higher interest rates will shift the demand for dollars (to purchase financial assets) to the right. Both actions will bring the market-determined exchange rate up to the OER. There is an obvious problem with this policy, however: the deficit country will be reluctant to slow economic growth and increase interest rates. Instead, the country will have an incentive to adopt *beggar-thy-neighbor* policies designed to deal with its economic problems by adversely impacting the economies of other countries.

The deficit country will have an incentive to impose trade restrictions (tariffs and quotas) to shift the supply of dollars to the left; subsidize the export sector (tax credits and low interest rate loans) to shift the demand function to the right; or launch "buy domestic" campaigns to shift the supply function to the left. All of these actions will bring the market exchange rate up to the ORE; however, they induce retaliation from other countries. If other countries adopt the same type of beggar-thy-neighbor policies, their actions will result in opposite changes in the supply and demand functions, so that the initial beggar-thy-neighbor policies are nullified. Ultimately, beggar-thy-neighbor polices end up discouraging international trade – the very objective of the fixed exchange rate system.

A most severe and damaging beggar-thy-neighbor policy is devaluation; that is, the deficit country simply changes the OER to equal the market exchange rate and eliminates the CA deficit. The deficit country simply revalues its currency against the dollar or, in the case of the United States, increases the dollar price of gold. Devaluation has a serious adverse impact on other countries, however. Any financial assets issued by the deficit country to finance its CA deficit have now been reduced in value overnight. There is a real possibility other countries will retaliate and devalue their own currencies and nullify the initial devaluation. Ultimately, devaluations will reduce international trade and finance.

The basic flaw is not confined only to the deficit country under the fixed exchange rate system. Surplus countries are required to stimulate their economies to eliminate their own imbalance; however, there is reluctance to do this in many cases. Not only do surplus countries regard the surplus as a sign of economic power, but many countries adopt an export-based development strategy and view surpluses in the CA as verification of a successful industrial strategy, and, finally, surplus countries are reluctant to stimulate their economies for fear of creating inflation.

Unwillingness on the part of the deficit – and, to some extent, the surplus – countries to play the rules of the fixed exchange rate system are the fundamental problem of all fixed exchange rate systems, and, in particular, brought an end to the Bretton Woods system in 1973. There were other problems as well. The ability of governments and the IMF to determine the appropriate official exchange rate for countries was greatly exaggerated and, at the time, reflected a *Keynesian* perspective that activist government could manage the animal spirits of the private market both domestically and internationally. The United States as the major key currency country was especially burdened by the Bretton Woods system. As the dollar became widely used the United States had to conduct policies to maintain the convertibility of the dollar into gold but, within a short time, the United States simply did not have sufficient gold reserves to keep that commitment, thus requiring other countries to hold onto dollars. Largely because the United States under the Nixon administration became increasingly frustrated with the burden of being the major key currency country, the Bretton Woods system unraveled from 1971 to 1973, when fixed exchange rates were replaced with the flexible exchange rate system that persists to this day.

7.8 The Flexible Exchange Rate System

Since 1973 exchange rates between the industrialized countries have been determined by market forces and fluctuate from day to day; however, not all countries permit their currencies to float. The current system is not a pure market system, since central banks often intervene in the foreign exchange market; hence, the current system is sometimes referred to as a *dirty* flexible rate system, though, in practice, the ability of governments to influence even short-term movements in the exchange rate is often exaggerated. Exchange rates, for all practical purposes, for the majority of the economically important countries are determined by market forces, and even countries such as China are increasingly being pressured to permit a market-determined rate for their currency.

Under a flexible exchange rate system, market-induced changes in the exchange rate eliminate the CA imbalance; that is, if a country operates with a deficit (panel B) or a surplus (panel C), the exchange rate adjusts up or down to bring the CA into balance.

The flexible exchange rate system has several advantages over the fixed exchange rate system. First, market forces rather than government agencies determine the appropriate exchange rate. Second, a country's monetary and fiscal policy is more independent in that it is not constrained to maintain a specific exchange rate. This is not a license to conduct inflationary policy, because such a policy would generate CA deficits, but it does permit a country to conduct its own policies focused on domestic considerations. Third, the fixed exchange rate system's claimed advantage is to encourage international trade by reducing exchange rate risk; however, fixed exchange rates provide incentives for deficit countries to adopt beggar-thy-neighbor policies, which, in turn, interfere with international trade. Although exchange rates fluctuate under a flexible system, international trade and finance have grown significantly since 1973, and financial innovation has mitigated much of the exchange rate risk inherent in a flexible standard in the form of futures markets in foreign exchange.

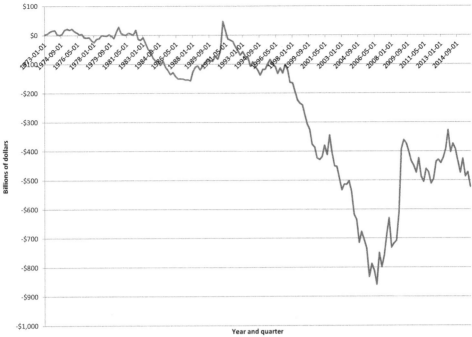

Figure 7.4. Balance on Current Account, 1973:1 to 2016:1. *Source:* FRED, Federal Reserve Bank of St. Louis.

7.9 Persistent U.S. Current Account Deficits and the Flexible Exchange Rate System

The United States has experienced trade and current account imbalances for the past several decades (Figure 7.4) as well as a major depreciation of the dollar against most currencies (Figure 7.5). This raises the question as to whether the flexible exchange rate system functions as advertised. If the flexible exchange rate system works, why has the U.S. CA deficit persisted at the same time that the dollar has depreciated over time?

The response to this apparent contradiction is based on a general relationship between any country's internal and external balance. Once the internal–external balance relationship is presented it's a straightforward matter to explain why the U.S. CA deficit persists despite a general depreciation of the dollar.

First, start with the definition of a country's GDP in terms of output:

$$GDP = C + I + G + (X - M) \tag{7.3}$$

where GDP is equal to current spending on consumption (C), investment (I), government spending (G) and the difference between exports (X) and imports (M) of goods and services. Exports are added to GDP because they represent domestic production and imports are subtracted from GDP because they are included in C, I

Figure 7.5. Trade-Weighted Dollar Index: Major Currencies, January 1973 to June 2016. *Source:* FRED, Federal Reserve Bank of St. Louis.

and G but represent spending on foreign-produced goods and services. The variable (X – M) is, essentially, the CA.

Second, GDP can also be considered from the perspective of the income that was earned producing GDP and how that income was used. That is, GDP represents not only the country's output but the country's income earned in producing the output. Hence, the following expression indicates how the country's income earned from producing GDP is used:

$$GDP = C + S + T \qquad (7.4)$$

where GDP is allocated to consumption (C), saving (S) and taxes (T).

Third, the term (X – M) is the CA balance and can be referred to as the country's external balance:

$$\text{External Balance} = (X - M) \qquad (7.4)$$

and, keeping in mind the relationship between the CA and FA,

$$\text{External Balance} = (X - M) = \text{Financial Outflow (Payments)} - \text{Financial Inflow (Receipts)} \qquad (7.5)$$

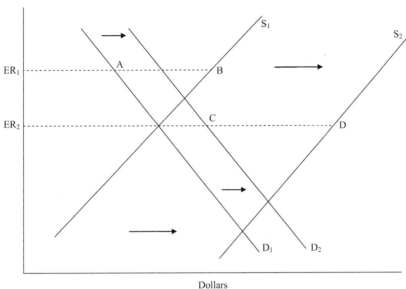

Figure 7.6. Persistent Current Account Deficits and a Depreciating Dollar.

Fourth, setting Expressions 7.3 and 7.4 equal to each other, rearranging terms and substituting Expression 7.4 and 7.5 generates the following relationship:

$$(S - I) + (T - G) = (X - M)$$
$$(S - I) + (T - G) = \text{External Balance}$$
$$(S - I) + (T - G) = \text{External Balance} = \text{Financial Outflow} - \text{Financial Inflow}$$
$$\text{Internal Balance} = \text{External Balance} = \text{Financial Outflow} - \text{Financial Inflow}$$
$$(7.6)$$

Expression 7.6 illustrates the relationship between a country's internal balance, defined as $(S - I) + (T - G)$, and its external balance, defined by the SIT. If a country has an internal balance that is negative because the government is running a deficit $(G > T)$ and/or investment exceeds saving $(I > S)$, then, according to Expression 7.6, the country must be running a negative external balance, indicated by a deficit in the CA and a surplus in the FA. Some claim that there is a relationship between government deficits and CA deficits, often referred to as the "twin deficits"; however, Expression 7.6 suggests the "twin deficit" concept may be correct for some periods, but a CA deficit can also occur without government deficits when investment exceeds saving. While a government deficit contributes to a CA deficit, a CA deficit can also occur in the absence of a government deficit depending on the relationship between investment and saving.

The relationship between the internal and external balances suggests two important points about CA deficits. First, CA deficits are as much the outcome of a country's domestic decisions regarding saving, investment, government spending and taxes as they are the outcome of the actions of other countries. Thus, blaming the behavior of other countries for the continuing U.S. CA deficits is intellectually unbalanced. A major part of the problem is that "we have met the enemy and the enemy is us!" Second, the continuing internal and hence external negative balance experienced by the United States over the past decade suggests why the flexible exchange rate system has not resolved the external deficit issue.

Figure 7.6 shows that, over time, the United States continues to spend more than it produces domestically, imports the difference and thus shifts the supply function for dollars to the right more than the demand for dollars shifts to the right. Starting with an exchange rate of ER_1, the U.S. CA deficit is AB with supply of dollars S_1, and demand for dollars D_1. The exchange rate falls to ER_2 to eliminate the deficit, but this will occur only if the demand and supply functions remain unchanged. They do not. Over time the supply of dollars shifts further to the right (S_1 to S_2) than the demand function (D_1 to D_2), so that at the lower exchange rate the CA deficit (CD) is actually larger than under the higher exchange rate; that is, CD is larger than AB. Hence, the exchange rate declines (the dollar depreciates), but the CA balance continues to increase. To put it simply – the United States is on a spending binge, in that it spends more than it produces, and as long as this continues it is unlikely that depreciation of the dollar with reverse the CA deficit.

Part III

The Role of Government in the Financial and Monetary Regime

Chapter 8

The Basic Roles of Government in the Financial and Monetary Regime

8.1 Introduction

In Chapter 2 the evolution of monetary systems was outlined. The monetary system has evolved from commodity money to representative commodity money and, finally, to the current stage of the modern monetary system. The modern monetary system is based on depository institutions that issue promises to pay, represented by bank notes in Hickenlupper's Bank, and checking accounts, in today's system based on depository institutions. In the modern system, depository institutions hold only a fraction of their promises to pay as reserves; the promises to pay and the fractional reserve maintained by the depository institution are both fiat money in which the face value is defined independently of any commodity; depository institutions issue new promises to pay when they lend and invest; and the modern system imposes a fiduciary responsibility on depository institutions to conduct their operations so as not to adversely affect the public's willingness to use their promises to pay as money.

The modern system is essentially an inverted pyramid that eliminates many of the problems of a commodity and representative commodity system; however, there is never a free lunch. The modern system itself has several inherent problems that require government to take a more active role in the nation's financial and monetary regime than required in the commodity and representative commodity systems.

This chapter focuses on inherent problems in commodity-based systems and the modern monetary system that rationalize a role for government in the nation's financial and monetary regime. In fact, government financial regulation and supervision through regulatory agencies is now considered one of the three components of the nation's financial and monetary regime. This role significantly influences the private aspects of the nation's financial system. In addition, the government even becomes a part of the financial system, setting up government-sponsored enterprises that provide subsidized credit to certain parts of the economy deemed economically and politically important. Not only does the second component consist of government regulation and supervision, the third component, represented by the nation's central bank and central bank policy, is under the control of the government.

The history of money started as a market innovation, then at an early stage incorporated government, which remained relatively small for many centuries, until the twentieth century. Today government is a major part of the nation's financial and monetary regime.

The commodity money, representative commodity money and, finally, modern money systems were developed as market innovations. Each represented an effort by the market to first overcome the limitations of barter and then the limitations of a commodity-based system. Each step improved the efficiency of the nation's money supply system and allowed the nation's financial and monetary regime to evolve to the current stage. Despite difficulties, the modern system has supported an impressive record of economic growth throughout the world.

The development of monetary systems in a three-stage framework presented in Chapter 2, however, is a pedagogical device meant to emphasize the essential elements of the evolution of the monetary system, but in reality the historical development of the U.S. money system was not a smooth process. In fact, until the establishment of the Federal Reserve in 1913, the U.S. money system was a hodgepodge of different forms of money incorporating elements of all three stages of monetary development. Starting with the Federal Reserve, the money supply has increasingly become unified, completely disconnected from gold or any commodity, and it is essentially under the control of the government through the central bank.

Likewise, the role of government did not evolve over time in a linear fashion but responded to problems that emerged in each monetary standard stage. In addition, the role of government in the nation's financial and monetary regime was driven not only by inherent problems with the different monetary systems but also by economic ideas, historical events and political considerations.

This chapter outlines the various elements of the basic role of government in the nation's financial and monetary framework from historical, institutional and political perspectives. These elements are as follows.

1 The early involvement of government in minting coin in a commodity system.
2 The inherent problem of a commodity or representative commodity monetary system.
3 The inherent problems of an inverted pyramid monetary system, whether based on a commodity or a purely fiat system.
4 The three basic responsibilities of government to deal with the inherent problems of commodity-based and inverted pyramid systems.
5 Extended government responsibilities.
6 An institutional overview of the government's role in the U.S. financial and monetary regime.

7 The influence of economic ideas, historical events and political considerations in the evolution of government involvement in the nation's financial and monetary regime.

8.2 The Beginning of Government Involvement: Minting Coin and Gresham's Law

Money, until the printing press became widely available, consisted of commodity money, in which the money supply depended on the supply of the commodity. The preferred commodity was gold or silver, or both. Government did not invent commodity money but, rather, commodity money was a market innovation introduced to eliminate the inefficiency of barter. However, there was a degree of market failure, in that coins based on the commodity were not of uniform measure, weight or commodity content. The lack of uniformity was due to a lack of standardization in producing coins, but also because of the incentive in the private market to debase the commodity money by counterfeiting coins, overstating weight or "shaving" some of the commodity off the coins. Any such debasement of the money supply brought into play Gresham's law, named after the English financier Sir Thomas Gresham (1519–1579), though references to the law can be traced to Copernicus and others. According to Gresham's law, "Bad money drives out good money." Debased money is spent while good money is hoarded, thereby reducing the benefits of money in general.

This problem was recognized very early in recorded history and, as a result, governments began very early to take responsibility to ensure a uniform coinage by ensuring weight, measurement and commodity content. Government minting of coins provided a uniform commodity money the public could confidently use, but government frequently abused its power and debased the commodity money. Government would reduce the amount of gold and silver in a coin relative to other materials that made up the coin, but maintain the stated value on the coin. This essentially increased the money supply, which in turn, according to the quantity theory of money, generated inflation and debased the entire commodity money system. Gresham's law would come into play as the market hoarded coins of full value and used the less than full-valued coins and, in some cases, resorted to other forms of money. An interesting example of this is in pre-modern Japan. In Japan, around 1000 AD, the imperial court in Kyoto debased the commodity money it produced over many years to such a degree that the coins it minted were no longer accepted. Instead, people resorted to using Chinese coins, which were obtained via trade with China, because they were more likely to be full-valued. In addition, privately minted coins also were used instead of official coins.

There is a long history of governments during the period of commodity money debasing the coinage, causing inflation and generating much economic and political distress for the nation. Copernicus was one of the first to highlight, in a study on the minting of coin published in 1525, that the debasement of the coinage was one factor among a short list of factors that caused the decline of the nation. The important point here is that, while there is a generally accepted rationalization for government control over the minting of coins under a commodity standard, there is no guarantee the government will not abuse the power to expand the money supply to support government spending. The debasement problem did not disappear with the establishment of the modern monetary standard.

Article 1, Section 8, Clause 5 of the U.S. Constitution gave the federal government the authority to mint coins from commodities such as silver and gold and to regulate the value of the minted coins. It is was not clear, however, whether the federal government could print money, and until the U.S. Civil War (1861–1865) the government did not print fiat money. The U.S. money supply up to the Civil War was a mixture of government-minted coins, actual gold and silver, privately minted coins, foreign coins and banknotes issued by institutions such as Hickenlupper's Bank, discussed in Chapter 2. The government did start to print fiat money during and after the Civil War, though for all practical considerations the U.S. money supply was tied to the supply of gold. The establishment of the Federal Reserve System in 1913, however, significantly changed the role of government in the nation's money supply, but it wasn't until the Great Depression that the major upward movement in government involvement in the nation's financial and monetary regime commenced.

The Federal Reserve issued a new national currency, called the Federal Reserve note, which for all practical purposes is the nation's currency. The Federal Reserve note is pure fiat money since it is not backed by any commodity and has value only because it is defined to have value by the Federal Reserve. Coins minted by the U.S. Treasury are, likewise, pure fiat, since the face value of any coin far exceeds the value of the material used to produce it. The major part of the money supply is promises to pay issued by depository institutions and retail money market funds, which, again, are pure fiat money since they are not backed by any commodity. Some argue that Article 1 does not permit the government to play such an important role in the nation's money supply; however, this debate is over, whatever the merits of the two sides. The government now is responsible for supplying the nation's money supply, which, in turn, is entirely fiat-based.

8.3 The Inherent Problem of a Commodity-Based Monetary System: Money Not Responsive to Needs of Trade

Commodity and representative commodity standards were sensitive to the supply of the commodity and, in turn, the supply of the commodity tended to be accidental and not always well timed to the needs of the nation for money to finance its transactions. The limitations of a commodity-based system in this regard could be resolved by giving the government greater control over the nation's money supply through a central bank.

No example better illustrates the limitations of the commodity-based standard than the monetary problems of the United States in the last third of the nineteenth century. In fact, in the opinion of many scholars, the limitations of the commodity-based standard and the resulting political upheaval during this period are the background for one of American's most beloved fairy-tale movies, *The Wizard of Oz*, released in 1939. *The Wizard of Oz* and another well-known movie, *Gone with the Wind*, also released in 1939, were the first two major color movies, and they have achieved the status of "classics". The movie is based on L. Frank Baum's 1900 publication of *The Wonderful Wizard of Oz*.

A number of scholars claim that *The Wonderful Wizard of Oz* is more a political and monetary allegory of the economic and political events in the last part of the nineteenth century than a fairy tale for children. There is circumstantial evidence to support this view, though Baum never explicitly said his work was political or monetary comment. Setting aside this issue, the interpretation of *Oz* as political and monetary allegory provides great background to understand the limitations of a commodity-based standard and one of the main reasons for the establishment of the Federal Reserve System in 1913. The historical events stand on their own merit; however, the events and the juxtaposition of *The Wizard of Oz* make for a most interesting story.

Prior to the Civil War the United States was on a bimetallic commodity standard, in that both gold and silver were the foundation of the nation's money. In 1873 Congress passed the Coinage Act, which demonetized silver and placed the United States on a single commodity standard – gold. The nation's money supply, which at the time was a mixture of commodity, representative commodity and elements of the modern system, became directly related to the nation's supply of gold. The nation's supply of gold, however, did not keep pace with the growing economy in the latter part of the nineteenth century, and, even though the money supply expanded, it was not sufficient to prevent deflation taking into account trends in velocity and real output. Figure 8.1 illustrates the U.S. monetary gold stock from 1880 to 1906. The gold stock was constant from 1880 to 1888 but started to increase in 1889, and by 1906 the gold stock was nine times the amount it had been in 1880.

Table 8.1 presents the average annual percentage changes in the money supply, velocity, real output, general prices and farm prices for two periods: 1870–1896 and 1897–1906. The average growth rates for each period in Table 8.1 can be interpreted in the context of the quantity theory of money. Real output grew at 3.8 percent in the first period, but while the money supply grew at 4.8 percent, combined with a 2.6 percent decline in velocity, the price level declined 1.7 percent. At the same time, farm prices declined on average by 2.6 percent; that is, farmers were receiving less for their products than they had to pay for commodities to produce and live, and, at the same time, farm debt increased in value since it was fixed in nominal terms. As a result of the relatively slow money growth due to fewer new discoveries of gold, the United States experienced deflation and a decline of farm prices relative to

Table 8.1. *Percentage Changes of Money, Output, and General and Farm Prices,*
1870 to 1906

Period	General price level	Farm price level	M2 money	Real output	M2 velocity
	Year-to-year percentage change				
1870 to 1896	−1.7	−2.6	4.8	3.8	−2.6
1897 to 1906	2.1	3.8	9.8	6.1	−1.3

Source: Calculations based on data presented in Rockoff (1990).

the general price level, which generated much economic, financial and political distress.

In an economy in which agriculture played a much larger role than at present, the decline in farm prices relative to the general price level generated much social and political distress, especially in the Midwest, where farmers were operating with large amounts of debt. The situation generated a populist reaction to large banks on the East Coast (as well as politicians in Washington, D.C., including President McKinley (1897 to 1901)), who were viewed as responsible for allowing this to happen by insisting on adherence to the gold standard.

The conflict created by the more than two decades of deflation pitted farmers and debtors against creditors such as banks and those who supported the gold standard

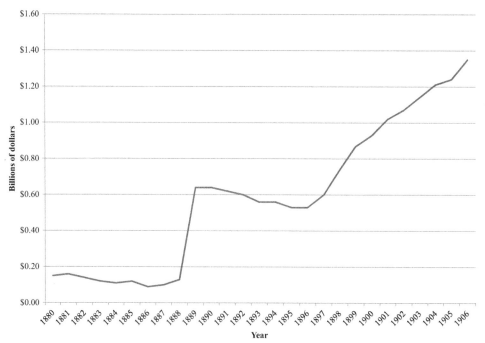

Figure 8.1. Monetary Gold Stock, 1880 to 1906. *Source:* U.S. Bureau of the Census (1975).

as a constraint on over-issuing money and causing inflation. Increased pressure was brought to monetize silver, increase credit, increase the money supply to reverse the relative fall of farm prices and increase the inflation rate to asset debtors by reducing the real value of debt. Large banks and many politicians resisted this pressure for fear easy money would lead to inflation and instability, and in general creditors benefited from deflation, as their financial assets increased in value since they were fixed in nominal value.

The pressure cumulated at the 1896 Democratic National Convention to select the Democratic presidential nominee, when William Jennings Bryan gave his famous "cross of gold" speech. Bryan passionately argued the gold standard limited economic opportunity and crucified mankind upon "a cross of gold". A broader commodity base that included both gold and silver was necessary to resolve the nation's economic and financial distress. "Having behind us the producing masses of this nation and the world, supported by the commercial interests, the laboring interests and the toilers everywhere, we will answer their demand for a gold standard by saying to them: 'You shall not press down upon the brow of labor this crown of thorns, you shall not crucify mankind upon a cross of gold.'"

Bryan emerged from the convention as the Democratic nominee for president, but he lost the 1896 election. Despite the impressive rhetoric of Bryan's cross of gold speech, the economic issues had already been resolved by that time, according to Table 8.1. As the nineteenth century came to a close, the money supply growth rate increased from 4.8 to 9.8 percent, the rate of velocity decline slowed from 2.6 to 1.3 percent, and real output growth increased from 3.8 to 6.1 percent, thus the price level increased at a rate of 2.1 percent. Just as important, farm prices not only reversed their decline but now increased at a rate of 3.8 percent, which was higher than the general inflation rate of 2.1 percent. As a result of these trends, the economic foundation for the populist movement ended.

Why did the money supply expand significantly in the second period relative to the first period? It expanded for much the same reason money had grown slowly after the Civil War. Money grew slowly in the first period and faster in the second period because of the changes in gold supply. The increase in the gold supply, and hence money supply, after 1890 was the result of two factors: first, new discoveries of gold in South Africa, Alaska and Colorado; and, second, the application of new methods of mining gold. Together these two factors supported almost a doubling of the average annual growth rate of money in the second period. This was a worldwide phenomenon, because the world was connected by a common monetary standard.

How does *The Wizard of Oz* fit into this historical period? Political scientists see it as an allegory of the political conflict between the West, farmers and debtors, on one side, and the East Coast large creditor banks and Washington, D.C., on the other. Economists, in particular, see it as a monetary allegory that fits into the quantity theory of money framework.

Dorothy represents traditional American values of family, farmers and hard work. Scare Crow represents farmers, who are smarter than those in the East. Tin Man represents industry, rusted shut from insufficient oil (liquidity, money and credit). Cowardly Lion is Bryan, who led the populist movement for expanded money in 1896, but in 1900, again as the Democratic presidential nominee, shifted attention to other issues, such as the American–Spanish War. Dorothy, Scare Crow, Tin Man and the Lion set out on the yellow brick road to the Land of Oz, which represent the gold standard and Washington, D.C., respectively. They seek the all-knowing Wizard (President McKinley and his advisors), who turn out to be more smoke and mirrors than knowledgeable. The solution to all these problems consists of two elements: first, water, which represents liquidity, credit and money; and, second, Dorothy's silver slippers. In the book, Dorothy's slippers were silver, but in the movie they were ruby, to better highlight the new color technique. Water saves Scare Crow, when the wicked witch sets him on fire, and water destroys the wicked witch. At the end, Dorothy can go home again to her farm, family and traditional values by simply clicking her silver slippers together. That is, the solution to all problems was close at hand – or, better, close at foot – all the time: monetize silver and expand the money supply.

It is not really important whether Baum intended his book to be political and monetary allegory, though many do think Baum meant it to be so. The story does seem to fit the economic and political events fairly well. At a minimum, the juxtaposition of the events in the last third of the nineteenth century and *The Wonderful Wizard of Oz* and the movie helps us understand the limitations of any commodity-based monetary system. This is an important reason why commodities such as gold and silver in the first part of the twentieth century became less and less important in influencing the nation's money supply. Today, commodities play no meaningful role in any nation's money supply. The nation's money supply is now ultimately under the control of the government through the central bank.

8.4 Two Inherent Problems of an Inverted Pyramid Monetary System

As the monetary system began to incorporate fractional reserves and began to emerge as the modern monetary system of today, two inherent problems or elements of market failure became apparent because of the fractional reserve nature of the standard. A fractional reserve system is like the inverted pyramid in Chapter 2. By definition, there is only a fraction of base reserve. Under a commodity standard the base is gold, silver or both, while under today's inverted pyramid the base consists of reserves under the control of the central bank.

The first problem is called the *contagion problem*, because the failure of one or a small group of depository institutions, irrespective of the cause, can contaminate the rest of the system. The second problem is referred to as the *money supply problem*, because individual actions by depository institutions in the aggregate can over-expand credit and the money supply. Both are examples of market failure, in that the individual depository institution follows its own self-interest without taking into account the impact those actions have on the entire system.

The contagion problem: Checkable or deposit money is efficient but it relies on the confidence of the public to hold and use deposit money, which, in turn, depends on the willingness of the public to accept deposit money for goods and services they sell, workers to accept deposit money for labor, and creditors to accept deposit money for debt service. That is, the willingness of the public to hold deposit money and use deposit money for their transactions instead of base money (gold, silver or reserves) is the foundation of the inverted pyramid, but there's a catch. There is only a fraction of base money backing deposit money. As long as the public have confidence they can withdraw deposit money in the form of base money without difficultly, then they are willing to use and hold deposit money, because it is more efficient than base money. If the public lose confidence in deposit money and attempt to convert deposit money into base money en masse, the pyramid collapses and generates intense economic and financial distress. It collapses because the fractional reserve nature of the system means there is insufficient base money to convert most deposits into base money.

What would cause the public to lose confidence? Assume one or several depository institutions have failed through no fault of their own. Perhaps they are located in a tourist area, and tourism has declined, so that many of its borrowers have defaulted and bankrupted the depository institutions. Depositors of those institutions no longer have access to their base money, since the institution's reserve can cover only a fraction of the deposits. Depositors of other institutions, who are not experiencing any difficulty, will start "runs" on their depository institutions to withdraw their deposits in the form of base money. The public lack the ability to distinguish between "good" and "bad" depository institutions, and when they witness the failure of another depository institution, or several institutions, they are likely to run to their institution and withdraw deposits. However, again, there are insufficient reserves, and these institutions go bankrupt, which, in turn, induces more deposit withdrawals for other healthy institutions – and they fail, and so on. This is called contagion because, like a disease, the failure of one or a small number of institutions induces deposit withdrawals from other institutions no matter what their economic health, and, because the system is based on fraction reserves, the entire system collapses.

This is exactly what happened during the Great Depression from 1929 to 1933, when the public lost confidence in deposit money and converted deposits into base money, which consisted primarily of Federal Reserve notes and gold certificates at the time. The 1929–1933 period of the Great Depression was so dramatic in terms of the collapse of the economy and financial system that it is referred to as the

Figure 8.2. Ratio of Currency to M2 Money Supply, 1929 to 1940. *Source:* U.S. Bureau of the Census (1975).

Great Contraction. The average reserve held by banks was about 10 percent at that time, so that for every $1.00 of deposit money there was only $0.10 of base money. Banks were simply unable to meet the withdrawal demands.

Figure 8.2 illustrates the ratio of currency held by the public to M2 money and illustrates the dramatic increase in the ratio from 1929 to 1933; the ratio then declines as the Federal Deposit Insurance Corporation, established in 1934, restores public confidence in the nation's money supply. Notice, however, that after 1933 the ratio declines but remains higher than in 1929, indicating continued concern about the safety of the nation's banking system. The direct result of the increase in currency held relative to M2 from 1929 to 1933 was widespread bank bankruptcy and a major decline in the number of banks (Figure 8.3). Banks were unable to meet the demands to convert deposits into currency and failed in large numbers across the nation. In 1929 there were 25,686 banks in the United States, while by 1933 the number of banks had declined to 14,771. This is a decline of 42 percent, and clearly provides one of the reasons why the period from 1929 to 1933 is called the Great Contraction and why the entire decade of the 1930s is called the Great Depression.

This example assumes that institutions that initially failed were subject to a shock beyond their control; that is, they had fulfilled their fiduciary responsibility to make good-quality loans that had a high probability of being repaid, but were

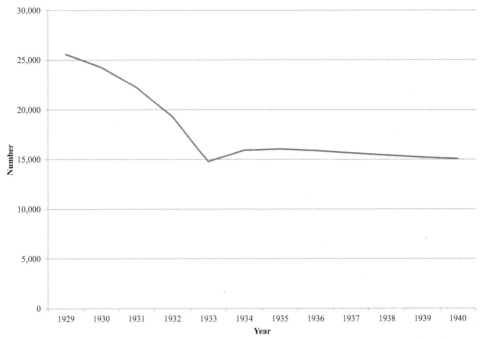

Figure 8.3. Number of Commercial Banks, 1929 to 1940. *Source:* U.S. Bureau of the Census (1975).

adversely impacted by a bad local economy or some other event beyond their control. The same sequence, however, would occur if the initial failures had been of incompetent bank management, fraud or imprudent lending and loan management. Even under the best of intentions, an individual depository institution has an incentive to assume imprudent levels of risk. As risk increases, the probability of failure increases and, hence, the probability of contagion increases.

Depository institutions are highly leveraged financial firms with an incentive to assume imprudent levels of risk because they don't take into account what impact their actions will have on the rest of the system. An individual depository institution has an incentive to operate with low levels of reserves because reserves earn no or little interest while loans earn much higher interest; an individual depository institution has an incentive to make riskier loans because they earn higher interest rates than less risky loans; and an individual depository institution has an incentive to operate with a small level of capital, which protects the institution from declines in the value of its assets on the balance sheet. Any of these actions increases the risk of the depository institution to bankruptcy and, if one or a few institutions go bankrupt, they can contaminate the entire system; that is, they generate a contagion process.

The money supply problem: Depository institutions are highly leveraged institutions and use this advantage to enhance profit. As a group, each depository institution has an incentive to over-expand lending, and hence the money supply is driven by self-interest, but, at the same time, individual institutions don't take into account the impact of their increased lending on the system and the fact that all depository institutions are behaving in much the same manner. Increased lending can be supported by reduced holdings of reserves, making riskier loans as the quantity of low-risk loans runs out or reducing capital. These actions increase the risk of failure, which can lead to contagion, as discussed above, but they also generate an excessive amount of lending and money supply in the aggregate. Excessive money supply can then generate inflation, which in turn lowers the value of the given money supply, reducing public confidence in money.

8.5 Government Resolution of the Problems of Commodity-Based Systems and Fractional Reserve Systems

The three problems identified above – money supply not responsive to needs of trade in commodity-based systems; the contagion problem in the inverted pyramid system; and the money supply problem in the inverted pyramid system – together rationalize the basic role of government in the nation's financial and monetary regime.

The difficulties of a commodity-based money supply that is not always responsive to the needs of trade can be solved by disconnecting the money supply from a commodity. This is accomplished by establishing a central bank that supplies reserves and regulates the demand for reserves by depository institutions by setting the reserve requirement; hence, the central bank controls the money supply by setting the reserve ratio and the reserve base.

The central bank also solves the money supply problem of the inverted pyramid system since the overall money supply is under the control of the central bank rather than the combined actions of individual depository institutions.

The solution to the contagion problem involves the government becoming a lender of last resort and the financial and regulatory authority limiting risk taking by depository institutions and providing deposit quarantines to maintain public confidence in deposit money.

Central bank control of the nation's money supply: The United States was a latecomer to the club of countries with central banks. The United Kingdom, many European countries and Japan, for example, established central banks well before the Federal Reserve was established in 1913. While periods such as the deflation in the last part of the nineteenth century generated calls for a more manageable money supply, the political and economic traditions of the United States made it difficult to establish a central bank. The United States had been established with a much larger degree of economic and political freedom than most countries and had a deep distrust of concentrations of economic and political power; hence, calls for a central bank and greater control of the nation's money supply were met with resistance. It is rather amazing that the United States in the last part of the nineteenth century was one of the few industrial economies that did not have a central bank. The

United Kingdom designated the Bank of England, which had been established as a private bank in 1694, as the country's official central bank in 1844. Japan, which began its modernization much later than the United States when in 1868 it commenced the Meiji Restoration, established the Bank of Japan in 1882, three decades before the United States got around to establishing the Federal Reserve System in 1913. It was a rather intense but short financial panic in 1907 that provided the catalyst, which, combined with a progressive President Wilson, produced the economic and political conditions needed to set up a central bank.

While a central bank may be able to achieve a more stable monetary growth than a commodity-based system in theory, history has shown that the central bank solution to commodity money or the money supply problem in the inverted pyramid stage has not always generated the expected results. Central banks can make policy errors based on faulty models of the economy and faulty procedures. Central banks such as the Federal Reserve are often organized to be formally or *de jure* independent of the government, but history shows that institutional independence is an easy wall to breach when government wants the central bank to expand the money supply. Thus, like the justified role of the government in minting coin, there is no guarantee that central banks will generate a significantly better output than when the money supply is tied to a commodity. Some argue for a return to a commodity system, but this is not realistic, for a number of reasons. The most important is that few countries would be willing to permit their money supply to be determined by the supply of a commodity such as gold. Instead, it is better to focus on reforms to the existing system, so that central banks accomplish the job they are designed for and capable of doing: providing a monetary growth that meets the needs of trade and maintain price stability without allowing the money supply to grow too fast or too slowly. The central bank has the potential to be a meaningful improvement over a commodity system, but whether the end result is a stable financial and monetary environment depends on how the central bank conducts policy.

Lender of last resort: Shifting from a commodity-based to a fiat-based reserve system in the inverted pyramid system provides the government not only with the ability to control the money supply but with the ability to function as a lender of last resort to prevent contagion. If there is any loss of confidence in deposit money, the government can provide whatever level of reserves is needed by individual depository institutions to meet deposit withdrawals. When the public realize they can convert their deposits into money without difficulty, they no longer have an incentive to convert, and go onto their normal daily business. That is, the government sets itself up as a lender of last resort to depository institutions experiencing runs, which, in turn, stops the run. Runs on depository institutions are largely driven by fear of an inability to convert deposit money into base money, and once that fear is removed there is no longer any desire to convert, and the inverted pyramid remains stable.

The central bank is the government institution responsible for lender of last resort services because it has the ability to control base money and the money supply.

Regulatory and supervisory authority: Regulatory and supervisory authority by the government covers a wide range of roles basically designed to limit risk taking by individual depository institutions and maintain public confidence in deposit money. These objectives can be accomplished by regulation and supervision, to limit imprudent lending by depository institutions; ensure that an adequate level of reserves and capital is maintained; monitor the operations of depository institutions through frequent reporting requirements on asset and liability operations; monitor operations of depository institutions via on-site examinations; and provide deposit insurance backed by the full faith and credit of the government.

The central bank is responsible for monetary control and lender of last resort services, but there is no inherent reason why central banks should play a major role in financial regulation and supervision. The reason central banks are most often assigned the responsibility of monetary control and lender of last resort is because, in a modern inverted pyramid monetary system, the central bank controls the reserve base. Managing the reserve base permits the central bank to thus function as a lender of last resort and provide overall control of the money supply. How this is done will be discussed in a later chapter.

The institutionalization of regulation and supervision, however, varies to a greater degree among countries. In the United States, the Federal Reserve is an important regulatory and supervisory agency, along with the U.S. Treasury and other federal regulatory agencies, as well as regulatory and supervisory agencies at the state level. In contrast, the central bank in many countries does not possess the degree of regulatory and supervisory responsibility the Federal Reserve does; for example, the Bank of Japan, Bank of Korea, Bank of England and European Central Bank play lesser roles in both regulation and supervision.

There has been a long-standing debate about the degree to which a central bank should be involved in regulation and supervision. Central banks argue that they need to have their hands on information regarding the financial system provided by at least some degree of regulation and supervision, such as on-site examinations, in order to carry out their monetary control and, especially, lender of last resort responsibilities. Others counter this argument in two ways. First, they point out that the central bank can easily obtain from other agencies the information needed to carry out its basic responsibilities without actually being a regulatory and supervisory authority over financial institutions and markets. Second, conflicts of interest arise between monetary policy and regulation as central banks become more concerned with the stability of those elements of the financial system they have responsibility for than the overall direction of monetary policy.

8.6 Institutionalization of Government's Role in the U.S. Financial and Monetary Regime

Table 8.2 lists, in order of the dates of their establishment, the most important agencies responsible for lender of last resort, prudential regulation and monetary control

Table 8.2. *Monetary, Regulatory and Supervisory Authorities*

Federal level

Office of the Comptroller of the Currency (1863)	The OCC is the first national regulatory authority established to regulate and supervise federally chartered banks. Organized as part of the U.S. Treasury.
Federal Reserve System (1913)	The Federal Reserve is the nation's monetary authority that controls the money supply; conducts monetary policy; sets reserve requirements for all federally and state-insured depository institutions; serves as a lender of last resort; provides wide-ranging regulatory and supervisory authority over banks and the banking system; and enforces a wide range of consumer protection laws.
Federal Deposit Insurance Corporation (1933)	The FDIC insures the deposits of commercial banks, S&Ls and savings banks up to $250,000 per account backed by reserves and the full faith and credit of the federal government. Federally and state-chartered banks, S&Ls and savings banks alike are eligible for FDIC insurance.
Securities and Exchange Commission (1934)	The SEC regulates and supervises the organized financial markets to maintain transparency and eliminate inside trading.
National Credit Union Administration (1971)	The NCUA regulates and supervises federally chartered credit unions and provides deposit insurance to both federal and state-chartered credit unions.
Commodities Futures Trading Commission (1974)	The CFTC regulates and supervises futures trading in commodities and financial assets in much the same manner that the SEC regulates and supervises organized financial markets.
Federal Housing Finance Agency (2008)	The FHFA supervises Freddie Mac, Fannie Mae and the Federal Home Loan Bank System. Freddie Mac and Fannie Mae are government-sponsored enterprises that establish a secondary market for residential mortgages. The Home Loan Bank System is a system of 11 government-sponsored enterprises or banks that provide loans to depository institutions to make residential mortgages.
Consumer Financial Protection Bureau (2010)	The CFPB has broad powers to regulate and supervise consumer credit provided in the United States.
Financial Stability Oversight Council (2010)	Consisting of representatives of the Federal Reserve, SEC, CFTC, OCC, FDIC, FHFA, NCUA, CFPB, the insurance industry, and chaired by the U.S. Treasury, the FSOC is responsible for identifying excessive risk taking in the financial system.

State level

Each state has one (e.g. Nevada) or a large number (e.g. California and New York) of regulatory and supervisory agencies that oversee financial activity within their state. Most of the above functions are duplicated at the state level to some degree, with the exception of deposit insurance, lender of last resort and monetary control. States focus their attention on state-chartered depository institutions and often share responsibility with federal agencies, especially over branching, even for federally chartered depository institutions.

There is one area of regulation and supervision that is exclusively at the state level. The insurance industry is regulated and supervised at the state level. There are no federal agencies directly responsible for overseeing the insurance industry.

functions in the United States. The regulatory structure of the United States differs from that of other countries in two important respects. First, the United States operates with a multiplicity of regulatory authorities, often with overlapping responsibilities; and, second, the regulatory structure of the United States is a *dualistic system*, based on the fact that the United States is a federal republic consisting of 50 state governments and a federal government at the center. The federal government dominates, but states retain considerable responsibility primarily as financial regulatory authorities. These two characteristics – the multiplicity of regulatory authorities and the dualistic structure of regulatory authorities – are unique. No other country is quite like the United States in this regard.

The multiplicity of regulatory authorities and dualistic structure reflect the history and political structure of the United States. The multiplicity characteristic reflects the checks and balance foundation of the political structure and reflects the nation's inherent distrust of concentrations of economic, political and regulatory power. The dual system reflects the original structure of the United States in the Constitution.

8.7 Extended Rationales for Government Involvement

The above three roles are the basic rationale for government becoming a part of the nation's financial and monetary regime, to offset the problems of commodity-based systems and fractional reserve systems. However, over time the three roles have been increasingly redefined and extended, to the point where, now, the government has become, for all practical purposes, the major force in the nation's financial and monetary regime. In the following, four specific extensions of government are noted.

Activist monetary policy and limiting systemic risk: At the start central banks were intended to merely ensure a stable monetary growth so as to maintain price stability, provide lender of last resort services on occasion and provide other services to establish a national payments system. However, central banks almost from the beginning began to conduct activist policies to offset shocks to the economy by conducting countercyclical monetary policy. The Federal Reserve is now responsible by congressional statute for achieving price stability, maximum employment and moderate long-term interest rates. In fact, central banks have now become the most important stabilization instrument of government to manage aggregate demand. At one time, fiscal policy – government spending and taxing – was regarded as an important instrument of stabilization, but that has changed significantly in the past few decades. For all practical purposes, monetary policy is *the* instrument of economic stabilization, with objectives assumed by the central bank or imposed on the central bank that go far beyond merely focusing on long-run price stability. There is considerable debate as to whether this is a good or bad thing – a subject postponed to a later chapter.

Likewise, the lender of last resort function was designed to limit contagion among depository institutions, and in this regard the central bank was more passive than activist, but now central banks have been assigned responsibility for monitoring and responding to risk, broadly defined, in the financial system – also broadly defined. Now central banks are responsible for limiting "systemic risk", defined to mean the risk that portfolio activities of any large component of the financial system place on the entire financial system and economy. In this regard, the Federal Reserve and other government agencies are now responsible for ensuring that those systemically important parts of the financial system have the capital and liquidity needed to survive economic turbulence.

In the past, regulatory authorities and the Federal Reserve focused on *microprudential* regulation, which focused on the condition of an individual depository institution; however, in the past decade regulatory authorities and the Federal Reserve have expanded prudential regulation to include *macroprudential* regulation. This is a dramatic extension of the responsibilities and administrative control of government over the financial system. It involves a focus on how large groups of financial institutions defined as systemically important to the stability of the financial system should be regulated to prevent asset bubbles and to ensure they can withstand financial and economic shocks.

Protecting the consumer of financial services: A major focus of government regulation and supervision is the protection of the consumer of financial services, based on the assumption that the consumer is at a disadvantage due to a lack of knowledge of financial transactions as a result of their complexity and the fact that financial institutions possess a much higher degree of market power than the individual. The Federal Reserve is the most important agency protecting consumer transactions involving credit, charge and debit cards issued by both financial institutions and retail outlets; electronic transactions; deposit transactions; consumer loans; automobile leases; and mortgage and home equity loans. Consumer protection, starting in the 1960s, has become a major focus of government regulation and supervision. The Truth in Lending Act of 1968 was the first requiring creditors to provide detailed information as to terms, interest rates and other conditions of any loan and is implemented by the Federal Reserve's Regulation Z. Table 8.3 lists important consumer protection laws in chronological order since 1968 for which the Federal Reserve has established regulations.

The Federal Reserve also conducts a wide range of educational efforts, designed to inform consumers of financial services of their rights as well as their responsibilities with regard to financial disclosure. The Federal Reserve maintains a consumer complaint program that responds to complaints about the practices of financial institutions. The Federal Reserve's institutional structure in fact provides importance to consumer affairs. The Federal Reserve has established three advisory committees that directly advise the Federal Reserve, one of which, established in 1976, is the Consumer Advisory Council. All in all, the Federal Reserve is a major player

Table 8.3. *Consumer Protection Laws*

Fair Housing Act of 1968	Prohibits discrimination in mortgage credit markets.
Truth in Lending Act of 1968	Requires uniform methods for informing borrowers of the cost of credit and terms.
Fair Credit Report Act of 1970	Protects consumers from inaccurate information by credit rating agencies.
Flood Disaster Protection Act of 1973	Requires flood insurance for certain properties.
Fair Credit Billing Act of 1974	Regulates how creditors must respond to billing-error complaints.
Equal Credit Opportunity Act of 1974	Prohibits discrimination in credit transactions.
Real Estate Settlement Procedures Act of 1974	Requires transparency in real estate settlements.
Home Mortgage Disclosure Act of 1975	Requires mortgage lenders to provide public information about the geographic distribution of mortgage credit applications and ethnicity, race, sex, income and other details.
Consumer Leasing Act of 1976	Requires transparency in consumer leases, such as for vehicles.
Fair Debt Collection Practices Act of 1977	Prohibits abusive collection methods.
Community Reinvestment Act of 1977	Encourages financial institutions to meet the credit needs of all those who live in their community, especially low- and moderate-income areas in which financial institutions have a presence.
Right to Financial Privacy Act of 1978	Protects customers of financial institutions from unlawful actions by fund transfer services such as automated teller machines, etc.
Federal Trade Communications Act of 1980	The Federal Reserve, acting on behalf of the Federal Trade Commission, restricts certain activities of banks regarding late charges, wage assignments, etc.
Expedited Funds Availability Act of 1987	Establishes the amount of time in which depository institutions must make funds available to depositors after making deposits.
Women's Business Ownership Act of 1988	Extends certain rules for consumer credit applicants and to applicants for business credit, such as reasons for a loan denial.
Fair Credit and Charge Card Disclosure Act of 1988	Amended Truth in Lending Act to provide information regarding applications made available to the public, such as credit card applications provided via mail or telephone.
Home Equity Loan Consumer Protection Act of 1988	Requires transparency in credit extended based on the consumer's home dwelling.
Truth in Savings Act of 1991	Requires transparency about deposits offered by depository institutions, such as explicit statement of interest paid; prohibits certain types of advertising; and regulates advertising for savings accounts.
Home Ownership and Equity Protection Act of 1994	Amends Truth in Savings Act to include certain disclosures about home equity loans.
Gramm–Leach–Bliley Act of 1999	This Act removes restrictions on branch banking across state lines, and part of the Act restricts the information that can be provided to third parties when dealing with the disclosure of personal information.
Fair and Accurate Credit Transactions Act of 2003	Amends the Fair Credit Reporting Act to assist consumers in dealing with thief identification.

Source: Board of Governors of the Federal Reserve System (2005).

in regulation and supervision designed to protect the consumer in the financial system. Other agencies, such as the Securities and Exchange Commission or the Office of the Comptroller of the Currency, provide similar services to those areas of the financial system not covered by the Federal Reserve. Each state also plays a role in protecting the consumer of financial services.

The protection of consumers function was significantly expanded in 2010 when the Consumer Financial Protection Bureau was established by the Dodd–Frank Act. The CFPB is an independent agency within the Federal Reserve structure, but not subject to Federal Reserve influence, and it has been granted wide-reaching powers to regulate and supervise consumer credit through the entire economy.

Establishing a level playing field and regulating the structure and performance of the financial system: Regulation and supervision are directed toward establishing a "level playing field" in the financial system, through a wide range of regulations on the part of the Federal Reserve and other agencies to regulate entry and exit, competitive practices, etc. Unlike many activities in the real economy, such as establishing a small business, for which entry, exit and competition are relatively unregulated, the government imposes extensive regulations on the structure and performance of the financial system. Establishing a new depository institution, establishing a new branch, especially across state lines, and introducing a new financial product or service all fall under the supervision of the Federal Reserve and other regulatory authorities, including those at the state level. While liberalization of the financial system in the past four decades has changed attitudes about regulating the structure and performance of various elements of the financial system and now permits greater competition than previously, the structure and performance of the financial system is subject to far greater regulation than all but a few other parts of the U.S. economy.

Subsidizing favored sectors of the economy: Governments, almost from the start of their involvement in the nation's financial and monetary regime, have used their power to subsidize favored sectors of the economy, such as real estate, especially residential real estate; export industries; agriculture; small businesses; and low-income households. There is a complex system of government regulations, government agencies and government-sponsored agencies designed to subsidize credit to these sectors. One of the more important involvements of the government in this regard is the Community Reinvestment Act (CRA) of 1977.

The CRA requires depository institutions, especially banks, to provide credit to all consumers in the community in which they operate, especially low- and moderate-income households. The CRA is based on two perspectives. First, depository institutions benefit from government deposit insurance and government restrictions on exit and entry, and, hence, their profits are partly dependent on government regulation. Second, depository institutions then should be responsible for serving all individuals in their communities, especially low- to moderate-income households. Over the years, especially starting in the 1990s, the CRA influenced the lending decisions of depository institutions, particularly with regard to consumer and mortgage credit.

8.8 Government Involvement Has a Downside: Government Failure Is as Important as Market Failure

The case for government involvement at some level in the nation's financial and monetary regime in the three basic areas is strong. In this regard, government policy is designed to mitigate elements of market failure. Milton Friedman (1959), one of the most influential conservative economists of the twentieth century, long ago argued that government had certain responsibilities to regulate and supervise the financial system to prevent the "economic equivalent of counterfeiting". By this, Friedman meant that government had responsibility to ensure confidence in the nation's money supply and that government had responsibility to ensure that only enough money be created to meet the needs of trade and maintain long-run price stability. However, government's role in the nation's financial and monetary system has gone far beyond preventing the economic equivalent of counterfeiting. Intense debate continues as to how far government involvement in the nation's financial and monetary regime should extend. Many argue for more extension while others argue for retrenchment.

Even at the minimal level of government involvement in the nation's financial and monetary regime, there is no free lunch. Government involvement comes with a price, and there is ample evidence government involvement has been a destabilizing force at times. A more balanced approach to understanding the role of government in the nation's financial and monetary regime is to recognize that, while market failure does exist, requiring government involvement, there is also government failure, which can be as serious as, or more serious than, the market failure it is designed to mitigate. On occasion, government involvement in the financial and monetary regime has generated periods of intense economic, financial and political distress.

There is no doubt that well-designed government policies to carry out the basic responsibilities of lender of last resort, prudential regulation and monetary control assist the nation's financial and monetary regime to fulfill its obligations, but four perspectives on government involvement suggest that an intellectually honest approach requires us to recognize there is government policy failure and that focusing only on the benefits lacks reality. The four perspectives are *moral hazard*; *crony capitalism and politicization of regulation*; *politicization of monetary policy*; and *public choice incentives*. The public choice perspective is not so much a separate issue, but offers a theoretical framework to understand the second and third perspectives.

Moral hazard: Moral hazard is a technical term used to describe human behavior in the presence of insurance or guarantees. Insurance of any type is subject to moral hazard; that is, the existence of insurance provides incentives to the insured that are adverse to the insurer. Car insurance, for example, makes you less concerned about parking the car in an area where there is a probability of damage or theft, as when you lock the car and walk away you tell yourself that "the car's insured". In the private sector, insurance companies have been aware of moral hazard for a long time and try to price their products to minimize moral hazard. In the public sector, and especially with regard to government involvement in the financial and monetary system, moral hazard is a real problem that is difficult to minimize. Two examples illustrate this point.

First, deposit insurance has moral hazard, because it removes concern by depositors about how the depository institution manages its portfolio, and, instead, they are concerned only with how much interest is earned on deposits. The depository institution now has less depositor discipline to worry about and thus has more incentive to adopt riskier portfolio behavior. Hence, deposit insurance, designed to increase public confidence in the nation's money supply, ends up providing incentives for depository institutions to take greater risks and thereby generate greater instability. Moral hazard is a serious problem, and, though there are policies to reduce the moral hazard of deposit insurance, they are difficult to implement for political reasons. One approach to reducing the moral hazard of deposit insurance, for example, is to impose risk-based deposit insurance premiums; however, this has proved to be difficult. Depository institutions know a good deal when they see one. After much resistance from depository institutions, however, deposit insurance was modified in 1991 to incorporate risk-based pricing. Unfortunately, the risk-based pricing has not been used to any great extent, nor has it had much practical impact on the behavior of depository institutions.

Politicians and government regulatory authorities tend to play down moral hazard because it does not have a direct measurable cost when guarantees are offered by the government. This way politicians have little difficultly passing laws that provide guarantees because they appear to be a real free lunch, since the guarantee adds nothing to the budget. Another reason why governments offer guarantees is because any future cost due to their unsustainability can be dealt with by issuing debt, raising taxes or increasing the money supply. Most often, when the real cost of an unsustainable guarantee becomes apparent, few if any government agencies experience any meaningful penalties.

Second, regulatory authorities are likely to err on the side of caution when dealing with troubled depository institutions, because of concern over contagion and not wanting a repeat of what happened in the first part of the 1930s to occur on their watch (Figure 8.2). Hence, there is a tendency to delay resolution of troubled depository institutions and declare them bankrupt. Instead, there is an incentive to provide time for institutions to work their way out of the problem or to delay implementing existing regulations. This policy is called *forgiveness and forbearance*, but, like deposit insurance, it has a moral hazard impact.

Depository institutions that are operating with negative net worth or close to negative net worth should be closed, but permitting them to continue operation only provides them incentives to adopt riskier loan and investment policies. This is a rational strategy, since the institution is already bankrupt or close to bankrupt, and a policy of forgiveness and forbearance is politically easier and, essentially, is taxpayer-assisted support. The problem is it seldom works. As a result of forgiveness and forbearance, depository institutions adopt riskier loan and investment strategies because the institution is being supported by taxpayers. The riskier loan and investment strategies only increase the ultimate cost of closing the institution down. This was a major issue in the S&L crisis in the 1980s. It was estimated that, had the government resolved the S&L problem in the early 1980s, the cost to taxpayers would have been around $25 billion in current dollars. Political pressure from the S&Ls and the real estate industry, which benefited from S&L lending, led to extensive forgiveness and forbearance policies by those agencies that regulated the S&L industry. The proper policy would have been to close many S&Ls, recapitalize those that were viable and cut the losses to the taxpayer; however, this was not done. Like zombies from the cult movie *Night of the Living Dead* (1968), a large number of S&Ls were permitted to remain open and operate even though they were insolvent by any reasonable accounting standard. When this policy was no longer possible, the government by 1989 was forced to bail out the S&L industry. The total cost, based on an FDIC study (Curry and Shibut, 2000), is about $214 billion in 2014 dollars.

The forgiveness and forbearance policy is not always applied equally to all depository institutions. Regulatory authorities have a tendency to focus on the larger institutions and adopt what amounts to a "too big to fail" policy for large institutions, which impose a risk to the financial system if they collapse. The "too big to fail" institutions, however, become aware of this special concern and have an incentive to adopt riskier loan and investment strategies because they know that, if problems occur, the government regulatory authorities will regard them as too big to fail. In practice, regulatory authorities often view small financial institutions as "too small to save"!

Crony capitalism or the politicization of regulation and supervision: Adam Smith in *The Wealth of Nations*, published in 1776, pointed out that businesses are seldom fans of competition. In fact, businesses will make every attempt to limit competition in order to enhance market share and profits. One of the rationales for expanded government, in not only the nation's financial and monetary regime but in the real sector, is to prevent restrictive business practices that limit competition and impose higher prices on the consumer. This rationale for government involvement is fine in theory, but the reality is somewhat different.

Once government has become a major regulatory presence in the nation's financial and monetary regime, the private sector has an incentive to establish relationships with regulatory agencies and politicians to ensure regulation is favorable to the sector. Regulatory agencies have an incentive to provide favorable regulation. Regulatory agencies are often run by individuals drawn from the very industry they regulate, and many who leave the agencies end up working in the industry they regulated. This close relationship between the private sector and the government is referred to as crony capitalism, in that there is a close relationship between the government regulatory authorities and the entities that they regulate, being beneficial to the regulated industry but often adverse to the public. This is not a right versus left issue in politics, as crony capitalism relationships are invariant to political party; that is, crony capitalism is an equal opportunity activity. Government regulation over the years has been politically sensitive to special interests representing financial markets, depository institutions, real estate, education, agriculture, consumers, etc. While much government regulation, even though influenced by special interests and crony relationship with the regulated entity, is in the general interests of the nation, a significant part of financial regulation is not in the best interests of the nation.

The use of regulation to support the housing sector has been a particularly serious problem, and over the years the government has employed many policies to encourage homeownership. There have been times Federal Reserve policy has been directed toward supporting housing. It might be worth the cost of the support if the outcome was more homeownership. But that is not the case. Homeownership rates in the United States since 1950 have averaged around 65 percent, peaked in 2005 at about 69 percent and have recently fallen back to around 65 percent. The United States compares poorly with other countries in terms of homeownership. The Pew Research Center in 2013 reported that, of the 42 countries that were members of the Organisation for Economic Co-operation and Development and the European Union, plus Singapore, the United States ranked 34th (DeSilver, 2013).

The cost is even much higher than the misallocation of resources to the housing sector. Government regulations to support housing have played a key role in the collapse of the S&L industry in the 1980s, the asset bubble in housing prices from 2001 to late 2005 and the collapse of the housing bubble in 2006 and the Great Recession. That is, the politicization of government regulation in this regard has come at a high price, with questionable benefits.

Politicization of monetary control: While an argument can be made for government control of the money supply, instead of permitting the money supply to be determined by a commodity such as gold, there is no guarantee the government will control the money supply with the objective of price stability. Central banks may be pressured to pursue other goals, such as employment or industrial policies to support specific sectors of the economy, or to monetize the government debt.

Monetizing government debt has been a main source of conflict between central banks and government in general. When the government increases spending, there are only three methods to finance spending in excess of existing tax revenue:

raise taxes, issue government debt or print money. Raising taxes is always politically difficult, and, while issuing more government debt is easier, issuing more
debt generates higher interest rates. In order to encourage the public to hold government debt, the interest rate offered on government debt must be increased.
Higher interest rates, however, adversely impact the economy and bring attention
to the government's deficit spending. Governments most of the time don't print
money themselves, but pressure the central bank to expand the money supply to
monetize the debt and keep interest rates from increasing. While such a policy is
difficult to maintain over long periods to time, it does work for short periods of
time.

The most frequently offered solution to this potential conflict between the government and central bank is to establish an independent central bank to minimize
or prevent political considerations playing a role in its management of the money
supply. Central bank independence is often held up as an important institutional
design to ensure that control of the money supply is protected from political considerations. As will be discussed later, however, legal independence from the government is far more complex than it appears at first sight. Central banks can seldom be made truly independent, and history demonstrates that independent central
banks do not necessarily generate a stable monetary policy. In fact, the evidence
shows that central banks, including the Federal Reserve, are sensitive to their political environment irrespective of their institutional design, and often do the government's bidding.

Public choice perspective of government: The greatest expansion of government
involvement in the monetary system as well as in the economy in general started
during the Great Depression under the Roosevelt administration. The interpretation
of the expanded role of government then and into the first few decades of the post-
WWII period was that government involvement was in the public good, designed
to offset market failure, which was often driven by the quest for profit. The market
failure view of government continues to be emphasized; however, in the 1960s
and 1970s a number of economists questioned the view that government policy is
always directed toward the public interest. Their perspective is now referred to as
the public choice perspective of government. Public choice economics has become
an important part of our understanding of government policy.

According to the public choice perspective, government agencies function much
like the individual consumer or business firm, pursuing their self-interest. Government agencies have utility functions that include the public welfare as a param-
eter, but, like individuals, government agencies operate with self-interest. Their
main concern is to enhance their budget, and individuals within the government
agency are concerned with enhancing their post-retirement careers. The problem
comes from the fact that government agencies supply regulation, but special interests demand regulation to enhance their profits and protect them from competition.
That is, government regulatory agencies become captured by special interests, and

much government regulation is designed not for the public good but for a special interest.

In a sense, public choice is another way to understand the politicization of government regulation and monetary policy; however, it provides a deeper understanding of the incentives possessed by government agencies and the central bank, explaining why public policy is not always in the public interest. Government institutions, for obvious reasons, are not fond of the public choice perspective, because it views a government agency as a self-interested entity, in the same vein as a consumer maximizing a utility function subject to a budget constraint, or a business maximizing profit subject to a cost function.

8.9 The Influence of Economic Ideas, History and Politics on Government Involvement in the Nation's Financial and Monetary Regime

The evolution of government involvement in the nation's financial and monetary regime is complex, to say the least, and any discussion of the important developments is beyond the scope of this contribution; however, in closing we can briefly highlight some of the major factors that have influenced the evolution of government in the nation's financial and monetary regime.

Prevailing theories of how the economy works: Government involvement is motivated and rationalized based on the prevailing theories at the time of how the economy functions. There have been four important historical periods that have importantly influenced government involvement in the economy.

The period from 1776 to 1936 is referred to as the Classical period, which viewed a private economy as inherently stable and requiring only a limited role for government to protect private property, provide national defense, provide certain types of public goods, such as infrastructure, and provide a stable financial and monetary regime.

The period from 1936 to the 1970s witnessed the rise of Keynesian economics, which in turn was strongly influenced by the Great Depression. The Great Depression started in 1929 and lasted a decade and, to many, contradicted the Classical view that markets were inherently stable and required only minimal government involvement. The Great Depression destroyed faith in the market system. The political response was to expand government to offset the then perceived market failure. *The General Theory* by Keynes, published in 1936, provided the theoretical foundation for attributing the Great Depression to market failure and provided the policy solution in the form of expanded government. The view shifted from one of stable markets and limited government to one of unstable markets and expanded government. This period lasted until the 1970s.

In the 1970s the Classical School reemerged but expressed in modern mathematics and econometrics. Markets again were viewed as stable and government efforts to administer and regulate markets, especially financial markets, were again viewed as destabilizing. While there were few serious arguments to return to the limited role of government before the Great Depression, this period witnessed the dismantling of many of the policies enacted during the 1930s that limited the role of market forces in the financial system. This period witnessed significant deregulation and liberalization policies, which changed the institutional design of the nation's financial and monetary regime. Like the previous period being named after Keynes, this period was often referred to as the age of Fredrick von Hayek and Milton Friedman, two prominent economists who advocated the importance of markets and emphasized the limitations of government involvement.

Starting in the 1990s and continuing into the first decade of the new century, the Keynesian perspective has returned to some degree. Markets, especially financial markets, again were viewed as inherently unstable and requiring government regulation and supervision. As a result, government has again expanded its role, but, as in the previous period, there have been few serious efforts to eliminate many of the reforms that were established during the deregulation phase of the last part of the twentieth century.

Historical events: Historical events play an important role in the evolution of government involvement. The growth of federal government involvement in the nation's financial and monetary regime started in earnest during the Civil War. The federal government attempted to replace state with federal regulation of the nation's banking system, but failed. Eventually the country ended up with a dualistic system, in which the federal and state governments both regulate financial matters. The deflation in the last third of the nineteenth century combined with a serious financial panic in 1907 are responsible for the establishment of the Federal Reserve System in 1913. The Great Depression is responsible for a major expansion of the role of government in the economy and, especially, in the nation's financial and monetary regime. The Great Inflation was responsible for a shift away from the Keynesian perspective back to the Classical perspective. The Great Recession is responsible for a shift back to the Keynesian perspective to some degree.

Political influences: And, finally, political considerations have been a major driving force behind government involvement. Politicians have an incentive to use the nation's financial and monetary regime for purposes that go far beyond the original rationale for government involvement, to control the money supply, provide lender of last resort services and provide financial and supervisory regulation. In fact, in a democracy in which elected individuals are the ones who institutionalize the government's role in the nation's financial and monetary regime, it would be naive to believe that politics has not been a main driver of government involvement in the nation's financial and monetary regime. To borrow a line from the movie *Casablanca*, one would be "shocked, shocked", to see that politics has been an important force behind the growth of government control over the money supply, lender of last resort function and prudential regulation of the nation's financial and monetary regime.

References

Board of Governors of the Federal Reserve System (2005). *The Federal Reserve System: Purposes and Functions*, 9th edn. Washington, D.C.: Board of Governors of the Federal Reserve System.

Curry, Timothy, and Lynn Shibut (2000). "The Cost of the Savings and Loan Crisis: Truth and Consequences". *FDIC Banking Review*, 13: 26–35.

DeSilver, Drew (2013). "Around the World, Governments Promote Home Ownership". Pew Research Center, August 6, www.pewresearch.org/fact-tank/2013/08/06/around-the-world-governments-promote-home-ownership.

Friedman, Milton (1959). *A Program for Monetary Stability*. New York: Fordham University Press.

Rockoff, Hugh (1990). "The 'Wizard of Oz' as a Monetary Allegory". *Journal of Political Economy*, 98: 739–60.

Smith, Adam (1776). *An Inquiry into the Nature and Causes of the Wealth of Nations*. London: W. Strahan and T. Cadell.

U.S. Bureau of the Census (1975). *Historical Statistics of the United States: Colonial Times to 1970*. Washington, D.C.: U.S. Bureau of the Census.

Chapter 9

Regulation and Supervision of the Financial System

9.1 Introduction

Government regulation and supervision of the financial system constitute one of the three components of the nation's financial and monetary regime. Chapter 8 discussed how government regulation and supervision evolved over time as the nation's monetary standards shifted from commodity to representative commodity and, finally, to fiat-based standards. That discussion was designed to explain how government emerged as a major force in the nation's financial and monetary regime. The discussion in Chapter 8 was necessarily broad. This chapter is more focused, in two ways: First, the rationale for government regulation and supervision is expanded to incorporate different perspective of market failure; and, second, the important and specific types of government regulation and supervision are outlined.

9.2 Asymmetric Information, Adverse Selection and Lemons

The rationale for government regulation and supervision can now be extended to incorporate two other types of market failure that interfere with the ability of the nation's financial and monetary regime to operate smoothly. The two new perspectives of market failure are referred to as the *asymmetric information* and *adverse selection* problems. These are general problems in any market, and can be introduced by considering a market for a commodity such as a used car or home. George Akerlof (1970) is credited with bringing attention to how asymmetric information and adverse selection render the used car market less inefficient. His analysis is now referred to the "lemon problem" in the used car market. The principles, however, are general.

Asymmetric information refers to the fact the buyer and the seller of the used car do not have the same information set. The seller generally has more information about the car than the buyer. The seller knows the car engine burns too much oil or has a weak transmission even though the car drives well for short distances. The buyer does not have this knowledge, and, while the buyer can pay to have a mechanic examine the car, this is expensive and time-consuming and may not provide reliable information if the defect is subtle. That is, the seller knows the car is a lemon but the potential buyer does not. As a result, the potential buyer assumes the used car is of average quality irrespective of how well it is represented and, hence, will offer a price based on that assumption alone. If in fact the car is a lemon, the seller will be willing to accept the price based on average quality, but, if the car is above average quality, the seller is not likely to sell at the average price the buyer is willing to pay. The asymmetric information problem is made worse because of adverse selection. Adverse selection is the tendency for sellers with lemon cars to be overrepresented in the market as they have a greater incentive to sell the car than the individual has with a good used car. As a result, the market will be overrepresented by lemons and, because buyers have incomplete information, buyers will be underrepresented. In the context of symmetric information there is no lemon problem, as there is no adverse selection problem. That is, the more information that is available on both sides of the transaction, the more efficient the market.

The asymmetric information problem and adverse selection are particularly important in the financial system, because transactions are complex, reliable information is difficult to collect and assess and financial transactions occur at a more rapid pace than most real transactions. Lemon borrowers – that is, those with higher risk – have more incentive to borrow than those with less risk, and, because of asymmetric information, lenders are at a disadvantage. In lending and borrowing transactions, the asymmetric information and adverse selection problems in direct financial markets make it difficult for small lenders and borrowers to complete a transaction.

In fact, indirect finance can be viewed as a market innovation designed to resolve the two problems. The financial institution offers the lender a promise to pay tailored to the lender's needs but, more important, the promise to pay is liquid and with low or zero default risk. The financial institution is able to diversify its loan portfolio to reduce risk and devote resources to credit evaluation and monitoring, thus reducing the adverse selection problem. This is why indirect finance is, by and large, the most important channel of finance in developed and developing countries alike. In financial intermediation it's not important for the lender to the financial institution to have the same information set about the borrower as the financial institution since the institution has the incentive and resources to obtain symmetric information. The financial institution also is able to deal with adverse selection effectively by becoming an expert at credit evaluation.

Asymmetric information and adverse selection in the direct financial markets, in contrast, cannot be resolved by an intermediary. There is no intermediary other than a broker and agent, who merely brings lenders and borrowers together, collects a fee for the complete transaction and has no economic interest in the underlying promises to pay. As indirect finance was a market innovation to resolve the asymmetric information and adverse selection problems for small lenders and borrowers, there has been a market response to these problems in the direct financial markets. First, small lenders and borrowers play a limited role in direct financial markets; and, second, credit rating firms have evolved to provide information so lenders can evaluate the creditworthiness of debt and equity issued in open markets. Credit rating information, however, depends on a financial disclosure system for those issuing debt or equity in the direct markets. The requirements of a transparent and meaningful financial disclosure system and the limited role played by small lenders and borrowers in the direct markets under any circumstances account for the fact only about 30 percent of the flow of funds in the United States is transferred through the money and capital markets. In other countries, the role of direct markets is much smaller.

Indirect finance and credit rating systems are market solutions to asymmetric information and adverse selection; however, there is still a need for government regulation and supervision to render the financial system a component of a stable financial and monetary environment. Financial institutions have incentives to assume risk and expand credit that require some degree of government regulation and supervision, especially in the case of depository financial institutions. Financial markets benefit from government regulation and supervision, which ensures a level playing field between the lender and the borrower and a meaningful financial disclosure system in the direct money and capital markets. However, there is a fundamental difference between the objectives of government regulation and supervision of indirect finance and direct finance. Limiting systemic risk and maintaining a stable financial environment are the objectives of government regulation and supervision of financial institutions. In contrast, government regulation and supervision are not concerned with risk taking in the direct markets, but ensuring that there is adequate information to assess risk and ensuring confidence the direct markets are not rigged.

9.3 Government Regulation and Supervision of Indirect Finance

The institutions of indirect finance are among the most extensively regulated and supervised in any economy because of their role in the transfer of funds from lenders to borrowers, especially depository institutions, because their promises to pay constitute the major part of the M2 money supply. The majority of funds borrowed by the private sector are from financial institutions even though U.S. direct markets are relatively more important than in other developed countries. Based on data from 1970 to 2000 (Hackethal and Schmidt, 2004), nonfinancial businesses obtained 56 percent of their external financing from depository institutions and non-bank financial institutions, 32 percent by issuing bonds and 11 percent by issuing equity. In other countries the reliance on indirect finance by nonfinancial business is even higher; for example, in Germany and Japan nonfinancial businesses obtained 86 percent of their funding from depository institutions and nondepository institutions, 7 percent and 9 percent, respectively, from issuing bonds and 8 percent and 5 percent, respectively, from issuing equities. In the United States, households obtain virtually all of their borrowing from depository institutions and finance companies, while government, at all levels, issues debt in the direct markets.

Among financial institutions, depository institutions are the most heavily regulated and supervised, because of their role in the nation's money supply. Depository institutions are subject to frequent on-site audits; must satisfy reserve requirements and capital–asset requirements; are subject to asset and liability portfolio restrictions; have access to lender of last resort services; and operate with federal deposit insurance backed by the full faith and credit of the U.S. government. Nondepository financial institutions are also subject to a variety of similar regulations, with the exception of deposit insurance and frequency of on-site audits. The promises to pay issued by nondepository financial institutions do not, with the exception of money market funds, function as money.

Government regulation and supervision of indirect finance are not confined to prudential objectives to limit systemic risk, but have other objectives focused on the structural characteristics of the financial system in terms of numbers of firms; exit and entry and branching; consumer protection; and industrial policies designed to provide subsidized credit to politically important sectors of the economy.

In the following we first focus on the more important aspects of government regulation of depository institutions and then, second, comment on government regulation and supervision of nondepository financial institutions.

9.4 Government Regulation and Supervision of Depository Financial Institutions

9.4.1 Deposit Insurance

Government deposit insurance is designed to ensure public confidence in deposit money in order to prevent contagion. Deposit insurance was first authorized by the Banking Act of 1933 in the aftermath of the Great Contraction and collapse of the banking system from 1929 to 1933. Today deposit insurance is provided and administered by the Federal Deposit Insurance Corporation. The FDIC insures deposits of banks, savings banks and S&Ls while the National Credit Union Administration insures credit union deposits. The combined checking, saving and time deposits under a specific ownership name at one institution are covered up to $250,000. Several decades ago some individual states insured the deposits of S&Ls;

Table 9.1. *FDIC Deposit Insurance Limits, 1934 to 2015*

Year	Current dollars	Adjusted for inflation
1934	$2,500	$2,500
1935	$5,000	$2,635
1950	$10,000	$4,635
1966	$15,000	$6,231
1969	$20,000	$7,058
1974	$40,000	$9,481
1980	$100,000	$15,846
2008	$250,000	$41,404

Source: Federal Deposit Insurance Corporation.

however, these systems were not viable and are no longer part of the deposit guarantee system. Only the federal government has the resources to make credible the claim that "the full faith and credit of the government" stands behind deposit insurance. Deposit insurance is mandatory for any federally chartered depository institution and available for any state-chartered institution, and, for all practical purposes, every depository institution in the United States is federally insured.

Deposit insurance was originally designed to cover small depositors who lacked knowledge, opportunities and resources to monitor their institutions, but over the decades deposit insurance coverage has increased to cover virtually all depositors. Table 9.1 lists the deposit insurance limits established by the FDIC at various times since 1934 and what the insurance limits would have been had they been adjusted for the inflation rate. The current deposit limit of $250,000, established in 2008, would have been $41,404 ($82,808) had the original limits of $2,500 ($5,000) been adjusted over time for inflation. Thus, there has been a rather significant expansion in government deposit guarantees in real terms. As already mentioned, while deposit insurance is an effective method in dealing with contagion, its downside is moral hazard.

One component of the money supply, however, is not federally insured. Retail money market funds are part of M2 money, but not federally insured. They thus possess a degree of default risk, which became apparent during the 2008/2009 financial crisis. The fact they were not federally insured raised concern at the time that both retail and institution funds would be withdrawn en masse and intensify the financial and economic distress. In response, the U.S. Treasury temporarily extended federal deposit insurance to money market funds, and in 2014 the Securities and Exchange Commission established new rules for the transparency of money market funds and how their value is reported, to make it clear to the public that money market funds are not federally guaranteed. The public did get the message, and the role of money market funds in the M2 money supply has declined significantly since 2008 (Figure 2.1).

Deposit insurance does work, and many regarded it as a major improvement in the monetary system when first offered in 1934. Today, countries have increasingly adopted the explicit deposit insurance scheme used in the United States. Deposit insurance eliminates the probability of contagion as long as the public believes the "full faith and credit" of the government stands behind deposit insurance; however, deposit insurance does have its own problem – moral hazard.

The moral hazard embedded in deposit insurance subsidizes risk taking by depository institutions since deposit insurance eliminates depositor discipline. Depositors have no interest in the economic health of the institution or whether it is making imprudent loans, being interested only in the services and return they receive for their deposits. This was recognized at the time deposit insurance was debated before the 1933 Banking Act was passed; President Roosevelt raised the issue and was not completely enthusiastic about signing the legislation establishing the FDIC. It was believed at that time, however, that the regulatory and supervisory oversight of the government and the willingness to close troubled depository institutions would restrain imprudent lending and limit or remove any moral hazard incentives. This view was mistaken.

The S&L crisis in the 1980s, banking problems in the early 1990s and the housing bubble in the first decade of the new century were all in part the result of risky lending, especially residential mortgages. There is little doubt moral hazard played a role. Can the moral hazard of deposit insurance be reduced?

There are two approaches to reducing the moral hazard. First, lowering the deposit insurance limit to, say, $50,000 would still cover most deposits and, at the same time, be consistent with the original intention of deposit insurance to cover only small deposits. This is not practical, however. The public has come to regard deposit insurance as an entitlement and would greatly resist any reduction in the limit. Politicians likewise would resist any reduction in the limit. They think deposit insurance is a "free lunch", because raising the limit does not appear to have any budgetary cost, but moral hazard is the cost, and the cost is high. Research has shown that moral hazard is real and has played a role in the financial problems not only of the United States but of many countries, especially Japan.

Second, risk-based deposit insurance premiums would reduce moral hazard and would invoke less resistance from the public and politicians. Historically, all depository institutions paid a premium to the FDIC based on the premium percentage factor times covered deposits. The premium percentage was flat across all institutions at any point in time; that is, the premiums were not adjusted for the risk of the individual institution. This was at variance with common practice in the private insurance industry. Car insurance, for example, is adjusted according to one's driving record as an indicator of risk.

The government and depository institutions have historically resisted risk-based deposit insurance premiums in general, but the environment for deposit insurance reform changed with the collapse of the S&L industry in the 1980s. In

1987 the Government Accounting Office declared the Federal Savings and Loan Insurance Corporation (1938–1989) insolvent. In addition, the FDIC for a few years lost money, in that payoffs for deposits at failed banks exceeded premium revenue. There was great concern FDIC would follow the way of the Federal Savings and Loan Insurance Corporation. The 1991 Federal Deposit Insurance Corporation Improvement Act was designed to place federal deposit insurance on a sounder foundation. The Federal Savings and Loan Insurance Corporation was eliminated, with its functions transferred to the FDIC; deposit insurance premiums were increased; a variety of new approaches to dealing with troubled depository institutions, known as Prompt Corrective Action (PCA), were adopted; and, as part of the reform effort, risk-based deposit insurance premiums were introduced for the first time. Since 1991 deposit insurance premiums have been adjusted for risk, but the range of adjustment is rather minor and, for all practical purposes, in the United States and most countries, deposit insurance premiums are not very sensitive to the risk of the individual depository institution.

9.4.2 Reserve Requirements

All federally insured depository institutions are required to satisfy reserve requirements established and administered by the Federal Reserve irrespective of their size or whether they operate under a federal or state charter. Reserve requirements specify the amount of funds an institution must maintain against specific deposits. The current reserve requirement system was established in 1980 and can be summarized by the following questions and answers.

What are the specific deposits subject to reserve requirements? Reserve requirements apply only to net checking or what are officially labeled net transactions accounts (demand deposits, NOW accounts and credit union share drafts). Net transactions accounts are total accounts less amounts due from other depository institutions. Saving and time deposits are not subject to reserve requirements and, while reserve requirements can be imposed on large CDs and Eurodollar deposits, the reserve requirement on these deposits was set to zero in 1990. So, for all practical purposes, only checking deposits are subject to reserve requirements.

What are the reserve requirements? Table 9.2 indicates the reserve requirements as of January 2015. There are three rate levels. First, deposits from zero to $14.5 million for an institution are exempt from reserve requirements because of the relatively small size of any depository institution with $14.5 million or less in deposits. The "exemption level" of deposits is adjusted each year based on the past year's deposit growth. Second, deposits more than $14.5 million up to $103.6 million are subject to a 3 percent reserve requirement. The upper deposit level, or "low-reserve tranche", is adjusted for deposit growth in the previous year. Third, deposits above $103.6 million are subject to a 10 percent reserve requirement.

Table 9.2. *Reserve Requirements, January 2015*

Deposit type	Percentage of deposit
Net transactions accounts	
$0 to $14.5 million	0
More than $14.5 million to $103.6 million	3
More than $103.6 million	10
No personal time deposits or large CDs	0
Eurocurrency deposits	0

Source: Federal Reserve.

Who sets the reserve requirements? The Federal Reserve has no independent authority to change the first two reserve requirement levels; however, the Federal Reserve can change the third reserve requirement from 8 percent to 14 percent. Reserve requirements have been changed only twice since the current system was established in 1980. In 1990 the requirement for large CDs and Eurodollar deposits was set at zero and in 1992 the requirement on transaction deposits was lowered from 12 percent to 10 percent. Even though the reserve requirement has not been changed since 1992, the effective reserve requirement has declined because depository institutions have established "retail sweep programs". Retail sweep programs shift funds from deposits subject to the reserve requirement into deposits that are not subject to reserve requirements.

How does the depository institution satisfy the reserve requirement? Required reserves must be held in the form of vault cash. If vault cash is insufficient to satisfy the requirement, the balance must be held as a reserve deposit at the Federal Reserve. The depository institution can maintain a reserve deposit either with the Federal Reserve or at another depository institution on a "pass-through relationship". Banks that are official members of the Federal Reserve must maintain a reserve deposit at the Federal Reserve. At one time the status of "official member" of the Federal Reserve was important, but since 1980 the distinction between member and nonmembers of the Federal Reserve has been economically meaningless and more a leftover from the early days of the Federal Reserve. This issue will be discussed when we introduce the organizational structure of the Federal Reserve in a later chapter.

Do the reserve balances at the Federal Reserve earn interest? In 2008 the Federal Reserve commenced paying interest on reserve deposits held by depository institutions. The interest rate as of January 2015 was 25 basis points on required reserves and 25 basis points on excess reserves. Excess reserves are total reserves held less required reserves. The two rates are determined by the Federal Reserve and do not have to be identical. The Federal Reserve decided to pay interest on required reserves to compensate banks for the opportunity cost of satisfying the reserve requirement and views the payment of interest on excess reserves as a new tool of monetary policy.

Are excess reserves "unwanted reserves"? The answer is a clear "No". "Excess reserves" is merely the technical name for reserves above required reserves. The amount of excess reserves desired by a depository institution is determined by economic factors and varies over time, especially with respect to changes in interest rates. In the late 1930s the Federal Reserve made a serious policy error, because it viewed the then high level of excess reserves held by banks as "unwanted", which could easily be "mopped" up by raising reserve requirements. In fact, the high level of excess reserves was desired. Imagine yourself as a bank that had survived up to that point. You would, understandably, have little confidence the Federal Reserve was able to prevent another banking collapse. You would be much more risk-averse and would have an incentive to hold liquidity and limit lending. Based on this misunderstanding of the level of excess reserves, the Federal Reserve doubled reserve requirements in a six-month period and caused a sharp recession as banks reduced lending to reestablish desired levels of excess reserves.

9.4.3 Capital–Asset Requirements

Depository institutions are subject to a minimum capital–asset ratio. The capital–asset ratio is like a shock absorber in your car. Like a shock absorber that softens the bumps on the road, the amount of capital relative to assets provides a cushion to offset declines in the value of assets. A 10 percent capital–asset ratio, for example, means the value of assets can fall by any amount less than 10 percent and the institution continues to operate with positive capital. In the absence of government-required capital–asset ratios, depository institutions would still operate with some capital, but it would likely be far below prudent levels to enhance profit. The same can be said for reserve requirements. In the absence of government-required reserves, depository institutions would still operate with some reserves, but they would be far below prudent levels to enhance profits.

Depository institutions have always been subject to minimum capital–asset requirements; however, three events have elevated the importance of these requirements and generated a more uniform set of capital–asset requirements for depository institutions.

First, in 1988, the Basel Committee on Banking Supervision, headquartered in Basel, Switzerland, and consisting of representatives of 12 major central banks and regulatory authorities, recommended that countries adopt a standard set of risk-based capital–asset ratios, especially for large banks with significant international operations. The specific recommendations are known as Basel I.

The Basel I capital–asset requirements are based on first computing a risk-weighted level of assets for a specific bank. The weights are based on the credit risk of the various assets; for example, cash and home Treasury securities are assigned

Table 9.3. *Prompt Corrective Action and*
Tripwire Capital–Asset Ratio Adequacy

Tripwire description	Tripwire ratio
Well capitalized	$\geq 10\%$
Adequately capitalized	$\geq 8\%$
Undercapitalized	$< 8\%$
Significantly undercapitalized	$< 6\%$
Critically undercapitalized	$\leq 2\%$

Source: Federal Deposit Insurance Corporation.

a risk weight of 0; mortgage-backed securities are assigned a risk weight of 0.2; and corporate bonds are assigned a risk weight of 1.0. Capital is divided into tiers depending on its liquidity. The ratio of risk-adjusted assets to total capital is the bank's risk adjusted capital–asset ratio. The recommended Basel I capital–asset requirement was 8 percent for banks engaged in significant international operations.

The Basel I recommendations were incorporated into the banking regulations of a large number of countries to varying degrees. In 2004 and 2010 the recommended requirements were revised to correct defects in the Basel I requirements and provide regulatory authorities with a broader range of capital adequacy measures to better assess bank risk. The expanded requirements are known as Basel II and Basel III, the latter of which is still being implemented. The United States adopted the Basel I, II and III recommendations for all depository institutions above a certain size.

Second, in light of the collapse of the S&L industry in the 1980s and the $214 billion taxpayer bailout (in 2014 dollars), as well as serious banking problems in the early 1990s, a new approach to dealing with depository institutions was established, referred to as Prompt Corrective Action. Many countries have adopted similar PCA policies based on the U.S. model. PCA is a policy designed to deal with institutions well before they fail, partly based on the Basel I type of capital–asset ratio requirements combined with a "tripwire" system of regulatory responses based on the ratio. As the total capital–asset ratio falls, the primary regulatory authority for the depository intuition is required to impose regulatory and supervisory pressure of increasing intensity until the final tripwire of 2 percent or less is reached. At that point, the institution is placed into receivership, to be closed or merged with another better-capitalized institution. Table 9.3 indicates the tripwire system for FDIC-insured depository institutions.

Third, the financial crisis in 2008/2009 and the Great Recession raised concerns the existing capital–asset requirements needed to be enhanced to reflect the complex portfolios of depository institutions in the new environment of deregulation and internationalization of finance. Basel III is currently being implemented over the next few years and the 2010 Dodd–Frank Act has also revised capital adequacy requirements and established new government agencies to monitor any financial institution deemed to pose systemic risk to the economy. There is a general consensus that depository institution capital has been insufficient in the new environment of deregulation and financial liberalization and that depository institutions, along with other financial institutions, need to have "more skin" in the game to limit imprudent lending and investing. Hence, capital requirements are likely to continue to be increased in the future, and regulatory authorities will be increasingly inclined to use the capital requirements, along with other measures of financial health, as the basis for a tripwire system of responses to changes in the health of any major part of the financial system.

9.4.4 Supervision and Oversight: CAMELS Rating System

Depository institutions are subject to continuous review of their financial performance and subject to on-site examinations by their respective regulatory agencies. The CAMELS rating system is used by the Federal Reserve, Comptroller of the Currency and National Credit Union Administration to summarize the institution's financial health. Along with the capital asset adequacy measurements, the CAMELS rating system is an important input into the PCA policy.

CAMELS is an acronym for the quality of the institution's capital (C), assets (A), management (M), earnings (E), liquidity (L) and sensitivity to market risk (S). Each component is assigned a score from 1 (best) to 5 (worst) and an overall composite score ranging from 1 to 5 is assigned; however, the composite score is not an average of the individual scores but an overall assessment of the quality of the depository institution by the on-site team. Every federally insured depository institution is assigned a CAMELS rating.

A composite score of 3, 4 or 5 places an institution on a "problem" list. The institution is then subject to a wide range of regulatory actions, from written warnings to closure of the institution. The number of institutions on the list and their assets are published; however, individual institutions on the problem list are not made public, nor are the CAMELS scores made public for any institution. Figure 9.1 presents the number of FDIC-insured depository institutions, and their asset value, that were placed on the problem list in each year from 1990 to 2014. Note that the problem list and value of assets was actually larger in the early 1990s than since 2008.

CAMELS ratings and the composite score are not made public, and there has been debate as to whether they contain information beyond what the market knows and whether they should be made public. There is little doubt that, for the very large depository institutions, especially large banks, the public is aware of the institution's financial health, and the CAMELS ratings would provide little additional

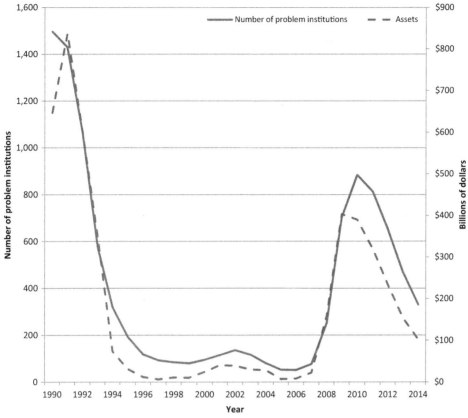

Figure 9.1. Number and Assets of Problem FDIC Insurance Depository Institutions, 1990 to 2014 (September). *Source:* Federal Deposit Insurance Corporation.

information even if they were made public; however, for middle-sized to small institutions, the CAMELS scores do have information the public is not likely to be aware of. There has been debate over whether the CAMELS should be publicized, but regulatory authorities are reluctant to publish this information for fear it would generate contagion and reduce the willingness of the management team of any institution to come forward with issues that need to be resolved. On balance, the argument for confidentially is stronger than the argument for public disclosure.

9.4.5 Supervisory Stress Testing

A new supervisory and oversight tool is becoming important as a result of the 2010 Dodd–Frank Act. The Act is complex and continues to be subject to debate as to whether it improves oversight, expands moral hazard by defining financial institutions systemically important or involves the government in micromanagement of the financial system. In any event, the Act now requires the Federal Reserve to conduct an annual stress test of the bank holding companies with $50 billion or more in assets as well as for those nonbank financial institutions defined to be systemically important; a systemically important financial institution is one that is so large and integrated in the financial system that problems at that institution impact the entire financial system and economy. The Act also requires the target financial institutions to conduct their own stress tests and report the results to the Federal Reserve.

The Federal Reserve stress test is simple in concept but complex in implementation. The stress test projects key elements of the institution's balance sheet and income statement over a nine-quarter planning horizon using a set of capital action assumptions specified in the Act. The projections are computed for three macroeconomic scenarios: baseline, adverse and severally adverse. The institutions are required to use the same set of capital action assumptions and macroeconomic scenarios.

The objective of the stress testing is to provide financial institutions, the public and the regulatory authorities with forward-looking information about the susceptibility of the financial system to adverse macroeconomic developments by determining the ability of large and important financial institutions to absorb losses. Unlike the CAMELS, the results of the individual and Federal-Reserve-conducted stress tests are made available to the public in summary form.

9.5 Government Regulation and Supervision of Nondepository Financial Institutions

Nonbank financial institutions are subject to extensive government regulation and supervision, though not to the same extent as the regulation and supervision directed at depository institutions. Nonetheless, they are subject to many of the same regulations over their portfolio activities, capital adequacy, reserves and liquidity, as well as being subject to on-site audits. A review of the various regulations for the different nondepository institutions would be far beyond the scope of this writing, but two aspects of the regulation of nondepository financial institutions are worth mentioning: state-based insurance regulation and transparency in money market funds.

State-based insurance regulation and supervision: Insurance companies are the only financial institution not subject to federal regulation and supervision. They are regulated and supervised only at the state level, whereas every other financial institution is regulated to some degree at the federal level. The National Bank Act of 1863 authorized the federal government to begin regulating and supervising the banking system through what is now the oldest federal regulatory agency as part of the Treasury – the Comptroller of the Currency. This represented a major shift from state governments to the federal government, which has continued to the present; however, the federal government, for all practical purposes, does not regulate or supervise the insurance industry.

A few years after the National Bank Act was passed the Supreme Court, in 1869, declared that an insurance policy was not commerce and thus not subject to federal legislation. In 1939 the Supreme Court overturned this decision, but Congress passed a law in 1945 declaring that insurance regulation was best left to the states. In the 1970s and 1980s, with deregulation and financial liberalization of the nation's financial and monetary regime in full force, increased attention was devoted to whether it was in the public interest to continue with state-based regulation and supervision of the insurance industry. In the past few decades the federal government has made some efforts to extend its reach to the insurance industry, such as requiring minimum standards for state regulation. But two events in the past decade have intensified interest in adding the insurance industry to federal regulation and supervision responsibilities.

First, the growth of financial derivatives and the role played by the insurance industry in certain types of derivatives. Financial derivatives have become important financial innovations far larger in value than the bonds, equities and mortgages on which they are based. Some experts have indicated that, as of 2014, the total size of the global derivative market is $1,200 trillion. A derivative is, essentially, a financial instrument whose value is derived from or based on another financial instrument or commodity. Three important financial derivative are collateralized debt instruments, mortgage-backed bonds and credit default swaps (CDSs). Collateralized debt instruments are promises to pay the interest and principal earned by the underlying assets serving as collateral. Collateralized debt instruments can be divided into "tranches", in which the highest grade offers the lowest risk of payment and the lowest grade offers the highest risk of payment. Mortgage-backed bonds are collateralized instruments based on a pool of mortgages. CDSs are instruments that insure the default risk of a set of obligations. CDSs can be purchased by anyone whether or not they have a property right to the underlying obligations being insured against default.

The CDS market has largely been unregulated, nontransparent and complex as well as a large part of the total derivative market. The market played an important role in the housing price bubble from 2002 to 2006, as insurance companies and others issued CDS to insure the default risk of pools of mortgages, especially pools of subprime mortgages. Subprime mortgages were those made to high-risk borrowers, with no or little down payment and little documentation on the borrower's earnings. At the same time, CDSs were issued for many other types of obligations; for example, CDSs were sold to pension funds to insure default of their underlying obligations. The CDSs were issued without adequate reserves because they were based on the view that default had only a small probability of occurrence. Insurance companies in particular came to be on both sides of the market. On one side, insurance companies sold CDSs to obtain revenue, and, on the other, they purchased CDSs to limit the risk on their own portfolios of bonds and mortgages.

CDS exposure played the key role in the collapse of American International Group (AIG), the largest U.S. insurance company. AIG had issued large amounts of CDSs, which required AIG to increase reserves if there was a decline in AIG's credit rating. As housing prices fell and lowered the value of AIG's holdings of mortgage-backed bonds, AIG was required to set aside reserves that it did not have nor could raise in the market. At the same time, defaults throughout the economy increased and required AIG to pay off CDSs it had sold. AIG did not have sufficient reserves to meet their obligations; hence, AIG collapsed in late 2008 and required an $85 billion loan from the U.S. Treasury to continue operation, so that it could be reorganized to limit any further damage to the financial system.

Second and third, the passage of the Affordable Care Act and Dodd–Frank Act in 2010 has elevated the regulatory and supervisory interest of the federal government of the insurance industry. The Affordable Care Act elevates the role of the insurance companies as part of a government-directed effort to oversee the health industry, estimated to represent about 20 percent of the U.S. economy. The Dodd–Frank Act extended government regulation and supervision to any firm or industry deemed to expose the economy to any significant degree of systemic risk, and, by any reasonable definition, the insurance industry, as the largest financial institution, meets this standard.

Hence, the role of the insurance industry in the CDS market, the role of the insurance industry as part of a semi-nationalization of the health industry and the importance of the insurance industry to the stability of the nation's financial and monetary regime together suggest that the historical state-based regulation of the insurance industry is likely to come to an end in the future. The state-based system has strong supporters, however. The state insurance regulatory authorities are not enthusiastic about giving up authority or sharing authority with federal regulatory authorities, and the insurance industry will resist federalization because it can play off one state against the other. While there are strong arguments in favor of ending the state-based system, the ultimate outcome will be determined by politics.

Transparency in money market funds: Those who hold money market funds have historically assumed that those funds would always have a $1.00 net asset value (NAV); that is, if they purchased a share of a fund at $1.00 the share would always be available at $1.00 and would not "break the buck". History seems to support this assumption, as the only money market fund failure occurred in 1994, and for the entire history of the money fund market few firms broke the buck. As a result, those who held money market funds accepted money funds as equivalent to federally insured deposits. The money fund industry made no effort to correct this perception. This perspective was unrealistic, and reality has finally changed the public's perception of the liquidity of money market funds.

The financial crisis starting with the Lehman Brothers bankruptcy in September 2008 revealed that money market funds were not equivalent to insured deposits. As a result of the collapse of Lehman, Reserve Primary Fund was forced to write off $785 million of Lehman debt purchased with money market funds issued by Reserve Primary Fund. Reserve Primary Fund was the oldest money market fund in the nation, but as a result of the write-off of Lehman debt its NAV fell to $0.97 and it was forced to suspend withdrawals for a short period of time. This caused panic, and, while no other money market funds actually "broke the buck", the 20 largest funds were close to breaking the buck. There was widespread concern that the realization the assumption of a constant $1.00 NAV was unrealistic would generate a run on money market funds in general. As a result, the U.S. Treasury extended a temporary one-year guarantee of $250,000 per named account as of September 8, 2008, much like deposit insurance.

The experience raised issues about the transparency of the money market fund industry, especially how funds reported the value of their shares sold to the public. The Securities and Exchange Commission in 2014 announced new rules for money market funds. They were required to report a floating NAV starting in 2016; however, there is a difference in treatment between retail and institutional funds. The NAV of retail funds will be reported rounded to the nearest penny, which, for all practical purposes, means a stable $1.00 NAV. The NAV for institutional funds will report the value at four decimal places. Government funds are exempt from the floating NAV requirement. In addition, funds can impose a "liquidity gate" in two ways to prevent runs on the fund. First, the fund can suspend withdrawals for up to ten days; or, second, the fund can impose a 2 percent withdrawal fee. The new rules also require more transparency in the underlying portfolio and require a shorter maturity than in the past.

These reforms are in the right direction. The structure of the money market fund industry, its performance over the past several decades and the new rules should continue to render retail money market funds a highly liquid financial asset and a component of M2 money. At the same time, the public has become aware that money market funds are not like deposits at depository institutions and there is an element of risk. As already discussed, money market funds have significantly declined since 2008 as a component of M2 money.

9.6 Ensuring Transparency in the Money and Capital Markets

The market response to the asymmetric information and adverse selection problems in money and capital markets has come in two forms: first, the participants in these markets are confined to large and knowledgeable lenders and borrowers; and, second, a variety of credit rating services have become available to provide information on the creditworthiness of borrowers. The market solution, however, has been augmented with government regulation and supervision of the money and capital markets. Whereas government regulation of indirect finance is designed to limit risk taking, government regulation of direct finance is designed to ensure the money and capital markets are competitive.

The difference resides in the role of promises to pay in the money supply issued in different parts of the financial system. Promises to pay issued in direct financial markets are not part of the money supply; hence, financial markets are regulated to ensure a competitive and transparent market. Promises to pay issued by non-depository financial institutions, with the exception of retail money market funds, are not part of the money supply; hence, while they are subject to government regulation to limit risk taking, they are not subject to the same level of regulation as depository institutions. The promises to pay issued by depository institutions, however, are the nation's money supply; hence, depository institutions are subject to the greatest degree of government regulation and supervision.

In contrast, regulations directed toward financial markets are designed to ensure transparency so that lenders have access to any relevant information needed to assess the risk of the borrower's instrument. To establish a financial disclosure system the SEC requires any issuer of a promise to pay to provide quarterly and annual information about all aspects of its operations that would be needed to assess risk as well as ensure that financial markets are operated openly without insider trading.

This public information, combined with other information, is the basis of a widely used credit rating industry designed to limit the asymmetric information and adverse selection problems for those who lend in the direct markets. The industry is dominated by three private firms that, combined, represent 90 percent of the credit rating market – Standard & Poor's (S&P), Moody's Investor Services and the Fitch Group. Fitch is a distant third, with only about 15 percent of the market; nonetheless, Fitch is considered part of the "Big Three".

The Big Three rate the debt obligations of a wide range of private and government borrowers, both domestically and internationally. Their status is strengthened by being designated as a nationally recognized statistical rating organization (NRSRO) by the Securities and Exchange Commission. This designation was established in the 1970s during a period of intense financial and economic distress, when many financial institutions and bond issuers were seeking ways to provide the public evidence they were financially sound. In an effort to meet the higher regulatory standards that were being implemented in the 1970s, bond issuers, insurance companies, commercial banks, pension funds and money market funds were permitted some regulatory relief if they issued debt obligations or held debt obligations rated by an NRSRO.

The Big Three all have a similar rating system in which the default ratings range from high investment quality securities ("A" rating) to very speculative, close to default or in default ("C" rating). Each uses different upper- and lower-case letters and variations, sometimes with a "+" or "−", to indicate a range of default ratings.

The credit rating industry has been the subject of debate since it began to assume a large role in the 1970s. Some claim the rating firms perform a useful function, while others claim they have too close a relationship with the government because of their NRSRO status and others claim there is a conflict of interest with borrowers because the Big Three firms often underwrite the bonds sold in the open market. The debate and controversy, however, accelerated after the stock bubble and the bursting of the bubble in the late 1990s, and especially since the 2008/2009 financial crisis. This is because many of the high ratings given to debt, especially mortgage-backed bonds, proved to be widely incorrect. Let's review some of the issues.

First, the market is considered noncompetitive because it is dominated by essentially two rating agencies – S&P and Moody's.

Second, the credit rating agencies have a conflict of interest with bond issuers because they generate almost 50 percent of their revenue by underwriting bonds and have an incentive to generate higher ratings than justified by the fundamentals of the firm.

Third, the designation of NRSRO by the government provides an incentive for the rating industry to generate higher rates for federal government debt, debt issued by government-sponsored organizations and state/local governments. Assigning a higher value to NRSRO-rated debt by regulatory agencies in general generates systemic risk because it renders the financial system more fragile.

Fourth, the past three decades, which witnessed a stock market bubble in the late 1990s and a housing bubble in the first part of the new century, have raised questions about the accuracy and quality of the ratings, irrespective of potential conflicts. In the run-up of equity prices from 1996 to 2000, the ratings assigned to debt issued by many private entities, state and local governments and by government-sponsored enterprises were overstated, in hindsight, after the equity bubble burst in early 2000. More significant, the ratings assigned to bonds, especially the mortgage-backed bonds that provided the foundation for financing the bubble in housing prices from 2002 to 2005, were grossly exaggerated. Many asked the following question: "How could a bond backed by subprime mortgages in a market dominated by 'bigger fool' price expectations be rated as A or better?"

The Big Three were signaled out for special attention by *The Financial Crisis Inquiry Report* of 2011, which attempted to determine who and what caused the financial crisis of 2008/2009 and the Great Recession:

> The three credit rating agencies were key enablers of the financial meltdown. The mortgage-related securities at the heart of the crisis could not have been marketed and sold without their seal of approval. Investors relied on them, often blindly. In some cases, they were obligated to use them, or regulatory capital standards were hinged on them. This crisis could not have happened without the rating agencies.

There were no doubt gross mistakes and serious lapses of judgment made by the credit rating agencies in the run-up of housing prices; however, there is another perspective than that suggested by *The Financial Crisis Inquiry Report*.

First, the essential nature of an asset bubble is that just about everyone becomes part of the process, including government regulatory authorities, and most accepted the bigger fool theory of asset pricing. "I know I am a fool for paying $500,000 for a track home in Las Vegas, NV, but a bigger fool will pay me $750,000 in one year!" This is especially true if they are making profits in the process or see the agenda of expanded homeownership being realized. The Financial Crisis Inquiry Commission's conclusion that the crisis could not have happened without the rating agencies is dubious. Government regulatory agencies are responsible for monitoring the financial system, and the Securities and Exchange Commission confers special status on the Big Three, raising the question as to why regulatory agencies permitted such serious lapses of judgment in rating a bond with low-quality mortgages as A or better. That is, why didn't the dog bark in the middle of the night when there was a threat to property? The answer is partly due to the role of housing in the U.S. economy.

Second, government policy from the early 1990s, under both Democratic and Republican administrations, was to encourage homeownership, especially among low- to moderate-income households. Government regulation and supervision designed to encourage mortgage lending, along with support from Fannie Mae and Freddie Mac, played a major role in the housing bubble. In this environment, the credit rating agencies would have faced a difficult political problem if they had been more realistic about the quality of the mortgage-backed bonds that financed the bubble and lost significant value when the bubble burst, especially as the agencies were dependent on the government's blessing as NRSROs. Hence, government failure likely plays as much a role here as market failure on the part of the credit rating agencies.

Third, the report failed to devote any attention to the historically easy monetary policy of the Federal Reserve, which contributed the liquidity to support the housing price bubble as a factor. The Federal Reserve permitted historically low interest rates on mortgages from 2002 to 2005.

The *Inquiry Report* was more a political document to blame the private sector for the housing bubble, the bursting of the bubble and the subsequent Great Recession and absolve government policy. A more intellectually honest review would have emphasized government policy errors as well as market failure.

At the same time, the willingness of the Big Three, given their fiduciary responsibility, to assign high ratings to mortgage-backed bonds that, by any reasonable standard, were essentially junk is difficult to justify. Either it was incompetence, "bigger fool" thinking about never-ending real estate values or an unwillingness to raise an adverse issue about a market that had broad public and political support – or, more likely, a combination of the three. While the credit rating debacle did not cause the bubble and burst of the bubble in housing prices, as claimed by the *Inquiry Report*, it did become a contributing force. The topic is addressed again in the closing chapter.

9.7 The Expanded Role of the Federal Reserve as a Regulatory and Supervisory Agency

Central banks are well positioned, because of their ability to control the monetary base, to provide lender of last resort services so as to prevent contagion and control the money supply to achieve long-run price stability. Many argue the central bank should be concerned with goals in addition to price stability, such as full employment, minimizing the fluctuations of actual output around potential output and supporting the industrial policies of the government. However, this debate is about the goals of monetary policy. There is another issue worth discussing in that, namely: what role should the central bank play in financial regulation and supervision?

Central bankers argue they need to be an important part of the regulatory process in order to fully appraise the performance of the financial system, to conduct lender of last resort services and to formulate and execute monetary policy in general. There are good arguments to support this view, but one must keep in mind that it's natural for any government agency to argue that its powers should be expanded. The size and influence of any government regulatory agency are valued goods and there is an inherent incentive to rationalize expanded influence. The real issue is whether the central bank's role in financial regulation and supervision adversely impacts its other responsibilities.

Critics of the extensive role of the Federal Reserve in regulation and supervision emphasize the "industry perspective" problem. Regulatory authorities tend to adopt an industry perspective when they have a close regulatory relationship with an industry, such as the banking industry. Tight monetary policy imposes pressures on financial institutions and markets as interest rates increase, and may even weaken the balance sheets of financial institutions. As a result, the central bank may become overly cautious in raising interest rates. That is, the "industry perspective" may end up being more important for the conduct of monetary policy than the more appropriate "public perspective". The Federal Reserve, of course, denies any such influence, but economic theory and history suggest the "industry perspective" issue is far from trivial.

Even in the absence of an "industry perspective" problem critics of the Federal Reserve's role in government financial regulation and supervision argue that monetary policy is taxing enough, and for the Federal Reserve to assume other responsibilities that can be handled by other entities diverts resources from its main responsibilities – lender of last resort and price stability. The Federal Reserve can easily obtain whatever information is needed from other agencies in fulfilling its lender of last resort responsibilities.

As a reflection of this debate, central banks have been assigned varying degrees of regulatory responsibilities, ranging from minimal responsibilities, such as the Bank of Japan and the Bank of Korea, to being a major regulatory authority, such as the Federal Reserve. The Federal Reserve is responsible for regulating banks, bank holding companies and foreign banks and for enforcing a wide range of regulations designed to protect consumers in the financial system. Whatever the arguments against such a role, the institutional design of the Federal Reserve is not likely to change toward less regulatory authority. In fact, the Federal Reserve's role as a prudential regulatory authority was significantly increased as a result of the Great Recession and the 2010 Dodd–Frank Act.

Prudential regulation and supervision for decades focused on individual institutions and markets designed to limit financial crisis and maintain public confidence in deposit money. This type of regulation was intended to apply a set of rules and principles that did not vary over time; that is, they were not to be used as an economic stabilization tool. Their goal instead was to maintain stability in the inverted pyramid of the monetary system by limiting risk taking by individual institutions and ensuring transparent financial markets.

As a result of the housing bubble and burst of the bubble, the financial crisis of 2008/2009 and the Great Recession, central banks, including the Federal Reserve, have advocated an expanded approach to regulation and supervision now referred to as *macroprudential* regulation and supervision, in contrast to the traditional *microprudential* regulation and supervision focus. Macroprudential regulation is a policy to be implemented not only by central banks but by all major government regulatory and supervisory agencies working together. The objective of macroprudential regulation is twofold: first, to identify asset bubbles, speculative excesses and overheated financial markets; and then, second, to employ regulations over capital–asset ratios, liquidity and margins on trading securities and place restrictions on credit underwriting.

Macroprudential policies essentially mix the two functions of maintaining financial stability and macroeconomic policy, which have traditionally been separate, in the sense that financial stability regulations are not intended to vary with the business cycle while macroeconomic policy was intended to smooth out the business cycle and limit the fluctuations of actual output around potential output. Macroprudential policies constitute a fundamental shift in policy that is increasingly being discussed at the Federal Reserve, and to a degree, has been institutionalized in the 2010 Dodd–Frank legislation.

At this time it is unclear to what degree and how macroprudential policy will become a part of the operations of central banks and other regulatory agencies. There are some fundamental problems with the approach, however. First, it is based on the ability of the central bank to identify an asset bubble or some other type of speculative excess; however, central banks have an extremely poor record in such identification. Not only did key Federal Reserve officials fail to comprehend the housing bubble in the first few years of the new century, they continue to deny that the central bank played any significant role in generating and supporting the housing bubble when the evidence suggests otherwise. Second, macroprudential policy imposes additional responsibilities on the central bank that it is not well designed to carry out and, in the opinion of a number of economists, not capable of carrying out. Third, central bank policy is intended to be independent of government and the financial system; however, to extend monetary policy into virtually every important direct and indirect channel of finance not only renders the central bank all-powerful, but increases the interrelationships with other government agencies and the financial system that will likely become part of monetary policy. Fourth, once central banks and other government regulatory authorities begin to vary prudential regulations, the government has moved into the business of allocating credit and substituting government decisions for market decisions, in the quest for stability. The history of credit allocation policies in every country, including the United States, should give pause to macroprudential policy. The focus of government regulation and supervision on nondepository institutions, as well as the financial system in general, has expanded since the collapse of housing prices in 2006 and the 2008/2009 financial crisis. In other words, government prudential regulation now takes a more expanded view in its efforts to limit systemic risk than previously.

References

Akerlof, George (1970). "The Market for 'Lemons': Quality, Uncertainty and the Market Mechanism". *Quarterly Journal of Economics*, 84: 488–500.

Financial Crisis Inquiry Commission (2011). *The Financial Crisis Inquiry Report.* Washington, D.C.: U.S. Government Printing Office.

Hackethal, Andreas, and Reinhard H. Schmidt (2004). "Financing Patterns: Measurement, Concepts and Empirical Results", Finance and Accounting Working Paper no. 125. Frankfurt: Goethe University.

Chapter 10

A Short History of the U.S. Financial and Monetary Regime in Transition

10.1 Introduction

It is important to understand the historical evolution of the nation's financial and monetary regime for three reasons.

First, one cannot consider oneself educated in financial and monetary issues – or, for that matter, general economic issues – unless one has some basic understanding of the historical evolution of the nation's financial and monetary regime.

Second, a historical perspective provides lessons for how best to design a financial system, government regulation and supervision and central bank policy. The often quoted philosopher George Santayana emphasized the importance of historical perspective in this regard: "Those who cannot remember the past are condemned to repeat it." Much has been learned from the past, but sometimes there is a sense of *déjà vu* in that government regulation and supervision and central bank policy fail to learn from the mistakes of past policy decisions.

Third, the historical evolution of the financial and monetary regime provides insights into major economic problems experienced by the United States, especially the three periods of intense economic and financial distress – the Great Depression, the Great Inflation and the Great Recession. These three periods provided the catalyst for major institutional redesigns of the nation's financial and monetary regime and manifested the interplay between government policy failure and market failure. It is important to have a balanced view of the causes of major periods of economic and financial distress and far too convenient to simply attribute them to market failure, as is the common practice. An intellectually balanced approach requires that both market and government failure be considered, but, since government policy makers often set the regulatory parameters and have greater access to the pulpit, the public gets an unbalanced view. Fourth, an understanding of the interplay between government policy and market behavior helps us understand the broader debate about the role of government in the nation's economy and whether we have come to expect too much from government regulation and supervision, fiscal policy and monetary policy. Much of the education system provides a one-sided view of the role of government in the economic and monetary affairs of the U.S. economy. Not only does it emphasize market failure over government policy failure but it presents an unrealistic view of the ability of government to solve economic and financial problems. This is not to claim government does not have important roles to play in the nation's financial and monetary regime, but only to point out a more balanced perspective of government is required to be considered educated. A more accurate historical account would provide a better balance to the debate.

Fifth, an understanding of the historical evolution of the U.S. financial and monetary regime provides a framework to understand regimes in other countries. This is especially important in reviewing the financial and monetary transitions that have been in progress since the 1970s throughout the world. Large numbers of developed and developing economies are opening up their real and financial sectors to competitive forces, and the process of transition has not been that much different from what was experienced in the United States. The differences between those cases and the United States pale in comparison to the similarities.

This chapter provides a framework for understanding the transition of any nation's financial and monetary regime; identifies the major turning points in the transition of the U.S. financial and monetary regime; and identifies the major legislative and administrative events that have shaped the nation's financial and monetary regime since 1776.

10.2 A Taxonomy of a Changing Financial and Monetary Regime

Every financial and monetary regime shares five basic responsibilities: it institutionalizes the saving and investment process; provides an efficient flow of funds from lenders to borrowers; provides a stable environment for the flow of funds from lenders to borrowers; provides an adaptable environment responsive to the needs of lenders and borrowers; and provides a platform for central bank policy to achieve and maintain price stability. The institutionalization of these five responsibilities differs from country to country, reflecting each country's culture, history and national policy, and, as each country's monetary system evolves from commodity-based to fractional reserve money, government becomes a more active and important part of the regime.

As long as the financial and monetary regime carries out the basic responsibilities there is little pressure for institutional redesign; however, if one or more of the basic responsibilities is not being satisfied, pressures for redesign emerge. Financial redesign takes place through two channels: first, and the most visible, are government or regulatory innovations; and, second, there are market innovations.

Government or regulatory innovations are manifested by changes in the regulatory parameters of the financial system, as with new agencies enforcing new rules that define the portfolio diversification powers of different financial institutions, rules that regulate loan and deposit rates, rules that regulate entry and exit from specific financial markets, rules that regulate direct financial markets and rules that regulate the inflows and outflows of capital, etc. Most often, government innovations are manifested by legislative acts, but administrative rule making can also play an important role in government innovations.

Market innovations are manifested by new financial assets and services introduced by market participants, designed to circumvent constraints that limit profit and, in many cases, to circumvent government regulations that limit profit opportunities. The introduction of money to replace barter was largely a market innovation, as was the shift from commodity-based monetary systems to fractional reserve standards.

Market innovations have always been an important force in the evolution of financial and monetary regimes, but their role in shaping the institutional design of the nation's financial and monetary regime has been enhanced because of the advances in computer and telecommunications technology starting in the 1960s. The ability to increase the productivity of financial transactions, open up new lending and borrowing channels both domestically and internationally and provide financial services to all who use the financial system has accelerated greatly in the past few decades. The post-WWII period has witnessed a revolutionary expansion of computing and telecommunications technology, which seems to grow exponentially each year. Financial transactions are especially adaptable to this expanding technology and increase the incentives for the market to innovate around a restriction on profit. Computer technology reduces the transactions cost of introducing new financial assets and services, thereby increasing the number of restrictions worth circumventing. This, in turn, is making it more difficult for government to enforce financial regulation and conduct central bank policy.

The two channels of change are often in conflict, especially in the past few decades with the advances in technology and the growing complexity of the financial and monetary regime, making it increasingly easier to circumvent government regulations. Government regulation tends to be passive and frequently more focused on maintaining the status quo, even when there is widespread recognition that institutional redesign of the financial system is necessary. To illustrate, government maintained interest rate ceilings on savings and time deposits (Regulation Q) from 1933, when they were first introduced, to 1980, when a phase-out over a six-year period was enacted. By the late 1960s it was obvious the ceilings were responsible for major economic and financial distress, and especially disruptive to the S&L industry, yet it took a decade or more after these problems had become apparent for government to change the rules. Government regulation as a reflection of political institutions is often dominated by "special interests", which frequently resist change for fear they will lose their influence in any new institutional environment. Government itself often takes its own "special interest" into account, because for any given regulatory agency, whether it be the Comptroller of the

Currency or the Federal Reserve, redesign of the nation's financial and monetary regime brings some uncertainty as to whether it will retain as much regulatory power as it had beforehand. This is a truth that needs to be understood.

Market innovations are more active, flexible and intended to get around the status quo, which limits profit making, but, at the same time, there are elements in the private sector that resist change. Banks, for example, resist expanded money and capital markets for fear they will reduce their role in the flow of funds, while securities companies resist any effort by depository institutions to become active in the direct markets. Depository institutions resist any change in government subsidization of real estate or consumer lending for fear it will reduce their profit opportunities. Until the early 1970s banks, for all practical purposes, had a monopoly on checking accounts, as demand deposits were the only generally available checking accounts. Demand deposit accounts were prohibited from paying interest and were legally offered only by a bank. As nonbank depository institutions began to issue NOW deposits in the 1970s, banks resisted their efforts in every way possible, because NOW accounts not only provided a competing checking deposit to demand deposits but paid interest at least up to the interest rate ceiling set for savings deposits. Banks at first used the legal channel, but when that failed they played a major role in convincing the government to prohibit NOW accounts for several years outside the six New England states in which they had first been introduced, so that the impact of NOW accounts could be studied.

Thus, government innovation tends to be passive and based on maintaining the status quo, while market innovation is more active and willing to change the status quo. But there is a part of the market itself that resists change and often uses its influence with government to maintain the status quo. This is a good example of both government and market failure combining to limit the ability of the nation's financial and monetary regime from fulfilling its responsibilities. While there are elements within the market that resist change, they tend to pale in importance compared to those elements that actively pursue change, so that market innovation is a driving force of institutional change in the nation's financial and monetary regime.

The different characteristics of government and market innovations often generate intense conflict between the government and the market, which has been best described by Edward Kane (1979) as a *regulatory-market dialectic*. The regulatory-market dialectic is applied to financial regulation but based on a philosophical conception of change introduced by George F. Hegel, the nineteenth-century German philosopher, and utilized by Karl Marx to describe the evolution of economic systems over time.

Market innovations are generally the first sign that the nation's financial and monetary regime is not fulfilling its responsibilities. They are introduced to limit some restriction; for example, nonbank depository institutions in the 1970s started issuing checking accounts (NOW deposits and credit union shares) to expand their sources of funds, meet the public's desire for more competition in checking accounts and provide the public with a checking account that paid interest.

Government often reacts to a market innovation by extending regulation to limit or control the innovation; for example, in the case of NOW accounts, the government actually prohibited NOW accounts for several years outside the New England states, and, even when they were permitted, attempted to subject them to interest rate ceilings. The market in response re-innovates to avoid the new restrictions; for example, the emergence of money market funds was an effort to circumvent the government's interest rate ceilings on checking, saving and time deposits by offering a type of checking account backed by high-quality money market instruments that, most importantly, paid a market rate of interest. The government may then reregulate to limit the market innovation; for example, when money market funds became more important and competed with deposits of depository institutions, there was some consideration of subjecting money market funds to reserve requirement, but, fortunately, money market funds were not required to meet reserve requirements.

At some point the government accepts the market innovations and becomes an active partner to institutionalize the innovations and incorporate them into its regulatory and supervisory system. It would not be too bold to claim that most government redesigns of the financial system, especially during the past four decades throughout much of the world, are, essentially, official recognition of market innovations that were the first to respond to the failures of the financial system to achieve one or more of its basic functions. Governments do not like to admit they are less dynamic than the market, but, in the case of the nation's financial and monetary regime, market innovations have been a powerful force for change.

The following sequence of five steps provides a general taxonomy of how financial and monetary regimes evolve over time that can be applied to almost any country at any time.

Five Steps to Financial and Monetary Regime Transition
Start with the Existing Financial and Monetary Regime
There is a given institutional design of the nation's financial and monetary regime, consisting of private and government financial institutions, financial markets, government regulatory authorities and central banking institutions.

↓
Catalysts for Transition
New economic, political and/or technological environments generate conflicts with the given institutional design, which interfere with the ability of the financial and monetary regime to carry out its basic responsibilities. The conflicts can be manifested in a variety of ways, ranging from failures of financial institutions in markets, disruptive flow of funds movements and price instability.

↓
Market and Government Innovations
The resulting financial disruptions and inefficiency stimulate market and government innovations. Market innovations usually occur before government innovation responds.

↓

Resistance to the Transition

Market and government innovations are not always welcomed, because various elements of the financial and monetary regime had adapted to the old system. Some elements of government resist the innovations because they might reduce their regulatory and political influence. Some elements of the private sector resist the innovations because they might reduce their economic power.

↓

Outcome of the Transition

The transition of the financial and monetary regime is successful or not depending on the type of and completeness of government innovations, the degree of resistance to the transition by some elements of the government and private sector and the general economic, financial and political environment.

This is a general taxonomy that helps us understand the transition of the nation's financial and monetary regime over time. Not every element is represented in every period of transition, but the taxonomy will help highlight the most important aspects of the transition and avoid us getting bogged down in a detailed account of a complex economic and political process over long periods of time.

10.3 Major Turning Points in the Transition of the U.S. Financial and Monetary Regime: A Brief History from 1776 to the Present

To review the history of the financial and monetary regime in detail would be difficult, boring to the majority of readers (and to the writer) and not very productive in achieving the objectives of this book. Rather than provide a running summary of changes in the financial and monetary regime, it is more productive to identify historical periods that differ from each other in important ways and summarize each in terms of the type of institutional change, the reason for the institutional change and other key characteristics of the period. In addition, aspects of each period that fit into the taxonomy above will be highlighted. The following six historical periods define the transition of the U.S. financial and monetary regime.

1 1776 to 1863: commodity money standard; no central bank; limited direct finance; indirect finance dominated by banks regulated at the state level; and free banking after 1837.
2 1863 to 1913: national banking system; expanded federal government; market innovation; emergence of a dualistic structure of indirect finance; and insufficient money growth.
3 1913 to 1929: Federal Reserve System replaces national banking system; federal government expands role; and the quiet before the storm for the new central bank.
4 1929 to 1965: Great Depression; major expansion of government at both the federal and state levels; restrictions on market forces in the financial system; expanded power and centralization of the Federal Reserve; and the Age of Keynes.
5 1965 to 1979: Great Inflation; monetary policy clashes with the structure of the financial and monetary regime; and the rise of the Age of Hayek and Friedman and decline of the Age of Keynes.

6 1980 to the present: disinflation and the Great Moderation of monetary policy; limits of the Keynesian/activist approach to government; deregulation of the economy, especially the financial system; and the Age of Milton Friedman.

Table 10.1 lists the most important legislative and administrative events for each of the six periods to accompany the narrative.

10.4 1776 to 1863

The existing financial and monetary regime: The commodity money supply was originally based on gold and silver before 1834, and then only on gold, until the establishment of the Federal Reserve in 1913. The nation suspended the gold standard during the Civil War, but soon returned to it afterward. Gold, silver, gold certificates, banknotes and even privately minted coins constituted the nation's money supply during the period up to 1863.

In terms of the flow of funds, the majority of funds were transferred through banks. Other financial institutions and direct financial markets playing a relatively minor role in the flow of funds. Banks not only made the majority of loans but operated as investment banks, to the extent that borrowers issued debt or equity in the direct markets.

In terms of government regulation, regulation and supervision were limited and there was no dual system, as banks were chartered, regulated and supervised at the state level. Organizing a state bank required a legislative act and, hence, limited bank competition. Criticism of this system of protected banks led to the first Free Banking Act, passed in Michigan, with other states following up to the start of the Civil War. The era of free banking, from 1837 to 1863, meant that many states made it relatively easy for anyone to establish a bank as long as they met the minimum capital requirement and adhered to other regulations imposed by the state banking authority. The Free Banking Acts permitted a much more competitive banking system than existed previously.

The federal government attempted to involve itself in the banking system on two occasions by supporting and owning 20 percent of the capital of the First (1791–1811) and Second (1816–1836) Bank of the United States. The two banks provided fiscal agent services to the government – receiving and disbursing funds. They operated as private banks but, because of their large size relative to other banks and the influence of the federal government, used their financial strength to impose discipline on the behavior of other banks to maintain sound banking practices and public confidence in banknotes. The First and Second Banks of the United States, however, had a turbulent existence, because of complaints from other private banks, which resented their attempts to impose prudential regulations, and criticisms from those who opposed federal government involvement in what was viewed then as essentially a state rights issue.

Table 10.1. *Major Legislative and Administrative Events in the U.S. Financial and Monetary Regime*

First Bank of the United States (1791–1811)

    Charter by Congress for 20 years with the federal government contributing 20 percent of the capital

    Board of directors included representatives of the federal government

    Large bank for its time acted as fiscal agent for the federal government and imposed regulations on other private banks to maintain quality loans and convertibility of banknotes

Charter not renewed

Second Bank of the United States (1816–1836)

    Charter by Congress for 20 years with similar structure and responsibilities as first Bank, but larger with $35 million in capital compared to $10 million in capital of the first Bank

Charter not renewed

First Free Banking Act, 1837, Michigan, and other similar Acts

    No longer need a legislative charter to establish a bank

    Only a minimum amount of capital required to charter a bank with the relevant state authority and willingness to meet requirements regarding reserves and convertibility

By 1860, 17 other states had enacted Free Banking Acts

National Bank Act of 1863

    National banks to replace state banks to unify the banking system under federal regulations

    National banks subject to higher minimum capital and reserve requirements, along with reporting requirements

    The national banknote replaced state banknotes to unify the currency system, and only national banks could issue national banknotes, which required a national bank to have on deposit at the Comptroller; government bonds equal to 90 percent of the issued national banknotes

    The Office of the Comptroller of the Currency established as part of the U.S. Treasury

Federal Reserve Act of 1913

    The Federal Reserve was originally designed to resolve the problems of the national banking system by establishing a central bank to provide lender of last resort services, an efficient national payments system and improved banking supervision

    One of the original objectives of the Federal Reserve Act was for "other purposes", and, as the Federal Reserve evolved over time, the "other purposes" now cover a wide range of activities that include extensive regulation, supervision and central bank policy

    Weakened the dual system to some degree

McFadden Act of 1927

    National banks permitted to branch subject to the branch rules of the state within which located

    Interstate bank branching prohibited

    Strengthened the dual system to some degree

Banking Act of 1933 (also referred to as the Glass–Steagall Act) and Banking Act of 1935

    Established the Federal Deposit Insurance Corporation

    Zero interest rate ceiling on demand deposits issued by banks and non-zero ceiling on savings and time deposits

    Commercial and investment banking separated, so that commercial banks could no longer underwrite securities except government securities

Securities Act of 1933 and Securities Exchange Act of 1934

    Standardized disclosure of all issuers of debt required and equity sold on any organized exchange

    Rules established to prevent insider trading and misrepresentation

    Securities and Exchange Commission established

Investment Company Act of 1940 and Investment Advisors Act of 1941

    Regulation of investment companies and mutual fund companies and investment advisors

Employment Act of 1946

    Federal government given responsibility to promote maximum employment

    Established the Council of Economic Advisors to the President and the annually published *Economic Report of the President*

(continued)

Table 10.1 *(continued)*

Treasury–Federal Reserve Accord of 1951
  Released the Federal Reserve from pegging government security interest rates at low level that had been adopted in 1942 to support government spending in WWII
  Widely interpreted to provide the Federal Reserve independence in monetary policy
Bank Holding Company Act of 1956 and Douglas 1970 Amendment to Bank Holding Company Act
  Federal Reserve authorized to regulate and supervise multibank and single bank holding companies
National Credit Union Administration established in 1970
  Independent agency to regulate and supervise federally chartered credit unions
  Credit union insurance for both federal and state credit unions on same basis as other depository institutions
Depository Institutions Deregulation and Monetary Control Act of 1980
  Regulation Q ceilings on savings and time deposits phased out from 1980 to 1986
  NOW and sweep accounts permitted
  Thrifts given expanded asset diversification powers
  Many usury laws (loan interest rate ceilings) eliminated
  Deposit insurance increased from $40,000 to $100,000
Depository Institutions Act of 1982
  Expanded authority given to deal with troubled thrifts
  Money market deposit accounts permitted
Competitive Equality Banking Act of 1987
  Officially affirmed that deposit insurance was backed by the full faith and credit of the United States
  Funds to recapitalize the Federal Savings and Loan Insurance Corporation provided
Financial Institutions Reform, Recovery, and Enforcement Act of 1989
  Taxpayer funding provided to resolve the S&L problem
  Federal Savings and Loan Insurance Corporation eliminated, its function transferred to the FDIC
  Federal Home Loan Bank Board eliminated, its responsibility transferred to the Office of Thrift Supervision
  Deposit insurance premiums increased
Federal Deposit Insurance Corporation Improvement Act of 1991
  Tripwire system and Prompt Correct Action established
  Risk-based insurance premiums introduced
  FDIC recapitalized
Riegle–Neal Interstate Banking and Branching Efficiency Act of 1994
  Interstate and intrastate bank branching permitted
Gramm–Leach–Bliley Financial Services Modernization Act of 1999
  Wall between commercial and investment banking removed
Sarbanes–Oxley Act of 2002
  Oversight of money and capital markets increased
  Increased transparency and responsibility for accuracy of financial statements provided to public required
Federal Deposit Insurance Act of 2005
  S&L insurance fund and the bank and savings bank insurance fund merged into one FDIC insurance fund
  Deposit insurance limit increased to $250,000 on individual retirement accounts
Dodd–Frank Wall Street Reform and Consumer Protection Act of 2010
  Consumer protection increased, especially for mortgage credit
  Regulation over derivative products increased
  Proprietary trading by banks limited
  Government responsibility for assessing risk increased, identifying financial institutions deemed "systemically important" and subjecting those institutions to increased regulation and supervision
  Two new agencies established: Consumer Financial Protection Bureau and Financial Stability Oversight Council
  Office of Thrift Supervision abolished, responsibilities transferred to Comptroller of the Currency, Federal Reserve and FDIC

Catalysts for reform emerge: After 1837 free banking, in the sense that it was easy to establish a bank, dominated most of the banking system, though some banks continued to operate without free banking laws. The banking system was competitive and operated with minimal state government regulation. There was frequent criticism of the system because of the limited regulation (which varied widely from state to state), bank failures and the large number of state banknotes that circulated at various rates of discount. Many argued that the lack of a unified currency system limited economic growth, and many claimed the state banking system was dominated by "wildcat" banks that disrupted the U.S. economy. Wildcat bank were ones that made low-quality loans and issued banknotes that were difficult to redeem in commodity money because they were located only "where wildcats lived". Research has shown, however, that the claims of wildcat banking were overstated.

Overall, despite the lack of extensive regulation and a varied banking and currency system, the financial and monetary regime from 1776 to 1863 supported an impressive record of economic growth that meant that, by the start of the Civil War (1861–1865), the United States had emerged as a major industrial power in the world. At the same time, the lack of a unified currency, minimal regulation and supervision in most states and the asymmetric information between depositors and banks because of a lack of bank transparency suggested that improvements to the nation's financial and monetary regime could be achieved.

10.5 1863 to 1913

Catalysts for reform generate transition: Despite the fact that the U.S. economy grew rapidly from 1776 to 1863, suggesting the nation's financial and monetary regime was at least adequately performing its job, by the late 1850s there was increasing concern about the number of bank failures, fraud and disarray in the nation's money supply, with many state banks operating, with different and sometimes minimal regulations, and a large number of state banknotes in circulation, estimated at 10,000 by 1860. Added to this was the need for the federal government to finance the Civil War. The existing money and capital markets were far too small to raise the funds needed. Borrowing from Europe was not a meaningful solution, as many European countries would rather sit back and let the Civil War weaken the United States. As a result of problems with the state banking system and the need to finance the war, the federal government moved to fundamentally change the structure of the U.S. financial and monetary regime, solving both problems.

Government innovation: The National Bank Act of 1863 fundamentally altered the role of government in the U.S. financial system, and, even though it was designed to establish a unified banking system under the federal government, the Act instead established a dualistic system of depository institutions and government regulation and supervision that continues to the present. The Act was rationalized by the alleged inefficiency and instability of the state banking system, but the need to finance the Civil War was at least as important.

The Act established a unified currency for the country – the national banknote – that could be issued only by nationally chartered banks. National banknotes were required to have a 90 percent reserve of government bonds. The Act established the first federal government regulatory agency – the Office of the Comptroller of the Currency, as part of the U.S. Treasury – to issue national charters, regulate and supervise the national banking system and establish reserve and capital requirements. To ensure the success of the new unified national banking system and national banknotes, a 10 percent tax was imposed on state banknotes.

Market innovation limits the success of the national banking system: The new system appeared successful in the first decade. A large number of state banks converted to national banks and the total number of state banks declined significantly. Those who wanted to operate a state bank, either because of their allegiance to state rights or because they wanted to operate with a less restrictive set of government regulations, innovated around the national banking system. The banknote was the primary promise to pay instrument issued by banks. State banks shifted from issuing banknotes subject to the 10 percent tax to issuing checking deposits, which were not subject to the 10 percent tax. This is a clear example of a market innovation designed to circumvent a restriction that limited profit. As a result, the number of state banks began to increase, and, as the end of the nineteenth century approached, the number of state banks outnumbered national banks. In 1896 there were 3,689 national banks and 7,785 state banks; however, national banks were larger, with fewer than a half them holding 54 percent of total bank assets.

When it became clear to the federal government the shift from banknotes to checking accounts gave state banks a second life, there was little enthusiasm on the part of the federal government to make another attempt to unify the banking system in the country after the carnage of the Civil War. The federal government gave in to state rights on the issue of banking. Hence, the Act actually established a dualistic system, which continues to the present. Depository institutions operate under either a national or state charter and, in many instances, state regulation continues to be important. Over time, however, the federal government increased its relative role, and, while the dualistic structure is an important feature of the U.S. financial system and regulation, it is a pale shadow of what it was under the national banking system.

The irony here is that the effort of the federal government to establish a financial system under federal control provided incentives to innovate sooner rather than later and, as a result, in fact established a dualistic system of depository institutions and regulatory agencies to oversee the operations of depository institutions. This event illustrates not only how market innovation circumvents restrictions but how ingrained state rights are in the U.S. political system despite the defeat of the Confederacy.

An unsuccessful reform and new catalysts for reform: The national banking system was a failure, for four reasons. First, it did not unify the banking system nor replace state with federal regulation and supervision. Second, national banknotes did simplify the currency system, but the Act established no mechanism to adjust the currency to the public's demand for currency. In addition, the monetary system was still under the influence of the supply of gold. The gold standard did not provide sufficient monetary growth in the last part of the nineteenth century and generated a two-decade period of deflation that imposed economic, financial and political distress on the nation. Third, the Act failed to foresee the growth of checkable deposits and, as a result, failed to establish a national check-clearing mechanism, which generated as much inefficiency in the money supply as the large number of state banknotes in the free banking era. Fourth, the absence of a central bank ensured that the inherently defective reserve requirement system established by the national banking system would generate financial instability, and, on several occasions, generated financial panics.

In sum, the nation's financial and monetary regime did not fulfill its basic responsibilities from the end of the Civil War to the first decade of the twentieth century. The national banking system was a failure. It was responsible for several periods of financial and economic distress, the country experienced deflation under the gold standard, and the continued absence of a central bank with lender of last resort powers rendered contagion a continuing problem. This became increasingly clear to many as the United States started the twentieth century. The turning point was reached with the 1907 financial panic. The absence of a lender of last resort contributed to a loss of public confidence in deposit money and a number of bank failures that shocked the nation.

10.6 1913 to 1929

Catalysts for reform: A number of periods of financial distress were caused by the inherent structural defects of the national banking system, but it was the banking panic of 1907 and the contagion it generated, coming after a long period of price deflation, that combined to generate the political momentum to redesign the national banking system and establish a central bank.

Government innovation – two legislative events: A National Monetary Commission, established by Congress from 1909 to 1912, extensively studied the nation's financial and monetary regime and recommended a number of institutional changes to fundamentally redesign the regime. The major recommendation was to establish the Federal Reserve as the nation's first central bank. The Federal Reserve Act was signed by President Wilson in December 1913. The United States had finally joined the club of other industrial and many developing countries that already had central banks. The United States was a latecomer by any standard.

Japan presents an interesting comparison. At the end of the Civil War the United States emerged as a major world industrial and military power. Japan, in contrast, was a feudal, agrarian and isolated country until the 1868 Meiji Restoration, which was Japan's turning point in becoming a modern nation. The objective of the Meiji

Restoration was to first achieve industrial and military parity with the West, and then to surpass the West. Japan adopted the U.S. national banking system in 1872, but found the system wanting, for many of the same reasons it failed in the United States. In 1882 Japan established its central bank, the Bank of Japan – some 30 years before the United States came to the same conclusion.

The original four objectives of the Federal Reserve Act were rather modest by today's Federal Reserve. First, the Federal Reserve was established to provide an elastic currency responsive to the needs of the public by replacing the national banknote issued by private banks with the Federal Reserve note, issued by the Federal Reserve. The Federal Reserve note is today's standard currency. While not mentioned as an objective in the first part of the 1913 Act, the Federal Reserve also established a national check-clearing system. Providing currency and check clearing were the key elements of a national payments system that continues to the present. Second, the Federal Reserve was established to provide lender of last resort services by discounting commercial paper held when reserves were needed. Third, the Federal Reserve was to provide more effective supervision and regulation of national banks. Fourth, the Federal Reserve was established for "other purposes". As history unfolded, the "other purposes" became far more important than the three specific objectives of the 1913 Federal Reserve Act, as will be discussed in subsequent chapters.

The 1913 Federal Reserve Act represents a major event in the evolution of the nation's financial and monetary regime. Not only did it establish the nation's first central bank after over a century of economic development, but it greatly expanded the federal government's role in the financial system, which continued to be dominated by the banking system. By the turn of the century money and capital markets were increasingly important, but there was a close relationship between these markets and banks. Banks not only functioned as traditional commercial banks – accepting deposits and making commercial loans – but also acted as investment banks, underwriting debt and equity promises to pay to be sold in the direct markets.

The Federal Reserve Act did not eliminate the dual system. National banks were required to be members of the Federal Reserve; however, state banks were not required to become official members unless they applied for membership and met the requirements imposed by the Federal Reserve. Few state banks joined the Federal Reserve, because they had the option of operating under a less restricting set of regulations, especially lower reserve requirements at the state level. It would not be until 1980 that state banks and all nonbank depository institutions became part of the Federal Reserve System and subject to the same reserve requirements with the same access to services provided by the Federal Reserve. The dual system continues, but, again, it pales in comparison to what it was before the establishment of the Federal Reserve.

The second major legislative event was the 1927 McFadden Act, which permitted greater competition among banks by allowing national banks to establish branches. Prior to 1927 national banks had been required to conduct their operations from one location, but from 1927 they could branch to the same degree permitted by the state. That is, if a national bank were located in a state that prohibited branching (called a unit banking state) it was prohibited from branching even though it operated under a national charter. If it was located in a branching state it was permitted to branch but subject to the regulations at the state level. Hence, the dual system remained in place. The McFadden Act explicitly prohibited interstate branching by recognizing that states had the ultimate authority over branching by banks or any other financial institution. In the 1990s more and more states became branching states, and some even allowed interstate branching within their borders. In 1999 the restriction on interstate branch was removed, and now there is fairly complete intrastate and interstate branching of banks.

The Federal Reserve in the first five years of its existence was occupied with establishing its infrastructure, administration and operations, and then it was occupied with assisting the government in financing the war effort after the United States declared war on Germany in April 1917. WWI ended in November 1918, and from that point onward the Federal Reserve began to operate as a central bank. There is general agreement that, after a short postwar adjustment period, the 1920s were a period of rapid economic growth and stable prices that presented few serious challenges to the new central bank. Near the end of the 1920s it appeared the Federal Reserve had become a successful part of a stable financial and monetary environment, but this turned out to be no more than the calm before the storm.

10.7 1929 to 1965

The date 1929 is the starting point for this period because the Great Depression started in August of that year, according to the NBER, and the October 1929 collapse of the stock market manifested the weakness of the U.S. economy. The date 1965 is the ending point of the period because it marks the start of the Great Inflation, the second major period of economic and financial distress. At this point we are not concerned with a detailed discussion of these two periods, or the Great Recession, but only to highlight how they became catalysts for a major redesign of the nation's financial and monetary regime.

The catalysts: The Great Depression and the collapse of the financial system were then viewed as the outcome of market failure and, hence, required expanded and a more activist government to stabilize the economy. The British economist John Maynard Keynes provided the intellectual foundation for this new approach to government in his 1936 book *The General Theory of Employment, Money and Interest.* Keynes argued the Great Depression was the outcome of market failure, "animal spirits" that drove investment and led to speculation and insufficient private spending. The solution was obvious. Expand government regulation and supervision to deal with market failure, especially in the financial system; use government spending to offset insufficient and unstable private spending; use government taxes to stimulate private spending and use monetary policy to stimulate private spending. Only in this manner would the economy be able to grow at its potential.

Some claim the Roosevelt administration's New Deal was drawn from the pages of Keynes; however, this is incorrect. *The General Theory* was not published until 1936. The Roosevelt administration's New Deal was rationalized on the same arguments and adopted some of the policies advocated by Keynes, but the New Deal was a political response to what appeared to be major market failure. Keynes, however, came to provide the intellectual foundation for the type of activist government initiated by the Roosevelt administration. This was a major transformation in perspective. Previously, private and unregulated markets had been viewed as stable and not in need of much government involvement, but now they were viewed as inherently unstable, requiring activist government intervention to generate market outcomes consistent with the general public good. This perspective and the foundation provided by Keynes dominated public policy in the United States and through much of the Western world until the 1970s. It would not be an exaggeration to call the period from the 1930s to the 1970s the *Age of Keynes*.

Government innovation: A series of legislative events in 1933, 1934 and 1935 fundamentally redesigned the nation's financial and monetary regime in three ways: first, the federal government dramatically increased its role in regulating and supervising the financial system; second, the Federal Reserve was redesigned to concentrate power in the Board of Governors, located in Washington, D.C., and provided with new tools of monetary policy; and, third, while the dual system of regulation continued to be an institutional feature of the U.S. financial system, responsibility for regulation and supervision was significantly shifted to the federal level.

The legislative events were based on the view that the Great Depression and collapse of the financial system were due to too little regulation and supervision, too much competition in the financial system, too close a relationship between banks and bond and equity markets and the limited ability of the Federal Reserve to conduct monetary policy. In the absence of regulation and supervision, banks made imprudent loans, operated with inadequate capital and reserves and engaged in behavior that took advantage of their position as the nation's provider of money. In the absence of a centralized Federal Reserve, the Federal Reserve was not able to stabilize the economy.

Too much competition in the financial system provided incentives for banks to offer higher interest rates to attract deposits, which, in turn, required them to adopt riskier loan and investment portfolios in search of higher interest returns. Competition increased systemic risk in the financial system. Too close a relationship between banks and indirect markets exposed banks to imprudent risks, since they were the providers of the nation's money supply and exposed banks to conflicts, in that banks would encourage their larger depositors to purchase bonds and equities that they had underwritten to sale. Structural problems and the lack of a wide range of tools of monetary policy prevented the Federal Reserve from effectively reversing the decline in economic activity after 1929.

The new financial and monetary regime was based on greatly expanded government regulation and supervision at both the state level and, especially, the federal level; designed to limit competition by limiting portfolio powers, preventing competition among different depository institutions and imposing interest rate ceilings on bank and nonbank deposits; separated commercial banking from investment banking; and redesigned the Federal Reserve to concentrate decision making at the federal level, providing new tools to implement a more activist monetary policy. This approach to redesign the nation's financial and monetary regime was part of the general view the Great Depression was the result of speculative excesses in the 1920s, financed by easy credit and money, combined with a fragile financial system in the absence of government regulation and supervision that permitted imprudent competition, lending and borrowing. The stock market bubble and its dramatic collapse in October 1929 were the poster child of the then accepted interpretation of the Great Depression. Unregulated financial institutions and markets generate instability; hence, the solution resided in an expanded role of government prudential regulation, lender of last resort services and more active and powerful central bank policy.

Outcome: Despite these changes in the nation's financial and monetary regime, combined with increased regulation and supervision of the rest of the economy and deficit spending by the government, the economy remained distressed throughout the decade. In 1938 the unemployment rate stood at 19 percent and the economy was operating with a large negative output gap. The build-up for war through lend-lease starting in early 1941, then the declaration of war on Japan on December 9, 1941, two days after the December 7 Japanese attack on Pearl Harbor, and Germany's declaration of war on the United States on December 11, 1941, generated a major increase in economic activity. The unemployment rapidly fell, to stand at less than 1 percent by the end of WWII in 1945.

After a few years of postwar adjustment, shifting from wartime to peacetime production, the U.S. economy achieved a decade of stable and noninflationary economic growth in the 1950s. Federal Reserve policy was successful in stabilizing the price level and the financial system was stable. During the 1950s and into the 1960s bank failures had declined to only a few in any given year. By this standard, it appeared the major redesign of the nation's financial and monetary regime had been successful.

Government innovation in the 1950s: There were three further important developments that continued the reforms of the 1930s. First, an administrative agreement or accord between the Treasury and the Federal Reserve in 1951; second, legislation that further expanded the role of the Federal Reserve as a financial regulatory authority and further reduced competition in banking; and, third, the Full Employment Act of 1946, which officially made the U.S. government responsible for economic stability.

Treasury–Federal Reserve Accord of 1951: The Federal Reserve lacked the operational independence to maintain price stability as the economy began to grow in the late 1940s. It lacked operational independence because, since 1942, it had been required to support the prices (interest rates) of government bonds. In April 1942 the Federal Reserve was required to maintain Treasury bill rates at 0.375 percent and longer-term securities at 2.5 percent. This was accomplished by expanding the money supply to purchase any government debt offered to finance the war, and, for all practical purposes, the Federal Reserve became an agent of the government. The loss of independence during wartime is acceptable and proper; however, the interest rate support program continued after the end of hostilities in 1945 for six years, and ended only with the accord of March 1951.

There was considerable pressure to continue the policy of supporting government bond interest rates because of the large outstanding debt and concern that higher interest rates would increase the refinancing cost, impose large capital losses on holders of government debt and make it difficult for the economy to grow. The Federal Reserve showed little enthusiasm to challenge the Treasury, for two reasons: first, the Federal Reserve had failed to prevent or reverse the decline in the 1930s, losing reputation and credibility; and, second, the Federal Reserve operated in a professional climate adverse to monetary policy. Monetary policy and money were regarded as impotent in the original Keynesian model. Several generations of students were taught that fiscal policy, not monetary policy, was the government's primary instrument of stabilization.

Nonetheless, there was growing pressure to end the support program and return independent monetary policy to the Federal Reserve. The pressure resulted in the March 1951 Treasury–Federal Reserve Accord, in which a joint statement was released to the public that the Federal Reserve would no longer support the prices of government bonds and begin normal monetary policy to stabilize the economy.

Expanded regulatory power of the Federal Reserve: Banks were restricted in the products and services they could offer as well as their geographic locations. In the 1950s banks innovated around these restrictions by forming bank holding companies. The first innovation was the multibank holding company, consisting of at least two banks that could include activities such as leasing, management consulting, other financial institutions such as finance companies, and loan services, as well as including banks that operated in different geographic locations. The multibank holding company could then circumvent restrictions on products and services and restrictions on intra- and interstate branching. In 1956 the Federal Reserve was authorized to regulate the operations of multibank holding companies, which were officially defined as holding companies consisting of at least two banks. The banking industry re-innovated by using the single bank holding company structure, which was brought under the regulatory sphere of the Federal Reserve in 1970.

Government officially responsible for promoting employment and economic stability: Government assumed it now had the responsibility to regulate, supervise and stabilize the economy, based on the experience of the Great Depression, the effect government spending had on unemployment during WWII and the widely accepted theories and policies of *The General Theory*. As a result, an effort was made to legitimize this responsibility by legislation. The 1946 Employment Act was considerably weaker than the originally proposed legislation; for example, the 1945 version was titled the "Full Employment Act" rather than just the "Employment Act". The 1945 version stated individuals had a right to a job and required the government to "assure" full employment rather than "promote" full employment. The final wording from Section 2 follows: "The Congress hereby declares that it is the continuing policy and responsibility of the Federal Government to use all practical means . . . in a manner calculated to foster and promote free and competitive enterprise and the general welfare . . . to promote maximum employment, production and purchasing power." In addition, the Act established a Council of Economic Advisors to the President and required the president to report to the public on the economy annually. The Council and the *Economic Report of the President* continue to the present.

Even in its watered-down version, the Act made it clear the federal government had a responsibility to promote full employment through its regulatory, supervisory, spending, taxing and central bank powers. Price stability was not explicitly emphasized, other than a reference to "maximum purchasing" power. The Act has never been viewed as anything but emphasizing the employment goal, and it set the tone for government intervention that employment was a more important goal than price stability, which continues to the present. This would present serious challenges to the Federal Reserve, since only in the short run do central banks have the ability to influence employment.

10.8 1965 to 1979

The catalyst for transition: The date 1965 marks the start of the Great Inflation, which is now viewed as the result of excessively easy monetary policy, based on a flawed economic model called the Phillips curve, and the politicization of Federal Reserve policy in the 1960s and 1970s. The Phillips curve will be discussed in later chapters, as well as central bank independence and politicization; however, the reader can accept the statement that there is considerable evidence to support the monetary policy causes of the Great Inflation, not only in the United States but for inflation throughout much of the world in the 1960s and 1970s. The basic idea of the Phillips curve is that you can purchase more employment with more inflation. The Phillips curve is now largely rejected as a long-run relationship, but in the 1960s and 1970s it held a prominent place in economic policy.

The excessively easy monetary policy in the 1960s and 1970s not only failed to increase employment but, instead, led to stagflation, as both the unemployment rate and the inflation rate increased. The easy policy also clashed with the existing structure of the nation's financial and monetary regime and revealed fundamental defects in the regime as a result of the reform legislation of the 1930s. The financial and monetary regime's institutional design involved extensive government regulation and administrative control over the domestic and international flow of funds, designed to suppress market forces. Thus, the Great Inflation not only included economic distress caused by inflation but financial distress caused by a clash between easy monetary policy and a flawed financial system.

The end of fixed exchange rates: The Bretton Woods fixed exchange rate system, established in 1944, was set up to permit governments to control exchange rates in an orderly fashion with international policy cooperation channeled through the newly formed International Monetary Fund. This became difficult to achieve given the differing inflation rates among countries, because a higher inflation rate in one country relative to another country generated trade deficits. Trade deficits over time under the Bretton Woods system required the deficit country to slow its pace of economic growth; however, this was politically difficult. It was politically easier to blame other countries for unfair trading, impose restrictions on imports, provide subsidies to exports and even adopt exchange control policies. The deficit countries were not willing to slow economic growth and surplus countries were unwilling to inflate. The United States was in a particularly difficult position, because the dollar was a "key" currency used as an international investment and reserve asset. The 1960s witnessed interest conflict between the United States, Germany and Japan as a result of the structure of the Bretton Woods fixed exchange rate system.

The fixed exchange rate system's days were numbered by 1970, and in 1973 the system was replaced with a flexible exchange rate system, which continues to the present. The end of the fixed exchange rate system was, essentially, a rejection of the view that government policy could regulate the price of a financial asset. Efforts by government to ignore market forces by setting exchange rates that conflicted with market forces had the same outcome that you get if you ignore the wind and tides. The end of the fixed exchange rate standard in 1973 was not only a rejection of the government policies designed to tame market forces but a rejection of Keynesian economics, and the beginning of the end of the *Age of Keynes.*

Financial distress: Inflation clashed with a number of elements of the existing financial structure, some of which are as follows: interest rate ceilings on deposits, permitting only commercial banks to issue checking deposits, limiting the portfolio powers of different depository institutions, subsidizing housing by maintaining S&Ls as specialized mortgage lenders and separating commercial from investment banking. Of these, the interest rate ceilings and the protected status of the S&L industry were particularly important, and they generated much financial distress, which lasted two decades and imposed a major cost on U.S. taxpayers.

By 1966 savings and time deposits at all depository institutions were subject to Regulation Q interest rate ceilings administered by the Federal Reserve. These interest rate ceilings had no economic effect in the 1950s and early 1960s because the market-determined interest rates of those deposits were lower than the ceiling; however, the inflation starting in 1965 increased unregulated interest rates in the money and capital markets while the Federal Reserve maintained deposit ceilings below what would have been a market interest rate on savings and time deposits.

As market interest rates rose above the Q ceilings, depositors withdrew their funds and invested them directly in money market instruments. At first, only large depositors had the funds and technical knowledge to purchase money market instruments, but the market innovation of money market funds allowed even small depositors to purchase money market instruments. The money market fund in a sense democratized access to the direct markets, much as the mutual fund industry that emerged in the 1950s had provided greater access to investing in equities and bonds. This process of withdrawing funds from depository institutions and transferring them to the direct market was the opposite of intermediation, and, hence, is referred to as disintermediation. Disintermediation generated several severe credit crunches as depository institutions lost funds and were unable to lend at any interest rate.

Disintermediation was particularly difficult for S&Ls. S&Ls by regulation were specialized mortgage lenders and relied on saving and time deposits for the majority of their funds. Disintermediation was the beginning of the end for the S&L industry, which collapsed in the 1980s and required a taxpayer bailout of $214 billion (in 2014 dollars) to salvage some part of the S&L industry. In the 1970s there were over 3,000 S&Ls. In 2015 there were fewer than 600.

Increasing criticism of Federal Reserve policy as contributing to the economic and financial distress in the 1970s brought greater congressional oversight over the Federal Reserve. The Full Employment and Balanced Growth Act of 1978 revised the 1946 Employment Act and extended the number of economic goals: full employment; economic growth; price stability; and balanced trade and government budget. The Act required the Federal Reserve to conduct policy to achieve full employment and price stability and provide greater transparency in the formation and conduct of policy by presenting to Congress two reports – a preliminary report for the coming year in July of the current year and a final report in February. The 1978 Act is credited with requiring a dual mandate for the Federal Reserve and elevating the goal of price stability on a par with employment and economic growth; however, the actual language in the Federal Reserve Act indicates three goals: maximum employment, stable prices and moderate long-term interest rates.

The economy was in deep economic and political distress by 1979: inflation; high unemployment; high interest rates; increasing gold prices; declining value of the dollar; disintermediation of funds from depository institutions to money markets; insolvency of the S&L industry; financial scandal involving an effort to manipulate the silver market; and the need for a large federal loan guarantee to keep Chrysler from bankruptcy. On the political front the Iranian hostage crisis further generated a sense the government was unable to influence its environment. As the 50th anniversary of the Great Depression passed a large number of policy makers asked whether "it" could happen again. The catalysts for another transition of the nation's financial and monetary regime were in place.

10.9 1980 and Beyond

In sharp contrast to the Age of Keynes period and the expanded role of government to restrict market forces in the financial system and stabilize the economy, the period starting in 1980 reflected a different approach that might be called the *Age of Hayek* and *Age of Friedman*. These two economists provided the theoretical and empirical perspectives, respectively, that emphasized the benefits of market forces and the downside of government intervention. Their views seemed to be borne out by the economic and financial distress starting in the late 1960s and becoming increasingly intense by the late 1970s. The Great Inflation and its associated collapse of the S&L industry and banking problems are viewed by many as a reflection of government failure – flawed financial regulation, financial supervision and central bank policy. This is not to deny any market failure, but the evidence suggests that policy errors on the part of the Federal Reserve, combined with a flawed institutional design of the financial system, played the major role in what is now called the Great Inflation.

Starting in 1980 a number of government innovations redesigned the nation's financial and monetary regime to permit market forces to play a greater role in the flow of funds and allocate more financial resources to the economy than previously, as well as requiring the Federal Reserve to focus more on price stability. Many of the institutional changes in the nation's financial and monetary regime were intended to eliminate or modify a number of key elements of the legislative agenda in the 1930s that restricted competition. As a result, the legislative process is referred to as deregulation of the financial system, in contrast to the regulation of the financial system in the 1930s. The term "deregulation" is not really accurate, since government regulation and supervision continued, but market forces were permitted to play a more important role in the allocation of credit than previously. Nonetheless, the term "deregulation" continues to be used.

The various government innovations that started in 1980 and continued for the next three decades can be viewed as a response to specific problems and were designed to achieve these objectives.

Improving monetary policy: As the money market fund and NOW market innovations grew rapidly in the 1970s, the Federal Reserve found it increasingly difficult to control the money supply. In addition, the dualistic system of reserve requirements provided incentives for a number of banks to leave the Federal Reserve and avoid the higher and more restrictive reserve requirements imposed by the Federal Reserve compared to state requirements. In response, in February 1980 the Federal Reserve under a new governor, Paul Volcker (1979–1987), announced new measures of the money supply to incorporate the market innovations that rendered the previous measures inadequate. The Deregulation and Monetary Control Act of 1980 eliminated the dual reserve requirement system and, essentially, made all federally insured depository institutions *de facto* members of the Federal Reserve. Combined with the greater transparency of Federal Reserve policy making required by the 1978 Full Employment and Balanced Growth Act, the Federal Reserve was redesigned so as to be better able to achieve price stability. The outcome of these institutional reforms resulted in a period of stable monetary policy and price stability from about 1985 to the first few years of the twenty-first century that is called the Great Moderation.

Removing competitive constraints on depository institutions: A series of Acts – the Monetary Control and Deregulation Act of 1980; the Depository Institutions Act of 1982; the Competitive Equality in Banking Act of 1987; the Riegle–Neal Interstate Banking and Branching Efficiency Act of 1994; and the Gramm–Leach–Bliley Financial Services Modernization Act of 1999 – reversed most of the competitive constraints on the financial system that had been established in the 1930s. This was a fundamental shift in perspective.

1 Regulation Q ceilings were phased out by 1986, though the zero ceiling on demand deposits remained in place until 2010.
2 All depository institutions were permitted to issue interest-paying checking deposits, as well as a new type of deposit called the money market deposit account, to compete with money market funds.
3 Nonbank depository institutions were permitted to diversify and function more like banks in terms of the type of loans they offered.
4 Interest rate ceilings on loans in general were eliminated.
5 The wall between commercial and investment banking was removed.
6 Restrictions on intra- and interstate bank branching were eliminated.

These and other changes fundamentally shifted the financial system toward one more responsive to market forces than government regulation and administration.

Deposit insurance: The deposit insurance system had to all intents and purposes collapsed by the 1980s. S&Ls had been insured by their own system (the Federal Savings and Loan Insurance Corporation) administered by the Federal Home Loan Bank Board. The S&L insurance corporation was bankrupt by the mid-1980s by any reasonable accounting standard. The FDIC was in better condition, but in the early 1990s it was losing money and on the way to bankruptcy. It was widely recognized both deposit insurance corporations had adopted a "too big to fail" perspective for dealing with large institutions and a "too small to help" perspective for small institutions, and their preferred policy response to troubled institutions was one of forgiveness and forbearance, hoping they would be able to "work their way out of difficulty" if only given sufficient time. The crisis in deposit insurance was dealt with by the following.

1 Deposit insurance limit raised from $40,000 to $100,000 on all deposits (1980), limit on individual retirement accounts increased (2005), and increased to $250,000 for all accounts (2008).
2 Federal Savings and Loan Insurance Corporation and Federal Home Loan Bank Board eliminated, FDIC responsible for insuring S&L deposits, and newly created Office of Thrift Supervision responsible for regulating and supervising S&Ls.

3 FDIC recapitalized, insurance premiums raised, risk-based insurance premiums introduced, regulatory discretion reduced by Prompt Correct Action and tripwire system of capital–asset ratios, and the potential for "too big to fail" policy reduced.

4 Generally accepted view that federal deposit insurance is backed not only by FDIC reserves but by the "full faith and credit of the United States" officialized.

These reforms placed the FDIC, as well as credit union insurance, on a firmer foundation, but deposit insurance continues to be subject to moral hazard, as explained earlier.

Resolving the S&L problem: The S&L industry was insolvent by the mid-1980s, and had fallen victim to Regulation Q and disintermediation and, when interest rate ceilings were phased out, to interest rate risk, as the industry lent long and borrowed short. The S&L was dissolved as a specialized mortgage lender for all practical purposes, but the resolution of the S&L problem took a decade (1989 to 1999) with a $214 billion taxpayer cost. The S&L industry today is much smaller than previously, and institutions function more like banks than the traditional mortgage lending and saving institutions they once were.

Disruptions in the first decade of the new century: By the start of the new century the government innovations of the past two decades and the market innovations of the private sector had fundamentally changed the nation's financial and monetary framework. The financial system was more competitive, open and transparent than previously. Government regulation and supervision did not decline, as suggested by the term "deregulation", but changed to permit market forces to play a greater role in the flow of funds. Federal Reserve policy was more transparent and more focused on price stability, though it was constrained by the dual mandate to achieve both maximum employment and price stability.

As the twentieth century came to an end, however, new economic and political events became catalysts for further transition, though, in this instance, the transition was back toward enhanced government regulation, supervision and activist central bank policy. Three changes in the environment are notable: the equity bubble and burst from 1996 to 2000; the housing bubble and burst from 2001 to 2006; and the Great Recession.

A bubble in equity prices from 1996 to 2000 and the collapse in mid-2000 brought back memories of market failure and the financial distress it could cause. It was during this bubble that the then governor of the Federal Reserve coined the well-known phrase of "irrational exuberance" to characterize equity prices. The collapse not only adversely impacted large numbers of individuals, especially through their retirement accounts, but revealed a number of misrepresentations about the value of individual equities and several outright frauds. In 2002 the Sarbanes–Oxley Act created a new government authority (the Public Accounting Oversight Board) to impose accurate reporting requirements and require certification by CEOs and CFOs of the accuracy of financial statements released to the public.

The bubble and burst of housing prices and the subsequent Great Recession renewed concerns that the market is inherently unstable and requires greater regulation and supervision, and, at the same time, some questioned the wisdom of the deregulation process since 1980. The probable causes of the housing bubble have already been mentioned and will be discussed in a later chapter; however, at this point, we need only understand that the housing bubble and Great Recession were the catalysts for the most recent government intervention in the financial system – the Dodd-Frank Wall Street Reform and Consumer Protection Act of 2010.

The Act is a complex, not completely implemented (amounting to a work in progress) piece of legislation, and it ranks as significant as the financial legislation passed in the 1930s and the Deregulation and Monetary Control Act of 1980. The Act has been controversial in at least five respects. First, it assumes the government is capable of identifying systemic risk such as the start of an asset bubble when, in fact, the government completely missed the housing bubble. Second, it assumes the government is capable of identifying systemically important financial institutions, which amounts to identifying institutions that are "too big to fail", when, in fact, the Act claims to reduce the "too big to fail" perspective. Third, the Act is based on the view that the housing bubble and Great Recession were due to market failure and ignores any role of government policy. Fourth, the Act and the implementation of the Act involve the government in micromanagement issues of the private market, and its emphasis on regulation and reporting might reduce the efficiency of the private financial system and reduce incentives to innovate. Fifth, the Act offers no recommendations for the two large government-sponsored enterprises, Fannie Mae and Freddie Mac, which importantly contributed to the housing bubble and subsequent Great Recession. In this regard, one might view the name of the Act as black humor, in that Christopher Dodd (D-Senate, Connecticut) and Barney Frank (D-House of Representatives, Massachusetts) were two of the most important proponents of subsidizing homeownership for low- to moderate-income households, reducing the prudential regulation of mortgage lending, encouraging subprime mortgage lending – and Fannie Mae and Freddie Mac.

The following are only a few of the provisions of the Act, which dramatically extends the role of government in the financial system: the government is responsible for identifying firms that pose systemic risk to the financial system and economy; the Act requires standard derivative products (financial instruments whose payoff is linked to other securities) to be traded and cleared through clearinghouses; it provides regulatory authorities with enhanced powers to seize and close failing institutions deemed to be systemically important; it expands the Federal Reserve's regulatory authority over financial institutions determined to be systemically important; it reduces the ability of banks to trade with their own funds (proprietary trading) in financial instruments and prohibits banks from any significant ownership of private equity firms; it weakens state-based insurance regulation by making insurance companies susceptible to the label "systemically important financial institutions"; and it extensively expands the consumer protection authority of the government over consumer lending, broadly defined.

The Act has made three changes to the institutional structure of government regulation and supervision. First, it has established the Consumer Financial Protection Bureau, which is housed in and funded by the Federal Reserve, but is completely independent of the Federal Reserve. Second, the Act has established the Financial Stability Oversight Council, consisting of all of the major regulatory authorities, chaired by the Treasury, to assess risk, identify asset bubbles and determine which financial institutions are systemically important. Third, the Act abolishes the Office of Thrift Supervision and transfers its powers mainly to the Comptroller of the Currency and, to a lesser extent, the Federal Reserve and the FDIC.

At the time of this writing, in mid-2017, considerable discussion continues about the structure of the nation's financial and monetary regime. The three areas of focus are as follows.

First, redesign of the Federal Reserve to increase its transparency and accountability and reflect concern about its increasing emphasis on macroprudential regulation. By any standard, the Federal Reserve's adoption of quantitative easing and zero-interest-rate policy for almost a decade starting in 2008 has not generated the anticipated outcomes. The recovery has been slow by historical standards and only began to pick up pace in late 2016.

Second, revisions of the Dodd–Frank Act because of concern the Act has gone too far in managing too many financial institutions and because the Act makes it difficult for smaller financial institutions to deal with the increasing complexity of regulations. There is concern the Act has limited the growth of credit because its regulatory reach has rendered banks and other lenders more risk-averse than necessary.

Third, there remains considerable debate about the role of the government's socialization of risk taking in mortgage lending by supporting the social contract for homeownership. There is some discussion of reforming Freddie Mac and Fannie Mae to prevent another run-up of housing prices, which generated the Great Recession. Of the three areas, this is likely the one that will receive the least attention because of the role of housing in the U.S. economic and political system. It is the "third rail" in U.S. politics.

Whether significant changes in any of the three areas will occur is difficult to determine, but student needs to keep in mind that the nation's financial and monetary regime is an evolutionary set of institutions and markets. The regime is in constant motion because of market forces, government policy and economic and political events.

Part IV

Five Steps to Understanding Central Banks and Central Bank Policy

Chapter 11

The Five Steps and Step 1: The Institutional Design of the Central Bank

11.1 Introduction

The country's financial and monetary regime consists of the financial system, financial regulation and supervision over the financial system, and the central bank and central bank policy. The previous chapters have focused on the first two elements of the regime, bringing into that discussion central banks and central bank policy only when appropriate. It is now time to focus attention on central banks and central bank policy.

The institutional design of central banks and central bank policy differ to some degree from country to country, but, on balance, the differences pale in comparison to the similarities. The institutional design of central banks, the way they formulate and implement monetary policy, the fundamental model of the economy they rely on and the policy targets they attempt to achieve are fairly consistent in their essential elements. There are five basic steps to understanding central banks and central bank policy in most countries, and, once the five steps are presented, the framework can be used to gain an overall understanding of the Federal Reserve and monetary policy in the United States.

A nation's central bank and central bank policy can be outlined in the following five steps.

Step 1: The institutional design of the central bank.
Step 2: The tools of monetary policy used by the central bank to influence base money, the money supply, credit and interest rates.
Step 3: The policy instruments or intermediate targets utilized by the central bank to guide the tools of monetary policy.
Step 4: The model of the economy used to guide monetary policy, which connects the policy instruments to the indicators of overall economic performance – employment, real GDP and prices.

Step 5: The final policy targets of the central bank, in terms of desired levels of employment, real GDP growth and prices.

The five steps provide a framework to understanding central banking in general. In fact, while we focus on the Federal Reserve, most of what we discuss applies to virtually any central bank. This chapter focuses on Step 1 – the central bank itself. Subsequent chapters focus on the four other steps.

11.2 The Institutional Design of the Central Bank

The central bank is an important public institution, with specific responsibilities in the nation's financial and monetary regime. The modern central bank influences the nation's money supply, credit and interest rates to achieve the following outcomes: long-term price stability; stabilizing the economy (reducing fluctuations in the GDP gap); acting as a fiscal agent of the government; maintaining the nation's payment system, by providing currency and a check-clearing system; providing lender of last resort services; and, in many cases, administering regulatory and supervisory responsibilities over the financial system.

Every nation has a central bank or similar government institution that carries out the functions of a central bank. Table 11.1 presents a list of the 69 central banks that are members of the Bank for International Settlements (BIS), located in Basel, Switzerland. The BIS is an international association of central banks, established in 1930. Other countries have central banks but are not members of the BIS.

There are five general aspects of the institutional design of a nation's central bank to review before attention is turned to the Federal Reserve: first, the reason central bank functions are housed in a government institution; second, ownership of the central bank; third, the role of the central bank as a financial regulatory and supervisory authority; fourth, the institutional relationship between the central bank and the government – the issue of central bank independence; and, fifth, the two significant institutional redesigns of central banks in the past several decades: greater legal independence from government and greater transparency.

After discussing each of the five general aspects of central bank institutional design, attention is then turned to the Federal Reserve.

11.3 Why a Government Central Bank?

Some central banks, such as the Bank of England, started as private for-profit commercial banks that were designated by the government to issue national banknotes and provide other central bank functions. Experience demonstrated, however, that there is a fundamental problem with a bank that operates as the nation's central bank and at the same time conducts operations to make a profit. Central banks, by and large, are designed to offset certain types of market failure in the financial and

Table 11.1. *Bank for International Settlements Central Bank Members, 2015*

Bank of Algeria
Central Bank of Argentina
Reserve Bank of Australia
Central Bank of the Republic of Austria
National Bank of Belgium
Central Bank of Bosnia and Herzegovina
Central Bank of Brazil
Bulgarian National Bank
Bank of Canada
Central Bank of Chile
People's Bank of China
Bank of the Republic (Colombia)
Croatian National Bank
Czech National Bank
Danmarks Nationalbank (Denmark)
Bank of Estonia
European Central Bank
Bank of Finland
Bank of France
Deutsche Bundesbank (Germany)
Bank of Greece
Hong Kong Monetary Authority
Magyar Nemzeti Bank (Hungary)
Central Bank of Iceland
Reserve Bank of India
Bank Indonesia
Central Bank of Ireland
Bank of Israel
Bank of Italy
Bank of Japan
Bank of Korea (South Korea)
Bank of Latvia
Bank of Lithuania
Central Bank of Luxembourg
National Bank of the Republic of Macedonia
Central Bank of Malaysia
Bank of Mexico
Netherlands Bank
Reserve Bank of New Zealand
Central Bank of Norway
Central Reserve Bank of Peru
Bangko Sentral ng Pilipinas (Philippines)
National Bank of Poland
Bank of Portugal
National Bank of Romania
Central Bank of the Russian Federation
Saudi Arabian Monetary Agency
National Bank of Serbia
Monetary Authority of Singapore
National Bank of Slovakia
Bank of Slovenia
South African Reserve Bank
Bank of Spain
Sveriges Riksbank (Sweden)
Swiss National Bank
Bank of Thailand
Central Bank of the Republic of Turkey
Central Bank of the United Arab Emirates
Bank of England (United Kingdom)
Board of Governors of the Federal Reserve System (United States)

Source: Bank for International Settlements (www.bis.org/about/member_cb.htm).

monetary regime and need to have an economy-wide perspective. Experience with private banks issuing national banknotes has not been encouraging. The U.S. national banking system established in 1863 was an effort to provide a unified national currency through private banks. The national banking system, however, was unable to provide a flexible national currency, and changes in the demand for currency and other problems caused several financial panics. The most severe was in 1907 and was the catalyst for establishing the Federal Reserve. Japan, as it started its modernization with the Meiji Restoration in 1868, adopted the U.S. national banking system model in 1875, with private banks issuing national banknotes. It was a failure, because the private banks over-issued national banknotes and generated inflation. Japan realized the error and the need for a central bank much sooner than did the United States. The Bank of Japan was established in 1882, to issue national banknotes and provide other functions. The Federal Reserve was not established until 1913, a little over 50 years after the national banking system had been established in 1863.

There are some advocates of "free" banking who argue that government central banks are not required to achieve a stable financial and monetary environment and that many of the functions of central banking can be satisfied by private institutions. These are interesting views, but, for all practical purposes, they make unrealistic assumptions about the ability of private institutions to deal with the nation's money supply, which in many respects is a public good. The arguments for central banks and their responsibilities being institutionalized as government entities outweigh the arguments for "free" banking; however, that does not mean that government institutions are problem-free.

The rationale for a central bank is based on the presence of certain types of market failure inherent in a private banking system based on fractional reserves – the contagion and money supply problems. Hence, only a standalone non-profit central bank that has an economy-wide perspective can provide services to prevent the economic equivalent of counterfeiting. There are some functions performed by a central bank, such as check clearing and transfers of funds domestically and internationally, that are shared with private entities and could be handled by the private sector, but the basic functions of controlling the nation's money supply and providing lender of last resort services can be adequately provided only by a central bank. Likewise, financial regulation and supervision need to be provided at the government level with an economy-wide perspective, but, in the case of this function, there is no inherent reason why these functions should be provided by the central bank.

Over time government has redesigned the nation's financial and monetary regime to make it easier for central banks to carry out their responsibilities. Today, the modern monetary system is pictured as an inverted pyramid (Figure 11.1) that consists of three components: first, the base, which consists of central-bank-issued liabilities (currency and reserves) used as currency and reserves of depository institutions; second, the reserve requirement; and, third, the nation's money supply,

Part 3: the money supply, M2

Part 2: reserve requirements on
checkable (transaction) deposits

Part 1: central bank fiat money:
currency and reserves – referred to as base money,
high-powered money or monetary base

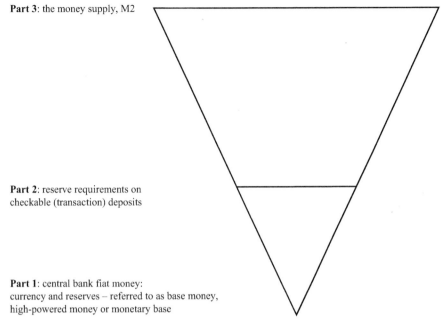

Figure 11.1. Three Parts of the Modern Inverted Pyramid Monetary System and Central Bank Monetary Policy and Lender of Last Resort Services.

measured by M2 money. The base is referred to as *base money, high-powered money* or the *monetary base*. In this context, it is straightforward to see how the central bank provides lender of last resort services and controls the money supply.

The central bank increases base money (the liabilities of the central bank) by purchasing financial assets and/or making loans to depository institutions and decreases base money by selling financial assets and/or reducing loans to depository institutions. For all practical purposes, the central bank can increase or decrease base money at will, much like "Monopoly money", in the Monopoly game that has been around since it was introduced in the 1930s. How this is done will be treated later in more detail in Chapter 13, on the tools of monetary policy (Step 2 of the five-step sequence), but at this point the reader needs only to accept the fact the central bank has the ability to change base money in the inverted pyramid framework with few constraints.

By being able to change base money, the central bank can be a lender of last resort to any specific depository institution, or, as in the case of the 2008/2009 financial crisis, can be a lender of last resort even to nondepository financial institutions. While lender of last resort actions will influence the nation's money supply, given that any change in base money will result in multiple changes in M2 money, the focus of lender of last resort operations is on a specific depository institution or group of depository institutions. The central bank has the option of offsetting the base money created by lender of last resort operations by reducing base money in other parts of the financial system so that the net effect is no change in the nation's money supply.

11.4 Ownership of the Central Bank

Central banks are organized as public corporations with an income and balance sheet statement. About 75 percent of the central banks in the world are directly owned by the government. The rest are jointly owned by the government and the private sector or, in a few cases, completely owned by the private sector; however, private ownership of the central bank does not confer any of the same benefits that ownership of a private corporation provides. Private entities that hold central bank stock have no ability to influence policy, and, if they play any institutional role in the structure of the central bank, that role is minimal. Irrespective of the corporate structure and ownership, the central bank is a *de facto* government institution under the control of the government.

The Federal Reserve and Bank of Japan are two interesting exceptions to government ownership of the central bank. The Federal Reserve is technically "owned" by member banks. National banks must be official members of the Federal Reserve and state-chartered banks can apply for official membership in the Federal Reserve System. A national bank is chartered by the federal government while state banks are chartered by the state in which their head office is located. Any bank that holds Federal Reserve stock is referred to as a member bank. At one time membership status was important, but as a result of the 1980 Deregulation and Monetary Control Act there is no meaningful difference between member and nonmember depository institutions in terms of central bank policy.

All federally insured depository institutions are required to have the same economic relationship with the Federal Reserve in terms of reserve requirements and access to Federal Reserve services. Even though some private banks "own" the Federal Reserve, they enjoy none of the usual rights of ownership. They do not play any meaningful role in the formulation and execution of monetary policy; they do not receive special treatment in the provision of any Federal Reserve services; they receive a statutory annual dividend of 6 percent on paid-in stock; they cannot sell the stock, as there is no secondary market for Federal Reserve stock; and they must surrender the stock at par when they leave the Federal Reserve System. Member banks are permitted to post a sign at their bank locations indicating Federal Reserve membership, but, for all practical purposes, this has no practical significance for the bank customer.

Why was the Federal Reserve established as a central bank "owned" by private banks? The establishment of the Federal Reserve was controversial, as many argued it would be under the control of the federal government. To allay this concern, the Federal Reserve would not be owned by the government but by private banks, and thus be a "bankers' central bank". Of course, this was political theater, and

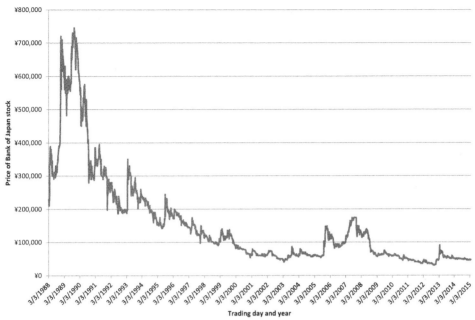

Figure 11.2. Bank of Japan Stock Prices, March 3, 1988, to March 24, 2015. *Source:* The Institute of Monetary and Financial Economics, Bank of Japan.

it was clear to everyone, at the time of establishment, the Federal Reserve was a government institution.

The Bank of Japan is another exception to government ownership. The capital of the Bank of Japan is jointly owned by the government and the public, with the restriction that the public cannot not own more than 45 percent of the outstanding Bank of Japan stock. Unlike Federal Reserve stock, however, Bank of Japan stock is traded on the Japanese capital market (Figure 11.2). Like Federal Reserve stock, Bank of Japan stock provides none of the usual ownership rights that pertain to stock held in any private corporation. Despite the fact the private sector in Japan has a significant ownership interest in the Bank of Japan, the Bank of Japan has always been a government institution. The Bank of Japan was based on the Bank of Belgium, established in 1850 with 100 percent of its capital provided by the private sector.

Thus, history and political considerations at the time a central bank was established account for the different types of corporate ownership of the central bank, but, for all practical purposes, central banks, even if entirely owned (Federal Reserve) or partly owned (Bank of Japan) by the private sector, are government institutions under the control and influence of the government.

One final comment to drive home the point that central banks are government institutions. Central bank operations are not conducted to make a profit in the traditional sense; however, central banks generate revenues far above their costs of operation, because they issue fiat money to purchase financial assets (mainly government securities) and make loans to depository institutions that generate interest income. The marginal cost of an additional unit of fiat money is close to zero while the marginal revenue of an additional financial asset or loan is positive; hence, central banks can't help but make money when they make money! Central banks also provide a variety of services to the private financial system, for which they receive fees. As a result, because central banks create money, they also create significant revenues and generate large profits. The large majority of revenue generated by the central bank, however, is transferred to the government budget as an intergovernmental transfer. The Federal Reserve transfers about 80 to 90 percent of its revenue to the U.S. Treasury each year, which is typical.

11.5 Central Banks as Financial and Regulatory Authorities

Central banks are well positioned, because of their ability to control base money, to provide lender of last resort services to prevent contagion and control the money supply to achieve long-run price stability. Central banks have long argued that, as part of their responsibilities for lender of last resort and monetary control operations, they should play a meaningful role in the regulation and supervision of the financial system, either as the primary financial regulatory authority or, at least, playing a major role, along with other government agencies responsible for financial and supervisory regulation of the system.

Central banks argue that they need to be an important part of the regulatory process in order to fully appraise the performance of the financial system, to conduct lender of last resort services and to formulate and execute monetary policy and, in general, ensure a stable financial and monetary environment. Irrespective of the arguments to support this view, one must keep in mind that any government agency has an incentive to expand its powers. The size and influence of any government regulatory agency are valued goods in government service and there is an inherent incentive to rationalize expanded influence. The real issue is whether the central bank's role in financial regulation and supervision contributes to or detracts from its basic responsibilities.

Central banks argue their regulatory and supervisory responsibilities do not conflict with their monetary policy responsibilities, but others point out at least four problems with central bank involvement in the regulation and supervision of the financial system.

First – the argument is weak: The argument that the central bank needs to be a major financial regulation and supervisory authority to conduct monetary policy or even lender of last resort functions is weak at best. Monetary policy in general does not require financial regulation and supervision, since it is based on controlling base money and setting the reserve requirement. Being lender of last resort does require information about depository and other financial institutions, but this information is not dependent on the central bank being a major regulatory and supervisory authority. Detailed information on financial institutions is routinely provided to many government agencies and can easily be shared with the central bank, and, in those cases in which depository institutions require a lender of last resort, the central bank can obtain any additional information required.

Second – central banks are at risk of being captured by the regulated entity: When the central bank becomes involved in the regulation and supervision of the financial system, it becomes exposed to an *industry perspective* problem. There is extensive research to suggest regulatory authorities tend to adopt an industry perspective when they have a close regulatory relationship with an industry, such as the banking industry. As the central bank becomes more of a regulatory authority, the industry perspective can interfere with its monetary control responsibilities. Tight monetary policy imposes pressures on financial institutions and markets, as interest rate increases will weaken the balance sheets of financial institutions. As a result, the central bank may become overly cautious in raising interest rates. That is, the industry perspective may end up being more important for the conduct of monetary policy than the more appropriate *public perspective*. Central banks deny any such influence, but economic theory and history suggest the "industry perspective" issue is far from trivial.

Third – central banks have increased exposure to political pressure: Financial regulation is subject to much political influence because financial regulation and how it treats specific types of financial institutions and markets influences the allocation of credit; for example, financial regulation in the United States has often been designed to ensure a steady flow of credit into housing, while, in Japan and South Korea, financial regulation has often been designed to ensure a steady flow of credit to the large corporations, especially those in the export sector. The greater the role of the central bank in financial regulation, the greater the potential for political influence over the central bank; that is, like the industry perspective, the central bank comes under the influence of a *credit allocation* perspective defined by political forces.

Fourth – monetary policy and managing the nation's payments system are hard enough: Monetary policy is taxing enough, along with the other central bank responsibilities to manage the payments system and be the fiscal agent for the government. The simple facts are: the larger the bureaucracy, the larger the administrative staff; and the greater number of responsibilities, the increased risk of diseconomies. Even if the regulatory responsibilities do not conflict with lender of last resort and monetary control responsibilities, they compete for the central bank's resources. Too many cooks in the kitchen! David Ricardo in 1817 introduced the concept of comparative advantage for international trade; that is, even though a country can produce any good more cheaply than any other country, the country should focus only on those export goods for which it has a comparative advantage over other countries. Likewise, a central bank should focus its resources on those activities for which it has a comparative advantage and leave other activities to other agencies.

As a reflection of this debate, central banks have been assigned varying degrees of regulatory responsibilities, ranging from limited responsibilities, as with the Bank of Japan and the Bank of Korea, to being a major regulatory authority, as with the Federal Reserve. The Federal Reserve is responsible for regulating domestic banks, bank holding companies and foreign banks and enforcing a wide range of regulations designed to protect consumers in the financial system. Whatever the arguments against such a role, the institutional design of the Federal Reserve is not likely to change toward less regulatory authority.

In fact, the regulatory role of central banks has steadily increased over the past few decades, especially in response to the financial distress in 2008/2009, the Great Recession and the 2010 Dodd–Frank Act. Central banks have assumed or been assigned increased responsibilities for managing systemic risk in the financial system – the risk that a specific or group of specific financial institutions pose for the stability of the entire financial system and economy. These new responsibilities go far beyond those of traditional *microprudential* regulation, which focused on troubled depository financial institutions and their risk to the financial system. The new *macroprudential* policy is a significant expansion of central bank financial and supervisory responsibilities.

The objective of macroprudential regulation is twofold: first, to identify asset bubbles, speculative excesses and overheated financial markets; and then, second, to employ regulations over capital–asset ratios, liquidity, margins on trading securities, and restrictions on credit underwriting to all financial sectors deemed "systemically" important. There are many issues as to whether this expansion is well advised and whether the central bank is assuming responsibilities for which it is not capable of achieving, and, in the process, reducing its ability to perform the traditional central bank responsibilities, which it has a reasonable degree of probability of achieving.

11.6 Central Bank Independence from Government

At first glance central bank independence from political influence is a straightforward concept. Of course the central bank should be independent in order to perform its basic responsibilities, because there are obvious conflicts between a central bank that controls the money supply and the fiscal program of the government. Governments spend money and are subject to intense pressure by various groups to spend money. Governments realize they can maintain and enhance political power by positively responding to these pressures and, hence, have an incentive to influence the central bank to accommodate their spending with money creation. Thus, central bank independence appears to be a desirable institutional feature of any central bank.

However, the issue is far more complex than it appears, as illustrated by considering the following five issues related to central bank independence. First, can a central bank really be independent? Second, is "independence" the best term, despite its common use, to institutionally assist the central bank in achieving those goals it can achieve? Third, what is the difference between *de jure* and *de facto* independence and why is the distinction important? Fourth, what is the evolution of views about central bank independence? Fifth, are central banks independent?

Can a central bank be independent? No. A central bank is a government institution established by government, and, while the central bank can be given degrees of independence from government in formulating and executing its responsibilities, the central bank can always be redesigned by government. Hence, independence from government is not absolute under any condition, and, paraphrasing the characterization of Federal Reserve independence by Governor McChesney Martine (1951–1970), the central bank has independence "within" government rather than independence "from" government. Independence is best understood as institutionalizing the central bank in such a manner that, even though it is a government institution, the central bank is permitted to formulate its own policy objectives and conduct its own operations to achieve those policy objectives without direct influence by the government, even if the objectives conflict with other government policies. To the extent that central bank objectives and operations are influenced by government policy, the less independent or dependent the central bank.

There's a story that goes like this. A new research staff member to the Board of Governors asked one of the board members if the Federal Reserve was independent. The board member responded: "Yes, of course, the Federal Reserve is independent." The new staff member then asked: "Does that mean the Federal Reserve can raise interest rates to prevent inflation even if that causes the unemployment rate to increase, say, from 5 to 5.5 percent?" The response: "Yes, of course, that's what independence means. We can pursue a policy that might conflict with the government." The new staff member persisted and asked: "What about if the unemployment rate increases from 5 to 6 or 6.5 percent?" The board member took more time to respond: "Probably not, because then we would lose our independence!"

Is "independence" the best term? No, but unfortunately the term "independence" is so commonly used it is difficult to substitute a more meaningful term. No central bank can be fully independent, since it is a government institution. The term "independence" is meant to describe an institutional design that permits the central bank to carry out its responsibilities without direct government influence. A better term would be "accountability" – an institutional design of the central bank that would ensure it was "accountable" for the objectives for which a central bank is designed: price stability and, on occasion, lender of last resort. An institutional design that provides a framework and incentives for the central bank to be accountable for what it is capable of achieving shifts the emphasis from the relationship between the central bank and government to the more important issue of how best to ensure the central bank achieves policy objectives for which it was designed and is capable of achieving.

In fact, history suggests that the formal relationship between the central bank and government is not a very good predictor of monetary policy that contributes to a stable economic and financial environment. The independent Federal Reserve played a major role in causing the Great Inflation and the Great Recession while, in other periods such as the 1950s and the Great Moderation (1985 to 2000), the same independent Federal Reserve achieved positive policy outcomes of low and predictable inflation. Yet, throughout each of these periods, the Federal Reserve remained a formally independent central bank. A focus on the institutional design that renders the central bank accountable would thus be more helpful than the issue of whether a central bank is independent, or dependent, from or within government. Central bank independence is a sideshow.

De jure and de facto independence: Independence is almost always in the *de jure* meaning, namely the formal or legal relationship between the central bank and the government as defined by the enabling legislation that established the central bank, such as the Federal Reserve Act, the Bank of Japan Law, etc. In contrast, *de facto* independence refers to the actual reality of central bank operations, which may or may not be consistent with *de jure* independence. The Federal Reserve is one of the world's more *de jure* independent central banks, but there are periods when it accommodated government policy, whereas the Bank of Japan, until 1998 one of the world's most *de jure* dependent central banks, operated with a fair degree of independence from the government at various times.

Evolution of the concern with central bank independence: The concern with central bank independence emerged as the nation's money supply became more dependent on the actions of the central bank and the nation's money supply became less dependent on a commodity standard. In theory, central bank independence was neither necessary nor sufficient for stable monetary policy as long as the country adhered to the fixed exchange rate standard, because, in this case, monetary policy is dictated by external considerations, ensuring the central bank will generate a noninflationary money supply over time.

If the central bank increased the money supply more than required by the needs of trade, the economy would grow above its potential in the short run and lead to inflation in the short and long run. Assuming the perspective of the United States, increased growth and inflation would shift the demand for dollars to the left and the supply of dollars to the right, depreciating the currency and generating a current account deficit. At a fixed exchange rate, there would be an excess supply of dollars in the foreign exchange market. In order to maintain the fixed exchange rate, the United States would use its international reserves to purchase the excess supply of dollars to offset the current account deficit with a surplus in the financial account (selling international reserves generates receipts to offset net payments in the current account). As international reserves were used to purchase dollars, this signals that monetary policy has been too easy and indicates the need to tighten monetary policy. The central bank would then reduce the rate of monetary growth to slow the growth of the economy and inflation.

If the central bank increased the money supply less than required by the needs of trade, the economy would grow below its potential in the short run and lead to lower inflation or deflation in the short and long run. Decreased growth and lower inflation would shift the demand for dollars to the right and the supply of dollars to the left, appreciating the currency and generating a current account surplus. At a fixed exchange rate, there would be an excess demand of dollars in the foreign exchange market. In order to maintain the fixed exchange rate, the deficit countries would use their international reserves to purchase dollars (buying international reserves generates payments to offset net receipts in the current account). As international reserves flow into the United States, this signals that monetary policy has been too tight and indicates the need to loosen monetary policy. The central bank would then increase the rate of monetary growth to increase the growth of the economy and inflation.

Of course, this worked only if countries adhered to the rules of the fixed exchange rate system. In this system the central bank is held accountable for providing a stable monetary environment by the requirement to conduct policy to maintain the fixed exchange rate system. But even in this environment central banks could be pressured by government to persist too long in easy policy and pressured to maintain tight policy for too short a period of time. This potential conflict was recognized even under the fixed exchange rate standard, and some attention was given to designing central banks to be independent; for example, the Federal Reserve was designed to be independent in 1913.

The issue of independence became important in the post-WWII period for three reasons. First, the connection between gold and the nation's money supply waned, and by 1973 the world had shifted to a flexible exchange rate system. This freed the central bank from conducting monetary policy to maintain a fixed exchange rate. Second, the Great Inflation in the United States was part of a worldwide inflation problem, with only a few exceptions (such as Japan), and in order to bring the inflation rate down many recommended more independent central banks. Third, the deregulation and financial liberalization process in the last part of the twentieth century, the breakup of the Soviet Union and the establishment of the European Monetary Union provided opportunities to redesign and/or design new central banking institutions.

The long-held *conventional wisdom* that independent central banks generated better policy outcomes rapidly became public policy in the 1980s and 1990s. Central bank independence was increasingly recommended as the best institutional design for ensuring that a central bank would contribute to a stable financial and monetary framework and, hence, contribute to economic stability and growth.

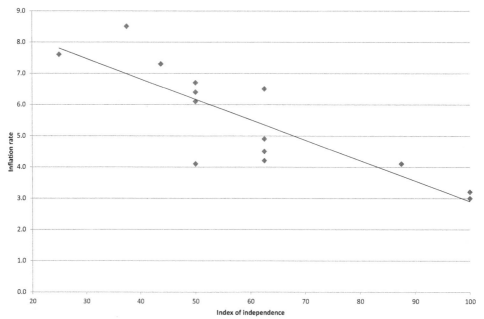

Figure 11.3. Index Based on *De Jure* Central Bank Independence and Inflation, 1955 to 1988. *Sources:* The line is based on a regression presented in Cargill (2013); the data were originally used in Alesina and Summers (1993), and put into the form used here by Carlstrom and Fuerst (2009).

The conventional wisdom received empirical support in the 1980s and 1990s as researchers developed measures of central bank independence and estimated correlations between inflation and the measures over time and across countries. Figure 11.3 presents a typical regression between inflation and measures of central bank independence for 16 central banks over the period from 1955 to 1988 (Alesina and Summers, 1993), which appears to support the conventional wisdom; however, some researchers regard these types of statistical relationships as fundamentally flawed and misleading (Cargill, 2013).

Central bank independence – reality or myth? The conventional wisdom has been challenged by some researchers, but, nonetheless, the conventional wisdom remains intact, and the relationship between inflation and central bank independence as expressed in Figure 11.3 is widely accepted. The BIS and IMF, central banks and many economists argue that independent central banks provide better monetary policy outcomes than less independent central banks, and often refer to empirical results such as in Figure 11.3 to support the conventional wisdom. Is the support for the conventional wisdom justified? A balanced view of the historical record of central bank policy and the statistical foundation suggests the conventional wisdom is not as solid as claimed.

First, Bank of Japan postwar history, especially in comparison with the postwar history of the Federal Reserve, contradicts the conventional wisdom, and, in light of this history, it is difficult to understand the continued acceptance of the convention wisdom. The Federal Reserve played a major role in the Great Inflation by pursing excessively easy monetary policy for almost two decades, significantly influenced by government policy, and yet the Federal Reserve is ranked in the measurement literature as one of the world's most independent central banks. In sharp contrast, the Bank of Japan pursued a price stabilization policy during the same period even in the presence of large government deficits in the 1970s, and yet the Bank of Japan was ranked during this period as one of the world's most dependent central banks. Advocates of the conventional wisdom either regard the U.S.–Japanese comparison an aberration that does not change the general relationship between independence and price stability or, more often, ignore the contradiction.

Second, the many detailed examinations of policy making show beyond dispute that central bankers are aware of their broader political conditions and constraints despite their formal independence, are never as insulated from their political environment as the language or measures of central bank independence suggest and often incorporate political considerations in the formulation and execution of monetary policy. There is documented evidence the Federal Reserve, for example, was subject to political pressure during the 1970s and conducted monetary policy accordingly despite its formal independence. One needs only to turn to the pages of a diary kept by Governor Arthur Burns (1971–1978), published in 2010 and discussed in Cargill and O'Driscoll (2013).

Burns summarizes a meeting on March 21, 1971, with President Nixon, who was focusing on his reelection campaign in 1972. Burns writes: "He agreed with my policy, that he preferred a slow start of the recovery which may then gather momentum in 1972." Burns continues: "He wants to rely primarily on me and [John] Connally in monitoring policy, that McCracken and Shultz – while able economists – did not understand politics, that I could handle both economics and politics, and that Connally was good at politics and therefore a great asset" (Ferrell, 2010, p. 40). Connally was Secretary of State. McCracken and Shultz were economic advisors to the president. More recently, Governor Alan Greenspan was asked why the Federal Reserve had kept interest rates at historical lows from 2001 to 2005 that, in the opinion of many, contributed to the housing bubble and subsequent Great Recession. Greenspan was quoted in the news media as follows (Frank, 2010): "[H]e [Greenspan] argued that if the Federal Reserve had tried to slow the housing market amid a 'fairly broad consensus' about encouraging homeownership, 'the Congress would have clamped down on us'" (Gustafson, 2010).

In Japan, the Bank of Japan became a focal point in the run-up to a national election in 2012, as major parties campaigned that, if they were elected, they would force the Bank of Japan to adopt a more easy policy and significantly increase liquidity in the economy. The Liberal Democratic Party won, and the prime minister, Shinzo Abe, replaced the governor and two deputy governors of the Bank of Japan with new management in early 2013. Base money significantly increased in 2013 and 2014 as a result of direct influence by the government. What makes the Japan case so interesting is that, in 1998, the Bank of Japan had significantly increased its independence from the government and joined the club of the more independent central banks in the world. Nonetheless, the independence of the Bank of Japan was a wall easily breached by government via a change in management to force the central bank to accommodate government policy.

Third, the statistical foundation of the widely accepted inverse correlation between measures of central bank independence and inflation is fundamentally flawed. The measures are based on *de jure* independence while the correct perspective should be on *de facto* independence. In fact, not only do the *de jure* measures of independence provide little information about the *de facto* relationship of the central bank to the government, some of the measures are incorrect. At a more technical level, the regression results are not statistically robust and far too simple to represent a complex relationship between the central bank and the government over time and across countries. How can one then explain the widespread acceptance of the simple correlation?

The measurement literature originated in the economics profession, which has a bias toward focusing only on variables that can be measured. This is an important reason why the measures are based on *de jure* independence; it's much easier to develop a measure based on the enabling legislation of the central bank than to attempt to measure the far more relevant *de facto* independence, which changes over time. In the effort to construct independence measures for a large number of central banks, researchers have not always been careful to understand the historical evolution of the relation between the central bank and government; for example, several researchers have actually ranked the Bank of Japan before 1998 at the same or close to the same independence assigned the Federal Reserve. This is incorrect. Until 1998 the Bank of Japan was regarded as one of the most dependent central banks in the world.

Another reason why the correlations are so widely accepted is that they are used by central banks to defend their independence or expand their independence. Central banks have a vested interest in the measurement literature, since any government organization regards "independence" as a valued attribute.

What's the bottom line? The historical and statistical foundation of the conventional wisdom is weak. The relationship between the central bank and government is far more complex than illustrated by Figure 11.3. The relative performance of the Bank of Japan and the Federal Reserve provide two important case studies that *de jure* independence is neither sufficient nor necessary for the central bank to achieve its primary objective of price stability. The "independent" Federal Reserve caused the Great Inflation and was clearly *de facto* dependent on the government, and the Bank of Japan during much the same time conducted *de facto* independent monetary policy in terms of price stability. Considering all of the evidence and the incentives for central banks to support the conventional wisdom, the conventional wisdom is more myth than reality! Despite this, the conventional wisdom continues to be held by many, especially central banks.

11.7 Two Important Institutional Redesigns of Central Banks

Central banks have been redesigned during the past several decades in two important respects. First, central banks have increasingly become more *de jure* independent as a result of the widespread acceptance of the conventional wisdom. A large number of central banks have either had their independence enhanced or been redesigned from dependent to independent central banks in the past several decades. Second, central banks have become more transparent in their operations than at any time in the history of central banking. In the following we focus on the second redesign, since the issue of central bank independence was discussed above.

Central banks until the last quarter of the twentieth century were rather nontransparent about their specific policy objectives and operations. In fact, in 1987 a book titled *Secrets of the Temple* (Greider, 1987) became a national bestseller. *Secrets of the Temple* was a discussion of how the Federal Reserve influenced economic activity during the turbulent Great Inflation years. The title meant to imply that central bank policy was nontransparent and under the control of a small group of "wise" individuals, who only infrequently informed the public as to their objectives and operations, often in vague language that left plenty of room for different interpretations.

Today the situation is dramatically different. Central banks are far more transparent, and information about their objectives and operations is now far more open to the public. Why the change, and what are the characteristics of the new transparency?

Why the change toward more transparency? The Great Inflation period in the United States and elsewhere imposed intense economic and financial distress, and efforts were directed to make sure the experience was not repeated. Central bank independence was one such effort, and greater transparency was another.

Economic theory suggests that the more information is available for any economic decision, the better the decision. If the central bank is more transparent about its objectives, more transparent about its own assessment of how well the objectives are being achieved, more transparent about how its objectives are being achieved from an operational perspective and more transparent about its underlying model of how the economy functions, the more effective monetary policy will be. This is because members of the public will have a more stable and predictable view of central bank policy, which, in turn, will form a stable part of their own current and future economic decisions. The economy will adjust more smoothly to shocks given that it has a more predictable and stable time path of central bank policy, especially future inflation. Current economic decisions are driven by expectations of the relevant variables for that decision in the future, and the more certain the expectations about the relevant variables, the more smoothly the economy functions and the more smoothly the economy adjusts to shocks.

While greater transparency in central bank policy is desirable, especially compared to the *Secrets of the Temple* days, it is difficult to draw specifics as to how much transparency is desirable and how that transparency should be communicated to the public. Too much transparency may be worse than little or no transparency; for example, there are many foods few would eat if they saw how they were processed and brought to the grocery store. Nonetheless, there is a widespread consensus that certain types of central bank transparency are a desirable feature of the institutional design of the central bank that contribute to better monetary policy outcomes.

Central bank transparency today: Dincer and Eichengreen (2007), in a comprehensive study of 100 central banks, define transparency in terms of political, economic, procedural, policy and operational transparency. *Political transparency* refers to an open and formal statement of central bank policy and, if there are several objectives, an open and formal ranking of those objectives. *Economic transparency* refers to the economic information and the underlying model of the economy the central bank uses to formulate and execute monetary policy. *Procedural transparency* refers to whether the central bank conducts policy by discretion or employs some type of rule to guide monetary policy. *Policy transparency* refers to the prompt disclosure of policy decisions, the justification for those policy decisions and likely policy decisions to be made in the future. *Operational transparency* refers to the specifics and technicalities of central bank operations.

Information about central bank policy is now communicated to the public in three ways. First, many central banks maintain a Web site in English (the world business language) providing detailed economic and financial data; policy statements; performance evaluations; operating procedures; economic research; their model of the economy; and information on the future course of central bank policy. Second, many central banks report to the government on a formal and frequent basis, with these reports available to the public. Many of these are on the Web site. Third, many central banks conduct policy in the context of policy objectives communicated to the public in varying degrees of detail.

The increased transparency is clearly evident for the major industrialized countries of the world, but the central banks of developing countries are also much more transparent than previously. By any standard, the days of the *Secrets of the Temple* are over!

11.8 The Institutional Design of the Federal Reserve System

The institutional design of the Federal Reserve is presented from three perspectives. First, what is the formal structure of the Federal Reserve System? Second, setting aside the formal organizational structure, who and what part of the Federal Reserve structure controls Federal Reserve actions and monetary policy? Third, is the Federal Reserve independent and transparent?

11.9 The Structure of the Federal Reserve System in the Broad Sense

The Federal Reserve in the broad sense is composed of five parts: Board of Governors; Federal Open Market Committee (FOMC); 12 Federal Reserve banks; advisory committees; and depository institutions that have an economic relationship with the Federal Reserve.

Board of Governors – 7/14/2: The Board of Governors of the Federal Reserve System, also referred to as the Federal Reserve Board, is the administrative head of the Federal Reserve and an important part of the decision-making process of the Federal Reserve. The term "7/14/2" describes the structure of the board. The board consists of seven members, appointed for 14-year terms staggered in such a manner that one term expires every two years. Board members are nominated by the president and subject to confirmation by the Senate. No board member can serve more than one full 14-year term; however, if a board member is appointed to an unexpired term, say one with ten years remaining, that board member can be reappointed for a full 14-year term once the unexpired term has ended. Alan Greenspan, for example, was a board member and chair of the board from 1987 through 2005, a total of 19 years, serving under Presidents Reagan, Bush-41, Clinton and Bush-42. The 7/14/2 structure was designed to reduce potential political influence by the president and/or Congress. The president nominates and the Senate confirms a board member to be chair and vice-chair for a four-year term.

The responsibilities of the board are broad. First, the board is the administrative head of the Federal Reserve System, with administrative responsibilities for the entire Federal Reserve System. Second, the board implements the financial regulation and supervision responsibilities of the Federal Reserve as well as administering a wide range of consumer protection laws. Third, the board is responsible for setting tier 3 reserve requirements, which can range from 8 to 14 percent of transaction deposits held by depository institutions. Fourth, the board sets margin requirements that specify the amount of cash down payment required to purchase equities (and convertible bonds) with credit. A margin requirement of 75 percent, for example, means that any purchase of stock with credit must consist of 75 percent cash and 25 percent credit. Fifth, the board "reviews and determines" the discount rate recommended by each of the 12 Federal Reserve banks. Essentially, the Board of Governors has the final word on the discount rate used by each of the Federal Reserve banks. Sixth, the board dominates the FOMC, the next component of the Federal Reserve to consider.

The Federal Open Market Committee – 12/7/4/1: The FOMC conducts open market operations by buying and selling securities, tradionally government securities, in the open money and capital markets. The exception to government securities occurred starting in 2008, when the Federal Reserve purchased almost as much in mortgage-backed bonds as it did in government securities. This unprecedented shift in open market operations will be discussed later. Open market operations are the most important, powerful, flexible tool of monetary policy used by the Federal Reserve to change base money and, hence, the money supply, credit and interest rates.

The term "12/7/4/1" describes the membership of the FOMC. The FOMC consists of 12 voting members, seven of whom are the members of the Board of Governors, four members are the presidents drawn from 11 Federal Reserve banks on a rotating basis, and one member is the president of the Federal Reserve Bank of New York. The permanent membership of the president of the Federal Reserve Bank of New York is due to the fact the actual buying and selling of securities are conducted by the Federal Reserve Bank of New York. The chair of the Board of Governors is the chair of the FOMC, and the president of the Federal Reserve Bank of New York is the vice-chair of the FOMC. Hence, the Board of Governors dominates the FOMC because it represents the majority of the voting members of the FOMC, the chair of the board is chair of the FOMC, and four of the other members are not permanent members.

The FOMC meets formally about eight times a year in Washington, D.C., at the Board of Governors. The 12 members are voting members, but the presidents of the other seven Federal Reserve banks participate in the FOMC meetings as nonvoting members.

12 Federal Reserve banks: There is a network of 12 Federal Reserve banks – one for each of the 12 geographic districts originally defined by the 1913 Federal Reserve Act. The 12 banks carry out many of the functions of the Federal Reserve System, including maintaining a national payments system by operating a nationwide check-clearing system, providing and absorbing currency in response to the needs of the public, making loans to depository institutions located in each bank's region and holding the reserve deposits of the depository institutions located in each bank's region. The Federal Reserve banks contribute to monetary policy in three ways.

First, the presidents of the Federal Reserve banks play an important role in the FOMC. The president of the Federal Reserve Bank of New York is a permanent member and four members of the Board of Governors are presidents of the other 11 Federal Reserve banks, and presidents of the seven other Federal Reserve banks participate in the FOMC as nonvoting participants. Thus, as part of the FOMC, the Federal Reserve banks play an important part in the FOMC.

Second, each Federal Reserve bank recommends to the board the discount rate each Federal Reserve bank will use in making loans to depository institutions in its district. The board then "reviews and determines" the discount rate each Federal Reserve bank will charge any depository institution in its district that borrows at the "discount window". The discount window is the primary channel through which the Federal Reserve serves as a lender of last resort.

Third, each Federal Reserve administers the discount window, makes a "Yes" or "No" decision to a loan request by a depository institutions and, if "Yes", decides the terms of the loan, including any additional basis points above the discount rate. That is, each Federal Reserve bank administers its own discount window within the general guidelines agreed to at the FOMC meetings.

Each Federal Reserve bank is managed by its own board of nine directors chosen from outside the Federal Reserve System, representing banking, commercial, agricultural, industrial and general public interests within each region. The board of directors appoints the president of each Federal Reserve bank.

The 12 Federal Reserve banks are a unique institutional design of a central bank that has no counterpart in the rest of the world. They were established to ensure regional representation and to ensure that the Board of Governors and/or the Federal Reserve Bank of New York did not dominate the Federal Reserve System. In the first two decades of the Federal Reserve, power was far more decentralized than today. The Federal Reserve Board was a relatively weak administrative head, and power was shared between the Federal Reserve Bank of New York and several of the Eastern Federal Reserve banks. The "decentralized" central banking structure of the Federal Reserve was a resolution of a political problem to allay concern the System would be dominated by Washington, D.C., and be responsive to the rest of the nation.

Advisory committees: There are three advisory committees that report to the Board of Governors on various matters. The oldest, and the one established in 1913, is the Federal Advisory Council, consisting of 12 members from the banking industry. Each member represents each Federal Reserve District. The Advisory Council meets with the board four times a year in Washington, D.C., to discuss a variety of issues relating to the nation's financial and monetary regime from the bankers' perspective.

The Consumer Advisory Council was established in 1976, advises the board on consumer protection issues in the financial system and meets with the board three times a year in Washington, D.C. The Thrift Institutions Advisory Council was established as a result of the 1980 Deregulation and Monetary Control Act, which extended reserve requirements to thrifts (savings banks, S&Ls and credit unions) and provided thrifts access to the discount window. The Thrift Institutions Advisory Council advises the board on the same types of issues as the Federal Advisory Council, but from the perspective of the thrift industry. Each Federal Reserve bank establishes its own advisory committees focusing on local issues.

Depository institutions that have an economic relationship with the Federal Reserve: All federally insured depository institutions have an economic relationship with the Federal Reserve in that they are subject to reserve requirements and have access to the discount window and other Federal Reserve services. The depository institutions, from the perspective of being part of the Federal Reserve System in the broad sense, are divided into member and nonmember institutions.

Member institutions actually "own" the Federal Reserve and, upon being granted membership status, must subscribe to Federal Reserve stock equal to 6 percent of their capital, 3 percent of which is paid and 3 percent subject to call by the Federal Reserve. As already discussed, this private ownership feature of the Federal Reserve was a political solution to allay concerns the Federal Reserve would be a government central bank. Instead, the stock ownership renders the Federal Reserve a "bankers'" central bank. Of course, this is a distinction without a difference, as the Federal Reserve from the start was a government-controlled central bank. Only two types of depository institutions can be official members: national banks must be members and state-chartered banks can apply for membership. In 2013 member banks included all 1,222 national banks and 829 state-chartered banks (17 percent of all state-chartered banks). Nonmember depository institutions include state-chartered banks that are not official members of the Federal Reserve and all other federally insured depository thrift institutions.

11.10 Where's the Power?

The Federal Reserve System in a broad sense consists of the Board of Governors, the FOMC, the 12 Federal Reserve banks, the advisory councils and the depository institutions that have an economic relationship with the Federal Reserve. Together they form a set of components that permit the Federal Reserve to control the money supply and influence credit and interest rates.

To answer the question "Where's the power?" one needs to ask a prerequisite question: "The power to do what?" Any central bank has essentially two functions: monetary policy and nonmonetary policy responsibilities. While there are some feedbacks between the two, they are separate, and distinguishing between the two helps us answer the question "Where's the power?" in the Federal Reserve.

The nonmonetary policy responsibilities focus on the nation's payment system, serving as a fiscal agent for the federal government, financial regulation and supervision, consumer protection and general economic research. These are referred to as nonmonetary policy responsibilities because they are not varied over time to influence economic activity. They are more of an ongoing responsibility of the Federal Reserve, and probably account for most of the Federal Reserve's resources and budget. While the Board of Governors is the administrative head of the Federal Reserve and sets broad guidelines for the various nonmonetary policy responsibilities, the majority of the nonmonetary policy responsibilities of the Federal Reserve are delegated to the large research staff of the Board of Governors and the 12 Federal Reserve banks. The nonmonetary policy of regulation and supervision, however, is concentrated at the Board of Governors.

The monetary policy responsibilities of the Federal Reserve, in contrast, focus on changing the money supply, credit and interest rates to influence economic activity to achieve specific final policy targets and providing lender of last resort services. In the past few years, however, the new macroprudential approach to financial regulation and supervision has become a new tool of monetary policy. Traditional microprudential policy is more a nonmonetary policy activity, but macroprudential policy is clearly part of monetary policy responsibilities. It is still too early to determine what, if any significant, role macroprudential policy will play in central bank policy for the Federal Reserve, or any central bank.

Surprisingly, only a fraction of the Federal Reserve's resources and budget are devoted to monetary policy responsibilities, but these responsibilities are the primary rational for establishing a central bank. When we think of a central bank, we immediately focus on its role to control the nation's money supply to influence economic activity and to achieve specific final policy targets and provide lender of last resort services. Who's in charge of monetary policy?

The apex of power to conduct monetary policy is concentrated in the FOMC, which, in turn, is dominated by the Board of Governors and especially the chair of the board, who is the chair of the FOMC. The chair has always been the most powerful member of the FOMC because of powers inherent in the chair's position and the fact the chair is the official representative of the Federal Reserve, but, over time, the power of the chair has increased relative to the rest of the FOMC – so that now, for better or worse, Federal Reserve policy is identified with the chair of the Board of Governors, who at present (2016) is Janet Yellen. To paraphrase George Orwell's *Animal Farm*, while each of the 12 voting members of the FOMC are technically equal, the seven board members are more equal than the other five members of the FOMC, and the chair is more equal than the other six members of the board.

There are two reasons why the power to conduct monetary policy is concentrated in the FOMC. First, the FOMC is responsible for the most important tool of monetary policy – open market operations. Second, while the FOMC is formally responsible only for open market operations, decisions about all of the tools of monetary policy are either made or discussed at the FOMC. That is, the full arsenal of the powers of the central bank to influence the economy are brought together in the FOMC.

11.11 The Federal Reserve and Central Bank Institutional Redesigns

Increased formal independence and increased transparency have been the two major institutional redesigns of central banks in the past several decades. How does the Federal Reserve fit into these institutional changes?

Independence: In terms of formal or *de jure* independence, the Federal Reserve is ranked by almost every observer as one of the more *de jure* independent central banks in the world. The Federal Reserve is designed to be legally independent. In the past Congress and/or the president have made efforts to become more involved with the Federal Reserve and influence monetary policy, but the Federal Reserve has largely been successful in preventing any meaningful breech of its wall of legal independence. As far as *de jure* independence is concerned, the Federal Reserve ranks high relative to other central banks. However, in terms of the more important concept of *de facto* independence, the Federal Reserve's independence is more debatable. The Federal Reserve and its defenders argue strongly the Federal Reserve conducts policy without outside influence, but the historical record suggests otherwise. The Federal Reserve on several important occasions has been strongly influenced by political considerations, especially pressure to accommodate government deficit spending and/or support specific sectors of the economy, such as housing. This should not be surprising given that the Federal Reserve was established by a government elected by the public.

The irony here is that efforts by the Federal Reserve to protect its *de jure* independence, which is a valued good in government, provide incentives for it to act *de facto* as a dependent central bank in order to protect its *de jure* independence. It is difficult to quantify this interaction between *de jure* and *de facto* independence, but any study of Federal Reserve policy since it was first established in 1913 suggests it is an important element of Federal Reserve interaction with the government and why, on occasion, the Federal Reserve has failed to achieve its basic responsibilities. Some might say the Federal Reserve is at times a "prisoner of its own independence".

Transparency: The Federal Reserve is far more transparent than it was even a few decades ago and provides much information to the public on its policy objectives and how those objectives are being pursued. Again, the *Secrets of the Temple* days are over. One can access the Web site of the Board of Governors or any of the 12 Federal Reserve banks and obtain detailed monetary policy reports, minutes of the FOMC meetings and, after five years, actual transcripts of the FOMC meetings, research reports on a wide range of policy issues, reports on models of the economy used by the Federal Reserve, as well as extensive databases, such as FRED.

References

Alesina, Alberto, and Lawrence H. Summers (1993). "Central Bank Independence and Macroeconomic Performance: Some Comparative Evidence". *Journal of Money, Credit and Banking*, 25: 151–62.

Cargill, Thomas F. (2013). "A Critical Assessment of Measures of Central Bank Independence". *Economic Inquiry*, 51: 260–72.

Cargill, Thomas F., and Gerald P. O'Driscoll Jr. (2013). "Federal Reserve Independence: Reality or Myth?". *Cato Journal*, 33: 417–35.

Carlstrom, Charles T., and Timothy S. Fuerst (2009). "Central Bank Independence and Inflation: A Note". *Economic Inquiry*, 47: 182–6.

Dincer, N. Nergiz, and Barry Eichengreen (2007). "Central Bank Transparency: Where, Why, and with What Effects?", Working Paper no. 13003. Cambridge, MA: National Bureau of Economic Research.

Ferrell, Robert H., ed. (2010). *Inside the Nixon Administration: The Secret Diary of Arthur Burns, 1969–1974*. Lawrence: University Press of Kansas.

Frank, Ryan (2010). "Greenspan Rejects Criticism of His Boom-Era Policies". *Oregonian*, April 7, http://blog.oregonlive.com/frontporch/2010/04/greenspan_rejects_criticism_of.html.

Greider, William (1987). *Secrets of the Temple: How the Federal Reserve Runs the Country*. New York: Simon & Schuster.

Gustafson, Dave (2010). "Greenspan Defends Fed's Role in Run-Up to Financial Crisis". PBS Newshour, April 7, www.pbs.org/newshour/rundown/greenspan-defends-feds-role-in-run-up-to-crisis.

Chapter 12

Central Banks, Base Money and the Money Supply

12.1 Introduction

The previous chapter outlined the institutional structure of central banks in general and the Federal Reserve in particular, thus completing Step 1. Before moving on to the tools of monetary policy (Step 2), we need to develop a more detailed understanding of the inverted pyramid monetary system. That is, we need to understand the money supply process in a modern financial and monetary regime as a prerequisite to understanding how central banks influence economic activity.

This chapter discusses the money supply process from two perspectives: first, the mechanics of the money supply process; and, second, the ability of the Federal Reserve to utilize the money supply process in conducting monetary policy.

12.2 The Money Supply Process in Two Parts

The money supply process is illustrated in two parts. Part 1 illustrates the process with a set of restrictive assumptions to illustrate the basic elements of a modern monetary system. Some of the restrictive assumptions are relaxed in part 1, but part 2 illustrates the process with all of the restrictive assumptions relaxed, and thus describes the money supply process in any modern monetary system.

12.3 Part 1: A Simple Illustration of the Inverted Pyramid

The restrictive assumptions: The following three assumptions are adopted in order to develop the basic insight into how the inverted pyramid works.

1 *Monopoly Depository Institution*; that is, there is only one depository institution, with many branches.
2 *Constant Level of Desired Currency Held by the Public*; that is, the public does not change the amount of currency it holds, no matter what happens to changes in the overall money supply. In terms of symbols, $\Delta C = 0$, where C represents currency held by the public.

3 *Constant Level of Desired Excess Reserves Held by the Monopoly Depository Institution*; that is, the monopoly depository institution does not change the amount of desired excess reserves (total reserves minus legally required reserves), no matter what happens to changes in overall money supply. In terms of symbols, $\Delta E = 0$, where E represents the desired level of excess reserves held by the monopoly depository institution.

All of the above three assumptions are unrealistic; however, they provide an easier path to understanding the money supply process, and, once this understanding is achieved, the restrictions can be removed.

Central banks create and destroy base money: The money supply process framework is based on the inverted pyramid model discussed at several points in previous chapters, and, in this framework, the central bank has the ability to increase or decrease base money in the inverted pyramid framework without any meaningful restrictions. Base money consists of reserves and currency created or destroyed by the central bank. The central bank, for all practical considerations, is not constrained by how much base money is created or destroyed, since base money is pure fiat money without any commodity reserve such as gold. The only "backing" of base money created by a central bank is the assets on the central bank's balance sheet, but in fact the assets are purchased with base money, so the assets provide no restriction on how much base money is created or destroyed.

To illustrate how this works, consider how the Federal Reserve can create $100,000 of base money by purchasing $100,000 of government securities in the open market from Joe Hickenlupper. How does the Federal Reserve pay for the securities? It could simply print $100,000 in Federal Reserve notes and hand them over to Joe, the seller of the government securities, as illustrated in the T account.

Federal Reserve balance sheet

Assets	Liabilities
Government securities	Federal Reserve notes
+$100,000	+$100,000

The Federal Reverse now owns the securities, as reflected by an increase in assets of $100,000, and has paid for the securities by issuing $100,000 in Federal Reserve notes, a liability of the Federal Reserve. This, however, is not the way the central bank normally purchases securities. Instead, the Federal Reserve writes out a check "payable to Joe", who in turn deposits the check in one of the branches of the monopoly depository institution at which he keeps his checking account. The monopoly depository institution sends the check to the Federal Reserve for payment. The Federal Reserve pays for the check by adding an equivalent amount to the reserve account of the monopoly depository institution. Technically, the securities purchased with the $100,000 in reserves "back" the created reserves, but, for all practical purposes, the promises to pay by the Federal Reserve are pure fiat money. The balance sheet in this case would change as illustrated.

Federal Reserve balance sheet

Assets	Liabilities
Government securities	Reserves of monopoly depository institution
+$100,000	+$100,000

In either case, base money increases by $100,000. Base money is also called *high-powered money*, because every $1.00 of base money in a fractional reserve system can support several dollars of checkable deposits; hence, base money is also high-powered money.

Now let's consider how the Federal Reserve can destroy base or high-powered money. The Federal Reserve destroys $100,000 of base money by selling to Joe $100,000 of its holdings in government securities in the open market. Holdings of government securities on the Federal Reserve balance sheet decrease. How does Joes pay for the securities? Joe could pay for the securities with Federal Reserve notes, in which case the balance sheet would change as illustrated.

Again, this would not be normal. Joe instead will write out a check payable to the Federal Reserve for the securities on a deposit account held at the monopoly depository institution. The Federal Reserve collects on the check by deducting the amount of the check from the reserve account held by Joe at the monopoly depository institution.

Federal Reserve balance sheet

Assets   Liabilities

Government securities   Federal Reserve notes

–$100,000   –$100,000

Federal Reserve balance sheet

Assets   Liabilities

Government securities   Reserves of monopoly depository
                                               institution

–$100,000   –$100,000

In either case, base or high-powered money decreases by $100,000.

The above example indicates why central banks are so powerful, because they can create and destroy base money by simply buying and selling securities by increasing and decreasing liabilities (central bank notes or reserves). While this involves a number of technical steps, the essential nature of the above example is that the central bank can create base money "out of thin air". Central banks don't like to describe their power in such simple terms, but, for all practical purposes, they do create base money out of thin air. Changes in base money then change the money supply.

Making an offer the market can't refuse: The reader might think the above example is unrealistic because it assumes Joe is willing to sell or purchase $100,000 of securities to or from the Federal Reserve. The above example works only if Joe is willing to sell securities to the Federal Reserve or purchase securities from the Federal Reserve. Is this realistic? Yes; one needs only to remember the famous line from the classic movie *The Godfather*: "I am going to make him an offer he can't refuse." In a sense, the Federal Reserve makes an offer to buy or sell securities the market can't refuse. In the case of buying securities, the Federal Reserve will simply bid up the price to purchase whatever securities it wants to purchase. In the case of selling securities, the Federal Reserve will simply lower the price to sell whatever securities it wants to sell.

One might object to this explanation by pointing out this is not a way to make a profit. Central banks do not conduct monetary policy to make a profit, however. Decisions to buy or sell securities are motivated by using monetary policy to influence economic activity. In any event, central banks can't help but be profitable, because they create base money out of thin air to purchase assets that, in turn, pay interest and principal. That is, a central bank can't help but make money, in terms of profit, when it makes money! In fact, central banks generate far more revenue than they require to conduct their operations, and they transfer back to government most of their revenues, because most was earned by holding government securities.

The money supply process with the three restrictions: Assume Joe sells $100,000 in government securities to the Federal Reserve. Joe deposits the check he receives from the Federal Reserve into his account at the monopoly depository institution. The institution sends the check to the Federal Reserve, which pays for the check by adding $100,000 to the institution's reserve account. The monopoly depository institution balance sheet will appear as illustrated

Monopoly Depository Institution balance sheet

Assets	Liabilities
Reserves	Transaction deposit of Joe Hickenlupper
+$100,000	+$100,000

Assume the reserve requirement, rr, on transaction deposits, T, is 20 percent. Total reserves have increased by $100,000, required reserves have increased by $20,000 and excess reserves have increased by $80,000. We have assumed the desired level of excess reserves is constant; hence, the monopoly depository institutions does not wish to hold the new excess reserves and would rather use them to make loans and earn a higher profit than earned on interest paid by the Federal Reserve on the excess reserves.

At first, one would think the institution would simply lend out the $80,000 – the level of excess reserves; however, this would not be optimal, because under a fractional reserve system much more than $80,000 can be loaned. The next balance sheet illustrates this point.

Monopoly Depository Institution balance sheet

Assets	Liabilities
Reserves	Transaction deposit of Joe Hickenlupper
+$100,000	+$100,000
Loans	Transaction deposit of Martha Murgatryod
+$80,000	+$80,000

A loan of $80,000 is made to Martha Murgatryod and the proceeds of the loan are made available to Martha by setting up a transaction deposit in her name in the amount of $80,000. How much have required reserves increased with transaction deposits now totaling $180,000? At rr = 0.20, required reserves increase from $20,000 to $36,000, which means excess reserves decline from $80,000 to $64,000. Clearly, more can be loaned to Martha. How much can the loan account increase?

Loans can be expanded until the reserve requirement on total transaction deposits is $100,000, because at that point excess reserves will be zero. What is the level of total transaction deposits at rr = 0.20 that will require $100,000 in reserves? If the institution makes a loan for $400,000 and credits that amount to Martha's new transaction deposit, total transaction deposits will be $500,000 (Joe's original deposit of $100,000 and the loan-generated transaction deposit of $400,000 for

Martha). Required reserves will be $100,000 and excess reserves will be zero. The balance sheet will appear as illustrated.

Monopoly Depository Institution balance sheet

Assets	Liabilities
Reserves	Transaction deposit of Joe Hickenlupper
+$100,000	+$100,000
Loans	Transaction deposit of Martha
+$400,000	+$400,000

Notice how the inverted pyramid works. The Federal Reserve created $100,000 in base money by purchasing $100,000 in securities from Joe, and the monopoly depository institution was able to loan out $400,000 to Martha and, in doing so, create $400,000 in transaction deposits. The total increase in M2 money is therefore $500,000, based on an increase in base money of $100,000. The relationship between the change in M2 and the change in base money is known as the *money multiplier.*

This process also works in reverse. If the Federal Reserve sold $100,000 in securities to Joe, Joe's transactions account would decline by $100,000, because the check he wrote to the Federal Reserve will be paid for by reducing the depository institution's reserve account at the Federal Reserve. The monopoly depository institution will now have no reserves to meet the reserve requirement for the $400,000 deposit created by the $400,000 loan to Martha and will need to reduce the $400,000 transactions account. As transaction deposits are reduced to pay off the loan, the institution will reduce its lending, so that loans and deposits will decline over time by $400,000. The end result would be a decline in M2 money by $500,000.

Dropping the first restriction of a monopoly depository institution: Instead of a monopoly depository institution we now assume the more realistic case of multiple depository institutions, each with separate balance sheets. How does this impact the above examples? The end result is the same. An increase (decrease) in base money by $100,000 will increase (decrease) M2 money by $500,000 over time. But the process to getting to the same end result differs.

In the monopoly case, the institution could make the maximum loan of $400,000 permitted with a reserve requirement of 20 percent without fear that any of the newly created transaction deposits will be transferred to other institutions. The funds would be spent, but those who received the funds would deposit the funds back into the same monopoly depository institution. In a multiple depository institutions system, however, the individual institution cannot loan out the maximum because it will be forced to transfer reserves it does not possess to other institutions that receive those checks. In a multiple system, and assuming that each dollar loan will be spent and likely be deposited in another depository institution, the institution cannot safely loan out any more than its excess reserves. By definition, the institution can lose its excess reserves to another institution and still meet its reserve requirements on the remaining transaction deposits. But the other institutions that receive funds will have excess reserves that can be loaned, and so on until the process is completed.

The balance sheets illustrate this point.

Depository institution no. 1 balance sheet

Assets	Liabilities
Reserves	Transaction deposit of Joe Hickenlupper
+$100,000	+$100,000
−$80,000	
Loans	Transaction deposit of Martha
+$80,000	+$80,000
	−$80,000

Depository institution no. 1 makes only an $80,000 loan to Martha, the amount of its excess reserve, because it assumes each dollar of that loan will end up in another depository institution. Martha spends the $80,000 on a classic car purchased from Flim Flam Motors. Flim Flam Motors deposits the $80,000 check in depository institution no. 2, which sends the check back to depository institution no. 1, which pays for the check by transferring $80,000 in reserves to no. 2. The reserve account at no. 1 is reduced to $20,000, which is sufficient to meet the reserve requirement

Depository institution no. 2 balance sheet

Assets	Liabilities
Reserves	Transaction deposit of Flim Flam Motors
+$80,000	+$80,000
−$64,000	
Loans	Transaction deposits of borrower
+$64,000	+$64,000
	−$64,000

Depository institution no. 3 balance sheet

Assets	Liabilities
Reserves	Transaction deposit of Flim Flam Travel
+$64,000	+$64,000
−$51,200	
Loans	Transaction deposit of borrower
+$51,200	+$51,200
	−$51,200

of the ramming transaction deposit of $100,000. The net increase in M2 money from no. 1 is $100,000.

The action now moves to no. 2, which has excess reserves of $64,000 as a result of receiving a deposit of $80,000 from Flim Flam Motors ($80,000 − 0.20*$80,000 = $64,000). No. 2 makes a loan for $64,000 and creates a transaction deposit for the borrower of $64,000, who, in turn, spends the funds on a excursion to Hawaii at Flim Flam Travel. Flim Flam Travel deposits the funds into depository institution no. 3, and so on. The net increase in M2 money from no. 2 is $80,000.

The action now moves to no. 3, which has excess reserves of $51,200 as a result of receiving a deposit of $64,000 from Flim Flam Travel ($64,000 – 0.20*$64,000 = $51,200). No. 3 makes a loan for $51,200, loses reserves of $51,200 in the check-clearing process when the borrower spends the funds, but retains reserves of $12,800, which is sufficient to satisfy the reserve requirement of the increased transaction deposits of Flim Flam Travel. The net increase in M2 money from no. 3 is $51,200.

The same transactions occur at depository institutions nos. 4, 5, 6 and so on, with each net increase in M2 money getting smaller and smaller because the available base money that is not being held as required reserves is getting smaller and smaller. Adding up all the net additions to M2 money will total $500,000 – the same result obtained with the monopoly depository institution assumption.

Hence, shifting from a monopoly to a multiple depository institution system makes no difference in the end result, only in the process of getting to the end result. Dropping the remaining two restrictions prevents us from using T accounts because they become too cumbersome and we need a more general framework to understand the relationship between the money supply process and monetary policy.

12.4 Part 2: The Money Supply Process in More Detail

The T accounts are not practical to develop the money supply process when we drop restrictions 2 and 3; however, they can be used to provide insight into how dropping restrictions 2 and 3 influence the money supply process. In the T accounts for depository institutions nos. 1, 2 and 3, we assumed that none of the deposits were withdrawn in the form of currency because we assumed the public did not change its holdings of currency despite the fact the M2 money supply changed. In the T accounts, we assumed that all of the excess reserves were used to support loans, since depository institutions did not change their desired level of excess reserves. Dropping these two restrictions significantly impacts the money supply process illustrated with the above T accounts.

Allowing for withdrawals of currency lowers the increase in M2 money supply in response to an increase in base money of $100,000; for example, if Joe withdraws $10,000 from his $100,000 deposit in the form of cash, depository institution no. 1 would have had to reduce its reserve by $10,000 to pay Joe $10,000 in currency. Total reserves will decline from $100,000 to $90,000. Required reserves would decline from $20,000 (0.20 × $100,000) to $18,000 (0.20 × $90,000) and, as a result, assuming no. 1 loaned its excess reserves, it would be able to loan Martha only $72,000 instead of $80,000. If we assume Flim Fan Motors withdrew some of the funds it received from Martha in currency, no. 2 would have fewer funds to lend, and so on. Thus, allowing for currency to increase as M2 money increases reduces the overall increase in M2 in response to the initial increase in base money of $100,000.

Allowing for changes in desired excess reserves also reduces the amount of M2 money that can be generated from an increase in base money; for example, assume no. 1 decided to hold onto $5,000 of the new reserves of $100,000 as desired excess reserves. Total reserves are still $100,000 and required reserves are still $20,000, but now desired excess reserves increase by $5,000, leaving $75,000 in excess reserves available for loans instead of $80,000. If no. 2 also decides to hold some of the reserves it receives as desired excess reserves, no. 2 will loan out less, and so on. Thus, allowing for increases in desired excess reserves in each depository institution as M2 money increases reduces the overall increase in M2 in response to the initial increase in base money of $100,000.

We can develop a money supply framework with some straightforward algebra that is general and allows for complications such as changes in currency and excess reserves by asking and answering two questions regarding the process described in part 1.

What starts the process? Answer: the process starts with a change in base money. While the change in base money in the above description was caused by the Federal Reserve purchasing securities from Joe, base money can change because of other actions by the Federal Reserve, as well as for other reasons besides actions of the Federal Reserve. Irrespective of the source of the change in base money, the process always starts from a change in base or high-powered money.

What stops the process? Answer: the process stops when the change in high-powered money is no longer available to support lending by depository institutions. In the above example, the change in high-powered money was absorbed by increased required reserves at each step. Once the entire change in high-powered money became required reserves, the process stopped. By dropping restrictions 2 and 3, withdrawals of currency and/or increased holdings of excess reserves also absorb the initial change in high-powered money.

Money multipliers: With the two questions and their respective answers, the entire money supply process can be represented by a series of expressions to derive money multipliers. We start first with an expression that defines the end of the money supply process in response to any change in base money:

$$\Delta H = rr\Delta T + \Delta C + \Delta E \qquad (12.1)$$

where the change in high-powered money, ΔH, is the initiating change that starts the process on the left-hand side of Expression 12.1 and on the right-hand side are the factors that absorb ΔH: changes in required reserves held against transaction deposits, $rr\Delta T$; changes in currency held by the public, ΔC; and changes in desired excess reserves held by depository institutions, ΔE. The absorbing factors reduce the availability of the initial change in H, as the process evolves over time and across different depository institutions to a point when the initial change in H is no longer supporting lending. At this point the equality between the initial change in high-powered money and the absorbing factors is the ending point and the process stops, as defined by Expression 12.1.

The change in required reserves is the reserve requirement times the change in transaction deposits subject to the reserve requirement. The reserve requirement is set by the Federal Reserve, and the change in required reserves is the reserve requirement, rr, times the change in transaction deposits, ΔT.

The change in currency held by the public is based on the assumption the public holds currency as a proportion of its transaction deposits:

$$C = kT \qquad (12.2)$$

where k is a fraction determined by economic, tax avoidance, technology and social/cultural factors. If k $= 0.25$, for example, for every $1.00 of transaction deposits the public will hold $0.25 in currency. How do economic, tax avoidance, technology and social/cultural factors influence the k ratio (C/T)?

Interest rates are an important economic factor influencing k. Since currency pays no interest, higher (lower) interest rates provide incentives to reduce (increase) the amount of currency held relative to transaction deposits; that is, k is inversely related to interest rates.

Higher (lower) income taxes provide incentives to increase (decrease) the ratio of "underground economy" transactions to "above the ground economy" transactions. Currency is the preferred medium of exchange in the underground economy. Drug dealers, for example, don't accept checks, and people who plan to avoid paying taxes on their receipts don't accept checks because they leave chicken tracks! That is, k is inversely related to income and related taxes, and, as such, k is often used as an indicator of the size of the underground economy.

Technology in the form of automatic teller machines (ATMs) influences k; for example, the increased spread of ATMs and their greater use by the public reduce the need for currency; that is, this type of technology reduces k.

An example of cultural and social considerations is the perception of safety and risk of being mugged. The higher (lower) the perception of risk, the lower (higher) k.

The change in desired excess reserves held by depository institutions is based on the assumption that depository institutions hold excess reserves as a proportion of their transaction deposits liabilities:

$$E = eT \qquad (12.3)$$

where e is a fraction determined by economic factors. The e ratio (E/T) is influenced by interest rates and risk. Lower interest rates and/or perceived higher risk tend to increase the e ratio while higher interest rates and/or perceived lower risk tend to decrease the e ratio. In addition, the interest rate paid by the Federal Reserve on excess reserves influences the e ratio.

Expressions 12.2 and 12.3 can be expressed in terms of changes as follows:

$$\Delta C = k \Delta T \tag{12.4}$$

$$\Delta E = e \Delta T \tag{12.5}$$

The next step is to rewrite Expression 12.1 so that the right-hand side variables are expressed in terms of ΔT:

$$\Delta H = rr \Delta T + k \Delta T + e \Delta T \tag{12.6}$$

Divide Expression 12.6 by ΔT and invert the resulting expression to obtain

$$\Delta T / \Delta H = 1/(rr + k + e) \tag{12.7}$$

The left-hand side of Expression 12.7 is called the transaction deposit multiplier, TM ($\Delta T / \Delta H$). TM indicates how much transaction deposits will change in response to a change in base or high-powered money; that is,

$$\Delta T = TM \Delta H$$

$$\text{where } TM = 1/(rr + k + e) \tag{12.8}$$

Based on the same reasoning, the currency multiplier, CM ($\Delta C / \Delta H$), and the desired excess reserve multiplier, ERM ($\Delta E / \Delta H$), can be derived:

$$\Delta C / \Delta H = k \Delta T / \Delta H = k/(rr + k + e) \tag{12.9}$$

$$\Delta C = CM \Delta H$$

$$\text{where } CM = k/(rr + k + e) \tag{12.10}$$

$$\Delta E / \Delta H = e \Delta T / \Delta H = e/(rr + k + e) \tag{12.11}$$

$$\Delta E = ERM \Delta H$$

$$\text{where } ERM = e/(rr + k + e) \tag{12.12}$$

The currency multiplier, CM, indicates the change in currency in response to a change in base money, and the excess reserve multiplier, ERM, indicates the change in desired excess reserves in response to a change in base money.

The money multiplier can be derived; however, the money multiplier depends on how one defines the money supply.

First, define the money supply as M1 (currency plus transaction deposits); then the change in M1 money supply is

$$\Delta M1 = \Delta C + \Delta T \tag{12.13}$$

Divide both sides of Expression 12.13 by ΔH, substitute the expressions for the currency and transaction multiplier and invert the resulting expression to obtain the M1 money multiplier, M1M $(\Delta M1/\Delta H)$:

$$\Delta M1/\Delta H = \Delta C/\Delta H + \Delta T/\Delta H$$

$$\Delta M1/\Delta H = k/(rr + k + e) + 1/(rr + k + e)$$

$$\Delta M1/\Delta H = 1 + k/(rr + k + e)$$

$$\Delta M1 = M1M\Delta H$$

$$\text{where } M1M = 1 + k/(rr + k + e) \tag{12.14}$$

The M2 money multiplier is based on an expanded definition of the money supply, and, for simplicity, assume that $M2 = C + T + MMF$, where MMF represents money market funds. Now that we have an additional component of the money supply, we need to indicate how the new component varies. Following the procedure used to indicate how currency and desired excess reserves fit into the money supply process, the following expression is used to incorporate MMFs:

$$MMF = mT \tag{12.15}$$

or

$$\Delta MMF = m\Delta T \tag{12.16}$$

The M2 money multiplier is thus defined in the following steps:

$$\Delta M2 = \Delta C + \Delta T + \Delta MMF \tag{12.17}$$

$$\Delta M2 = k\Delta T + \Delta T + m\Delta T \tag{12.18}$$

$$\Delta M2/\Delta H = k\Delta T/\Delta H + \Delta T/\Delta H + m\Delta T/\Delta H \tag{12.19}$$

$$\Delta M2/\Delta H = k/(rr + k + e) + 1/(rr + k + e) + m/(rr + k + e) \tag{12.20}$$

$$\Delta M2/\Delta H = (1 + k + m)/(rr + k + e) \tag{12.21}$$

$$\Delta M2 = M2M\Delta H$$

$$\text{where } M2M = (1 + k + m)/(rr + k + e) \tag{12.22}$$

12.5 An Illustration of the Money Supply Process

To illustrate how the money supply process works in terms of the various multipliers, assume the following:

1 Households desire to hold $0.25 in currency and coin for every dollar of checkable or transaction deposits; that is, $k = 0.25$.
2 Transaction deposits are subject to a 10 percent reserve requirement; that is, $rr = 0.10$.

3 Depository institutions desire to hold $0.05 in excess reserves for every dollar of checkable or transaction deposit liabilities; that is, e = 0.05.

4 Households desire to hold $0.50 in money market funds for every dollar of checkable or transaction deposits; that is, m = 0.50.

The values of the various multipliers can be determined by substituting the specific values in the appropriate expressions as follows.

The transaction deposit multiplier	TM	=	1/0.40	=	2.5
The currency multiplier	CM	=	0.25/0.40	=	0.625
The excess reserve multiplier	ERM	=	0.05/0.40	=	0.125
The M1 multiplier	M1M	=	(1 + 0.25)/0.4	=	3.125
The money market fund multiplier	MMFM	=	0.50/0.40	=	1.25
The M2 multiplier	M2M	=	(1 + 0.25 + 0.50)/0.4	=	4.375

To illustrate how these multipliers can be used to illustrate the money supply process, assume that $\Delta H = \$1,000$ and then calculate how each component of the money supply changes.

Transaction deposits	(2.5)($1,000)	=	$2,500
Currency based on k ratio	(0.25)($2,500)	=	$625
or currency multiplier:	(0.625)($1,000)	=	$625
Required reserves	(0.10)($2,500)	=	$250
Excess reserves based on e ratio	(0.05)($2,500)	=	$125
or excess reserve multiplier:	(0.125)($1,000)	=	$125
M1 money	(3.125)($1,000)	=	$3,125
Money market funds based on m ratio	(0.50)($2,500)	=	$1,250
or money market fund multiplier:	(1.25)($1,000)	=	$1,250
M2 money	(4.375)($1,000)	=	$4,375

All of the expressions developed and determined so far are based on the basic definition of the money supply process in Expression 12.1; that is, when the sum of the changes in the absorbing factors equals the initial change in base or high-powered money that started the process, the process is completed. To illustrate this point, the sum of the absorbing factors can be calculated and shown to be equal to the initial change in base money that started the process.

The absorbing factors are:

1 required reserves increase by $250;

2 currency increases by $625; and

3 desired excess reserves increase by $125.

Table 12.1. *Simple Central Bank Balance Sheet*

Assets	
	Loans to depository institutions, L
	Securities, S
	Foreign exchange, FE
	Other assets, OA
Liabilities	
	Central bank notes, CBN
	Reserve deposits held by depository institutions, RD
	Government deposits, GD
	Other deposits, OD
	Other liabilities, OL
Capital, CAP	
	Central bank stock
	Retained earnings

The sum of the absorbing factors is $1,000, which is the value of the initial change in base money. Notice that the addition of money market funds to the money supply process does not change the list of absorbing factors, since they are not subject to a reserve requirement.

12.6 Central Banks, Base Money, the Money Supply Process and Developments since 2007

The M2 money multiplier presented in Expressions 12.21 and 12.22 helps us understand how the money supply process and the inverted pyramid representation of a modern monetary standard work. The expressions are based on changes, but can just as easily be presented in terms of levels; that is, Expression 12.22 can also be presented as

$$M2 = M2M(H) \tag{12.23}$$

Can the Federal Reserve use the money supply process discussed to this point as the foundation for monetary policy? This question can be addressed by considering the following points.

First – can the central bank control base money, the monetary base or high-powered money? Yes. The Federal Reserve, as well as any central bank, essentially controls base or high-powered money even though base money has many non-Federal-Reserve influences. This point can be illustrated by a simple central bank balance sheet that applies to all central banks, though specific central bank balance sheets, such as that of the Federal Reserve, are far more complex. The simple balance sheet in Table 12.1 is sufficient to demonstrate how central banks control base money.

Central bank assets consist of loans made to depository institutions, L; securities, S; foreign exchange, FE; and other assets, OA. L represents lender of last resort services provided by the central bank; that is, when the central bank advances funds to depository institutions, L increases, and when these loans are repaid, L decreases. S represents securities held by the central bank and, most of the time, consists of government securities. When the central bank purchases securities, S increases, and when the central bank sells securities, S decreases. FE represent holdings of non-home-currency-denominated financial assets and OA represents other assets, such as buildings, etc.

Central bank liabilities consist of banknotes, CBN, such as Federal Reserve notes; reserve deposits, RD, held by depository institutions; government deposits, GD, since central banks are fiscal agents of their respective governments; other deposits, OD, such as deposits of other central banks, other governments or international government organizations; and other liabilities, OL.

The central bank, as a public corporation, has a capital account, CAP, consisting of paid-in capital stock and retained earnings.

The balance sheet in Table 12.1 can be rearranged to express RD in terms of all of the other components of the balance sheet as follows:

$$RD = (L + S + FE + OA) - (CBN + GD + OD + OL + CAP) \quad (12.24)$$

Expression 12.24 can be further simplified by eliminating OA, OL and CAP, because these accounts do not change as much as the other items and have little to do with the conduct of monetary policy:

$$RD = (L + S + FE) - (CBN + GD + OD) \quad (12.25)$$

Central bank notes outstanding, CBN, represent currency held by the public (C in the above expressions) and reserves held in the form of currency by depository institution; therefore, we can express central bank notes as $CBN = C + VC$, where VC is vault cash held by depository institutions. Therefore,

$$R = RD + VC = (L + S + FE) - (C + GD + OD) \quad (12.26)$$

where R represents total reserves held by depository institutions.

Base money or high-powered money is defined as $H = R + C$; hence, we can rearrange Expression 12.26 to show the relationship between H and the central bank's balance sheet:

$$H = (L + S + FE) - (GD + OD) \quad (12.27)$$

Do central banks control H? Yes. Let's first consider the determinants of H, with the exception of S. Central banks influence L through the discount rate and loan standards used to make loans to depository institutions, but depository institutions also play a role in the process; hence, central banks only partially determine L. Holdings of foreign exchange, FE, are largely determined by decisions of the government, since foreign exchange intervention decisions are made by government, not the central bank. Likewise, government deposits and other deposits are not under the control of the central bank.

In contrast, the central bank's holdings of securities, S, are under the control of the central bank for all practical purposes. This means the central bank can purchase or sell securities in the open market to offset or reinforce any other influence on base money to establish any desired level of base money. Central banks have significant control over base money, but does the central bank have the same degree of control over the money supply as suggested by the inverted pyramid?

Second – control over base money does not translate into control over M2 money: Does the ability to determine base money translate into significant control over the money supply? Not really, especially over shorter periods of time. The money supply is the product of the money multiplier and base money. While the central bank controls base money, the money multiplier is jointly determined by the public, depository institutions and the central bank. The only variable in the multiplier under the control of the Federal Reserve is the reserve requirement, rr. The k and m ratios are determined by the public; the e ratio is influenced by the Federal Reserve, because the Federal Reserve can set the interest paid on excess reserves, but the decisions of depository institutions play at least as important a role in determining the e ratio. Theoretically, if the central bank can statistically determine the value of the money multiplier over time, the central bank can predict the movement of the money multiplier and, combined with its control over base money, control the money supply. This has proved to be difficult, however. There have been periods when the Federal Reserve and other central banks focused on the money supply, but the instability of the money multiplier made it difficult to influence money in a predictable manner, especially over short periods of time. This is not to say the money supply is not tied to base money, but only to emphasize that the relationship is not sufficiently stable to provide a foundation for central bank policy.

Third – the M2 multiplier and the quantitative easing policy since 2007: According to Figure 12.1, the M2 multiplier (the large dashed line) trended upward from 1959 to the early 1980s, trended downward to the early 1990s, stabilized and then sharply trended downward starting about 2007. The period since 2007 is remarkable. The Federal Reserve adopted a quantitative easing policy (QEP) in 2008, designed to inject very large amounts of base money into the system to offset the decline in GDP. From 1959 to 2007 the monetary base increased on average by 6.7 percent and the M2 money supply increased 7.0 percent, suggesting a close relationship between changes in base money and money over a long period of time; however, from 2008 to 2015 base money increased 23.0 percent but M2 money increased only 6.5 percent.

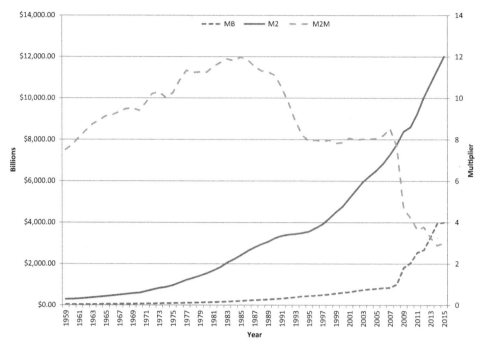

Figure 12.1. Monetary Base (MB), M2 Money Supply and M2 Money Multiplier (M2M), 1959 to 2015. *Source:* FRED, Federal Reserve Bank of St. Louis.

Base money since 2007 increased primarily because the Federal Reserve purchased large amounts of Treasury securities and mortgage-backed bonds. This is remarkable for two reasons: first, as a result of QEP, base money has increased more since 2007 than any time in the entire history of the Federal Reserve; and, second, QEP has not had the effect on the growth of M2 as predicted by past values of the money multiplier. Why?

The multiplier framework can provide some insight. An increase in the e ratio (excess reserves to transaction deposits) will lower the M2 multiplier so that, for any given increase in base money, the increase in M2 money is less. Until 2008 excess reserves earned zero interest, so that depository institutions had an incentive to maintain a low ratio of excess reserves to checking deposit liabilities. The average e ratio from February 1984 to August 2008 (Figure 12.2, solid line) was 0.002; that is, depository institutions held excess reserves on average equal to 0.2 percent of checking deposit liabilities. The sharp spike in the ratio in September 2001 is associated with the terrorist attack on the United States. The average e ratio from September 2008 to April 2016 was 1.3; that is, depository institutions since the financial crisis started with the collapse of Lehman Brothers in September 2008 are now holding excess reserves on average equal to 130 percent of checking deposit liabilities. This is one of the reasons for the significant decline in the value of the M2 multiplier in recent years, illustrated in Figure 12.1.

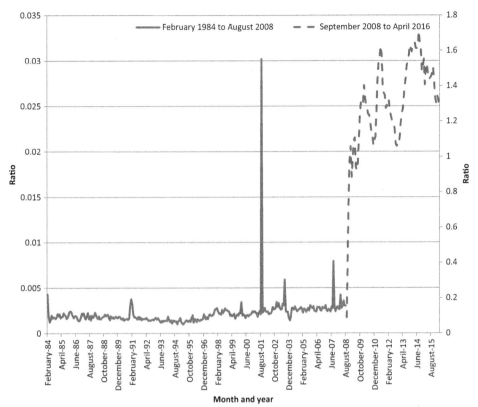

Figure 12.2. Ratio of Excess Reserves to Checking Deposits, February 1984 to April 2016. *Source:* FRED, Federal Reserve Bank of St. Louis.

There are two factors that account for the significant increase in excess reserves held by depository institutions since 2008. First, depository institutions have been reluctant to lend as the economy continues to operate below its potential even as of 2016; the Dodd–Frank Act of 2010 has imposed a number of restrictions that render depository institutions more risk-averse than previously; and the intense criticism of financial institutions as the cause of the Great Recession by many politicians has increased risk aversion. Second, since October 2008 the Federal Reserve has paid interest on both required and excess reserves. At present the rate on both required and excess reserves is 0.5 percent, or 50 basis points, and, combined with historically low interest rates and greater risk aversion, depository institutions have had an incentive to hold onto excess reserves that earn 0.5 percent.

The interest on required reserves is designed to offset the implicit tax on depository institutions for holding required reserves at zero interest. The interest on excess reserves is a new monetary policy tool, discussed in the next chapter, designed to assist the Federal Reserve in targeting the federal funds rate.

Fourth – are the inverted pyramid and money multiplier frameworks no longer useful for monetary policy? The inverted pyramid framework remains correct as a description of a modern monetary system, and, as predicted by the inverted pyramid framework, there is a positive relationship between base money and the money supply greater than one; that is, changes in base money generate a greater-than-one change in the money supply and, in turn, changes in the money supply influence economic activity.

At the same time, the framework is not sufficiently stable to be the foundation of monetary policy over the short run. In fact, the Federal Reserve, and central banks in general, have shifted attention away from the money supply to influencing interest rates as the channel for monetary policy to influence the economy, as discussed in the next chapter.

Chapter 13

Step 2: The Tools of Monetary Policy; and Step 3: Monetary Policy Instruments

13.1 Introduction

As part of the sequence of central bank policy, in Step 2 the central banks are seen to possess a set of tools used to influence base money, the money supply, credit and interest rates, and thereby influence general economic activity. The basic tools of monetary policy are the same for virtually all central banks. The tools of monetary policy are like the tool set used by a mechanic in an automobile repair shop. The mechanic knows how he/she wants to adjust the engine to improve performance (final target), but without a set of wrenches, sockets, electronic and other types of tools there is no way the intentions of the mechanic can be realized. Like the mechanic, central banks have a basic set of tools they apply to the financial sector, which, in turn, influences the overall economy.

The tools of monetary policy are directed to influence a policy instrument (Step 3), which in turn influences economic activity (Step 4), which in turn is designed to achieve the final policy target or targets (Step 5). There are two categories of policy instruments: first, measures of the money supply; and, second, key interest rates. Measures of the money supply are a quantity variable and include base money (the monetary base or high-powered money) and various measures of the money supply, such as M1, M2, etc. The key interest rate is a price variable, and is the interbank interest rate or the federal funds interest rate in the United States.

This chapter discusses the tools of monetary policy, issues regarding the choice of policy instrument, and the policy instruments used by the Federal Reserve.

13.2 The Tools of Monetary Policy and the Decline of Selective Tools

The tools of monetary policy are divided into three categories: general tools, selective tools and announcement tools, or what the Federal Reserve once referred to as "moral suasion", more recently referred to as "forward guidance".

The general tools are designed to influence the overall supply of loanable funds to the economy while the selective tools, in contrast, are designed to influence the supply of loanable funds to specific sectors of the economy. That is, the general tools are focused on the overall supply of credit, permitting the market to allocate the overall supply of credit, while the selective tools are focused on the allocation of credit determined by the central bank. Another analogy can help make the distinction. Consider a large forest. The general tools are focused on influencing the overall size of the forest and not concerned with how individual trees fall or grow to achieve an overall change in the size of the forest. The selective tools are focused on influencing specific trees in the forest, even though changes in specific trees impact the overall size of the forest.

In practice, the general tools emphasize the general impacts while selective tools highlight the selective impacts. At one time central banks relied on both general and selective tools; however, selective tools have become a relatively minor part of the tools of monetary policy used by most central banks. Setting margin requirements by the Board of Governors is the only remaining selective tool of monetary policy available to the Federal Reserve. At one time it was thought that increasing the margin requirement would limit credit going into the stock market while lowering the margin requirement would increase credit going into the stock market. This turned out to be incorrect, and, while margin requirements are still a selective tool of the Federal Reserve, the fact they have not been used since 1974 indicates their effective demise. In 1974 they were set at 50 percent, and they have not been changed since.

What accounts for the reduced reliance on selective tools of monetary policy? There are five reasons. First, they simply don't work very well. Credit is fungible, and any effort to influence the amount of credit in any part of the financial system is likely to generate innovations to circumvent the selective control. The margin requirement, for example, can be circumvented by using general credit to purchase equities rather than a security loan that uses the securities as collateral. Second, selective controls are administratively expensive and cumbersome to implement; they require a large amount of resources. Third, selective controls in the past have often had unintended consequences and generated economic and financial distress; for example, interest rate controls over consumer credit have hurt the very groups they were designed to protect, and Regulation Q interest rate ceilings on saving and time deposits were directly responsible for the collapse of the S&L industry in the 1980s. Fourth, selective credit controls are inconsistent with the open and competitive financial systems that have developed during the past four decades as a result of deregulation and financial liberalization. Fifth, the general tools, especially open market operations, are far more effective in influencing economic activity than any selective tool of monetary policy.

13.3 General Tools of Monetary Policy

The general tools of monetary policy are designed to influence base money, the money supply and interest rates. There are three traditional general tools and two new general tools that are utilized by the Federal Reserve. The traditional general tools are: open market operations; discount policy; and changes in reserve requirements. The two new general tools of monetary policy are: interest paid on excess reserves, introduced in 2008; and the term deposit facility, introduced in 2010. The two new tools have not been used to any great extent, there is uncertainty as to how they will be used in the future and there is debate as to whether they effectively contribute to the Federal Reserve's ability to conduct monetary policy.

Open market operations: Open market operations are reflected by the Federal Reserve's holdings of security (S in Table 12.1) and were used to illustrate the money supply process in the T accounts in Chapter 12. Whenever the Federal Reserve purchases securities, reserves of depository institutions increase and, hence, base money increases, dollar for dollar. Whenever the Federal Reserve sells securities, reserves of depository institutions decrease and, hence, base money decreases, dollar for dollar.

Open market operations are divided into permanent and temporary operations. *Permanent open market operations* involve the outright purchase and sale of Treasury securities, government-sponsored enterprise debt securities and mortgage-related securities without any commitment to the sellers and purchasers, respectively. *Temporary open market operations* include purchases of these securities under agreements to resell to the dealer at a set time, amount and price (*repurchase agreement, repo or RP*) and sales of these securities under agreements to repurchase from the dealer at a set time, amount and price (*reverse repurchase agreement, reverse repo or reverse RP*). The RP temporarily increases base money and the reverse RP temporarily reduces base money. Technically, RPs and reverse RPs involve buying to resell and selling to repurchase securities, but in essence they are short-term collateralized loans that rarely extend beyond 14 business days. In the past temporary open market operations were used to offset short-term movements in reserves, but, since QEP, RPs have become the primarily tool used to target the federal funds rate, as the Federal Reserve has not significantly engaged in permanent open market operations for a number of years since the 2008/2009 financial crisis.

Open market operations have historically been the most important tool of monetary policy for a number of reasons, discussed below; however, since 2007 the securities used in open market operations have changed significantly. Up through 2007 open market operations were confined mainly to operations in Treasury securities, but as part of the quantitative easing policy, starting in 2008, the Federal Reserve has not only greatly expanded its holdings of Treasury securities but also made open market purchases of mortgage-backed bonds to support the housing sector.

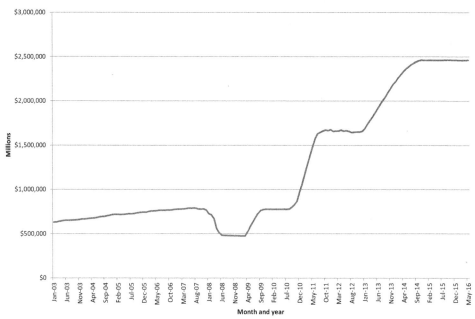

Figure 13.1. Holdings of Treasury Securities by the Federal Reserve, January 2003 to May 2016. *Source:* FRED, Federal Reserve Bank of St. Louis.

Figure 13.1 shows the Federal Reserve's holdings of Treasury securities from January 2003 to May 2016, and indicates a dramatic increase after 2007. Figure 13.2 indicates the Federal Reserve's holdings of mortgage-backed securities from January 2003 to May 2016. The Federal Reserve held no mortgage-backed securities prior to February 2009. The holdings of both Treasury securities and mortgage-backed bonds have changed little since late 2014 as the Federal Reserve has rolled over these securities to maintain their level. Since then the Federal Reserve has relied on temporary open market operations to target the federal funds rate, as well as using the two new tools discussed below.

Open market operations account for the overwhelming source of base money. Federal Reserve assets as of May 18, 2016, were $4.47 trillion; of this amount, Treasury securities represented 55.0 percent and mortgage-backed securities represented 39.4 percent.

Discount policy: This is, essentially, the lender of last resort function of the central bank, available to assist depository institutions to manage their liquidity requirements in times of distress. Discount policy actually consists of two components, referred to as the *cost effect* and the *administration effect*. The cost effect occurs when the Federal Reserve changes the discount rate to increase the cost or reduce the cost of borrowing from the Federal Reserve. The administration effect occurs when the Federal Reserve sets the loan standards for borrowing by depository institutions.

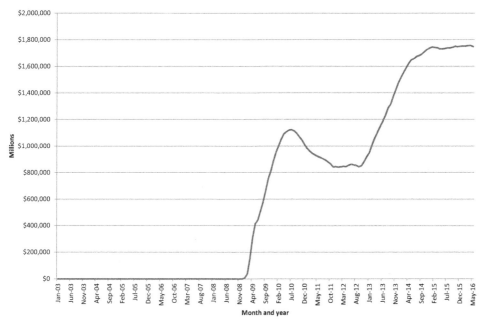

Figure 13.2. Mortgage-Backed Securities Held by the Federal Reserve, January 2003 to May 2016. *Source:* FRED, Federal Reserve Bank of St. Louis.

Increased lending by the Federal Reserve increases reserves dollar for dollar. In the following balance sheets, the Federal Reserve makes a loan to depository institution no. 1.

Federal Reserve balance sheet

Assets	Liabilities
Loan to depository institution no. 1	Reserve deposit of depository institution no. 1
+$100,000	+$100,000

Depository institution no. 1 balance sheet

Assets	Liabilities
Reserves	Loan from Federal Reserve
+$100,000	+$100,000

When no. 1 pays off the loan, reserves and base money decline. In the first decade of the Federal Reserve the discount policy was regarded as the primary tool of monetary policy, designed to serve two purposes: control the money supply and provide the channel for lender of last resort services. The discount policy was never a very effective general tool of monetary policy, because it is rather inflexible and the initiative does not reside completely with the Federal Reserve. The Federal Reserve can set the discount rate and loan standards, but the depository institutions have to come to the Federal Reserve in order for the discount policy to work.

The discount policy plays a relatively minor role in determining base money. As of May 18, 2016, outstanding loans to depository institutions represented only a fraction of a percent of Federal Reserve assets. During periods of economic and financial distress, however, such as in 2008 and 2009, loans can become a large component of base money.

Changes in reserve requirements: The Federal Reserve can set the tier 3 reserve requirement from 8 to 14 percent, and it has been 10 percent for over two decades. However, since the current reserve requirement system became effective in 1986, the tool has been used only once, in 1991 and 1992, when the reserve requirement on Eurodollar and large CDs was reduced from 3 to 0 percent and when the tier 3 reserve requirement on checking accounts was reduced from 12 to 10 percent. Changes in the reserve requirement, represented by rr in the above expressions, do not change reserves or base money but, rather, change the size of the money multiplier. Increasing rr reduces the size of the multiplier and reduces the money supply for any given level of base money. Decreasing rr increases the size of the multiplier and increases the money supply for any given level of base money.

Reserve requirements are not an effective tool of monetary policy. They are powerful – in fact, too powerful and inflexible. Even small changes in the reserve requirement generate large changes in the money supply; for example, using the value of the M2 money multiplier of 4.375 determined in the Chapter 12 example, if rr increases from 0.10 to 0.11, the money multiplier declines to 4.268 – and the money supply declines by 2.5 percent. More important, frequent changes in the reserve requirement would be burdensome to depository institutions and administratively difficult to implement, since depository institutions meet reserve requirements on a lagged basis. In other words, the current reserve requirement is based on an average of deposits over a past period, such as two weeks.

It is unlikely that reserve requirements will be used as a general tool of monetary policy given they have been unchanged for over two decades and the Federal Reserve has expressed no indication they will be used in a flexible manner in the future. Reserve requirements are important, however, because they are the major foundation of the inverted pyramid representation of a modern monetary standard.

Paying interest on excess reserves: The Federal Reserve pays interest on required reserves to mitigate the fact that a reserve requirement without interest is an implicit tax, since required reserves cannot be used to generate interest income. The Federal Reserve pays interest on excess reserves because, according to the Federal Reserve, paying interest provides it with better ability to target interest rates. If the target federal funds rate were 2 percent, depository institutions with excess reserves would have an incentive to supply excess reserves to the federal funds market at rates well below 2 percent, since excess reserves earned 0 percent. This would make it more difficult for the Federal Reserve to achieve a 2 percent federal funds rate; however, by paying interest on excess reserves, starting October 2008, the Federal Reserve can place a floor on the federal funds rate by providing a disincentive for depository institutions to supply funds at rates below the interest rate on excess reserves. This has become increasingly important since 2008 to the present. Until 2008 excess reserves held by depository institutions were small, generally representing less than 10 percent of total reserves, but starting with QEP, in late 2008, excess reserves have increased significantly (Figure 13.3) as a percentage of total reserves.

There are at least three rationales for the new general tool of monetary policy. First, paying interest on excess reserves allows the Federal Reserve to better target the federal funds rate in the presence of large holdings of excess reserves. Second, paying interest provides another method to influence money and credit by influencing the e ratio in the money multiplier, to provide incentives for depository institutions to hold excess reserves at a level appropriate for the goals of monetary policy. Third, the Federal Reserve has indicated that, at some point, it will reduce the historically high levels of assets and base money generated after 2008 so that the Federal Reserve will have better control over the level of excess reserves as it pursues an "exit strategy".

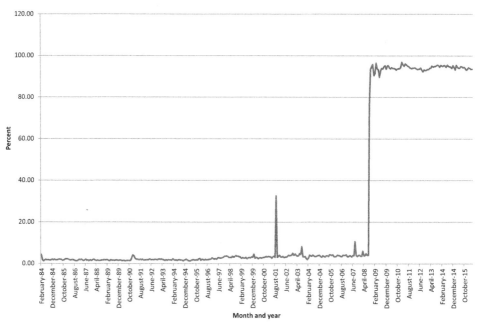

Figure 13.3. Excess Reserves as a Percentage of Total Reserves of Depository Institutions, February 1984 to May 2016. *Source:* FRED, Federal Reserve Bank of St. Louis.

Term deposit facility: The Federal Reserve offers term deposits to depository institutions, much like depository institutions offer large CDs to the public. By varying the interest paid on term deposits the Federal Reserve can influence the amount of deposits purchased by depository institutions. An increase in interest paid, which in the recent past has been slightly above the rate paid on reserves, provides an incentive for depository institutions to purchase term deposits, which, in turn, reduces reserves and base money. A decrease in interest paid has the opposite effect. To date term deposit transactions have been relatively small, and it is not clear what role they will play as a general tool of monetary policy in the future.

13.4 Moral Suasion and Forward Guidance

There is a long history of central banks trying to influence behavior in the financial system, through announcements ranging from closed-door meetings with representatives of the financial system to speeches by central bank officials and central bank announcements. At one time the Federal Reserve referred to this policy approach as "moral suasion", and defined the policy as an effort to persuade depository institutions and the financial system to behave in a certain manner without using the force of the traditional tools of monetary policy. The "moral" part of the policy is to remind depository institutions and the financial system to conduct their operations not only for individual profit but with an economy-wide or public policy perspective. The "suasion" part involves efforts to persuade depository institutions and the financial system to conduct their operations in line with the objectives of the Federal Reserve without having to make any change in the general or selective tools of monetary policy.

Moral suasion continues to be used by the Federal Reserve and many central banks, and, in some instances, has evolved into forward guidance, as used by the Federal Reserve and Bank of Japan. The difference between moral suasion and forward guidance is determined by differences in the degree of transparency of the intention and the degree to which the intention is binding. Moral suasion is a communication of a general intention or concern of the central bank, without details on the intended action of the central bank if the market does not follow the central bank's intension. A well-known and now famous example of this type of moral suasion is a speech given by then governor Alan Greenspan in 1996. Stock prices were increasing rapidly and there was concern both within and outside the Federal Reserve of a stock market bubble. Greenspan reminded his audience that the then current stock market appeared to be governed by *irrational exuberance* instead of economic fundamentals. The phrase quickly became a part of the economic and financial language. Despite Greenspan's warning, the Federal Reserve did nothing of significance to slow the increase in stock prices, which continued for another three years.

Forward guidance is much more specific and presents a public promise to follow a specific policy in the context of a specific set of conditions; for example, both the previous governor, Ben Bernanke (2006–2014), and the current governor, Janet Yellen (2014 to present), have made it clear in speeches and announcements that the Federal Reserve will maintain low interest rates for a period of time and indicated the conditions that would require an increase in interest rates. Forward guidance is thus a specific announcement of what the central bank intends to do under certain circumstances and is designed to anchor public expectations of what the central bank will do in the future.

Are moral suasion or forward guidance useful tools of monetary policy? While forward guidance is a form of central bank transparency, and thus contributes to improved central bank performance in general, both moral suasion and forward guidance suffer from two basic problems. First, the central bank is seldom clear as to what it will do under what conditions; that is, moral suasion is not always as transparent as claimed. Second, and more important, the impact of central bank policy is achieved through actual operation of the traditional tools of monetary policy. It is action rather than words that are important.

13.5 The Monetary Policy Instruments

There are two basic policy instruments used by central banks: the money supply and interest rates. The first is a quantity variable that includes base money and various measures of the money supply, and the second is a price variable represented by

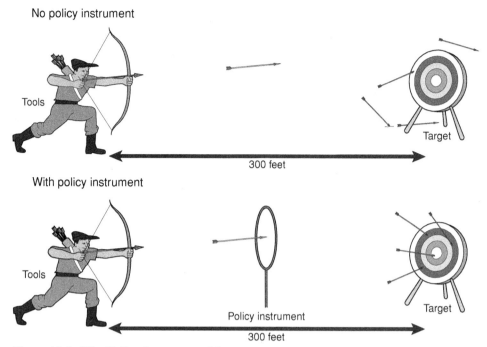

Figure 13.4. Why Policy Instruments Matter.

an interbank interest rate. Policy instruments are also referred to as intermediate targets of monetary policy, as opposed to final policy targets (Step 5). The policy instruments can be understood by considering the following four issues. First, why does the central bank target a policy instrument? Second, how does the central bank use the general tools to target the policy instruments? Third, can the central bank target both money and the interest rate at the same time? Fourth, which policy instrument is best?

Why policy instruments? Figure 13.4 illustrates why policy instruments are important. There is a great deal of "economic distance" between the central bank (Step 1) and the final policy targets (Step 5).

Think of the final policy target as an archery target at one end of the football field with the central bank at the other end. The tools of monetary policy (Step 2) are the arrows let loose by the central bank (Step 1), but 300 feet is a long distance. Many of the arrows miss the target surface entirely while those that hit the target surface have a low probability of hitting the bullseye. Also, the misses provide little information on how to adjust the pull of the bow and the angle of the arrow, because it takes a long time for an arrow to travel 300 feet and the target surface is not easily visible from that distance. This is monetary policy without policy instruments.

Now place an intermediate target at the 50-yard line in the form of a rod with a wire circle on top. The length of the rod and the circumference of the circle need to have a meaningful relationship with the bullseye at the end of the field on the target surface. Assuming the rod's length and size of the circle are designed properly, if the central bank can fire an arrow through the circle the probability is high the arrow will hit the target surface, and there is now a reasonable probability of getting a bullseye. The probability of hitting the intermediate target is much greater than hitting the final target. Also, failure to get the arrow through the intermediate target provides feedback information as to how the pull on the bow and angle of the arrow need to be adjusted to get the arrow through the intermediate target and achieve the final target objective. This is monetary policy with policy instruments. Figure 13.4 also illustrates why policy instruments are often referred to as intermediate targets of central bank policy.

The general tools and the policy instruments: The general tools influence the money supply and interest rates. First, consider how the tools influence the money supply.

The money multiplier framework shows how each of the tools influence the money supply. Open market operations and the discount policy change base money. Open market purchases increase reserves and base money while open market sales decrease reserves and base money. A lower discount rate and/or less restrictive loan standards increase reserves and base money while a higher discount rate and/or more restrictive loan standards decrease reserves and base money. Changes in reserve requirements change the value of the money multiplier rather than base money. Increases in reserve requirements decrease the money supply while decreases in reserve requirements increase the money supply for any given level of base money.

The two new tools also have predictable effects on the money supply. Higher (lower) interest on excess reserves decreases (increases) the money supply by decreasing (increasing) the money multiplier. Higher (lower) interest on term deposits offered to depository institutions decreases (increases) reserves and base money.

Second, to the extent that the general tools influence base money and the money supply, do they influence interest rates as well? Any increase in reserves and base money contributes to a rightward shift in the supply of loanable funds and reduces interest rates. Any decrease in reserves and base money contributes to a leftward shift in the supply of loanable funds and increases interest rates. Even though changes in reserve requirements do not change reserves or base money, they will still influence interest rates. A decrease in reserve requirements will shift the supply of loanable funds to the right since part of required reserves becomes excess reserves and is now available to support more lending by depository institutions. An increase in reserve requirements will shift the supply of loanable funds to the left, since any excess reserves will become required reserves and depository institutions will reduce lending.

Table 13.1 summarizes how each of the general tools influence the money supply and interest rates.

Table 13.1. *Response of the Money Supply and Interest Rates to the General Tools of Monetary Policy*

Open market operations	Money	Interest rate
Outright open market operations		
Purchase securities	↑	↓
Sell securities	↓	↑
Temporary open market operations		
RP (purchase securities with agreement to resale)	↑	↓
Reverse RP (sell securities with agreement to repurchase)	↓	↑
Discount policy		
Decrease discount rate and/or decrease loan standards	↑	↓
Increase discount rate and/or increase loan standards	↓	↑
Change reserve requirements		
Decrease reserve requirements	↑	↓
Increase reserve requirements	↓	↑
Interest on excess reserves		
Decrease interest on excess reserves	↑	↓
Increase interest on excess reserves	↓	↑
Term deposit facility		
Decrease interest on term deposits	↑	↓
Increase interest on term deposits	↓	↑

Can the central bank target both the money supply and interest rates at the same time? No. If the central bank targets the interest rate, the money supply will have to change to ensure that the interest rate target is met, while, if the central bank targets the money supply, the interest rate will have to change to ensure that the money supply target is met. Figures 13.5 and 13.6 illustrate this point.

In Figure 13.5, panel A, the central bank targets the interest rate at 10 percent, which we assume is the equilibrium interest rate determined by DLF_1 and SLF_1. SLF_1 has embedded in the function a \$10 billion M2 money supply. As we discussed earlier, however, there are many fundamentals that influence the demand for and supply of loanable funds: changes in income, institutional factors that influence demand and supply, uncertainty, risk and expected profits, government deficits, inflationary expectations, etc. As a result, the demand and supply functions will shift and change the equilibrium interest rate. If the central bank targets the interest rate at 10 percent it will be required to change the money supply to offset movements in the demand and/or supply function; for example, panel B indicates a shift in the demand function to the right from DLF_1 to DLF_2 as a result of an increased government deficit, causing the market interest rate to increase from 10 to 12 percent. The central bank is thus required to increase the money supply to, say, \$20 billion, and thus shifts the supply function to the right from SLF_1 to SLF_2 to offset the upward pressure on the interest rate and maintain the interest rate at the target

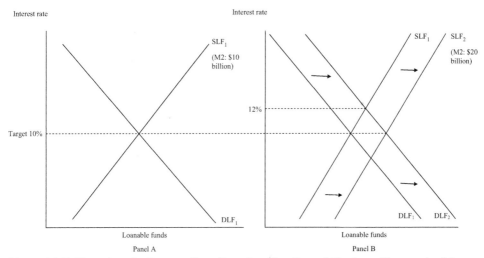

Figure 13.5. Targeting the Interest Rate Requires the Central Bank to Change the Money Supply to Achieve the Interest Rate Target.

level of 10 percent. Thus, targeting the interest rate requires the central bank to use the money supply to achieve the target.

Figure 13.6, panel A, illustrates a money supply target of $10 billion embedded in the supply function, SLF$_1$, but, again, demand and supply change over time and change the equilibrium interest rate. If the central bank continues to target the money supply at $10 billion, the interest rate needs to change to bring the demand for and supply for loanable funds into balance. Thus, targeting the money supply

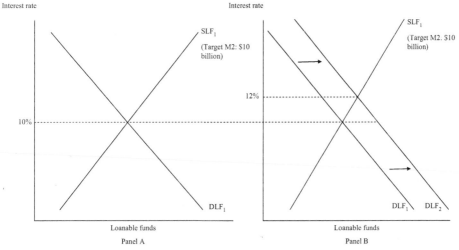

Figure 13.6. Targeting the Money Supply Requires the Central Bank to Permit the Interest Rate to Change to Achieve the Money Supply Target.

requires the central bank to permit the interest rate to fluctuate to achieve the money supply target. In panel B, the demand for loanable funds shifts to the right from DLF_1 to DLF_2 as a result of an increased government deficit. In order to target the money supply at the $10 billion embedded in the supply function, the central bank will have to allow the interest rate to increase from 10 percent to 12 percent, as illustrated in panel B. Thus, targeting the money supply requires the central bank to allow the interest rate to change to achieve the target.

Which policy instrument is best? Monetary policy can influence the real economy through either the money supply or the interest rate channel. One policy instrument is not correct and the other incorrect – both are correct; however, there are practical issues to determine a preference for one or the other.

In the past half-century central banks have largely used interest rates as the policy instrument, with the exception of a short period in the 1980s when central banks, including the Federal Reserve, focused on the money supply. That money-supply-focused policy was considered unsuccessful, and central banks returned to targeting interest rates. There are four practical reasons why central banks use interest rates as the policy instrument.

First – definitional issues: The money supply is not an easy variable to define, and, even if one can reasonably measure money at a point in time, financial innovation will likely change the definition of money over time. Even though M2 money stock is widely accepted as a reasonable definition of the nation's money supply, it remains an imprecise definition of money. Interest rates in contrast are easy to define.

Second – measurement issues: Even if one accepts M2 as "the" definition of money, statistically M2 cannot be accurately measured on a week-to-week or even month-to-month basis, seriously limiting its usefulness as a policy instrument. Interest rates can be measured accurately day by day and even within the day.

Third – control issues: Central banks have less control over the money supply than they did in the past as a result of variation in the money multiplier, which many attribute to the wider range of financial assets available to the public as the result of deregulation and financial liberalization. In contrast, central banks do have significant influence over short-term interest rates. At the same time, this advantage has a caveat. While central banks can influence very short-term interest rates, their influence over medium- and long-term interest rates is much less certain. The longer the term of the interest rate, the more important inflationary expectations.

Fourth – relationship to economic activity issues: At various times there has been a close and direct relationship between money and economic activity; however, the relationship between money and economic activity during the past several decades has become unstable for ongoing monetary policy. Central banks have turned to the interest rate channel in the belief it provides a better foundation connecting the tools of monetary policy with the final policy targets.

Despite arguments in favor of interest rates as the policy instrument, the money supply remains fundamentally important, because, over the longer run, inflation and deflation are inherently related to the growth rate of the money supply. A central bank that puts the money supply on the back burner and focuses only on interest rates is a central bank that will finds its policy to be one of "trouble in River City".

Chapter 14

Step 4: The Central Bank Model of the Economy

14.1 Introduction

Step 1 of the sequence of central bank policy focused on the institutional design of the central bank in general and the institutional design of the Federal Reserve in particular. The actual formulation and execution of monetary policy are concentrated in a central committee in most central banks. In the case of the Federal Reserve, the FOMC is the center point of the formulation and execution of monetary policy.

Step 2 of the sequence focused on the monetary policy tools and how the central bank, in the context of the money supply process, is able to influence the money supply, interest rates and credit. Central banks and the Federal Reserve possess a variety of general monetary policy tools, but for all practical purposes open market operations are *the* tool of monetary policy, because they are powerful and flexible and the initiative to use the tool resides solely with the central bank, whereas the other tools lack at least one of these characteristics.

In Step 3 of the sequence, the tools are directed toward one of two monetary policy instruments – the monetary aggregates or interest rates – in order to increase the probability of monetary policy achieving its final policy target or targets. The central bank can target only one instrument because the other instrument is required to change in order to achieve the target of the chosen instrument. Monetary aggregates are, ultimately, an important part of central bank policy, because in the long run inflation or deflation are directly related to the monetary aggregates, but in the shorter run the interest rate is the preferred policy instrument.

This chapter moves to Step 4 and provides an overview of the evolution, historical development and current version of macroeconomic models to understand the formulation and execution of monetary policy.

14.2 Macroeconomic Models of the Economy: Beginnings

Central bank policy from the time central banks began to function in the eighteenth and nineteenth centuries has always been conducted in the context of some understanding of the interrelationships between important macroeconomic variables of the economy – GDP, unemployment, prices, money, interest rates, credit, etc. – and how central bank policy actions influence specific variables (policy instruments) to influence other variables (final policy targets). Macroeconomic models of the economy first became part of the discussion of political economy as early as the late eighteenth century, when a group of French political economists developed the *Tableau économique* – a simple macroeconomic model of an economy. However, it wasn't until the early post-WWII period that macroeconomic models became an important part of economics and central bank policy. Two developments elevated the role of models for central bank policy.

First, in *The General Theory*, published in 1936, Keynes provided a set of building blocks or basic tools to develop macroeconomic models of the economy. While much of the original Keynesian model has not withstood the test of time, the lasting contribution of Keynes was to provide a set of tools or building blocks that permit the rigorous development of macroeconomic models used by central banks. Aside from the other contributions of Keynes, which continue to be debated, central bank policy owes a debt to Keynes for providing the framework to build macroeconomic models to guide monetary policy.

Second, in order to determine whether the macroeconomic model provides a reasonable description of the relationships between the variables in the model, the model must be subject to empirical verification. The verification involves a tremendous amount of complex estimation that was not possible until after WWII, when computer technology for the first time permitted economists to subject their various hypothesis about economic variables and models to empirical testing. By the 1960s macroeconomic modeling and estimation had become a standard part of central bank policy and economic research in general.

14.3 Why Models Are Important and the Historical Evolution of Models

The model used by the central bank is important for three reasons.

1 The model provides insight into the long-run equilibrium of the economy; for example, is there a tendency for actual real GDP to return to potential real GDP (PGDP) or is it possible for actual GDP to persist above or below PGDP for long periods of time? Or, if GDP has a tendency to return to PGDP, is the transition to equilibrium stable or unstable and is the transition rapid or slow? The answers to these questions are fundamentally important regarding the inherent stability or instability of a market economy and the need for an activist government to stabilize the market economy.

2 Governments attempt to influence the economy by fiscal and monetary policy to achieve specific goals, such as a specific GDP growth rate, inflation, etc., or to reduce the fluctuations in economy activity (for example, reducing the fluctuations in the GDP gap). Fiscal policy consists of changing government spending and taxes to influence aggregate demand while monetary policy consists of changing the money supply to change interest rates and credit and, thereby, change aggregate demand. The model provides insights into whether fiscal or monetary policy can influence the economy as claimed, the channels of influence and whether one government policy is preferable to the other. In this regard, the model provides insight into which final policy target is reasonable.

3 With regard to monetary policy, the model provides the "road map" of how to use the tools of monetary policy to target a policy instrument, which, in turn, influences the real sector with the objective to achieve the final policy target or targets.

There are three historical stages of the basic macroeconomic model used by central banks: the Classical period (1776 to 1936); the Keynesian period (1936 to 1970s); and the Neoclassical and Neo-Keynesian period (1970s to present).

Classical period (1776 to 1936): Adam Smith's *Wealth of Nations*, published in 1776, outlined a simple system of natural liberty. Self-interest and competitive markets in the context of limited government would provide incentives to individuals to maximize their own individual wealth and, hence, the nation's economic wealth, as if led by an "invisible hand". That is, competition would ensure that the nation's potential output was as high as possible given its resource base and technology, as well as provide incentives to innovate and expand markets to increase potential output over time. Some writers raised an issue that perhaps Smith's engine of production might produce too much, generate overproduction or underconsumption and generate a long-term "glut". In 1803 a French political economist, J. B. Say, answered this concern. Say hypothesized a law of supply and demand to answer this question that came to be known as Say's law of markets. Say's law states that "supply creates its own demand", because the act of production generates the income necessary to purchase the output, and, hence, while short-term gluts are possible, long-term gluts are not possible as long as competition and flexible prices and wages adjust in response to excess supply or demand in any market.

Say's law of markets is inherent in the QTM introduced in Chapter 2:

$$MV = PY \tag{14.1}$$

where M is the nation's money supply; V is the velocity of money, indicating how rapidly money is exchanged for goods and services; Y is real GDP; and P is the price level.

V is considered stable in the long run and Y is at its potential level in the long run as a result of flexible prices, wages and interest rates. Output in the long run is at its potential level because any difference between actual and potential GDP or difference between actual and natural unemployment would generate changes in prices, wages and interest rates to eliminate any excess supply or demand in the market. The essence of Say's law of markets is that departures of actual GDP from potential GDP are possible, but self-correcting forces will return GDP to its potential or natural equilibrium in the long run.

In the short run, changes in M impact V and Y as well as P, but, after markets adjust to the change in the money supply, V will return to its long-run level and Y will return to its potential level. P is the only variable in the QTM that will adjust to the change in the money supply in long-run equilibrium. That is, money is nonneutral in the short run, in that changes in M will impact both output and prices, but in the long run money is neutral in that it has no impact on the real performance of the economy other than to change prices (and nominal wages and nominal interest rates) in a one-to-one relationship.

Fiscal policy should focus on a balanced budget, and efforts to use government spending and/or taxes to generate deficits to stimulate the economy were not required and, if pursued, would have no net effect on the economy even in the short run because government deficits "crowded" out private spending.

The basic elements of the QTM were understood by the end of the nineteenth century, but the complete model with Say's law of markets would not be specified until the early post-WWII period. The Classical period lacked the macroeconomic model building blocks, which would not be developed until Keynes. Despite the lack of a detailed specification of the Classical model at the time of the Classical period, the implications of the model were widely understood and widely accepted.

1 A competitive market economy is inherently stable and does not require an activist government to achieve economic stability or economic growth.

2 Government should play a nonactivist and minimal role by providing for the protection of private property; certain public goods, such as roads, bridges and other infrastructure; and national defense.

3 Government budgets should be balanced, and efforts by government to use taxes and/or spending to influence the economy are not necessary because the economy is inherently stable and will grow at its long-run potential. In addition, any effort to influence the economy by increased government spending without changing taxes (deficit spending) is subject to "crowding out"; that is, a $1.00 increase in government spending is offset by a $1.00 decrease in private spending. The Classical model views government spending as neutral even in the short run because of these crowding-out effects. The Classical view of government budgets was to spend as little as possible and offset that necessary spending with tax revenues; that is, the government budget should be balanced over time.

4 Monetary policy is nonneutral in the short turn, but neutral in the long run.

5 Monetary policy, in the sense of controlling the nation's money supply, should be nonactivist and focus on providing a money supply that meets the needs of trade and maintains price stability over the long run; that is, in the context of the QTM, M should grow to satisfy any changes in V and P over time in such a manner that P remains constant. On occasion, the central bank should provide lender of last resort services to maintain financial stability.

6 The gold standard and fixed exchange rates are viewed as an effective constraint on excessive monetary and/or fiscal policy. Excessive monetary growth will generate current account deficits that, in turn, will lead to an outflow of gold to the surplus country and correct the excessive monetary growth. Insufficient monetary growth will generate current account surpluses, which, in turn, will lead to an inflow of gold and correct the insufficient monetary growth.

The industrialized world during much of the nineteenth century accepted these basic views of how the economy functioned, the limited role of government and the nonactivist role of monetary policy. During much of this period monetary policy was nonactivist and constrained by the need to maintain a fixed exchange rate.

The Keynesian period (1936 to 1970s): The Great Depression in the United States and much of the Western world was a major turning point in economic models and policy. The Great Depression officially started in the United States, according to the NBER, in August 1929, preceding the October 1929 collapse of the stock market. The deep collapse of the economy contradicted the Classical perspective: markets did not appear inherently stable and there was little evidence the economy would return to its potential level of output. There was intense pressure on government to shift from a nonactivist to an activist mode. The crisis was as much political as economic, given that four countries, based on different economic and political institutions, appeared to have avoided the Great Depression: Hitler's Germany, Stalin's Russia, Mussolini's Italy and Hirohito's Japan. These four countries were not based on competitive market economies, limited government and democratic political institutions; hence, the Great Depression was not only an economic crisis but a political crisis for market-oriented economies.

In *The General Theory*, Keynes rejected the Classical model, based on the QTM and Say's law of markets, offered an alternative model of how the macroeconomy functioned, explained why periods such as the Great Depression occurred and, most importantly, offered a set of policies rooted in expanded government that were required to stabilize a market economy. The model introduced by Keynes differed from the Classical perspective in the following ways.

1 The market economy was inherently unstable and required an activist government to achieve economic stability and economic growth. Say's law of markets was incorrect. Aggregate demand or total spending, not aggregate supply, determined economic activity.
2 The Great Depression was due to insufficient aggregate demand from the private sector, and, as a result, actual GDP would remain below its potential and actual unemployment would remain above its natural level as long as private spending was insufficient. There was no market mechanism to stimulate private aggregate demand, and, even if one existed, "[i]n the long run we are all dead", to quote Keynes.
3 Government should play a large and activist role in the economy beyond the basic functions accepted in the Classical period. In particular, governments needed to manage aggregate demand.

4 Government had a responsibility to use fiscal and monetary policy to stabilize the economy by managing aggregate demand. Fiscal policy could increase (decrease) aggregate demand by increased (decreased) spending or decreased (increased) taxes. Monetary policy could increase (decrease) aggregate demand by increased (decreased) money to then decrease (increase) interest rates. Fiscal policy had a direct effect on aggregate demand while monetary policy had an indirect effect on aggregate demand through the financial system.

5 Keynes suggested fiscal policy was a more effective tool than monetary policy because fiscal policy had a direct effect on aggregate demand while monetary policy's indirect effect was like "pushing on a string", because of certain relationships between money, interest rates and investment.

6 Fiscal and monetary policy had the ability to influence real output in both the short and long run; that is, unlike the Classical model, fiscal and monetary policy were nonneutral in both the short and long run.

It is difficult to overstate the impact *The General Theory* had on macroeconomic modeling and public policy in the first part of the post-WWII period. The view that government was able to manage aggregate demand and offset the inability of a private market economy to achieve economic stability, full employment and economic growth was widespread.

Neoclassical–Neo-Keynesian period (1970s to present): The Keynesian perspective dominated economic modeling, fiscal policy and monetary policy for several decades until the early 1960s, when a debate known as the monetarist–Keynesian debate emerged. The monetarist component of the debate refers to the fact the discussion was initiated by a debate over the role of money in the economy, but soon spread to a larger number of issues. The debate lasted about two decades, and by the late 1970s the Keynesian model and public policies based on the model were found wanting in many respects.

The original Keynesian perspective was replaced with a more rigorously restated version of the Classical model and QTM. The debate covered many economic issues and impacted macroeconomic modeling and public policy not only in the United States but throughout much of the world. The monetarist–Keynesian debate was part of a broader reevaluation of the role of government in the economy far beyond just monetary and fiscal policy. The debate focused on the role of government regulation and administrative influence over economic forces in general, and even over the structure of political institutions. In the last part of the twentieth century the outcome of the debate led to major institutional changes in the role of government, as most countries permitted a greater role for market forces in the allocation of resources, both domestically and internationally, than they had previously.

Four outcomes of the debate are particularly notable with respect to the Keynesian model and its policy implications.

First – no long-run glut: The Keynesian view that actual GDP could be in equilibrium below its potential – a long-run glut – was based on specific assumptions about labor markets. Flexible prices and wages were an important part of the self-correcting mechanism of a market economy in the Classical view. Keynes, however, argued that, while wages were flexible in an upward direction with increased demand for labor, they were rigid in a downward direction in the face of decreased demand for labor. This was due to "money illusion", or an inability on the part of workers to distinguish between nominal and real wages, with workers focused only on nominal wages. Workers resisted reductions in nominal wages even if the fall in wages was less than the fall in the general price level, which would increase real wages. The downward rigidity of nominal wages eliminated an important market mechanism for reducing any excess supply of labor.

Research suggested this assumption was inconsistent with economic theory, in that continued inability to distinguish between nominal and real wages was difficult to accept over time. The actual behavior of nominal and real wages also contradicted the assumption of downward wage rigidity. Once the assumption of downward wage rigidity was dropped, the Keynesian model became a more sophisticated version of the Classical model, with flexible wages and prices. That is, though the framework was Keynesian, the voice of the QTM and Say's law of markets emerged.

Second – monetary policy more powerful than fiscal policy: Keynes and many Keynesians regarded monetary policy as a weak tool of stabilization and instead emphasized fiscal policy as *the* stabilization tool. The view that monetary policy was impotent while fiscal policy was potent depended on specific assumptions about the channels of monetary and fiscal policy to influence total spending. Economic theory and empirical evidence, however, showed these assumptions to be incorrect. In fact, the empirical evidence suggested monetary policy even in the Keynesian model was far more powerful than fiscal policy. By the 1970s the crowding-out effects of fiscal policy were widely accepted, though considerable debate remains even to the present regarding the size of the crowding-out effect to increased government spending.

Third – fiscal policy and monetary policy do not determine the long-run growth path: Monetary policy and fiscal policy have both been shown to be neutral in the long run, and much of the research raised questions as to whether fiscal policy could be nonneutral even in the short run. In other words, neither policy could change the long-run growth of the economy by managing aggregate demand, and the long-run performance of the economy was more the result of aggregate supply, not aggregate demand.

Fourth – Keynesian activist policies contributed to economic and financial distress: The Keynesian perspective promised that activist government management of the economy would smooth out the business cycle, maintain full employment, encourage economic growth and achieve a reasonable rate of inflation. Keynesian activist policies based on both fiscal and monetary policy by the 1970s, however, were largely responsible for high and unstable inflation rates throughout much of the world. These policies were based on a version of the Keynesian model known as the Phillips curve, to be discussed below. Not only did the activist policies generate high rates of inflation, they also generated high rates of unemployment, or "stagflation": the worst of both worlds – high inflation and high unemployment. In the United States, policies based on Keynesian activist fiscal and monetary policy were directly responsible for the Great Inflation.

Nor did government management of financial flows fare much better. The managed fixed exchange rate system collapsed in 1973 and the extensive set of interest rate regulations and portfolio controls in domestic financial systems were responsible for intense financial and economic distress in many countries. In the United States, the collapse of the S&L industry can be directly traced to the combination of inflationary monetary policy and efforts to administer the financial system through interest rate ceilings and portfolio constraints.

In sum, these four outcomes – that the economy eventually returns to its potential output in the long run; monetary policy is a more effective tool of stabilization than fiscal policy; monetary policy is nonneutral in the short run but neutral in the long run; and fiscal and monetary policies based on the Keynesian model were largely responsible for the Great Inflation in the United States as well as inflation throughout much of the world for over two decades – are generally accepted. In addition, while the debate started over the role of money in the economy (hence the reference to the monetarist–Keynesian debate), the debate was far more extensive than one over money. As a result, it shifted to a debate between Keynesians and non-Keynesians. However, while there is general agreement about the above four issues, there are other aspects of the debate that remain unresolved. Two aspects of the continuing debate are especially important for the formulation and conduct of monetary policy.

First, a major difference between the new or neo-Keynesian and non-Keynesian perspectives that continues to the present is the degree to which the private economy is inherently unstable or stable and how long it takes the self-correcting mechanism of the market to return the economy to long-run equilibrium. Keynesians regard the private sector as unstable, and, even if the economy eventually returns to its potential performance, the process is not smooth nor rapid. It is not smooth because private spending, especially investment spending, is driven by "animal spirits" and, hence, is unstable. The phrase "animal spirits" was used by Keynes in the 1936 *General Theory* to characterize private investment spending. Keynesians no longer emphasize rigid wages but, instead, argue that "sluggish" wage and price adjustments due to "frictions" make any return to long-run equilibrium long and painful. Embedded in this view is a statement made by Keynes in 1923 regarding how long it took for the economy to adjust to a change in the quantity of money: "In the long run we are all dead." The Keynesian perspective now accepts the Classical view that, in the long run, Say's law of markets is correct; however, Keynesians regard this as an interesting theoretical result that has little importance for the role of government to manage aggregate demand to offset demand and supply shocks to the economy.

Non-Keynesians dispute these claims. In the absence of government policy, the private economy is far more stable and the return to equilibrium is far quicker than claimed by Keynesians. They attribute much of the instability and less than rapid return to equilibrium to government policy, not some inherent instability in the market. They argue that much of the apparent instability in the economy, especially the most intense periods such as the Great Depression, Great Inflation and Great Recession, are the outcome more of policy mistakes by the government than of any inherent instability in the private sector. That is, while Keynesians emphasize market failure and the need for government stabilization to offset market failure, non-Keynesians emphasize government failure and the need to shift to a nonactivist role for government.

Second, as a result of the Keynesian view that the private economy is inherently unstable and driven by "animal spirits", combined with the view monetary policy is a more effective stabilization tool than fiscal policy, Keynesians regard monetary policy as *the* stabilization tool, and believe monetary policy should be flexible, have more than one final policy objective and not be restrained by "rules". That is, monetary policy should be formulated and executed by "enlightened discretion" rather than any rule (Blinder, 1999, p. 49), or what has more recently been labeled "constrained discretion" (Bernanke, 2003).

In contrast, non-Keynesians regard "enlightened discretion" or "constrained discretion" as a source of many policy errors made by central banks. In particular, central banks under "enlightened discretion" have a tendency to emphasize employment over price stability, have a tendency to maintain easy monetary policy even when the evidence suggests a shift to tighter policy is desirable and have a tendency to overreact to demand and supply shocks because of lags in the effect of policy. The issue of lags is important, and will be discussed in the next chapter. In addition, "enlightened discretion" renders central banks more susceptible to political influence. As a result, non-Keynesians argue that central bank policy should be restrained by rules that clearly focus on final policy targets that the central bank is capable of achieving and for which it should be held accountable for achieving.

The two perspectives of central bank policy were most clearly stated over four decades ago by two of the major participants in the monetarist–Keynesian debate, Franco Modigliani and Milton Friedman.

Modigliani in his 1976 presidential address to the American Economic Association stated the Keynesian perspective as follows (Modigliani, 1977, p. 1, emphasis in original):

> In reality the distinguishing feature of the Monetarist school and the real issues of disagreement with non-Monetarists [Keynesians] is not monetarism but rather the role that should probably be assigned to stabilization policies. Non-Monetarists accept what I

regard to be the fundamental practical message of the *General Theory*: that a private enterprise economy using an intangible money *needs* to be stabilized, *can* be stabilized, and therefore *should* be stabilized by appropriate monetary and fiscal policies.

Friedman, a decade earlier in his 1967 presidential address to the American Economic Association, warned that the type of monetary policies advocated by Keynesians would have adverse outcomes on the economy (Friedman, 1968, p. 6):

> [W]e are in danger of assigning to monetary policy a larger role than it can perform, in danger of asking it to accomplish tasks that it cannot achieve, and, as a result, in danger of preventing it from making the contribution that it is capable of making.

The two perspectives persist to the time of this writing, but history and economic research suggest the Keynesian perspective has not fared well. History shows that monetary policy mistakes, especially during the Great Depression, the Great Inflation and, most recently, the Great Recession, have contributed to much economic and financial distress, not just in the United States but in other countries. In some cases, central banks have learned from their mistakes, but the tendency to manage the economy is difficult to resist, especially when governments use central banks to postpone making difficult structural reforms in the economy. We will return to this issue in the closing chapter of this book.

14.4 After Keynes: Evolution of the Central Bank Model of the Economy

It is now time to provide a detailed technical discussion of models in order to understand central bank policy as they evolved after the Keynesian assumption of downward wage rigidity was replaced with the Classical assumption of flexible prices and wages. There are two complementary model perspectives that provide insight into the model behind current central bank formulation and execution of monetary policy – the Phillips curve and the aggregate demand/supply model. Both illustrate the same points and provide the same policy implications, as well as provide a framework to understand the continuing debate between the Keynesian and non-Keynesian perspectives of central bank policy.

14.5 The Rise of the Phillips Curve

Keynesian models in the early post-WWII period began to move away from simply assuming downward wage rigidity to explain multiple macroeconomic equilibria, in which full employment was only one possible outcome, and the nonneutrality of monetary policy in the long run. Economics focused more on "frictions" in wage and price adjustments that prevented market forces to work as rapidly as claimed by the Classical economists. The most influential contributor to this new perspective of the Keynesian model was A. W. Phillips.

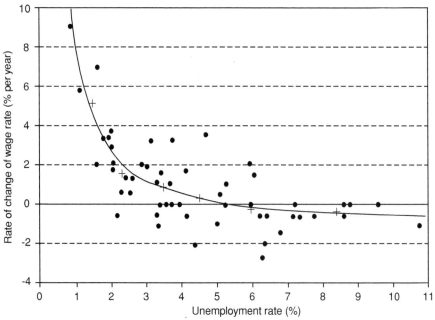

Figure 14.1. The "Old" Phillips Curve Relationship between Wage Inflation and Unemployment, Published by A. W. Phillips in 1958. *Source:* Phillips (1958), p. 295.

Phillips in 1958 suggested and estimated a statistical relationship between wage inflation and unemployment (Phillips, 1958). Phillips hypothesized the following relationship between wage inflation and unemployment:

$$w = f(UN) \tag{14.2}$$

where w is the annual percentage change in nominal wages; the unemployment rate, UN, is a measure of excess supply in the labor market; and the functional relationship is inverse – that is, higher (lower) unemployment generates lower (higher) inflation.

The original estimated relationship was based on percentage changes in nominal wages and the unemployment rate for the United Kingdom from 1860 to 1913, and is presented in Figure 14.1. The fitted curve is the solid line while the dots are the scatter points of data coordinates. It should be noted that Phillips was not the first to suggest such a relationship, but the 1958 paper by Phillips is considered the foundation paper for a body of literature on the Phillips curve that emerged in the first part of the post-WWII period.

The fitted relationship indicated a statistically significant inverse relationship between wage inflation and unemployment. Phillips expressed the hypothesis and estimated the curve in terms of wage inflation, but the relationship can just as easily be expressed in terms of percentage changes in the price level, making the reasonable assumption that there is a direct relationship between wages and prices.

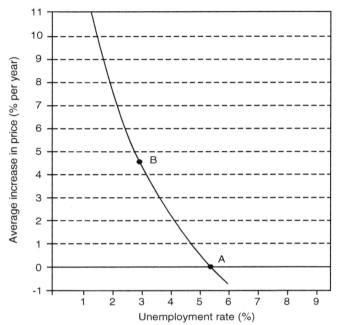

Figure 14.2. The Samuelson–Solow "Old" Phillips Curve Relationship between Inflation and Unemployment – an Approximation for 1960. *Source:* Samuelson and Solow (1960), p. 192.

In 1960 Paul Samuelson and Robert Solow, both eventual Nobel Prize winners, reviewed similar data for the United States and, based on 25 years of data on inflation and unemployment, offered their perspective on the Phillips curve (Figure 14.2). The Phillips curve in Figure 14.2 was not an estimated curve but an approximated curve based on a review of the data. Samuelson and Solow were among the first, however, to claim the Phillips curve could be used to guide demand management policies; for example, the government could manage aggregate demand to achieve either point A (lower inflation but higher unemployment) or point B (higher inflation but lower unemployment).

The two papers generated an intensive effort to estimate the Phillips curve for different countries, different time periods and different data sets, and within a few years the Phillips curve had become an important expression of the Keynesian perspective and Keynesian policies. Four reasons account for the widespread acceptance of the Phillips curve at that time.

First, the Phillips curve relationship appeared statistically robust, in that many studies found that a simple regression between price inflation (or wage inflation) and unemployment appeared to fit the data and appeared stable over time.

Second, the Phillips curve incorporated the Keynesian view an economy did not always equilibrate at full employment. Equilibrium in terms of inflation and unemployment could occur anywhere along the Phillips curve; that is, the economy could equilibrate at the upper left-hand part of the curve, with low unemployment and high inflation, or at the lower right-hand part of the curve, with high unemployment and low inflation. In other words, Say's law of markets did not apply, since equilibrium could occur at any point of unemployment (output), but only one point was associated with full employment. In technical terms, there were multiple equilibrium outcomes of the economy depending on aggregate demand only one of which was full employment.

Third, the Phillips curve focused on two important variables representing the economic welfare of the public – inflation and unemployment – and indicated that government aggregate demand management could "purchase" higher real economic performance (lower unemployment) by stimulating the economy with more inflation. Likewise, lower inflation rates could be "purchased" with slower economic growth by using aggregate demand management to reduce spending. The hypothesized relationship suggested a long-run tradeoff between two important indicators of economic welfare that governments could exploit with aggregate demand management.

Fourth, the Phillips curve suggested other government policies to better manage the economy and increase economic growth. Aggregate demand management could move the economy along a given Phillips curve, but institutional changes could shift the curve to the left so that any inflation rate would be associated with a lower unemployment rate. Institutional changes such as job training programs to increase skills; labor exchange information networks to better match jobs with those looking for work; better education; and wage and price controls were all advocated as policies to shift the Phillips curve to the left, thus improving economic welfare.

The Phillips curve became the foundation of monetary policy for over two decades in the 1960s and 1970s. It was widely used to illustrate the policy choices facing monetary policy and used to rationalize the role of government stabilization policy, as emphasized by Modigliani (1977). The Phillips curve was a standard and important part of textbooks in monetary economics and macroeconomics. It is difficult to overstate the influence the Phillips curve had on monetary policy and government demand management policy in general, as well as efforts to restructure the economy.

14.6 The Fall of the Phillips Curve and Rise of the "New" Phillips Curve

In the 1970s and 1980s the stable Phillips curve disappeared. Panel A of Figure 14.3 indicates the typical inverse relationship between inflation and unemployment for the 1960s, but in the 1970s and 1980s the Phillips curve relationship is no longer apparent (panel B of Figure 14.3). In fact, during much of the Great Inflation period, in the United States and other countries, there was a positive relationship between inflation and unemployment – stagflation. In fact, it was during this time that the

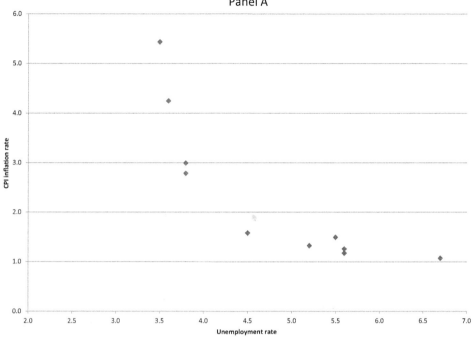

CPI inflation and unemployment rates, 1960 to 1969
Panel A

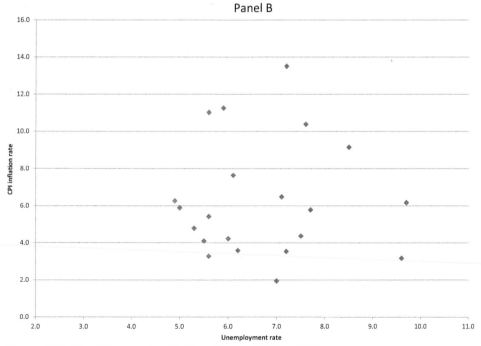

CPI inflation and unemployment rates, 1970 to 1990
Panel B

Figure 14.3. The Disappearing Phillips Curve, 1960 to 1990.

"misery index" was coined, defined as the sum of the inflation rate and the unemployment rate.

There were two reactions to the disappearance of the Phillips curve. First, those who regarded the Phillips curve as an important foundation for monetary policy attempted to reestablish the relationship by including various control variables – changing the demographics of the labor force, as females became a larger part of the labor force, or expected inflation – to reflect a shifting Phillips curve that might be better able to account for the type of inflation/unemployment coordinates illustrated in panel B of Figure 14.3. These efforts were largely unsuccessful, and, even if a set of control variables could have been identified to account for a shifting Phillips curve, the usefulness of the relationship for aggregate demand management was greatly diminished. The attraction of the Phillips curve was that it was a stable relationship between two important variables subject to influence by government policy.

Second, as part of the monetarist–Keynesian debate, Edmund Phelps and Milton Friedman, who would both eventually receive Nobel Prizes, demonstrated that the Phillips curve relationship was fundamentally flawed, as was the underlying Keynesian model, and could not be used as a foundation for monetary or fiscal policy. They revised the Phillips curve relationship in the context of the Classical macroeconomic model, referred to as the natural unemployment rate hypothesis, or, for simplicity, the "new" Phillips curve. In the "new" version, there is a short-run Phillips curve that is dependent on the expected inflation and a long-run Phillips curve that is independent of inflation. Combined, they show that monetary policy is nonneutral in the short run, but neutral in the long run. Hence, there is no way government demand management can exploit a claimed tradeoff between inflation and unemployment.

The "old" Phillips Curve was based on an inverse relationship between inflation and unemployment, as given in Expression 14.2; however, this expression implies an unrealistic view of how wage contracts are established. The demand for and supply of labor are dependent on real wages and not nominal wages, though, institutionally, the worker and employer can only bargain over the nominal wage. Nonetheless, it is the real wage that determines their willingness to supply and demand labor, respectively. Expression 14.2 needs to be rewritten as follows:

$$w - p = f(UN) \qquad (14.3)$$

where w is the percentage changes in nominal wages, p is the percentage change in the general price level and UN is the actual unemployment rate.

Expression 14.3 needs to be further rewritten, because it is not the current inflation rate that is of concern to workers and employers but the expected inflation rate over the period of the wage contract:

$$w - p_e = f(UN) \qquad (14.4)$$

where p_e is the expected inflation rate.

Expression 14.4 still needs further rewriting, because UN is not a reliable measure of excess supply or demand in the labor market. Excess demand or supply has meaning only with reference to a base, and that base is the natural unemployment rate, NUN. That is, if UN > NUN there is excess supply of labor and if UN < NUN there is excess demand for labor. Hence, the rewritten expression is

$$w - p_e = f(NUN - UN) \tag{14.5}$$

or, in terms of price inflation,

$$p - p_e = f(NUN - UN) \tag{14.6}$$

The "new" Phillips curve in Expression 14.5 or 14.6 is fundamentally different from the "old" Phillips curve. The Phillips curve incorporates expected and actual inflation, and the relationship between actual and natural unemployment depends on their relationship.

This can be illustrated in two steps. First, we consider the mechanical implications of Expression 14.6; and, second, we then provide a narrative of how the new Phillips curve functions to generate the mechanical results.

Mechanically, the new Phillips curve implies the following relationships between actual GDP and potential GDP, PGDP, and between actual unemployment, UN, and natural unemployment, NUN:

$$\text{If } p > p_e, \text{ then UN} < \text{NUN and GDP} > \text{PGDP}$$

$$\text{If } p < p_e, \text{ then UN} > \text{NUN and GDP} < \text{PGDP}$$

$$\text{If } p = p_e, \text{ then UN} = \text{NUN and GDP} = \text{PGDP} \tag{14.7}$$

These mechanical relationships can be understood by considering Figure 14.4. The vertical line is the long-run Phillips curve, LRPC, indicating there is no relationship between natural unemployment and the inflation rate. The natural unemployment rate is determined by the resource base of the economy, labor participation, productivity, capital accumulation, efficiency of the labor and product markets and technology. Changes in these fundamental determinants will shift the LRPC to the right or left, but the natural unemployment rate for which the LRPC is defined is not influenced by the inflation rate, since it is vertical at the natural unemployment rate.

To see why the LRPC is vertical at the natural unemployment rate, consider how equilibrium employment and the natural unemployment rate are determined in the labor market, illustrated by Figure 14.5. The demand for labor is an inverse function of the real wage rate (W/P); that is, as the real cost of labor declines, the quantity of labor demanded increases. The supply of labor is a positive function of the real wage rate; that is, as the real return from working increases, the quantity of labor supplied increases. The equilibrium employment is N_1 at $(W/P) = 1.0$. The amount of unemployment associated with N_1 determines the natural unemployment rate,

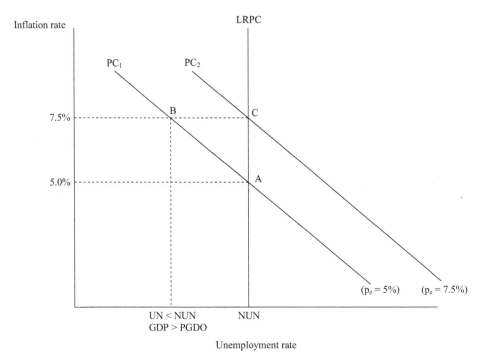

Figure 14.4. The "Old" and "New" Phillips Curves in the Context of Expansionary Monetary Policy.

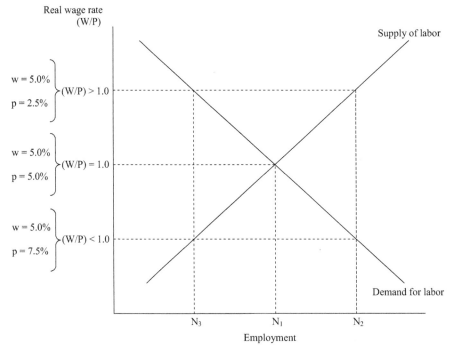

Figure 14.5. Equilibrium Employment in the Long Run and the Natural Unemployment Rate are Independent of the Inflation Rate.

NUN. If the actual inflation rate is 5 percent then, in order for the real wage to equal 1.0, wage inflation must also be 5 percent. That is, workers require 5 percent wage growth at a 5 percent inflation rate to supply N_1 workers. Employers are willing to employ N_1 workers at a 5 percent wage growth factor because they expect the prices of the products they sell and their nominal profit to also increase by 5 percent; therefore, a 5 percent wage growth factor maintains the real wage rate of 1.0. What happens if the inflation rate increases or decreases?

Assume the actual inflation rate increases to 7.5 percent. With a 5 percent wage growth factor the real wage rate declines to less than 1.0 and the quantity of labor demanded will increase from N_1 to N_2, but the quantity of labor supplied will decline from N_1 to N_3. There is now an excess demand for workers, which cannot be satisfied if wages continue to grow at 5 percent. The wage rate growth factor will be bid up to 7.5 percent and eliminate the excess demand. When the higher inflation rate of 7.5 percent is incorporated into wage contracts, the equilibrium employment remains unchanged at N_1. That is, the real wage rate remains the same whether the inflation rate and wage growth are 5 percent or 7.5 percent. Now assume the actual inflation rate decreases from 5 percent to 2.5 percent With a 5 percent wage growth factor the real wage rate increases above 1.0 and the quantity of labor demanded decreases from N_1 to N_3, but the quantity of labor supplied increases from N_1 to N_3. There is now an excess supply of workers, which drives down the growth of wages until the excess supply is eliminated. The wage growth factor declines from 5 percent to 2.5 percent, the equilibrium real wage is 1.0 and the equilibrium employment is N_1. That is, the real wage rate remains the same whether the inflation rate and wage growth are 5 percent or 2.5 percent.

Figure 14.5 shows that equilibrium employment and the associated natural unemployment rate are determined by real variables – the real wage rate and how the real wage rate influences the quantity of labor supplied and demanded. Whatever the inflation rate, the market will require the wage inflation factor to equal the inflation rate so as to maintain the equilibrium real wage rate. Hence, in the long run, after wages adjust to the excess demand for or supply of workers, the equilibrium employment and natural unemployment rate are independent of the inflation rate – the LRPC is vertical at the natural unemployment rate.

Back to Figure 14.4. PC_1 is a short-run Phillips curve with an embedded expected inflation rate of 5 percent. PC_1 intersects the LRPC at an actual inflation rate of 5 percent (point A); hence, the actual and expected inflation rates are the same, indicating UN = NUN and GDP = PGDP.

Why is the economy in equilibrium when the actual and expected inflation rates are identical in Figure 14.4 at point A? All economic decisions and economic contracts are determined by real rather than nominal prices; that is, the demand for and supply of labor are dependent on the real wage rate and not nominal wages, and the supply of and demand for loanable funds are dependent on the real interest rate and not the nominal interest rate. Focusing on these two markets in the economy, the labor market is in equilibrium when the real wage is equal to the demand for and supply of labor, and the real interest is equal to the supply of and demand for loanable funds. How do these two markets incorporate any given inflation rate?

The equilibrium real wage rate is consistent with any inflation rate as long as that inflation rate is the expected inflation rate that is incorporated into economic contracts. As already illustrated in Figure 14.5, as long as the wage growth rate is the same as the inflation rate, the equilibrium real wage rate is unchanged. How does this happen? The actual inflation rate eventually becomes the expected inflation rate and workers and employers incorporate the expected inflation rate into the labor bargain; that is, the long-run equilibrium employment level, N_1, is not impacted by the inflation rate as long as it is expected and incorporated into labor contracts. Workers and employers alike have an incentive to incorporate expected inflation into the wage contract since employment is ultimately determined by the real wage rate. Likewise, the equilibrium real interest rate is consistent with any inflation rate as long as the actual inflation rate is the expected inflation rate.

Therefore, point A in Figure 14.4 is the long-run equilibrium, as is any point along the LRPC when the actual and expected inflation rates are identical. Starting from point A, assume the central bank expands the growth of money, increasing aggregate demand. In the short run, inflation will increase, output will increase and unemployment will decline as the economy moves along the PC_1 from point A to point B. Why? Expected inflation remains at 5 percent even though the actual inflation rate has increased to 7.5 percent. As a result, both the real wage rate and the real interest rate decline below their equilibrium levels. Lower real wages increase employment above its natural level and lower real interest rates increase demand for loanable funds and investment above their natural levels. That is, at point B, UN < NUN and GDP > PGDP. This is only temporary, however. It takes time for markets to adjust their expected inflation rate to changes in the actual inflation rate, but, as the market begins to revise its expected inflation rate to the now higher 7.5 percent actual inflation rate, wages and nominal interest rates will be adjusted upward until they return to their original equilibrium levels.

Once the expected inflation rate is adjusted to the higher actual inflation rate of 7.5 percent, the short-run Phillips curve shifts from PC_1 to PC_2 and the economy returns to its natural equilibrium along the LRPC, where UN = NUN and GDP = PGDP, but at the higher inflation rate of 7.5 percent at point C. Hence, the short-run Phillips curve is ephemeral. It depends on the expected inflation rate and, as a result, cannot be used to obtain a long-run tradeoff between inflation and economic growth.

The process works the same for a tighter monetary policy (Figure 14.6). In this case, the economy moves from point A to point B, because economic contracts incorporate a 5 percent inflation rate (PC_1) but the actual inflation rate has declined to 2.5 percent. As a result, real wages and real interest rates increase, output declines

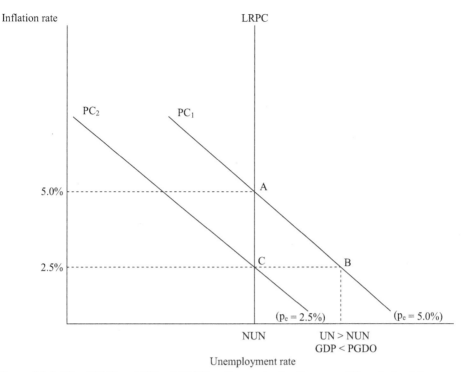

Figure 14.6. The "Old" and "New" Phillips Curves in the Context of Restrictive Monetary Policy.

and unemployment increases. Once the lower inflation rate is incorporated into economic contracts, however, the short-run Phillips curve will shift to PC_2 and return the economy to its long-run equilibrium in real terms at point C, but the actual and expected inflation rates are now 2.5 percent.

14.7 Policy Implications and Continued Debate

The new Phillips curve generates different policy implications for monetary policy from the old Phillips curve and the Keynesian model on which it is based.

First, Say's law of markets emerges as the long-run equilibrium for the economy. As long as one assumes flexible wages and prices, long-run equilibrium is characterized by the equality of UN and NUN and GDP and PGDP. The multiple equilibrium outcomes of the Keynesian model are simply incorrect in any model that assumes wages and prices are flexible and adjusts to eliminate excess supply and demand in product and labor markets. In the long run, Say's law of markets holds and Keynes' view of long-run gluts is rejected.

Second, monetary policy, fiscal policy or any government effort to manage aggregate demand can be effective only in the short run at best, in contrast to the Keynesian perspective. Monetary policy can move the economy along a given short-run Phillips curve (from point A to B in Figures 14.4 and 14.6), but, once inflationary expectations are adjusted to the changed inflation rate, the economy returns to its natural long-run equilibrium (from point B to C in Figures 14.4 and 14.6). That is, monetary, fiscal and other policies to change aggregate demand can be nonneutral only in the short run, but they are neutral in the long run. There is no Phillips curve tradeoff between inflation and economic activity that can be exploited by stabilization policy.

Third, the new Phillips curve indicates that the only reasonable final policy target for monetary policy (Step 5) is price stability. In the long run, central banks should focus their attention on the inflation rate, because there is a long-run relationship between monetary growth and inflation, and the central bank is unable to change the natural equilibrium of the economy. NUN and PGDP are dependent on real fundamentals and can be influenced only by institutional changes that improve the efficiency of the economy, technology, capital accumulation, changes in the composition of the labor force and changes in labor productivity. That is, asking central banks to achieve additional objectives to influence real economic activity is counterproductive and interferes with their ability to achieve their primary responsibility of long-run price stability. Another way to make the same point is that better monetary policy outcomes occur when central banks are less activist and focus instead on long-run price stability and being a lender of last resort on occasion.

The first two implications of the new Phillips curve are widely accepted; however, debate over the third continues. The neo-Keynesian perspective, which most central banks in the world operate under, is that the wage and price adjustments and the time it takes for actual inflation to be incorporated into economic contracts are neither smooth nor rapid. Many argue the short-run Phillips curve can be exploited to offset demand or supply shocks to the economy, smooth out the business cycle and still focus on long-run price stability. The Neoclassical view regards this as an overly simplistic view of how the economy works and ignores a number of problems faced by central banks in their attempt to balance short-run influence over output and employment with their primary responsibility to achieve long-run price stability.

We return to these issues in the next chapter, dealing with the formulation of monetary policy in the context of the new Phillips curve, the final policy targets and the rules versus discretion debate.

14.8 The Aggregate Demand and Supply Model

There is an alternative approach to the central bank model, based on the concepts of aggregate demand (AD) and supply (AS). AD is the total spending in the economy for output and AS is the total supply of output. The AD/AS approach complements the new Phillips curve discussed above. It provides not only an alternative approach

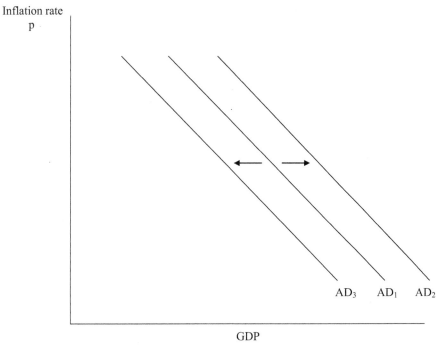

Figure 14.7. The Economy's Aggregate Demand Function.

to reaching the same point but a better foundation to see how monetary policy (and fiscal policy) influence the economy in the short run and long run.

Aggregate demand: The AD function concept is illustrated in Figure 14.7. AD_1 indicates the total amount of spending (real GDP) at different inflation rates, holding other things constant. The function is downward-sloping, and, while there is some similarity between the AD function in Figure 14.7 to market demand functions for a product, AD summarizes a rather complex macroeconomic model. Why is AD_1 downward-sloping and what causes aggregate demand to shift from AD_1 to either AD_2 or AD_3?

The AD function is downward-sloping because real spending increases with lower inflation. This occurs through a number of channels. Two are especially important. First, lower inflation at any given nominal interest rate lowers the real cost of borrowing and, hence, increases spending on any component of GDP sensitive to interest rates. Second, lower inflation increases the real value of any financial asset, such as bonds and stocks, increasing the wealth of financial portfolios, and thus it increases spending on a wide range of components of GDP. That is, lower inflation generates an increased amount of spending, other things held constant. Likewise, for the same reasons in reverse, higher inflation generates less total spending.

The AD function shifts when any factor held constant changes. Any autonomous or exogenous change in a variable that influences spending or autonomous or

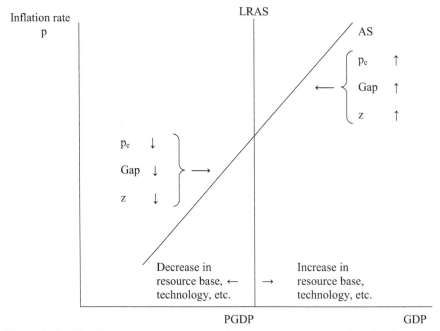

Figure 14.8. The Economy's Short-Run and Long-Run Aggregate Supply Functions.

exogenous change in spending itself will shift AD. The terms "autonomous" or "exogenous" refer to a change in a variable unrelated to the variables in the model. We illustrated this concept in Chapter 1 by distinguishing between endogenous and exogenous changes in consumption. The same principle applies here.

An autonomous or exogenous change in any of the following variables will shift AD to the right (AD_1 to AD_2) so that, at any inflation rate, output is higher: increase in the money supply; increase in government spending; decrease in taxes; increase in exports, increase in consumption or investment; and decrease in the distress in the financial system (referred to as financial frictions). An autonomous or exogenous change in any of the following variables will shift AD to the left (AD_1 to AD_3) so that, at any inflation rate, output is lower: decrease in the money supply; decrease in government spending; increase in taxes; decrease in exports, decrease in consumption or investment; and increase in distress in the financial system.

Shifts in the AD function in either direction are often referred to as "demand shocks", because the changes in spending are not dependent on the variables in the model or the model itself.

Aggregate supply: There is no difference between short- and long-run AD; however, in the case of AS, we need to distinguish between short- and long-run AS (Figure 14.8), because, even though wages and prices are flexible, it takes time for wages and prices to adjust to changes in output. Why is the short-run AS upward-sloping? What causes short-run AS to shift? Why is long-run AS, denoted as LRAS, vertical? Why does LRAS shift?

Short-run AS is upward-sloping because, as output increases, more workers are demanded, wages increase and, because wages are the largest component of cost of most products, prices and inflation increase. Short-run AS is dependent on expected inflation, the GDP gap and "supply price shocks", according to the following:

$$p = p_e + \alpha \, Gap + z \qquad (14.8)$$

where α determines how fast inflation responds to a change in the GDP gap and z is a price shock variable.

The smaller (larger) α, the slower (faster) prices adjust to changes in the GDP gap. According to Expression 14.8, AS shifts to the left with an increase in expected inflation, an increase in the GDP gap or an increase in the price of some important product or service. That is, the inflation rate is higher at any level of output. AS shifts to the right with a decrease in expected inflation, a decrease in the gap or a decline in the price of some important product, such as oil. That is, the inflation rate is lower at any level of output.

Long-run AS is vertical because, given sufficient time for prices and wages to adjust to excess demand or supply in any market, the economy will return to its natural equilibrium level. The LRAS is vertical at the potential GDP level for the same reason the LRPC is vertical at the natural unemployment rate. The LRAS function shifts for the same reasons the LRPC shifts – changes in the economy's resource base, changes in technology, etc.

Short- and long-run equilibrium: Short- and long-run equilibrium in the context of the Phillips curve are illustrated in Figure 14.4 and 14.6. The same point can be illustrated with AD and AS. Figure 14.9 illustrates long-run equilibrium at point A, where the short-run AS_1 intersects AD_1 along the vertical LRAS function at point A.

First, let's see what happens when AD shifts because of a demand shock. Assume monetary policy stimulates AD, shifting AD_1 to AD_2, by increasing the money supply. The economy moves from point A to point B and GDP > PGDP (UN < NUN); however, this is only a temporary equilibrium. Higher expected inflation and higher wages shift the short-run AS to the left, and the leftward shift will continue as long as GDP > PGDP. Eventually, short-run AS will shift to AS_2 and intersect AD_2 at a higher inflation rate on the vertical LRAS, at point C. This is exactly the same outcome as illustrated in the Phillips curve discussion; that is, in Figure 14.4 the economy moved from point A to B, and then, finally, to C, in response to an increase in the money supply. In fact, any demand shock that shifts AD to the right will generate the same sequence of events: higher output, lower unemployment and higher inflation in the short run, but a return to the original equilibrium output but with higher inflation (point C).

Likewise, any demand shock that shifts AD to the left will first reduce inflation and output and increase unemployment, but these outcomes will shift the AS to the right and return the economy to its natural equilibrium, but at a lower inflation rate than existed before the negative demand shock.

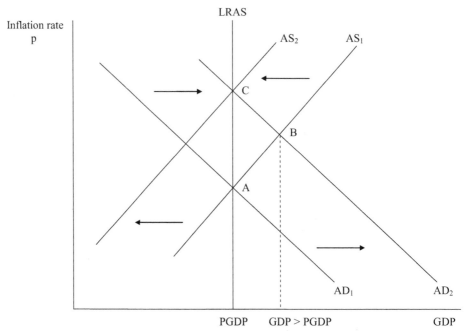

Figure 14.9. The Short-Run and Long-Run Responses to Expansionary Monetary Policy or Any Positive Demand Shock.

Figure 14.10 illustrates what happens when AS shifts, or what is referred to as a "supply shock". Assume oil prices increase and shift AS from AS_1 to AS_2. The leftward shift in AS intersects AD at point B, inflation and unemployment increase and output falls below its potential. The negative GDP gap reduces demand for workers, lowers wages and shifts the AS back to the right. How far will AS shift to the right? It will continue to shift until it returns to AS_1 and the economy returns to its potential level of GDP (point A). Keep in mind that the price shock assumes a one-time oil price increase. If oil prices decrease, the opposite sequence of events will take place: inflation decreases, output increases but eventually the positive GDP gap will increase wages and shift the AS back to its original position, at point A.

Implications: The implications drawn from the Phillips curve discussion are repeated in the AD/AS model. In the long run, the economy is in equilibrium at its natural level, determined by the resource base, technology, etc. Supply or demand shocks generate a GDP that can be greater or smaller than PGDP, but changes in prices and wages eventually return the economy to its natural equilibrium. Again, Say's law of markets emerges as the economy's long-run equilibrium. Likewise, monetary policy is nonneutral in the short run, but not the long run. The only reasonable final policy target for monetary policy is price stability. As with the Phillips curve case, however, there remains considerable debate about how smoothly and how rapidly the economy adjusts to a demand or supply shock.

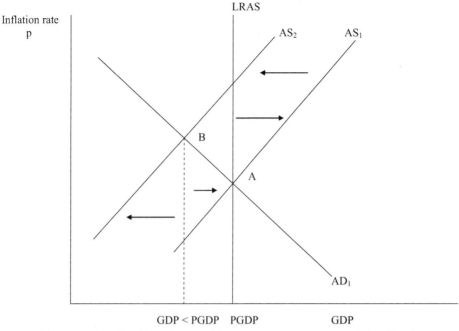

Figure 14.10. The Short-Run and Long-Run Responses to a Price Shock.

References

Bernanke, Ben S. (2003). "'Constrained Discretion' and Monetary Policy". Remarks at New York University, New York, February 3, www.federalreserve.gov/boarddocs/Speeches/2003/20030203/default.htm.

Blinder, Alan S. (1999). *Central Banking in Theory and Practice*. Cambridge, MA: MIT Press.

Friedman, Milton (1968). "The Role of Monetary Policy". *American Economic Review*, 58: 1–17.

Modigliani, Franco (1977). "The Monetarist Controversy, or, Should We Forsake Stabilization Policies?". *American Economic Review*, 67: 1–17.

Phillips, A. William (1958). "The Relationship between Unemployment and the Rate of Change of Money Wages in the United Kingdom, 1861–1957". *Economica*, 25: 283–99.

Samuelson, Paul A., and Robert M. Solow (1960). "Analytical Aspects of Anti-Inflation Policy". *American Economic Review*, 50: 177–94.

Chapter 15
Step 5: Final Policy Targets

15.1 Introduction

This chapter completes the sequence by discussing the final policy targets (Step 5) from four perspectives. First, the evolution of the final macroeconomic policy targets for central banks are identified in terms of the same three periods of the evolution of macroeconomic modeling: *Classical (1776 to 1936)*; *Keynesian (1936 to 1970s)*; and *Neoclassical and Neo-Keynesian (1970s to present)*. Second, the primacy of price stability as the final policy target in the last part of the twentieth century is emphasized by discussing the adoption of *explicit* and *implicit* inflation targets by central banks. Third, the final macroeconomic targets are then placed in the context of the other responsibilities of the central bank, such as lender of last resort services, financial regulation and supervision, and other goals. Fourth, the specific final macroeconomic policy targets of the Federal Reserve are discussed in the context of the Federal Reserve's "dual" mandate.

15.2 Evolution of the Final Policy Targets

The Classical period (1776 to 1936): Prior to Keynes, central banks had two basic responsibilities: first, to manage the money supply so as to achieve price stability; and, second, to provide lender of last resort services in order to maintain financial stability in the context of a fractional and fiduciary-based monetary system. If the central bank conducted policy to achieve price stability, not only would the economy grow more smoothly over time but it would grow at a stable rate of inflation, reducing the need to provide lender of last resort services. Central banks should resist the temptation to exploit the nonneutrality of money in the short run. The emphasis on a nonactivist central bank was consistent with the view the market was inherently stable and departures from potential output would be resolved by self-correcting economic forces. This approach to central bank policy did not claim that it would end the business cycle but, instead, that it would reduce fluctuations in the GDP gap over time and contribute to a stable financial and monetary regime that would support economic growth.

Likewise, fiscal policy should also be passive and nonactivist. In addition, even if there was a need for activist fiscal policy in the short run, it would not be effective because of the crowding-out effects of government spending. That is, government spending in the Classical period was regarded as not only neutral in the long run but also largely neutral in the short run. Fiscal policy should focus on a balanced and small budget limited to those specific roles required for government spending – protecting private property, providing certain public goods and national defense.

The Keynesian period (1936 to 1970s): The Keynesian period technically starts with the publication of *The General Theory* in 1936, but, for all practical purposes, it was not until the post-WWII period that the Keynesian model and perspective dominated public policy in the United States and elsewhere.

The Keynesian perspective emphasized the inherent instability of a market economy driven by business "animal spirits", in contrast to the inherent stability view of the Classical period; the Keynesian perspective emphasized multiple long-run equilibriums with regard to output and employment, in contrast to the unique long-run full-employment equilibrium output view of the Classical period; and the Keynesian perspective emphasized the need for activist monetary and fiscal policy to manage aggregate demand, as opposed to the Classical perspective of passive and nonactivist monetary and fiscal policy.

In the first few decades of the Keynesian period Keynesians focused more on fiscal policy than monetary policy as the major tool of economic stabilization, based on widely held views about key elements in the channels of how each policy influenced real output. Deficit spending had a *direct effect* on output since government spending directly increased output and lowered taxes directly increased consumption (and/or investment), which was a major component of output. In contrast, monetary policy had an *indirect effect* on output because changes in the money supply first impacted the financial system to change interest rates, which, in turn, would change spending, which was sensitive to interest rates.

The effectiveness of both policies depended on two relationships embedded in the model: first, how much the interest rate responded to government deficits and the money supply; and, second, how spending responded to changes in the interest rate. Let's consider government deficit spending first. An increase in government deficit spending shifted aggregate demand (AD) to the right, but without a change in the money supply the interest rate had to increase, since the demand for loanable funds function (DLF) shifted to the right in the presence of an unchanged supply of loanable funds function (SLF). However, because the supply of loanable funds was interest-elastic (supply function with a small slope, or flatter rather than steep), the rightward shift in the demand for loanable funds would result in only a small increase in the interest rate. It was also believed that investment spending (or other components of output) were rather insensitive to the interest rate, so that the small increase in the interest rate would have a small adverse impact on spending. Hence, government deficit spending had some crowding-out effects, but they were considered small, so that the net effect of government deficit spending was to increase total spending.

The same relationships that rendered fiscal policy potent rendered monetary policy impotent. An increase in the money supply shifted AD to the right, but not nearly as far to the right as fiscal policy. This was because the supply of loanable funds had a small slope because it was interest-elastic, so that any increase in the money supply would shift the supply function to the right only a small amount and generate only a small decrease in the interest rate. The insensitivity of spending to the lower interest rate would further weaken the ability of monetary policy to increase output.

The same holds true for restrictive fiscal and monetary policy. Tight fiscal policy would lower interest rates only a small amount, which would have a small positive impact on spending, so that tight fiscal policy could effectively lower total spending on a net basis. Tight monetary policy would be able to increase interest rates only a small amount, which would have a small negative impact on spending, so that tight monetary policy would not be very effective in reducing spending.

As part of the monetarist–Keynesian debate, the two relationships of the channels of how fiscal and monetary policy influenced output were subject to empirical investigation. It was only in the late 1960s and 1970s that economists had the computing power to test the two relationships with actual data. The original Keynesian perspective proved to be incorrect. The nature of the supply of loanable funds indicated that the interest rate was far more sensitive to changes in aggregate demand caused by either fiscal policy or monetary policy and that investment spending was far more sensitive to the interest rate than previously believed. Hence, empirical research demonstrated that monetary policy was the instrument of economic stability and that fiscal policy was subject to larger crowding-out effects than previously believed.

The shift in emphasis from fiscal to monetary policy did not, however, change the essential perspective of the Keynesian view, but only how Keynesian objectives would be achieved. By the 1970s monetary policy became *the* tool of economic stabilization in the Keynesian perspective. Central bank policy shifted from nonactivist to activist from both the long- and short-run perspective. There were several final targets of central bank policy in both the short and long run. In the long run, the central bank was able to select different combinations of inflation and employment in the context of a stable long-run Phillips curve tradeoff between inflation and employment. In the short run, the central bank could use monetary policy to offsets demand and supply shocks to minimize fluctuations in the GDP gap over time.

The Neoclassical and Neo-Keynesian period (1970s to the present): In the 1970s this approach to central bank policy was found wanting, ushering in the Neoclassical aspect of this period. In response, a Neo-Keynesian perspective emerged that accepted much of the Neoclassical perspective but differed in several important respects.

15.3 Neoclassical Perspective

Five developments ushered in the Neoclassical perspective and replaced the original Keynesian perspective, which had dominated public policy in the first part of the post-WWII period.

First – there is no long-run tradeoff between inflation and output: Central bank policy based on the Phillips curve did not generate the anticipated results. Easy monetary policy in the United States and throughout much of the world generated inflation but not much economic growth. In fact, many countries by the late 1970s were experiencing stagflation – high inflation and high unemployment at the same time. The inflation in the United States was so intense and the economic growth so low that the period from 1965 to 1985 is referred to as the Great Inflation and ranks as one of the three most intense periods of economic and financial distress in U.S. history, the other two being the Great Depression and, most recently, the Great Recession.

Second – only one long-run equilibrium: The Keynesian perspective of multiple equilibriums for output and employment was rejected, as the old Phillips curve was replaced by the new Phillips curve model and the assumption of downward fixed wages was replaced by the view that wages (and prices) were flexible in both directions. Modern macroeconomics based on Keynesian building blocks of AD and AS generated the same long-run results as the quantity theory of money. In the long run, any disturbance in the economy that caused actual output to differ from potential output (and actual unemployment to differ from natural unemployment) would generate economic forces to return the economy to a unique equilibrium in which actual and potential output (actual and natural unemployment) were identical. The long-run equilibrium of the economy as defined by potential output and natural unemployment were determined by the nation's resource base, technology and economic structure.

Third – the primacy of price stability: In the new framework, monetary policy was neutral in the long run and inflation was the only macroeconomic variable that could be influenced in the long run by central bank policy. Hence, the final policy target of the central bank should be the inflation rate, and by achieving price stability central banks could make their most important contribution not only to a stable financial and monetary environment but also to sustained economic growth. This view was supported not only by the revised macroeconomic models but by world history. The Great Inflation period showed that economies that operated with high and variable rates of inflation experienced low and uneven economic growth and intense periods of financial distress, such as the collapse of the S&L industry in the United States in the 1980s, which can be directly traced to flawed financial policy, interest rate ceilings on deposits and inflationary monetary policy by the Federal Reserve. The few countries that avoided the Great Inflation, such as Japan, experienced much smoother and higher economic growth without the financial distress that characterized most countries that attempted to purchase economic growth with easy monetary policy.

Fourth – fiscal policy is ineffective: Fiscal policy was nonneutral for all practical purposes in both the short and long run, as it was subject to significant crowding-out effects as well as other problems. Government should focus on a balanced budget and resist using the budget as an instrument of economic stabilization.

Fifth – the private market is inherently stable in the absence of activist government policy: The Keynesian perspective that the private economy was inherently unstable was challenged by both historical and econometric studies. These studies suggested government stabilization and financial policy generated as much economic and financial distress as, if not more than, any inherent instability in the private market. The Great Depression and Great Inflation were shown to be importantly caused by policy errors by the government in regard to fiscal, monetary and financial policy. As mentioned in the introductory chapter of this book, even former Governor Bernanke of the Federal Reserve admitted the role of the Federal Reserve in causing the Great Depression. Hence, the Classical view that the private economy was inherently stable reemerged and was the foundation of much of the deregulation and liberalization of economic institutions in the last part of the twentieth century.

As a result of these five developments, the Neoclassical view emphasized two objectives for central bank policy: first, focus on long-run price stability; and, second, exercise caution in responding to short-run demand and supply shocks. If these policies were followed, central banks would make a significant contribution to economic growth and would be less needed to function as a lender of last resort. Let's examine each of the two objectives.

15.4 A Steady and Low Rate of Inflation

Central bank policy should focus on long-run price stability, because the inflation rate is the only long-run variable the central bank can determine. Inflation and deflation in the long run are inherently a monetary phenomenon, and central banks determine the monetary growth rate over the long run; hence, price stability is the only final policy target the central bank can accomplish and be held accountable for. At times the central bank will need to provide lender of last resort services; however, if the central bank achieves price stability, the need for those services will be reduced.

How is price stability defined? There are two aspects to this question – price stability means low year-to-year variation in the inflation rate around the inflation rate target and a low inflation rate target. Hence, price stability is defined by achieving a specific inflation rate over time with a low variance.

An average inflation rate of 2 percent over time is consistent with little or great year-to-year variation; that is, an inflation target of 2 percent over two years can be achieved with either a 2 percent inflation rate in each year or a 0 percent inflation rate in the first year and a 4 percent inflation rate in the second year. The latter is not consistent with price stability. The central bank should achieve not only a specific inflation target but achieve that target with a rate whose year-to-year variation stays close to the target. This is because variation in the inflation rate, even if, on average, it equaled the inflation target, makes it difficult to formulate inflation expectations and incorporate them into economic contracts. High variation in the inflation rate on a year-by-year basis generates much uncertainty about the value of the nation's money supply and increases economic uncertainty.

The inflation rate target should be low. Today, most central banks define price stability as an inflation rate of 2 percent per year. Why a low inflation rate target? According to the new Phillips curve, as well as the AD/AS model, the economy can achieve long-run equilibrium at its potential output and natural unemployment rate at any inflation rate as long as the inflation rate is expected and incorporated into economic contracts. That is, these models suggest the central bank should be indifferent between a low and high inflation rate as long as it is steady and expected by the public. However, the higher the inflation rate, even if expected, the less efficient the economy in the long run. Another way to make the same point: the long-run Phillips curve has a slight positive slope and the long-run AS function has a slight negative slope, so that higher inflation, even if expected, generates higher natural unemployment and lower potential output than a lower inflation rate. Why?

Inflation, even if completely expected, imposes at least three costs on society: menu cost, shoe leather cost and tax bracket creep. *Menu cost* refers to the need to devote resources to posting new prices. The higher the inflation rate, the greater the need to post new prices more frequently. Resources devoted to posting new prices have an opportunity cost. *Shoe leather cost* refers to resources the public devotes to managing their currency and checking accounts that pay small or zero interest. Currency pays no interest, small checking accounts often pay no interest and other checking accounts pay positive but low interest. The higher the inflation rate, the more these components of M2 decline in real value and the greater the incentives for the public to find ways to reduce their holdings of currency and demand deposits. The resources devoted to this endeavor, however, have an opportunity cost. *Tax bracket creep* refers to the fact the tax system is not completely indexed to the inflation rate, so that the higher the inflation rate, the higher the real tax burden and the more resources are transferred from the private to the government sector. Government spends money less efficiently than the private sector in many cases, because government is spending other people's money. Tax bracket creep was significantly reduced in 1985 when the Reagan administration enacted legislation to adjust the tax brackets to the inflation rate, but important elements of the current U.S. tax system are still not indexed.

Menu cost, shoe leather cost and tax bracket creep impose a cost on society; however, estimates of these costs are generally low for the range of inflation rates experienced in the United States, especially as a result of the tax reforms in 1985. Nonetheless, these are real costs to inflation, even if they are quantitatively small; hence, a lower inflation target is better than a higher inflation target. Why not a 0 percent inflation target?

The generally accepted inflation rate of 2 percent as constituting price stability is based on the fact that price indexes have an upward bias. Depending on the size of the upward bias, a low positive inflation rate might actually mean deflation. Deflation of X percent has a much larger adverse effect on the economy than inflation of X percent because nominal interest rates are not less than zero under normal circumstances, though in Japan and some European countries, in 2015 and 2016, government bonds earned a small negative interest rate. Negative interest rates are the exception and depend on unusual circumstances that are not sustainable. Hence, the 2 percent inflation definition of price stability is widely accepted because it has only small resource cost effects on the economy and is sufficiently above 0 percent to reduce the probability of deflation.

15.5 Caution in Responding to Demand and Supply Shocks in the Short Run

Central banks should resist responding to short-run demand and supply shocks, for two reasons. First, the economy is complex, and economists overestimate their ability to build models that can guide monetary policy to offset demand and supply shocks. Second, and related to the first, the *lag in the effect of monetary policy* can render an activist monetary policy destabilizing. Economists overestimate not only their ability to model the economy but also their ability to take lags into account in the pursuit of activist monetary policy.

There are three components to the lag in the effect of monetary policy: the *recognition lag*; the *administrative lag*; and the *impact lag*. The three components are summarized in Figure 15.1. The recognition lag is the time from when a demand/supply shock occurs, at time t_0, to the time the central bank recognizes the demand/supply shock, at time t_1. The administrative lag is the time from when the need for a monetary policy response is recognized, at time t_1, to time t_2, when the monetary policy response is made by changing the central bank's policy instrument. The impact lag is the time from when the policy instrument is changed, at time t_2, until it has its major impact on real output, at time t_3. The first two lags are referred to as the *inside lag*, because they are within the central bank's decision-making process, while the third lag is referred to as the *outside lag*, because it occurs outside the central bank once the central bank has changed its policy instrument.

The lag problem has two aspects – the length of the lag and the variability of the lag. Let's focus first on the length of the lag. There is little issue with the inside lags (recognition and administration lags) for central bank policy. These lags are at most only a few months long, as central banks possess large staffs of highly trained economists and statisticians who have access to the world's most extensive

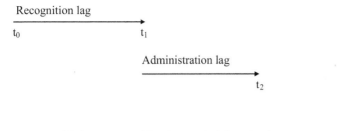

Inside lag = Recognition lag + Administration lag or t_0 to t_2

Impact or outside lag

t_3

Total Lag in Effect of Monetary Policy = Inside lag + Outside lag or t_0 to t_3

Figure 15.1. The Lag in Effect of Monetary Policy

databases and econometric models. Once the central bank recognizes the need for a policy change, the actual formulation and implementation of policy are accomplished in a short period of time. The impact lag is the critical issue – the time from when the central bank changes the policy instrument to the time when the change in the policy instrument has its major impact on the economy.

At one time central banks believed the impact lag was short, perhaps only a few months, but by the 1970s extensive econometric research had shown the impact lag was long, with estimates indicating at least a one-year impact lag. The longer the lag, the greater the probability the impact of any change in monetary policy will occur at the wrong time and destabilize rather than stabilize the economy in responding to demand and/or supply shocks.

Figure 15.2 illustrates the problem of countercyclical policy in the presence of lags. Line AA indicates the path of potential GDP while line BB indicates the actual path of actual GDP as it fluctuates above and below potential GDP over time.

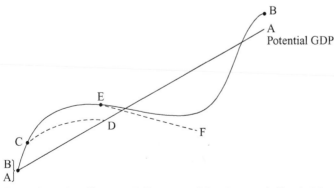

Figure 15.2. Central Bank Efforts to Offset a Positive Demand Shock May or May Not Stabilize the Economy Depending on the Length of the Lag in the Effect of Monetary Policy

The question is, can an activist monetary policy smooth out the business cycle? Lags render this difficult the longer and more variable the lag. At point A, actual GDP is equal to potential GDP, but the economy is subject to a demand/supply shock that increases actual GDP above its potential. Assume the Federal Reserve recognizes the economy is growing above its potential at point C and adjusts its policy instrument to slow the economy's growth at point C. Assume the lag is very short and almost immediately begins to slow GDP, and the path of GDP follows the dashed line CD.

Assume the lag is long. The central bank changes the policy instrument at point C, but, because of a long lag, the impact does not take place until point E. At point E the economy has already begun to slow and return to its potential path, but the tight monetary policy action at point C impacts the economy at the wrong time and further slows the economy, so it continues along the dashed line path EF.

The longer the lag in policy, the greater the probability policy will impact the economy at the wrong time and destabilize rather than stabilize the economy. The more variable the lag, the greater the probability policy will impact the economy at the wrong time and destabilize rather than stabilize the economy.

There is the additional issue of matching the magnitude of the central bank response to the magnitude of the demand/supply shock. Not only will a long lag increase the probability the impact of central bank policy will occur at the wrong time, but long lags make it more difficult to match the magnitude of the central bank action with the demand/supply shock. The problem becomes more complex when considering the fact that lags may be not only long but variable over time. Combined, these factors suggest that central banks need to be cautious about using the nonneutrality of money in the short run to offset demand and supply shocks.

The lags contribute to another problem in the ability of activist central bank policy to stabilize the economy aside from impacting the economy at the wrong time. The lags contribute to a tendency for monetary policy to overreact to a demand or supply shock, so there is a meaningful probability not only that the effect of policy will occur at the wrong time but that the magnitude of the policy response will be greater than the demand or supply shock. In response to a negative demand or supply shock the central bank is required to increase the money supply, but, because of the lag, not much happens. The central bank then increases the money supply to a greater extent, but not much happens, and so on. Eventually, when the economy begins to react to the expansionary monetary policy, the central bank has realized it expanded money too much and then starts to back off, but the economy continues to expand from the initial easy policy, so the central bank backs off even more, and so on.

To drive home the point with a common-sense example, consider the Federal Reserve is the captain of a boat in the sea, with its normal ups and downs, much like economic growth around its potential path. The people on the boat become concerned the boat is tipping too far to port. The captain announces that everyone should gather and move to starboard. The boat stops tipping to port, levels off and everyone congratulates the captain for stabilizing the boat, but now the boat begins to tip to starboard. The captain now calls for everyone to move to port, the boat levels, but now starts tipping to port more than previously. One can get the drift of what will eventually happen. The point is, not taking lags into account may destabilize rather than stabilize the economy.

15.6 Neo-Keynesian Perspective: Despite Agreement on Some Issues, Differences Still Exist

The Neo-Keynesian perspective now incorporates much of the Neoclassical perspective with respect to the neutrality of money in the long run; the unique long-run equilibrium of the economy; the importance of price stability as the final macroeconomic policy target of central bank policy; and the fact that monetary policy in the short run is a more powerful and flexible stabilization tool than fiscal policy. Nonetheless, three important differences remain.

First – activist monetary and fiscal policies are still needed: Neo-Keynesians emphasize the importance of demand and supply shocks, which require an activist monetary policy. Even if the economy eventually returns to full employment, neo-Keynesians still accept Keynes' observation that "[i]n the long run we are all dead". They continue to emphasize the animal spirits of the private market and its inherent instability. While they recognize the importance of crowding-out effects of fiscal policy they regard the crowding out to not be as large as in the Neoclassical perspective, and thus fiscal policy is still considered an important instrument of economic stabilization.

Second – wage and price adjustments are sluggish: Neo-Keynesians emphasize the importance of sluggish as opposed to fixed money wages and argue that wage and price adjustments simply don't occur rapidly enough to prevent the economy from long periods of high unemployment and low output. As a result, central banks need to take an activist approach to offset demand and supply shocks to the economy. Neo-Keynesians continue to believe monetary policy can exploit the short-run Phillips curve by making sure the public understands the central bank's commitment to long-run price stability.

Third – the lag problem is manageable: While Neo-Keynesians acknowledge the problem of lags and the difficulty of taking lags into account, they regard lags as manageable. Lags do not pose a serious problem to activist monetary policy. Lags can be modeled and can be incorporated into monetary policy decisions.

These are meaningful differences in how monetary policy is formulated and conducted; however, the differences between the Keynesians and non-Keynesians have diminished since the monetarist–Keynesian debate of the 1970s. The Keynesian perspective on monetary policy is less activist than it once was, and now emphasizes the need for long-run price stability more than was previously the case. In fact, price stability as the primary final policy target of central bank policy has become so widely accepted that many central banks now operate under formal inflation targets, established either by the central bank, the central bank and the government or, in some cases, just the government. We now turn to a discussion of inflation targeting.

15.7 The Primacy of Price Stability and Inflation Targeting

Inflation targets express a specific inflation target or target range of inflation in quantitative terms that is straightforward and transparent to the public. The inflation target is a public commitment by the central bank to focus on price stability and not attempt to exploit the Phillips curve relationship between employment and inflation. Inflation targets are not meant to be satisfied month by month, or even year by year, but to be achieved over the medium and long term while reducing the year-by-year variation in the inflation rate. Inflation targets can be formulated in terms of a specific inflation rate or specific price level; however, most inflation target discussion focuses on targeting the inflation rate.

The Reserve Bank of New Zealand in 1989, after a long period of inflation and general economic instability, adopted a formal inflation target to guide central bank policy, and since then 29 central banks, at the time of this writing, have adopted formal and explicit inflation targets as their final policy target (Table 15.1). While the Reserve Bank of New Zealand is the first in the post-WWII period to adopt an inflation target framework, the Swedish Riksbank, in 1931, was the first central bank of an industrial country to adopt a formal inflation target. The Riksbank targeted the price level, however, rather than the inflation rate. Targeting the price level is much the same as targeting the inflation rate if the price level is targeted to increase by certain amounts over time; however, there are technical differences. In any event, inflation targeting today is in the context of targeting an inflation rate rather than a price level even though some research continues to be devoted to price level targeting. While there are technical differences, the difference between inflation rate and price level targeting is a distinction without much of a difference.

Inflation targets do not exclude other final policy targets but do elevate price stability as the primary objective of central bank policy. The inflation target in some cases is decided by the central bank and in others is jointly determined by the central bank and the government. The absence of the Federal Reserve from the list of central banks operating with a formal inflation target in Table 15.1 is notable. The Federal Reserve has chosen to operate with an *implicit* rather than an *explicit* inflation target. An implicit inflation target permits the central bank to "have its cake and eat it too"; that is, the central bank focuses on price stability but is not formally committed only to price stability. There is a qualitative difference between an explicit and an implicit inflation target because explicit targets publicly commit the central bank to price stability whereas implicit targets provide more flexibility in the pursuit of other objectives.

Table 15.1. *Countries with Formal and Explicit Inflation Targets, 2012*

	Target set by	Target measure	Target 2012	Target type	Multiple targets?	Target horizon
Armenia	G and CB	H CPl	4% ± 1.5 pp	P+T	–	Medium term
Australia	G and CB	H CPl	2%–3%	Range	–	Medium term
Brazil	G and CB	H CPl	4.5% ± 2 pp	P + T	2012 and 2013	Yearly target
Canada	G and CB	H CPl	2% (mid-point of 1%–3%)	P + T	–	Six to eight quarters; current target extends to December 2016
Chile	CB	H CPl	3% ± 1 pp	P + T	–	Around two years
Colombia	CB	H CPl	2%–4%	Range	–	Medium term
Czech Republic	CB	H CPl	2% ± 1 pp	P + T	–	Medium term, 12 to 18 months
Ghana	G and CB	H CPl	8.7% ± 2 pp	P+T	End 2012 and 2013	18 to 24 months
Guatemala	CB	H CPl	4.5% ± 1 pp	P+T	2012 and 2013	End of year
Hungary	CB	H CPl	3%	Point	–	Medium term
Iceland	G and CB	H CPl	2.5%	Point	–	On average
Indonesia	G and CB	H CPl	4.5% ± 1 pp	P + T	–	Medium term
Israel	G and CB	H CPl	1%–3%	Range	–	Within two years
Mexico	CB	H CPl	3% ± 1 pp	P + T	–	Medium term
New Zealand	G and CB	H CPl	1%–3%	Range	–	Medium term
Norway	G	H CPl	2.5%	Point	–	Medium term
Peru	CB	H CPl	2% ± 1 pp	P + T	–	At all times
Philippines	G and CB	H CPl	4.0% ± 1 pp	P + T	–	Medium term (from 2012 to 2014)
Poland	CB	H CPl	2.5% ± 1 pp	P + T	–	Medium term
Romania	G and CB	H CPl	3% ± 1 pp	P + T	–	Medium-term target from 2013
Serbia	G and CB	H CPl	4.0% ± 1.5 pp	P + T	–	Medium term
South Africa	G	H CPl	3%–6%	Range	–	On a continuous basis
South Korea	CB (with G)	H CPl	3% ± 1 pp	P + T	–	Three years
Sweden	CB	H CPl	2%	Point	–	Normally two years
Thailand	G and CB	H CPl[a]	3.0% ± 1.5 pp[a]	P + T	Target set annually	Eight quarters
Turkey	G and CB	H CPl	5.0% ± 2 pp	P + T	2012 and 2013	Multi-year (three years)
United Kingdom	G	H CPl	2%	Point	–	At all times

Notes: CB = central bank; G = government; H CPl = headline CPl; P + T = point with tolerance band; pp = percentage point(s).
[a] Target proposed by central bank at start of 2012, pending Cabinet approval.
Source: Hammond (2012 version).

Why have so many countries adopted inflation targeting? There are five reasons. First, inflation targeting is a recognition that the rate of inflation is the only variable the central bank can influence in the long run and the only final policy target for which the central bank can be held accountable. Price stability is the only reasonable long-run final policy target of the central bank, according to both the Neoclassical and Neo-Keynesian perspectives. Second, the failure to achieve price stability has serious and adverse effects on the nation's economy and financial system. In contrast to the predictions of the Phillips curve, the high inflation rates during the Great Inflation, for example, generated stagflation and contributed to the collapse of the S&L industry in the 1980s. Third, inflation targeting helps the central bank achieve price stability by publicly committing the central bank to price stability and publicly announcing that government pressure will not interfere with the price stability objective. Fourth, the inflation target provides a transparent forward perspective of monetary policy so the public can understand that short-term decision making is anchored to the long-run goal of price stability. Fifth, the inflation target framework makes it more difficult for the government to pressure the central bank to accommodate government spending or to use easy monetary policy to postpone fiscal and/or structural reforms.

What has been the experience with inflation targeting? We now have almost three decades of experience with central bank inflation targets, and during that time the inflation rate and year-by-year variability of the inflation rate has declined from what it was in the 1980s. However, can this be attributed to inflation targeting? This is a difficult question, because inflation has also declined for countries that have not adopted an inflation target; countries without an inflation target may operate with an implicit target, as the Federal Reserve does; and, most importantly, the adoption of an inflation target may simply reflect a public announcement that the central bank has elevated price stability to be the primary final policy target. That is, the better inflation performance since the 1980s may simply be due to the fact that central banks pay more attention to price stability than in the past and that inflation targeting has been the result, and not the cause, of the commitment to price stability. More detailed analysis, however, suggests that even during the latter part of the twentieth century, when inflation was brought under control in most countries, inflation targeting provided a marginal difference, especially for developing economies, whose central banks often come under intense pressure from government to expand the money supply to finance government spending and substitute for structural reform.

In the first decade of the new century, however, the macroeconomic environment changed and provided new evidence of the benefits of inflation targeting. During the 2007–2010 period there were a series of global commodity price shocks and a global financial crisis. There is some evidence that inflation-targeting countries did a better job in keeping inflation under control despite sharp increases in commodity prices and were able to absorb the financial shocks better than non-inflation-targeting countries. This is consistent with economic theory, which argues that the more inflationary expectations are anchored and stable despite short-run demand and supply shocks, the more stable the macroeconomic environment.

All things considered, inflation targeting is not a panacea for central bank policy, but the limited experience to date suggests it is an important foundation for defining the only realistic final policy target of central bank policy: achieving price stability.

15.8 Final Policy Targets in the Context of Other Central Bank Objectives

The macroeconomic final policy targets occupy much of the attention of central banks, but central banks have other objectives that can be included in the final policy target step even though they are not directly related to the five-step sequence. To illustrate, the Federal Reserve lists the following objectives on its Web site.

1 Conducting the nation's monetary policy by influencing money and credit conditions in the economy in pursuit of full employment and stable prices.
2 Supervising and regulating banks and other important financial institutions to ensure the safety and soundness of the nation's banking and financial system and to protect the credit rights of consumers.
3 Maintaining the stability of the financial system and containing systemic risk that may arise in financial markets.
4 Providing certain financial services to the U.S. government, U.S. financial institutions and foreign official institutions, and playing a major role in operating and overseeing the nation's payments systems.

As already mentioned several times, central banks in response to the financial crisis of 2008 and 2009 have redefined their role as financial and supervisory regulatory authorities to include *macroprudential* regulation. Macroprudential regulation is a new concept, and even the term itself was seldom used before the 2008 and 2009 financial crisis. In the past, those central banks that had large financial regulatory responsibilities, such as the Federal Reserve, focused on *microprudential* regulation. Traditional central bank microprudential regulation focuses on individual depository institutions, with an emphasis on lender of last resort services and capital–asset requirements, etc. designed to limit the failure of one or several depository institutions from threatening the entire financial system and, hence, the economy. That is, microprudential regulation and supervision focused on maintaining confidence in deposit money in a fractional reserve monetary system. Macroprudential regulation differs in at least three respects.

First, macroprudential policy focuses on the entire financial system rather than individual elements of the financial system and maintaining confidence in deposit money. Second, macroprudential regulation expands regulation to all financial institutions to be deemed systemically important and is not just confined to depository institutions, the traditional focus of microprudential regulation. Third, macroprudential regulation is designed to limit asset bubbles, such as the real estate and equity bubble in Japan in the late 1980s and the real estate bubble in the United States from 2002 to 2006, by imposing regulations and supervision to limit financial behavior that generates such bubbles. In this regard, macroprudential regulation is designed to limit the "procyclical" tendency of the financial system to exacerbate the business cycle, by "stress tests" and building "financial cushions" in financial institutions during good times, so that they can be used as a shock absorber in bad times to limit systemic risk.

It is far too early to evaluate this new perspective, as it has been seriously discussed and applied only in the past few years; however, there already appear to be several problems. First, the concept is so vague that it removes almost any limit to the extension of central bank regulation, thus representing a major addition to central bank responsibilities that may conflict with its basic macroeconomic objective of price stability. Second, the notion that central banks are capable of preventing asset bubbles is dubious based on past history. Both the Bank of Japan and Federal Reserve were unable to prevent the two largest asset bubbles in post-WWII history among industrial countries, and, in fact, contributed to them. Third, central banks are not independent to any reasonable degree, and involving them further in the financial system, which is frequently used by government for industrial policy, will further reduce their ability to conduct price stabilization policy.

15.9 Evolution of Federal Reserve Final Policy Targets and the "Dual" Mandate

During the first few decades in the post-WWII period central banks were not transparent about their final policy targets and provided little information about their tactics and strategy to achieve whatever targets they regarded as important. Central banks expressed their objectives in general terms, such as price stability, exchange rate stability, economic stabilization, economic growth and financial stability, without reference to potential conflicts between these objectives; nor were central banks transparent as to which objectives were primary and which were secondary. This was especially the case with the Federal Reserve System.

A close reading of Federal Reserve publications and statements reveals the importance it has placed on orderly financial markets, economic growth and high employment. Price stability was mentioned, but any balanced reading of the Federal Reserve through the 1970s and review of Federal Reserve policies would have to conclude that employment and economic growth, as well as orderly financial markets, were more important than price stability. This is not surprising, given the political environment in which the Federal Reserve functioned. The 1946 Employment Act, which emphasized the importance of maximum employment, provided the operational political document to understand Federal Reserve policy through the 1970s. The Keynesian perspective adopted during this period, and especially the Phillips curve, provided the economic foundation for the Federal Reserve's belief it could manage employment in the long run, especially if it were willing to sacrifice price stability.

The monetarist–Keynesian debate, the emergence of the Neoclassical perspective and even the Neo-Keynesian perspective and especially the Great Inflation period from 1965 to 1985 convinced central banks to be more explicit about their final policy targets. As the old Phillips curve was replaced by the new Phillips curve and the cost of inflation in the United States and other countries during the Great Inflation period became apparent, central banks increasingly defined their final macroeconomic policy target as price stability. By the end of the twentieth century central banks emphasized price stability as the primary final policy target, and, while they continued to adopt activist policies to offset short-run demand and supply shocks on employment and output, they attempted to conduct these policies with long-run price stability as the final policy target. At the same time, focusing on offsetting demand and supply shocks on employment and output in the short run and focusing on long-run price stability has presented challenges to central bank policy that continue to be debated today.

The Federal Reserve has been somewhat of an outlier in this regard. First, the Federal Reserve has resisted an inflation target approach, instead operating with an implicit inflation target of 2 percent.

Second, the 1946 Employment Act was the operational framework of monetary policy through the late 1970s. The Act stated the "declared policy" of the U.S. government as follows: "The Congress hereby declares that it is the continuing policy and responsibility of the federal government to use all practical means . . . to promote maximum employment, production and purchasing power." Price stability is implied in the 1946 Act, but the emphasis was clearly placed on employment and output, and subsequent policy by the Federal Reserve and government in general in the decades after the Act demonstrated the primacy of employment over price stability. In 1977 the Act was revised when Congress amended the Federal Reserve Act to require the Federal Reserve to "promote effectively the goals of maximum employment, stable prices, and moderate long-term interest rates".

In contradiction to the three political mandates, the Federal Reserve refers to its responsibilities as the "dual" mandate of maximum employment and price stability without reference to long-term interest rates in most but not all announcements. On January 24, 2012, the Federal Reserve released a "Statement on Longer-Run Goals and Monetary Policy Strategy" that outlined the Federal Reserves' long-run final policy targets: "The Federal Open Market Committee (FOMC) is firmly committed to fulfilling its statutory mandate from the Congress of promoting maximum employment, stable prices, and moderate long-term interest rates." The same reference to interest rates is made in the two monetary policy reports to Congress made in February and July of each calendar year. Yet, in an April 29, 2015, public statement at the end of a two-day FOMC meeting, the Federal Reserve's mandate omitted reference to interest rates: "Consistent with its statutory mandate, the Committee seeks to foster maximum employment and price stability." This is the language the Federal Reserve uses most frequently in its FOMC reports and news outreach activities.

It is not clear what is meant by "maximum" employment. If the intent is to achieve an environment such that, over the long run, the unemployment rate will be at the natural unemployment rate, this will occur in any event, and be more likely the more successful the Federal Reserve is in achieving price stability. If the intent is to minimize fluctuations in the output gap and, hence, employment gap in the short run, there are conflicts between this and long-run price stability. More likely, Congress intended the Federal Reserve to permanently reduce the natural unemployment rate, currently estimated to range from 5 to 6.5 percent, to 3 or 4 percent; however, the Federal Reserve lacks the ability to accomplish this task. The lack of clarity as to the operational meaning of the dual mandate and the continued use of the phrase by the Federal Reserve make it difficult to determine the final policy targets of the Federal Reserve.

In sum, the dual mandate is problematical, for a number of reasons.

First – it is confusing at best: The dual mandate is confusing at best. It ignores the third mandate – moderate interest rates; ignores potential conflicts between the three mandates; ignores potential conflicts between employment and price stability; and provides no quantitative measure of the meaning of "maximum employment" and "price stability". Maximum employment might be interpreted as employment at the natural unemployment level, and this seems to be the view of the Federal Reserve, but it is likely not the view of politicians, since estimates of the natural unemployment rate range from 5.0 to 6.5 percent and most politicians think of full employment occurring only with a considerably lower unemployment rate. Price stability is generally defined by central banks at an inflation rate of 2 percent, and this seems to be the implicit inflation target of the Federal Reserve. Nonetheless, the Federal Reserve does not define what it means by maximum employment and price stability in a consistent and transparent manner. The confusion should not be surprising, as the dual mandate is a political mandate formulated by politicians on both sides of the aisle, based on short-run considerations rooted in unrealistic expectations as to what a central bank can accomplish and what it cannot accomplish. The Federal Reserve is a "prisoner of government" in this regard.

Second – it implies an exploitable short-run Phillips curve: The dual mandate implies that the Federal Reserve can influence both employment and inflation. In the short run the Federal Reserve can influence employment and inflation, but, as discussed above, even in the short run efforts by the Federal Reserve to respond to short-run shocks are complicated by long and variable lags in the effect of monetary policy. It is not at all a demonstrated fact that any central bank policy has predictable effects on employment and inflation in the short run that, on balance, can stabilize the economy. It is not a well-settled issue, despite the claims by the Federal Reserve that lags can be accommodated in the formulation and implementation of monetary policy.

In the long run, the Federal Reserve cannot change the level of employment and has the ability to determine only the inflation rate. Inflation (deflation) in the long run is a monetary phenomenon, and, hence, central banks can determine the inflation rate over time but can do little else despite political mandates the government imposes on the central bank. Simply put, requiring the Federal Reserve to achieve maximum employment amounts to imposing a final policy target that the Federal Reserve is incapable of achieving, and not only will the Federal Reserve fail to meet the mandate but it will likely find it more difficult to meet the price stability mandate that it does have the ability to achieve.

Third – what can the Federal Reserve be held accountable for? The dual mandate not only makes it difficult to hold the Federal Reserve accountable for goals it is not capable of achieving but subjects the Federal Reserve to political pressures that may influence policy away from long-run price stability. This was especially apparent in the early 1980s, as the Federal Reserve under Paul Volcker (governor from 1979 to 1987) sought to "slay" the inflation dragon with tight monetary policy. The Federal Reserve came under intense congressional and public pressure as, ignoring its mandate to achieve maximum employment, the disinflation process increased the unemployment rate above 10 percent in the early 1980s. One might respond by pointing out that, despite the pressure, the Federal Reserve was able to pursue price stability even though the unemployment rate rose in the short run and output declined in the short run. By 1985 the inflation rate had declined significantly, the unemployment rate had declined and the economy had begun an upward growth path that was not seriously interrupted until the financial crisis of 2008. This outcome, however, was only due to the Reagan administration's willingness to not interfere with Federal Reserve policy. It is not at all clear whether inflation would have been brought under control so effectively had there been another administration that placed more importance on maximum employment than price stability. In general, central banks subject to political pressure tend to have an inflation bias, and no institutional design based on *de jure* independence effectively insulates the central bank from political pressure.

Fourth – the time inconsistency problem: Even in the absence of political pressure, the dual mandate generates a *time inconsistency problem* for the Federal Reserve. Time inconsistency will be discussed in the next chapter, but it is a basic problem with any type of government policy that attempts to respond to short-run changes in the economy. Time inconsistency is doing what is *optimal in the short run but suboptimal in the long run*. Central banks that pursue both employment and price stability goals at the same time possess an inflation bias because it is optimal in the short run to emphasize employment targets and thereby sacrifice long-run price stability.

Hence, while the dual mandate sounds reasonable and appears straightforward, it is problematical. Its lack of clarity, its obvious omission of the interest rate mandate and the pressure it imposes on the Federal Reserve to exploit the short-run Phillips curve divert the Federal Reserve from achieving price stability. The Federal Reserve would better fulfill its fiduciary responsibility to the public to maintain a stable value of the nation's money supply (price stability) by having an open and frank discussion with Congress and the administration as to what central banks can accomplish and what they cannot accomplish. The dual mandate implies responsibilities that the central bank is not capable of achieving. Of course, if the Federal Reserve attempted to initiate such a discussion, it might lose its "independence".

References

Hammond, Gill (2012). "State of the Art of Inflation Targeting", Handbook no. 29. London: Centre for Central Banking Studies, Bank of England.

Chapter 16

Monetary Policy Tactics, Strategy and Rules versus Discretion

16.1 Introduction

The terms *strategy* and *tactics* are frequently used to describe the actual formulation and implementation of monetary policy designed to influence economic activity. The terms are sometimes used interchangeably; however, the terms are different in important ways, but, combined, they help us understand how monetary policy is formulated and implemented.

The strategy of monetary policy refers to the final policy targets – that is, the "what the central bank wants to accomplish" part of monetary policy. Strategy focuses on the final policy targets (Step 5) in the sequence of the central bank decision process. Central banks since the Great Inflation period have elevated price stability as the primary final policy target. A total of 29 central banks as of 2015 have adopted *explicit inflation targets* and conduct their day-to-day tactical operations in the context of that final policy target. The Federal Reserve and a number of other central banks instead utilize *implicit inflation targets*. While price stability has been elevated as a primary long-term goal of Federal Reserve policy, the Federal Reserve is constrained by its so-called "dual" mandate, which provides the operational and political framework that guides the Federal Reserve's final macroeconomic policy targets.

In contrast, the tactics of monetary policy refer to the "how the central bank accomplishes its strategic goals" part of monetary policy. Tactics refer to the choice of tools of monetary policy, choice of the policy instrument (money or interest rates) and how those policy instruments are used in the context of the macroeconomic model to achieve the final policy targets. Hence, tactics focus on Steps 2, 3 and 4 of the sequence of the central bank decision process.

The previous chapter focused on strategy. This chapter focuses more on the tactics of monetary policy, in three steps. First, this chapter reviews how the Federal Reserve formulates, implements and informs the public about its tactical and strategic operations. In this regard, the Federal Open Market Committee is the center of monetary policy in the United States. Second, the issue of tactics is broadened by considering the *Taylor rule* as a framework to understand tactically how the Federal Reserve, or any central bank, can achieve the objective of price stability as it formulates and implements monetary policy on a short-run basis. The Taylor rule is a much different tactical approach that is a substitute for the discretionary approach emphasized by most central banks. The rule introduces us to a much more general debate of the discretion versus rules approach to monetary policy. Third, the discretion versus rules debate is then discussed in detail. The debate has become rather intense at times, with the Federal Reserve and its supporters on the discretion side and critics of Federal Reserve policy on the rules side.

16.2 The FOMC and Monetary Policy

The FOMC is the focal point of the strategy and tactics of Federal Reserve policy. The structure of the FOMC was discussed in a previous chapter and emphasized as the focal point of Federal Reserve policy. The FOMC brings together at one time the Board of Governors (voting members) and the 12 Federal Reserve presidents (five of whom are voting members) and their research staffs. The FOMC brings together all of the tools of monetary policy in this regard. The FOMC formally meets eight times per year but can convene emergency meetings at any time. The meetings usually last two days and focus on two documents prepared by the Board's research staff and the research staffs of each Federal Reserve bank: the *Teal Book* and the *Beige Book*. The color refers to the color of the front/back cover of each book without any meaning attached to the color.

The *Teal Book*, prepared by the Board staff, is confidential and not available to the public until five years after the meeting at which it is utilized. The *Beige Book* is based on input from each of the 12 Federal Reserve banks and is publicly available prior to the FOMC meeting at which it is utilized.

The *Teal Book* consists of two parts. The first part is a summary and projection of domestic and international economic activity assuming no change in monetary policy, while the second part presents a projection of how the economy will perform under different types of monetary policy. The analysis is based on the Federal Reserve Board's econometric model, referred to as the FRB/US model. The FRB/US model represents the state of the art of econometric modeling, now consisting of some 300 equations representing almost a five-decade-long development.

Two weeks prior to each FOMC meeting the *Beige Book* is released to the public. The *Beige Book* is based on survey information, anecdotal information and statistical information compiled by each Federal Reserve bank regarding economic and financial activity in their respective districts. The *Beige Book* consists of 12 chapters, each devoted to one region, along with an executive summary.

The FOMC meeting is chaired by the chair of the Board of Governors, currently Janet Yellen. The chair has considerable influence over the meeting in terms of establishing the agenda, influencing the discussion and because the chair serves as the official spokesperson. It is hard to assign a specific weight to the influence of the chair because the chair's influence depends on his/her personality and the personalities of the other FOMC members, but it is always much greater than any one or several members. To paraphrase George Orwell's *Animal Farm*, "All FOMC voting members are equal, but some are more equal than the others."

The FOMC brings together all of the tools of monetary policy and the Federal Reserve officials responsible for all Federal Reserve operations, even though, from a narrow technical perspective, the FOMC is formally responsible only for open market operations. The actual open market operations and management of the Federal Reserve's portfolio of purchased securities are under the control of the Federal Reserve Bank of New York, which is the reason the president of the Federal Reserve Bank of New York is a permanent voting member of the FOMC.

The FOMC meeting can be summarized in the following five points.

First – what's the state of the economy? The FOMC forms an opinion about the current and future direction of the economy based on a wide range of economic indicators, including a complex model of the economy.

Second – the tactics and strategy of monetary policy are determined: The FOMC compares the current and future direction of the economy with its final policy targets, determines whether changes in policy are required and formulates a "forward guidance" narrative. "Forward guidance" refers to verbal and written statements as to the direction of future FOMC decisions with regard to the federal funds and other interest rates.

Third – setting the targets for the federal funds rate and other policy instruments: Decisions are made about whether to change the target value of the federal funds rate, the primary policy instrument used by the Federal Reserve. Changes in other monetary policy tools, such as the discount rate or interest paid on reserves, are also part of the dialogue. This step focuses on the tactics to achieve the strategic decisions in the previous step.

Fourth – the Federal Reserve Bank of New York, open market operations and the distinction between dynamic and defensive open market operations: The FOMC issues a directive to the manager of the Open Market Account at the Federal Reserve Bank of New York to conduct open market operations over the next few months to achieve the federal funds target. Traditionally, outright open market operations were used to target the funds rate. Since 2014 through 2016, however, the Federal Reserve has maintained a high level of securities held outright through rollovers as part of its quantitative easing policy and has not utilized changes in outright holdings of securities to target the federal funds rate. Temporary open market operations in the repurchase market have been the main tool used to target the federal funds rate, as well as the term deposit facility and setting the interest rate on excess reserves. In the following, however, we use the phrase "open market operations" in the broad sense to represent Federal Reserve efforts to target the federal funds rate.

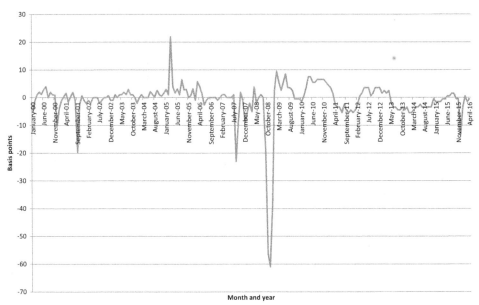

Figure 16.1. Actual Federal Funds Rate − Targeted Federal Funds Rate, in Basis Points, January 2000 to April 2016. *Sources:* Federal funds rate: – FRED, Federal Reserve Bank of St. Louis; targeted federal funds rate – based on Federal Reserve Board of Governors.

The Federal Reserve has been very successful in meeting the federal funds target over the years (Figure 16.1). The figure illustrates the difference between the monthly actual federal funds rate and the target federal funds rate for the month in basis points. One hundred basis points equal 1 percent; hence, the difference between an actual federal funds rate of 5.00 percent and a target rate of 5.10 percent is –10 basis points (500 – 510 = –10). Open market operations are designed to change base money to ensure the actual federal funds rate is close to the target. That is, if the actual rate exceeds the target, open market purchases, either through temporary or permanent operations, are made to bring the actual rate down to the target, and, if the actual rate is lower than the target, open market sales, either through temporary or permanent operations, are made to increase the actual rate.

The role of the federal funds rate can be summarized in the following:

Change in Target Federal Funds Rate = *f*(Actual Final Policy Target – Desired
Final Policy Target)   (16.1)

Change in Actual Federal Funds Rate = *f*(Target Federal Funds Rate – Actual
Federal Funds Rate)   (16.2)

To illustrate Expressions 16.1 and 16.2, let's start from equilibrium, in which the actual and targeted output growth rates are equal at 3 percent, and this is achieved with a 4 percent federal funds rate, equal to the target rate of 4 percent. The target and actual federal funds rate are equal, and, since actual output is equal to desired output growth, there is no need to change the targeted federal funds rate from 4 percent.

Now assume actual output growth declines to 2 percent because of a demand and/or supply shock. The negative output gap now requires a decrease in the target federal funds rate from 4 percent to 3 percent (Expression 16.1). The lower federal funds rate is intended to lower other interest rates, stimulate spending and increase output growth back up to the desired target rate of 3 percent. The actual federal funds rate is 4 percent and the new target is 3 percent, indicating the Federal Reserve will use open market purchases to reduce the current 4 percent federal funds rate to 3 percent (Expression 16.2). Open market purchases increase the supply of reserves, which, in turn, decreases the actual federal funds rate to the new target and thus increases output growth from 2 percent back to the desired rate of 3 percent.

In contrast, if we start from equilibrium and actual output increases to 4 percent, the target federal funds will be increased and the Federal Reserve will use open market sales to increase the actual federal funds rate so as to reduce output growth from 4 percent to the desired rate of 3 percent.

Dynamic and defensive open market operations: In this example, easier monetary policy is achieved with open market purchases and tighter monetary policy with open market sales; however, one needs to be careful in using open market operations as an indicator of monetary policy, because of the distinction between *dynamic* and *defensive* open market operations.

An example can illustrate the distinction. Assume the manager of the Open Market Account has determined that the current base money of $100 billion needs to be increased by $10 billion each month over the period until the next FOMC meeting to keep the federal funds rate equal to the target. Dynamic open market operations, assuming other things are held constant, would be to purchase securities of $10 billion each month. But other things are not constant. Base money is not only influenced directly by open market operations, which are under the control of the Federal Reserve, but also by many factors over which the Federal Reserve has some influence (such as borrowing from the Federal Reserve by depository institutions) or no influence (gold flows or decisions by the U.S. Treasury to change its account balance at the Federal Reserve). Assume these non-Federal-Reserve factors cause base money to increase from $110 to $120 billion in the first month; that is, the dynamic operations increased base money from $100 to $110 billion in the first month, but non-Federal-Reserve factors increased base money by a further $10 billion. The $120 billion in base money would cause the actual federal funds rate to fall below the target; thus, the Federal Reserve conducts defensive open market operations to defend the target of $110 billion. The Open Market Account manager would then conduct open market sales to bring base money down to $110 billion target for that month. Likewise, if base money decreased via non-Federal-Reserve factors from $110 to $105 billion, the manager would conduct open market purchases to bring base money up to $110 billion for that month.

The distinction between dynamic and defensive open market operations is important because it indicates why the direction of monetary policy cannot be determined by the direction of open market operations. Easy monetary policy might be accomplished as much with open market sales as with open market purchases, and, likewise, tight monetary policy might be accomplished with both sales and purchases. Instead of open market operations, the "Fed watchers" focus on the discount rate, targeted federal funds rate and forward guidance narrative provided by the FOMC.

Fifth – central bank transparency: The FOMC at the end of the meeting releases a statement to the public summarizing the decisions made by the FOMC and, after a few weeks, releases the minutes of the meeting to the public. The FOMC statement and minutes are an important component of central bank transparency and are both closely watched.

16.3 Transparency of the Tactics and Strategy of Monetary Policy

Central banks are dramatically more transparent about their tactics and strategy of monetary policy than a few decades ago. The Federal Reserve is transparent about decisions made at the FOMC and its overall approach to monetary policy in a number of ways.

First, a news statement is released immediately at the end of each FOMC meeting indicating the Federal Reserve's assessment of the economic condition, including a risk assessment of the economy in terms of unemployment, growth and inflation; any changes in the discount rate, the federal funds target or open market operations; a forward guidance narrative; and the record of the voting members' votes with regard to decisions made at the FOMC meeting. The chair also provides a press conference after the April, June, November and January FOMC meetings.

Second, the minutes of the FOMC meeting are released to the public about two weeks prior to the next meeting. The minutes are a fairly detailed record that provides the background discussion for the FOMC statement; for example, the minutes can provide information as to why certain members voted against the actions of the FOMC meeting as well as provide insight into the degree of the strength of any "Yes" vote. The minutes provide more detail about the FOMC's risk assessment of the economy.

Third, while the FOMC statement and minutes are the most closely watched by the numerous "Fed watchers" as to the direction of monetary policy, two other documents provide a longer-run perspective of Federal Reserve policy. In February of each year the Federal Reserve provides a *Monetary Policy Report* to Congress and testimony about past, present and future monetary policy concerns and decisions. The February report focuses on concerns and the direction of monetary policy for the coming year. In July of each year the Federal Reserve provides Congress with a preliminary report and testimony about past, present and future monetary policy concerns and decisions. The July report is a self-made report card as to how well monetary policy is accomplishing its goals for that year and what directions monetary policy might take in the next year. The February report receives the greater attention of the two reports to Congress.

Fourth, the FOMC statement, FOMC minutes and *Monetary Policy Reports* to Congress are the most important sources for the Federal Reserve's narrative of the tactics and strategy of monetary policy. However, the Federal Reserve also has a fourth channel of conveying its concerns and decisions to the public, in the form of *moral suasion*. News conferences, speeches and even sometimes research papers are used by the Federal Reserve to convey monetary and financial policy information to the public. The Federal Reserve assigns importance to this channel, but for all practical purposes moral suasion is not very informative, and most of the time has a "half-life" of only a few days after a specific moral suasion event.

16.4 Evolution of Federal Reserve Tactics

What are the tactics of Federal Reserve policy? How does the Federal Reserve develop a tactical procedure to achieve a strategic final policy target setting aside the ambiguity of the dual mandate? In the first few decades of the post-WWII period the Federal Reserve did not conduct monetary policy within the above five-step framework. The lack of a framework was not because the analytical framework of tools, policy instruments, model and final policy targets had not yet been developed. In fact, the analytical framework was well understood by economists in the 1950s. In the 1970s the Federal Reserve under the influence of Chairman Arthur Burns (1970–1978) devoted considerable resources to building an econometric model of the economy to offset criticism it had no formal model of the economy; however, the record indicates the Federal Reserve pursued a discretionary policy that was not rooted in a formal framework and was significantly influenced by political pressure that, combined, became a major cause of the Great Inflation. A number of observers at the time argued Burns used the model only as a public relations effort to defer the considerable criticism the Federal Reserve was receiving at the time for contributing to stagflation.

The Federal Reserve, like most central banks at the time, did not have a formal framework as represented by the five-step sequence. The Federal Reserve conducted policy on an FOMC meeting-by-meeting basis, without reference to what had been decided in previous meetings, and, rather than formulating any final policy targets and longer-term forward target determination, focused on short-run money market conditions and orderly financial markets. In fact, according to many critics of the Federal Reserve policy in the 1960s and 1970s, the Federal Reserve had no serious framework to formulate and implement monetary policy and was overly influenced by the "feel" and "tone" of the money market and the need to maintain an "even keel" in the money market during periods of Treasury financing – phrases once used by the Federal Reserve at that time to characterize how open market operations were conducted. While the Federal Reserve in the 1960s began development of a sophisticated econometric model of the economy that eventually evolved into the current FRB/US model, there is little evidence it played any meaningful role in the formulation and implementation of monetary policy through the 1970s.

The Federal Reserve began to develop a formal tactical and strategic approach to the conduct of monetary policy in the 1980s because of the following three factors. First, the Great Inflation that started in the mid-1960s indicated that the current operating procedures of the Federal Reserve had failed. The Federal Reserve's focus on short-run money market conditions in the absence of a clear final policy goal essentially rendered U.S. monetary policy rudderless in a turbulent sea. Second, the replacement of the old Phillips curve with the new Phillips curve elevated the primacy of price stability as the final policy target, elevated the role of expectations in how monetary policy influenced the economy and indicated the limitations of monetary policy to pursue employment objectives. Third, as part of the monetarist–Keynesian debate, much criticism was directed to the lack of any formal framework by the Federal Reserve for conducting monetary policy. In fact, in this regard, the Federal Reserve found itself on the losing end of a number of academic and public debates about then current monetary policy tactics and strategy.

In 1979, at the most intense period of the Great Inflation under the new leadership of Paul Volcker (1979–1987), the Federal Reserve began to develop and use a formal tactical framework to achieve final strategic policy targets that are now in practice not only at the Federal Reserve but at virtually every central bank in the world. First, monetary policy is conducted in the framework of a tools, policy instruments, model and final policy targets sequence; that is, the five-step sequence of central bank decision making is now the standard operating framework. Second, a set of goals is established that remain in place over time, so that, at each FOMC meeting, policy has a benchmark to determine whether it needs to be adjusted as conditions change to achieve those goals. Third, policy instrument choice is dependent on a well-researched relationship between policy instruments and final policy targets. The previous references to the "feel" and "tone" of the money market or an "even keel" are no longer mentioned in Federal Reserve policy or publications. Fourth, the tactical and strategic decisions of the Federal Reserve are made transparent to the public. Fifth, price stability is the primary final policy target.

The Federal Reserve, under the leadership of Volcker and with the formalization of tactics and strategy, was able to bring inflation under control by 1985, and the continuation of the price stabilization policy under Governor Greenspan (1987–2005) is largely regarded as generating almost two decades of price, financial and economic stability, which began to fall apart with the housing price bubble starting in 2002/2003. The period from 1985 to the first few years of the new century is referred to as the Great Moderation of central bank policy.

16.5 The Taylor Rule: Introduction to the Discretion versus Rules Debate

In 1993 Stanford University economist John Taylor developed a tactical framework to guide monetary policy to better enable central banks to make short-run decisions about the federal funds target in order to achieve the longer-run final policy target of price stability (Taylor, 1993). Taylor's objective was to suggest a tactical framework that anchored short-run decisions to set the federal funds rate to the long-run final policy target of price stability. While the framework is straightforward, it is based on a complex and complete macroeconomic model of the economy. The framework has become known as the *Taylor rule*, and it is used in various ways by many central banks. While few central banks use the rule as suggested by Taylor, the rule is often used as a benchmark to judge whether the current targeted federal funds rate is too high or too low.

The Taylor rule for setting the federal funds rate is expressed as follows:

$$\text{nffr}^* = \text{rffr}^* + p + 0.5(p - p^*) + 0.5(\text{GDP Gap}) \tag{16.3}$$

where nffr* is the target value of the nominal federal funds interest rate, rffr* is the equilibrium real federal funds interest rate, p is the actual inflation rate, p* is the target value of the inflation rate and GDP gap is the difference between actual GDP and PGDP as a percentage of PGDP. Instead of an output gap, Expression 16.3 could also be written by substituting an employment gap (natural unemployment rate minus actual unemployment rate) for the GDP gap.

The difference between actual and targeted inflation can be referred to as the *inflation gap* and the GDP gap can be referred to simply as the *output gap*. The equilibrium real federal funds rate is assumed to be 2 percent. The coefficients of 0.5 for the inflation and output gaps are approximations made by Taylor.

Here's how the Taylor rule works. Assume the economy is in long-run equilibrium at an inflation rate of 2 percent and a 0 percent output gap. At a 2 percent inflation rate, the expected inflation rate is 2 percent, the nominal federal funds rate is 4 percent and the inflation and output gaps are zero. To maintain this equilibrium inflation rate, the Federal Reserve needs to target the nominal federal funds rate at 4 percent, as indicated by the Taylor rule:

$$4\% = 2\% + 2\% + 0.5(2\% - 2\%) + 0.5(0) \tag{16.4}$$

since the inflation gap and output gap are zero. The Federal Reserve should target the actual federal funds rate at 4 percent. That is, if the actual federal funds rate exceeds the target federal funds rate, the Federal Reserve purchases securities to increase base money and thereby shift the supply of federal funds to the right, decreasing the federal funds rate to the target value of 4 percent. Instead, if the actual federal funds rate is lower than the target federal funds rate, the Federal Reserve sells securities to reduce base money and thereby shift the supply of federal funds to the left, increasing the actual federal funds rate to the target value of 4 percent.

In the absence of any change in the economy that might generate positive or negative inflation and output gaps the Federal Reserve maintains the actual federal funds rate at 4 percent. Under these conditions, monetary policy in the short run is designed to maintain price stability. If the inflation or output gap becomes negative or positive, the Federal Reserve should adjust the target federal funds rate. By doing so in the context of the Taylor rule, the public is assured that the primary goal is to maintain the inflation rate at 2 percent. A federal funds rate of 4 percent with a 2 percent inflation rate generates a real federal funds rate of 2 percent, consistent with the long-run equilibrium of the economy.

Assume a positive demand shock increases the actual inflation rate to 4 percent, generating an inflation gap of 2 percent and an output gap of 2 percent. According to the Taylor rule, the federal funds rate needs to be increased to 8 percent, according to the following:

$$8\% = 2\% + 4\% + 0.5(4.0\% - 2\%) + 0.5(2.0\%) \qquad (16.5)$$

At 8 percent, the nominal target generates a real federal funds rate equal to 4 percent, which is higher than the equilibrium rate of 2 percent and, hence, will close the inflation and output gaps. As the gaps close over time, the target federal funds rate should be reduced to 4 percent when the inflation and output gaps return to zero.

Notice the increase in the targeted federal funds rate is larger than the increase in the inflation rate; that is, the targeted federal funds rate is increased four percentage points, from 4 percent to 8 percent, whereas the inflation rate increased two percentage points, from 2 percent to 4 percent. This must be so because increasing the federal funds rate by the inflation rate increase or less will result in no change in monetary policy or represent easy monetary policy, respectively. To illustrate, if the target federal funds rate is increased two percentage points to 6 percent to match the increase in the inflation rate, the real federal funds interest rate equals 2 percent (6% – 4%) and results in no change in monetary policy. If the target federal funds rate is increased by less than the increase in the inflation rate, the real federal funds rate falls below 2 percent and represents easy rather than tighter monetary policy. Assume the target is increased by one percentage point from 4 percent to 5 percent. In this case the real federal funds rate will be 1 percent (5% – 4%). At 1 percent, the real federal funds rate is below the equilibrium rate and, despite the increase in the federal funds target, monetary policy is easy and inconsistent with price stability. Only if the federal funds rate is increased more than the increase in the inflation rate will monetary policy shift to a tighter policy and reduce the positive inflation and output gaps.

The need to increase the federal funds rate by an amount greater than the increase in the actual inflation rate is an important implication of the Taylor rule and is referred to as the *Taylor principle* – the federal funds rate needs to be adjusted upward more than the inflation rate. Anything less is not consistent with price stability and will not reduce the inflation rate back to the target.

The Taylor principle also applies to shifts to easier monetary policy. In the case of a negative inflation gap, when the actual inflation rate is lower than the target inflation rate, the federal funds rate needs to be adjusted downward more than the decline in the inflation rate to render monetary policy consistent with price stability. Assume a negative demand shock decreases actual inflation to 1 percent, generating a negative inflation gap of 1 percent and a negative GDP gap of 2 percent. The target federal funds rate needs to be lowered from 4 percent to 1.5 percent according to the following:

$$1.5\% = 2\% + 1\% + 0.5(1\% - 2\%) + 0.5(-2\%) \tag{16.6}$$

Notice that the decrease in the targeted federal funds rate is larger than the decrease in the inflation rate; that is, the inflation rate declined by one percentage point, from 2 percent to 1 percent, but the target federal funds rate declined 2.5 percentage points, from 4 percent to 1.5 percent. This must be so because of the Taylor principle. Lowering the federal funds rate by the decrease in the inflation rate would leave the real federal funds interest rate unchanged, and any decrease less than the decrease in the inflation rate would increase the real federal funds interest rate. To illustrate, reducing the target by one percentage point from 4 percent to 3 percent, to equal the decrease in the inflation rate, results in no change in monetary policy because the real federal funds rate would still be 2 percent ($3\% - 1\%$). Reducing the target by less than one percentage point, from, say, 4 percent to 3.5 percent, would result in a real federal funds rate higher than 2 percent; that is, the real federal funds rate would be 2.5 percent ($3.5\% - 1\%$). Only if the federal funds rate is decreased more than the decrease in the inflation rate will the resulting monetary policy be easy enough to eliminate the negative inflation and output gaps.

The Taylor rule has the advantage of a transparent and straightforward framework for the tactical decision on targeting the federal funds rate in the framework of strategic policy to achieve price stability. There are many issues with the Taylor rule, however.

The coefficient of 0.5 for the inflation and output gaps may not be accurate and, even if it is accurate at one point in time, may change over time; estimates of real GDP and, especially, potential GDP contain measurement errors that are not easily corrected even over medium periods of time; the data needed to compute the GDP gap are available only on a quarterly basis; and there may be other factors, such as financial distress, that influence the targeted federal funds rate. The Taylor rule is thus not a panacea, but, nonetheless, the Taylor rule and Taylor principle have become a standard part of central banks' tactical decision making.

In a review of the role of the Taylor rule in central banking provided by economists Pier Francesco Asso, George A. Kahn and Robert Leeson (2010), the following conclusion regarding the Taylor rule is rendered:

> The Taylor rule has revolutionized the way many policymakers at central banks think about monetary policy. It has framed policy actions as a systematic response to incoming information about economic conditions, as opposed to a period-by-period optimization problem. It has emphasized the importance of adjusting policy rates more than one-for-one in response to an increase in inflation. And, various versions of the Taylor rule have been incorporated into macroeconomic models that are used at central banks to understand and forecast the economy.

The Taylor rule provides a foundation for considering a broader issue of the tactics and strategy of monetary policy – the *discretion versus rules* debate. This debate is almost a century old, being first introduced by Henry Simons in the 1930s, but it continues to influence how central banks conduct monetary policy (Simons, 1936).

16.6 The Rules versus Discretion Debate

Under a rule approach to monetary policy, the tactics of policy are defined by a rule designed to achieve price stability. In a commodity-based system such as the gold standard, monetary policy was determined by the rule to maintain the fixed exchange rate. In fact, any fixed exchange rate system is a rule that guides policy with the objective of maintaining price stability.

Under a flexible exchange rate system with a fiat-based monetary system, the best-known examples of such rules are Milton Friedman's k% rule and the Taylor rule. The k% rule commits the Federal Reserve to increase the money supply (a policy instrument that can be represented by base money or one of the monetary aggregates) by a fixed percentage each year without any adjustment to changes in the economy to achieve price stability (the final policy target). This a rule without *feedback* from the economy, and, while it was debated at one time, it is not seriously considered as an effective rule for a variety of reasons. Nonetheless, it represents an important step in the debate over rules versus discretion.

The Taylor rule commits the Federal Reserve to set the target federal funds rate (policy instrument) over time defined by a rule desired to achieve price stability (final policy target). Unlike the k% rule, the Taylor rule takes into account changes in the current economic environment; that is, the Taylor rule is a rule with feedback from the economy. The rule approach is based on price stability being the only reasonable final policy target and the only macroeconomic variable for which a central bank can be held accountable. In the rules approach, central bank independence is a relatively unimportant institutional detail.

The discretion approach to monetary policy permits the central bank to use judgment and vary the tactics of monetary policy as conditions change to achieve strategic final policy targets. The discretion approach is consistent with price stability being the primary final policy, but, in reality, the discretion approach is more associated with multiple objectives of central bank policy. In the discretion approach, central bank independence is considered an important institutional design of the central bank to provide a full range of central bank discretion. It is needed to provide the central bank with a full range of discretion without outside influence as conditions change.

16.7 Arguments of the Advocates of Rules and Discretion

Advocates of rules emphasize the following points: First, while a rule will not generate complete economic stability, it will generate better outcomes than discretion, especially in achieving price stability. The record of central bank policy under discretion, especially the Federal Reserve, according to rule advocates, is not impressive. Central banks are far too confident in their ability to model the economy and use judgment to conduct monetary policy. Second, the rule provides a transparent framework to hold the central bank accountable for the one final policy target that a central bank is capable of achieving: price stability. Third, the rule prevents short-run considerations in the financial system or economy from overly influencing central bank policy and diverting it from its primary target – price stability. Fourth, the rule is the only way to render the central bank "independent" from political influence. *De jure* independence is an easy wall to breach by government, and, in reality, there is no guarantee that, in the absence of the rule, central banks will achieve price stability. In fact, the "political business cycle" is an outcome of discretion and the myth of independent central banks. Central banks under discretion are more likely to stimulate the economy in advance of an election because of pressure from the ruling party and, afterward, slow down the economy. A rule would go a long way in countering the political business cycle and other types of political influences on central bank policy. Fifth, central banks are managed by human beings, who make mistakes and possess an overoptimistic ability to understand a complex economy and, like any government agency, have an incentive to pursue policies that are perceived as important to the central bank but may be adverse to the general welfare of the public.

Advocates of discretion emphasize the following points: First, central bank policy is too complex, and short-run demand and supply shocks too numerous, to confine monetary policy to a rule. Conditions change and the rule approach limits the ability of the central bank to adjust to changing conditions and changing policy targets. Second, rules are far too simple and cannot incorporate the role of judgment; for example, the coefficients in the Taylor rule are not likely to remain constant over time, so that, even in the context of the Taylor rule, the central bank needs the discretion to adjust the coefficients. Third, rules are far too simple, because they cannot incorporate changes in the structure of the economy or provide the central bank with the flexibility to respond to a financial crisis or asset bubble. Fourth, central banks have the public good in mind when conducting policy, and a rule suggests a fundamental and unwarranted distrust of discretionary policy by a government agency. While central bankers are people who can made mistakes, discretion permits them to learn from their past mistakes.

There are three aspects of this debate worth consideration. First, what are the types of rules that have been proposed? Second, which view is the more reasonable? Third, how has the debate influenced the conduct of central bank policy today?

Type of rules: Commodity standards, such as the gold standard and the real bills doctrine, were rules that governed central bank behavior to ensure they maintained a monetary growth that generated price stability. We have previously discussed the gold standard, but not the real bills doctrine. This was another type of rule that required banks to lend only for purposes of supporting production or goods in process so that changes in money would be matched by changes in production. These rules, however, are not compatible with the financial and monetary regimes that have been in place for well over half a century around the world. The current debate focuses on the type of rules suggested by Friedman and Taylor.

The rules versus discretion debate started in earnest in the late 1950s, when Friedman challenged the Keynesians by alleging that Federal Reserve monetary policy would be better if Federal Reserve discretion were replaced by a fixed rule, to increase the M2 money supply by k% year after year, designed to achieve price stability (Friedman, 1959). As part of this view, Friedman claimed there was no reason to have an independent central bank if the central bank was governed by a rule and that independent central banks operating with discretion were more likely to generate instability than stabilize the price level. Essentially, Federal Reserve decision making would be replaced by an exponential function. The particular monetary growth rate was not as important as the rule itself. The Friedman k% rule is a no-feedback rule, since it remains fixed in the face of changes in economic activity. The Friedman k% rule had several variations, but has few advocates today. This is not because the concept of a rules approach is rejected by economists, but only because a no-feedback rule is too rigid and, in the case of the k% rule, it is difficult to determine an appropriate measure of money, and velocity is not sufficiently stable to ensure that a fixed percentage change in the money supply will generate price stability.

Taylor-type rules, however, have found much support, and, while central banks are reluctant to substitute an algebraic function for setting the interbank rate target for discretion, Taylor-type rules have influenced central banking practice far more than the Friedman k% type rule. Taylor-type rules are feedback rules, because they depend on current economic conditions and allow for judgment to play a role; for example, by changing the coefficients on the inflation and output gaps; changing the equilibrium federal funds rate based on economic modeling; or changing the target inflation rate. At a more basic level, Taylor-type rules are not regarded by central bankers as nearly as insulting as the Friedman k% rule.

Taylor-type rules, like the Friedman k% rule, have important implications for central bank independence. Central bank independence is more myth than reality, and the real issue is: how does a society hold the central bank accountable for price stability? A Taylor-type rule is a transparent tactical framework that has a reasonable probability of generating price stability and, for all practical purposes, is more likely to produce the results of an "independent" central bank than a central bank that is *de jure* independent but conducting policy by discretion and subject to political influence. Hence, in the Taylor rule, central bank independence is a relatively unimportant issue, since the rule provides the independence for the central bank to accomplish its primary final policy target – price stability.

Rules versus discretion – who can make the better case? Central banks are reluctant to hand over monetary policy to any rule and insist that rules are not a panacea and no rule can substitute for knowledgeable discretion. They make reasonable arguments against rules, especially the no-feedback rules, such as the Friedman k% rule. However, their arguments are overshadowed by three counter-arguments: first, the history of discretionary monetary policy is not as impressive as presented by the Federal Reserve; second, discretion generates unstable expectations about monetary policy and the inflation rate, according to the *Lucas critique*; and, third, discretion is subject to the *time inconsistency problem*.

Central banks, and especially the Federal Reserve, respond by admitting mistakes have been made, but, as long as the mistakes are understood, they are not likely to be repeated. The logic of the Lucas critique and time inconsistency is widely recognized by central banks, but, despite the logic, central banks argue that "enlightened discretion" or "constrained discretion" is still preferable, because any type of rule is too simple and too inflexible to guide monetary policy to contribute to a stable financial and monetary regime.

16.8 The Lucas Critique

Modern macroeconomic theory places heavy emphasis on the role of expectations about key economic variables in determining economic activity; for example, in the discussion of the term structure of interest rates in a previous chapter, expectations of short-term interest rates determine long-term interest rates. In the same vein, the public's expectations about monetary policy and other economic factors influence how the public will respond to any given monetary policy; hence, the response to any given monetary policy is not easily predictable. The new Phillips curve is importantly dependent on the public's expectation of inflation.

Robert Lucas, a Nobel Prize winner, formulated a set of models to illustrate the role of expectations and how they influenced the ability of economists to build complex econometric models such as the FRB/US model and the ability of discretionary policy to have predictable effects on the economy. The critique of econometric models and discretionary policy is now referred to as the Lucas critique.

The implications of the Lucas critique are important: first, any econometric model based on past macroeconomic relationships cannot be used to predict the future impact of any given monetary policy – the *Teal Book* discussed above is not informative; and, second, discretionary policy, because it changes in ways that are not predictable in the absence of a rule, increases expectation instability and, hence, increases economic instability.

An example of the Lucas critique can be illustrated with the discussion of how the interest rate responds to monetary policy at the end of Chapter 5. The response of the nominal interest rate is decomposed into a liquidity, income and price expectations effect. In response to an increase in the money supply, the decline in the nominal and real interest rates due to the liquidity effect is based on the public's expectation the inflation rate remains unchanged when the Federal Reserve increases the money supply. But, once the inflation rate increases as a result of the increase in the money supply (rightward shift in AD), expected inflation increases and, ultimately, the nominal interest rate increases by the increase in expected inflation and the real interest rate returns to its previous equilibrium. Thus, money is neutral in the long run with regard to the real interest rate when economic contracts are based on an expected inflation rate that is equal to the actual inflation rate.

Over time the public begins to understand that the nominal interest rate ultimately increases in response to easy monetary policy with each attempt of the Federal Reserve to lower interest rates, and under certain conditions, as in the last part of the Great Inflation in the late 1970s, nominal interest rates increased instead of decreased in response to an increase in the money supply as the price expectations effect commenced immediately. That is, the public became increasingly aware, such that, when the Federal Reserve expanded the money supply in an attempt to lower interest rates, they immediately adjusted their expected inflation rate up to incorporate the higher inflation rate that would come from the expanded money supply.

This example illustrates two implications of the Lucas critique. First, past statistical relationships between money and interest rates are not reliable, because expectations of how the economy responds to monetary policy change; and, second, the more discretionary the policy, the more unstable the expectations about the impact of any monetary policy. The implication of the Lucas critique is that a rules-based monetary policy is preferable to a discretionary-based monetary policy.

16.9 Time Inconsistency

Time inconsistency is a variation and extension of the Lucas critique rooted in the role of expectations. Time inconsistency is a straightforward concept – *pursuing a*

Table 16.1. *Matrix of Central Bank Policy Outcomes and the Public's Expected Inflation Rate*

	Public expect price stability: $p_e = 0$	Public expect inflation: $p_e = 1$
Central bank provides price stability: $p = 0$	(1,1) $p_e = p = 0$ and $y = y^* = 5$ $SW = -0^2 + 2(5 - 5) = 0$	(2,1) $p_e = 1; p = 0; y^* = 5;$ and $y = 4$ $SW = -0^2 + 2(4 - 5) = -2$
Central bank provides price inflation: $p = 1$	(1,2) $p_e = 0; p = 1; y^* = 5;$ and $y = 6$ $SW = -1^2 + 2(6 - 5) = 1$	(2,2) $p_e = p = 1$ and $y = y^* = 5$ $SW = -1^2 + 2(5 - 5) = -1$

policy that is optimal in the short run ends up being suboptimal in the long run. Every student has experienced a time inconsistency problem. The long-term goal is to achieve a good grade in a class, and that requires intense studying the weekend before a test, but something that is more appealing than studying often comes up that interrupts studying. A student often gives in, and goes to the party or concert with friends instead of studying. That seems optimal at the time, but the decision not to study reduces the probability of achieving the strategic objective of a high grade in the long run, which is a suboptimal outcome. This is time inconsistency.

Discretionary central banks are particularly prone to time inconsistency, because they are tempted to exploit the short-run Phillips curve tradeoff between inflation and unemployment even though, in the long run, the central bank cannot influence the level of unemployment and output. That is, central banks that conduct policy with discretion have an inflation bias.

Both the Lucas critique and the time inconsistency problem can be illustrated with a framework suggested by Alex Cukierman (1986). Assume the central bank and the public have a social welfare function in which social welfare, SW, is negatively related to inflation and positively related to an output gap according to the following:

$$SW = -p^2 + 2(y - y^*) \tag{16.7}$$

where p is actual inflation, y is actual output and y^* is potential output.

Table 16.1 illustrates a matrix of central bank policy outcomes in terms of p based on the public's expected inflation rate. Let's assume there are two central bank policy outcomes, $p = 0$ and $p = 1$, and two inflation expectations held by the public, $p_e = 0$ or $p_e = 1$. Further, assume $y^* = 5$. The value of y relative to y^* depends on whether inflation is equal to the public's expected inflation rate. There are four possible short-run outcomes.

1 If p = 0 and p_e = 0, the economy is defined by outcome (1,1) and SW = 0. The short-run Phillips curve defined for p_e = 0 intersects the long-run vertical Phillips curve at the actual inflation rate of p = 0.

2 If p = 1 and p_e = 0, the economy is defined by outcome (1,2) and SW = 1. The economy moves up along the given short-run Phillips curve defined for p_e = 0 and generates real output y = 6; that is, actual unemployment is less than natural unemployment and actual output is greater than potential output.

3 If p = 0 and p_e = 1, the economy is defined by outcome (2,1) and SW = –2. The economy moves down the given short-run Phillips curve defined for p_e = 1 and generates real output y = 4; that is, actual unemployment is greater than natural unemployment and actual output is less than potential output.

4 If p = 1 and p_e = 1, the economy is defined by outcome (2,2) and SW = –1. The short-run Phillips curve defined for p_e = 1 intersects the long-run vertical Phillips curve at the actual inflation rate of p = 1.

All four outcomes are possible in the short run, but only outcomes (1,1) and (2,2) are possible in the long run. Which of the two long-run outcomes is likely with central bank discretion?

The central bank has discretion to generate price stability (p = 0) or inflation (p = 1) in the absence of a rule; that is, its short-run decisions are not governed by a rule that anchors short-run decisions about the policy instrument to an inflation target. The simple social welfare function can be used to show that, if the central bank is not constrained by a rule, the central bank has a bias to inflate because of time inconsistency.

Assume the central bank has no knowledge of what the public expects and in the short run desires to pursue a policy that maximizes social welfare; that is, whether p_e = 0 or p_e = 1, the central bank will pursue a short-run policy that maximizes SW. If the public expect price stability (p_e = 0), the short-run optimal policy for the central bank is to inflate (p = 1), because social welfare is higher; that is, SW = 0 if p = 0 and p_e = 0, but SW = 1 if p = 1 and p_e = 0. If the public expect price inflation (p_e = 1), the short-run optimal policy for the central bank is to again inflate (p = 1), because social welfare is higher; that is, SW = –2 if p = 0 and p_e = 1, but SW = –1 if p = 1 and p_e = 1. Hence, in the absence of knowing what the public expect, as in the prisoner's dilemma, the central bank adopts a policy that it regards as optimal in the absence of a specific view of what the public expect. In this case, from the central bank's perspective the optimal policy is to inflate; that is, pursue a policy that is optimal in the short run but suboptimal in the long run.

As the Lucas critique emphasizes, the public adjust their expectations to take central bank policy into account. If the public expect a price-stabilizing central bank the central bank has an incentive to inflate, because the central bank can generate a positive output gap in the short run and maximize social welfare. The public will understand this inflation bias and incorporate expected inflation into their economic contracts. The economy will end up with policy outcome (2,2) in Table 16.1. If the public expect inflation the central bank has an incentive to inflate, because price stability will generate a negative output gap. The public will see that their expectations have been realized and continue to incorporate expected inflation into their economic contracts. The economy will end up with policy outcome (2,2).

In the long run, outcomes (1,2) and (2,1) are not possible, because in both cases a positive or negative output gap will generate changes in the economy to bring actual output into equality with potential output. The only long-run sustainable outcomes are (1,1) and (2,2), but which of these two is the more likely? The public over time will understand the central bank's bias to inflate to exploit the short-run Phillips curve and expect inflation; that is, over time $p_e = 1$ and the economy will end up with outcome (2,2) instead of (1,1). However, the long-run outcome generates a lower level of social welfare ($SW = -1$), because of higher actual and expected inflation than if the central bank achieved price stability and the public expected price stability ($SW = 0$).

16.10 Solutions to the Lucas Critique and Time Inconsistency

Four solutions have been suggested in the literature to solve the problem of the Lucas critique and time inconsistency. First, a rule that commits the central bank to price stability, ranging from setting inflation targets to adapting policy to a Taylor-type rule. Central banks have moved partly in this direction by incorporating both explicit and implicit inflation targets in their policies, but have been reluctant to rely extensively on Taylor-type rules. The second solution is the central bank establishes a reputation for price stability over time, the public understand the central bank's desire to maintain that reputation, and as a result expect a price-stabilizing central bank, and the economy ends up with outcome (1,1). The problem here is that reputation is fragile, especially in a political environment in which the central bank is pressured to pursue inflationary policies. The third solution is to simply structure a contract with the management of the central bank to generate price stability, and performance that does not meet the conditions of the contract results in either lower income or termination. The contract approach would have many practical problems even though it represents a theoretical solution to time inconsistency. The fourth solution is to appoint a conservative central bank management; that is, to appoint individuals who have a reputation for price stability and who would be unlikely to exploit a short-run Phillips curve. Again, like the contract approach, this has many practical problems.

Of the four solutions, some type of rule-based policy is the most practical solution. While central banks have adopted inflation targeting in one form or another, they resist the more constraining rule-based policies and prefer discretion.

16.11 Central Bank Response to the Lucas Critique and Time Inconsistency

The logic of the Lucas critique and time inconsistency is powerful and the policy implications important. The policy implications emphasize the benefits of rules over discretion, but rules are themselves problematic. In the past several decades central bank policy has incorporated a number of these policy implications in the following form:

1 greater transparency in central bank tactics and strategy;
2 primacy of price stability as the financial macroeconomic policy target;
3 explicit and implicit inflation targeting; and
4 utilization of the Taylor rule or variations of the Taylor rule to guide short-term tactics

Central banks, however, have remained reluctant to fully embrace the rules approach, and, even though they cannot deny the logic of the Lucas critique and time inconsistency, central banks regard the theoretical framework as too distant from the actual practice of central bank policy to be taken seriously. They have certainly moved in the direction suggested by the rules approach, but resist being constrained by rules and continue to use complex econometric models of the economy to guide policy.

The Federal Reserve, as well as other central banks, argue that they are more aware of the problems of activist monetary policy than in the past; have learned from their past policy errors; and have modified their tactics and strategy in response to the existence of lags in the effect of monetary policy and issues raised by the Lucas critique and time inconsistency. Nonetheless, discretion continues to be the preferred approach to central bank policy. In fact, the Federal Reserve has modified the traditional concept of discretion to what is now called "constrained discretion" (Bernanke, 2003), as a middle ground between the traditional rules and discretion approaches. Constrained discretion is a combination of the best elements of rules and the best elements of discretion. This sounds like "Do good and avoid evil", to which all would agree, but the problem comes when you have to define the meaning of "good" and "evil", and, for all practical purposes, constrained discretion (or what another former Federal Reserve official refers to as "enlightened discretion": Blinder, 1999, p. 49) is a more sophisticated discretion approach in the context of the five-step sequence discussed in this book, but discretion nonetheless. In the next and closing chapter we discuss the record of Federal Reserve policy and return to the issue of rules versus discretion in the closing comments.

References

Asso, Pier Francesco, George A. Kahn and Robert Leeson (2010). "The Taylor Rule and the Practice of Central Banking", Research Working Paper no. 10-05. Kansas City, MO: Federal Reserve Bank of Kansas City.

Bernanke, Ben S. (2003). "'Constrained' Discretion and Monetary Policy". Remarks at New York University, New York, February 3, www.federalreserve.gov/boarddocs/ Speeches/2003/20030203/default.htm.

Blinder, Alan S. (1999). *Central Banking in Theory and Practice*. Cambridge, MA: MIT Press.

Cukierman, Alex (1986). "Central Bank Behavior and Credibility: Some Recent Theoretical Developments". *Federal Reserve Bank of St. Louis Review*, 68: 5–17.

Friedman, Milton (1959). *A Program for Monetary Stability*. New York: Fordham University Press.

Lucas, Robert (1976). "Econometric Policy Evaluation: A Critique". *Carnegie-Rochester Conference Series on Public Policy*, 1: 19–46.

Simons, Henry C. (1936). "Rules versus Authorities in Monetary Policy". *Journal of Political Economy*, 44: 1–30.

Taylor, John B. (1993). "Discretion versus Policy Rules in Practice". *Carnegie-Rochester Conference Series on Public Policy*, 39: 195–214.

Part V

Performance of the U.S. Financial and Monetary Regime

Chapter 17

Five Important Periods in the U.S. Financial and Monetary Regime

17.1 Introduction

The concluding chapter reviews the performance of the nation's financial and monetary regime during five important periods of financial and economic change in the U.S. economy: the Great Depression (1929 to 1941); the Great Inflation (1965 to 1985); financial liberalization (1970s to); the Great Moderation (1985 to 2000); and the Great Recession (2006 to). Note the lack of ending dates for financial liberalization and the Great Recession. The pace of financial liberalization has slowed in the new century, but continues to change financial and monetary regimes throughout the world. The Great Recession officially ended June 2009, according to the National Bureau of Economic Research; however, the recovery has been weak, and the economy continues to operate below potential at the time of this writing in late 2016.

This chapter and Chapter 10 are historical and can be omitted without an adverse impact on understanding the country's financial and monetary regime, but knowledge of the historical evolution of the U.S. regime does add value and brings to light economic and political debates about the role of government in general and in the country's financial and monetary regime in particular. The five periods reveal important lessons about Federal Reserve policy.

The following discussion of the five periods is based on economic and historical research, some of which represents research by the author, and, while the basic outlines of the Great Depression, the Great Inflation, financial liberalization and the Great Moderation are generally accepted, debate continues over many of the details. This cannot be said of the Great Recession. Debate continues over whether the Great Recession was the result of *market failure*, *government failure* or some *combination* of the two.

Each of the five periods is addressed in turn.

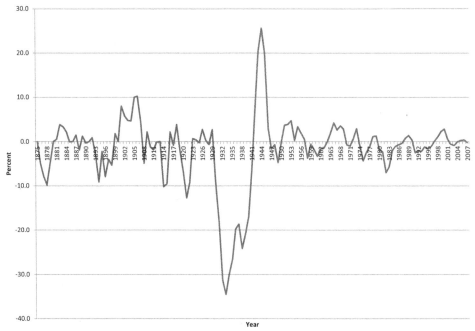

Figure 17.1. GDP Gap, 1875 to 2007. *Source:* Based on date provided by Robert J. Gordon.

17.2 Prelude to the Great Depression

It is difficult to overstate the economic shock to the nation and the world caused by the Great Depression. Figure 17.1 presents the U.S. GDP gap from 1875 to 2007 and Figure 17.2 presents the actual and natural unemployment rates from 1890 to 2007. The output and employment gaps and the economic distress the gaps imposed on the economy in the 1930s are remarkable. In Chapter 10, the collapse of the banking system was documented.

To better understand this period, the discussion starts with how the Federal Reserve evolved from its establishment in 1913 to the start of the Great Depression in 1929. The discussion then shifts to the Great Depression itself, the role of the Federal Reserve and the aftermath on Federal Reserve policy, which lasted until March 1951.

The Federal Reserve was established December 1913 in the environment of a financial system that was subject to minimal regulation and supervision by today's standard and a monetary system based on the gold standard. The first few years of the Federal Reserve's existence were challenging from several perspectives.

First, the infrastructure of the new central bank, with its unique structure of a decentralized central bank (Board of Governors and 12 Federal Reserve District banks), was a formable task in of itself.

Second, there was considerable debate between the Board of Governors, which was then referred to as the Federal Reserve Board, the New York Federal Reserve

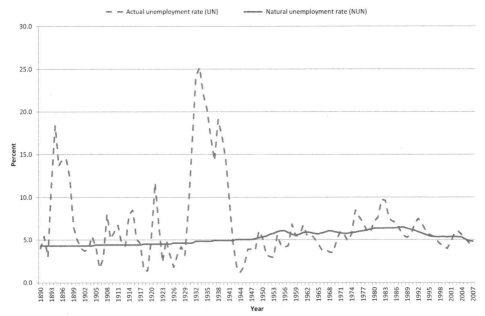

Figure 17.2. Actual Unemployment Rate and Natural Unemployment Rate, 1890 to 2007. *Source:* Based on data provided by Robert J. Gordon.

Bank and the 11 other Federal Reserve banks over the distribution of power. Until the late 1920s the New Federal Reserve Bank dominated decision making; in fact, a president of the Federal Reserve Bank of New York at one time stated that the system of 12 Federal Reserve banks was a system with 11 too many reserve banks!

Third, within a year of being established the Federal Reserve was dealing with large gold inflows from Europe that increased base money, and within a few more years it was being required to keep interest rates low to support U.S. Treasury borrowing to finance military spending during WWI. As a result, inflation increased rapidly after 1915. The average inflation rate measured by the CPI from 1916 to 1920 was 14.7 percent.

Fourth, the Federal Reserve in 1920 withdrew its support of U.S. Treasury securities and commenced a tight monetary policy with large increases in the discount rate. This is now considered a successful price stabilization policy, as inflation was quickly brought under control, but with a sharp decline in prices and output. The average inflation rate from 1921 to 1923 was 8.6 percent, but by 1923 the inflation rate was 1.8 percent. Inflation remained low and stable for the remainder of the 1920s and contributed to the prosperity of that decade. However, the negative political reaction to the Federal Reserve's aggressive discount policy had a lasting influence in tempering Federal Reserve interest rate policy that continues to the present. The Federal Reserve continues to be more willing to lower interest rates than raise interest rates.

The remainder of the 1920s was a successful period for Federal Reserve policy. The economy grew at a rapid rate in response to the direct and indirect effects of the new innovations of the radio and automobile. The business cycle was barely noticeable, employment was high and the average inflation rate was low. The average inflation rate from 1923 to 1930 was 0.3 percent. Nonetheless, the Federal Reserve on the eve of the Great Depression had a fractured decision-making structure in the form of a weak Board of Governors and decision-making process dominated, until 1928, by the Federal Reserve Bank of New York. In that year Benjamin Strong, who headed the Federal Reserve Bank of New York, died and was replaced by a much weaker leader. Thus, on the eve of the Great Depression the Federal Reserve decision-making process consisted of a weak board and 12 District banks with different views and competing for power and influence in the Federal Reserve.

17.3 The Great Depression

The Great Depression actually consists of four periods that span a decade: the Great Contraction, from 1929 to 1933, which witnessed the collapse of the U.S. financial and real sector; "recovery", from 1933 to 1937, in the technical sense that the economy began to expand after 1933; sharp recession in 1937; and continued recovery from 1938 to 1941 as the U.S. economy prepared for war. The Great Depression ended when the Japanese attacked Pearl Harbor on December 7, 1941. The United States declared war on Japan, and Germany and Italy declared war on the United States, and, as a result, the United States became an engine of war production unparalleled in world history.

The Great Depression started August 1929, according to the NBER. This is two months before the stock market crash on October 29, 1929. The stock market crash has been widely viewed as the start and cause of the Great Depression; however, the evidence is not consistent with the hypothesis, even though the crash continues to be assigned great importance as the cause. There are different opinions about what started the decline in August 1929, with most attention directed to a shift toward tighter monetary policy by the Federal Reserve. The recession was severe, but not out of line with previous downturns. The decline turned into the Great Contraction in late 1930 with a wave of bank failures as the public lost confidence in deposit money and there was a series of unwise policies by the federal government to raise taxes and restrict imports. To understand the wave of bank failures, keep in mind that federal deposit insurance was not established until 1934. The effort to convert deposits into currency (base money) had three immediate effects: first, by increasing the k ratio in the money multiplier, M2 money supply declined by 25 percent from 1929 to 1933; second, the contagion effect caused widespread bank failures, so that by 1933 the banking system had declined from about 40,000 banks to 30,000 banks; and, third, the banks that survived were much more risk-averse and less willing to loan funds.

The public's desire to hold currency instead of deposits, the resulting collapse of the banking system and the reduced supply of loanable funds; increased income taxes by the Hoover administration; and restrictions on imports by the Hoover administration (Smoot–Hawley tariffs) shifted AD to the left, resulting in a 27 percent decline in output and a 26 percent decline in the price level from 1929 to 1933.

The turning point in the Great Depression, in 1933, came in response to two factors. First, shortly after coming to power the Roosevelt administration declared a banking holiday, followed by an impressive series of financial reforms including establishing federal deposit insurance in 1934. The k ratio in the money multiplier declined and the money supply began to increase. Second, capital inflow from Europe caused a major increase in gold flowing into the United States. The U.S. Treasury monetized the gold inflow by issuing gold certificates to the Federal Reserve, which in turn increased base money.

The financial system stabilized in response to federal deposit insurance, other reforms and increased liquidity. The economy began to recover in 1933; however, the term "recovery" must be understood in the technical sense, because on the eve of the sharp decline starting May 1937 the economy remained depressed. In 1936 the output gap remained large at −19.8 percent and unemployment remained high at 17 percent. Unemployment was much higher, however, considering discouraged and marginal worker effects. Even in 1939 the economy remained distressed, with the output gap at −20.9 percent and unemployment at 17.2 percent.

The technical recovery ended May 1937 when the United States experienced a short but sharp decline, which bottomed in June 1938. The recession was short, and, starting June 1938, the economy continued to expand through December 7, 1941, and then expanded greatly thereafter (Figures 17.1 and 17.2). However, even in 1941 the economy was operating well below its potential. The output gap in 1941 was −6.3 percent and the unemployment rate was 9.9 percent.

17.4 Role of the Federal Reserve

Until the 1960s the widely held view of the Great Depression and the role of the Federal Reserve could be summarized in the following points.

First, the causes of the Great Depression were rooted in the unequal distribution of income; speculation in the stock market; business "animal spirits" in search of profit; excessive competition between banks for deposits and loans; and the close relationship between investment and commercial banking. That is, the economic and financial system were structurally weak, and any shift in AD would bring down the whole house of cards. The shift in AD was initially caused by a slowdown in private investment; hence, the Great Depression was the result of market failure.

Second, the New Deal policies of the Roosevelt administration were responsible for the recovery that started in 1933 and demonstrated the ability of activist government to mitigate market failure and stabilize the economy.

Third, the Federal Reserve conducted easy monetary policy, but the economy was in a liquidity trap in that providing money and lowering interest rates was like "pushing on a string", as the public lacked confidence and were unwilling to spend. The structural problems overwhelmed any easy monetary policy by the Federal Reserve. The Federal Reserve had its own structural issues because of the lack of central leadership, but, by and large, the Federal Reserve did everything in its power to reverse the decline.

Fourth, the war induced recovery in late 1941, demonstrating the correctness of the Keynesian model; that is, higher government spending ended the Great Depression.

This perspective, which emphasizes the ineffectiveness of monetary policy, the inherent instability of a market system and the need for an extensive expansion of government management of AD, regulation and supervision, was widely accepted into the first few decades after the end of WWII.

Then, in 1963, Milton Friedman and Anna Jacobson Schwartz published *A Monetary History of the United States: 1867 to 1960*, which challenged each of these widely held views. The challenge became an important part of the monetarist–Keynesian debate in the next two decades. Friedman and Schwartz (1963) offered an alternative view of the role of the Federal Reserve in the Great Depression.

First, policy errors by the Federal Reserve turned what would have been a normal recession into the Great Contraction by its failure to be an aggressive lender of last resort to individual banks and its failure to increase base money with open market operations. The errors were the result of dysfunctional decision making, a misunderstanding of how monetary policy impacted the economy and a lack of leadership.

Second, by any standard monetary policy was tight during the Great Contraction. Base money declined, the money supply declined and, while nominal interest rates were low, real interest rates were high because of deflation. The average real interest rate from 1930 to 1933 was 11.7 percent! Arguments by the Federal Reserve that regulations and rules governing discount policy prevented it from more aggressive action lacked merit and were ex post excuses for an ex ante lack of willingness to function as a lender of last resort. Had the Federal Reserve pursued a more active policy the Great Depression would not have been as deep nor as long.

Third, the recovery that started March 1933 had little to do with Federal Reserve policy or New Deal spending and more to do with federal deposit insurance reestablishing public confidence in deposit money (increasing the k ratio in the M2 money multiplier) and the decision by the U.S. Treasury to monetize the huge capital flight in the form of gold inflows from Europe as the winds of war became apparent.

Fourth, the sharp recession that started May 1937 was directly due to the Federal Reserve's decision to eliminate the large amount of excess reserves held by banks by doubling reserve requirements over a six-month period (Cargill and Mayer, 2006). The Federal Reserve assumed that the excess reserves were due to a lack of demand for loans and, hence, doubling reserve requirements would have no effect on bank lending. This was a policy error caused by the Federal Reserve's failure to distinguish between actual and desired excess reserves. The situation was just the opposite, however. The excess reserves were desired because of risk aversion by banks, and, as reserve requirements increased, banks reduced their lending.

Fifth, the Great Depression was due to government policy failure, especially Federal Reserve policy. The Great Depression is thus an argument against activist government policy rather than evidence to support an expanded role of government in the economy.

Sixth, the New Deal spending was ineffective, and many of the new policies to regulate the economy interfered with recovery.

Friedman and Schwartz ignited an intense debate, and, while some elements of their analysis have been modified and others reinforced, the weight of evidence is consistent with the view that policy errors by the Federal Reserve played an important role in causing the Great Contraction and the sharp recession in 1937 and 1938; that is, had the Federal Reserve pursued a more aggressive easy policy the Great Recession would have been shorter and not as deep. Robert Whaples (1995) illustrates this point in his survey of economists and historians. Whaples found that no more than 25 percent of both historians and economists would unconditionally reject the argument the Federal Reserve was a contributing factor. More recently Ben Bernanke (2002) has highlighted the negative impact the Federal Reserve had on the economy:

> The brilliance of Friedman and Schwartz's work on the Great Depression is not simply the texture of the discussion or the coherence of the point of view . . . For practical central bankers, among which I now count myself, Friedman and Schwartz's analysis leaves many lessons. What I take from their work is the idea that monetary forces, particularly if unleashed in a destabilizing direction, can be extremely powerful. The best thing that central bankers can do for the world is to avoid such crises by providing the economy with, in Milton Friedman's words, a "stable monetary background" – for example as reflected in low and stable inflation.
>
> Let me end my talk by abusing slightly my status as an official representative of the Federal Reserve. I would like to say to Milton and Anna: Regarding the Great Depression. You're right, we did it. We're very sorry. But thanks to you, we won't do it again.

The argument that New Deal government spending was ineffective is attested to by no other authority than Henry Morgenthau, President Roosevelt's secretary of the Treasury. On May 9, 1939, Morgenthau in a meeting with four other officials at the U.S. Treasury stated the following in his diary (Henry Morgenthau Diary, 1939):

> Now, gentlemen, we have tried spending money. We are spending more than we have ever spent before and it does not work . . . I want to see this country prosperous. I want to see people get a job . . . We have never made good on our promises . . .

This passage was made public only a few years ago, and it gives an uncomfortable perspective for those who hold the New Deal spending as good government policy despite the large body of economic evidence that the impact of the New Deal on the recovery is exaggerated.

17.5 Aftermath: Redesigning the Federal Reserve, Government Financial Regulation and the Financial System

The Federal Reserve was not held responsible for its role in the Great Depression for many decades. The Great Depression was viewed as the result of nonmonetary forces that could not be offset by monetary policy. The inability of the Federal Reserve to be more effective at that time was viewed as the result of a decentralized decision-making process, a lack of sufficient tools of monetary policy and a functionally unsound financial system because it permitted too much competition, allowed a close relationship between investment and commercial banking and was largely unregulated and unsupervised. Both issues were dealt with by a series of legislative and administrative actions from 1933 to 1935 that established the current structure of the Federal Reserve to the present and the financial system through the 1970s.

The redesign of the Federal Reserve: The Federal Reserve was subject to an extensive set of institutional reforms in 1935. Open market operations were centralized in the newly established Federal Open Market Committee; the tactics and strategy of monetary policy were concentrated in the Board of Governors, which dominated the Open Market Committee; and the monetary policy tools were revised and extended. In particular, the Board of Governors was provided with the ability to change reserve requirements and the ability to set margin requirements on stocks and bonds convertible into stocks.

As a result of the then perceived impotence of the Federal Reserve and the impotence of monetary policy in the early versions of the Keynesian model, Federal Reserve policy moved into the background and the Federal Reserve lost all flexibility to conduct monetary policy shortly after December 7, 1941, when it was required to target government security interest rates at a low level to assist U.S. Treasury sales of debt to finance the massive increase in government spending that would be required to wage war against Germany, Japan and Italy. This was a proper role for a central bank in times of national emergency; however, the Federal Reserve was required to continue targeting interest rates on government securities until March 1951. By that time there was growing concern Federal Reserve policy needed to be more flexible to deal with inflation and needed to be released from the requirement to support government security interest rates. In March 1951 a one-page Treasury–Federal Reserve Accord stated that the Federal Reserve would no longer support the interest rates on government debt, and these interest rates would henceforth be determined by market forces.

The Federal Reserve emerged from the 1951 accord diminished in reputation and relegated to a minor role as an instrument of stabilization, due to the increasing acceptance of the Keynesian model and the then popular nonmonetary theories of inflation. In fact, this episode illustrates the relative unimportance of *de jure* independence relative to *de facto* independence for a central bank. The formal independence of the Federal Reserve remained intact from 1942, when the interest rate support program was established, until March 1951, yet it was completely *de facto* dependent on the government. Despite the shift from a completely dependent central bank under the interest rate support program to some degree of *de facto* independence after the 1951 accord, Federal Reserve independence continued to be constrained by the 1946 Employment Act. The Federal Reserve, reflecting the political consensus to prevent a repeat of the high unemployment rates in the 1930s, placed a higher weight on employment than price stability despite publicly supporting price stability; developed a "flexible" concept of independence; and coordinated monetary policy with Treasury bond placements, referred to as "even keel" policies.

McChesney Martin became chair of the Board of Governors in 1951 and remained in that position until replaced by Arthur Burns in 1971. Martin publicly supported price stability, but in practice placed greater weight on coordinating monetary policy with the Treasury and viewed Federal Reserve independence as independence "within" rather than "from" government. This flexible view of independence amounts to *de facto* dependence on government policy.

The stable macroeconomic performance of the economy and price stability in the 1950s are often attributed to the independent Federal Reserve released by the 1951 accord; however, this view is not convincing, for two reasons. First, there is no evidence from a close reading of Federal Reserve documents during this period that the Federal Reserve understood the relationship between money and inflation, nor possessed anything but a shallow understanding of how monetary policy functioned. That is, the record is not consistent with the view of an independent Federal Reserve focused on price stability during this period. Second, the Federal Reserve found itself in a favorable environment with little pressure to depart from price stability. In fact, the 1950s were like the 1920s, which was also a successful period of Federal Reserve policy. Both decades followed wars, both decades experienced significant increases in potential output, both decades experienced a confident public and both decades had low government deficits.

The political environment changed in the 1960s, especially under the Johnson administration, when monetary policy became *de facto* less independent and set the basis for the Great Inflation.

Financial reform: The financial system was also subjected to significant institutional redesign. Federal government regulation and supervision expanded with the establishment of the Federal Deposit Insurance Corporation in 1934, the Securities and Exchange Commission in 1935 and a number of other new regulatory agencies to oversee different parts of the financial system. The number of financial reforms is large, and any detailed discussion would be beyond the scope of this chapter; however, three aspects of the redesign effort are important.

First, the financial system prior to the Great Depression was regarded as unstable, because it lacked federal regulation and supervision to limit imprudent lending by banks. Imprudent lending exposed banks to failure in the face of any economic decline and thereby reduced public confidence in deposit money. Hence, the rationale for a greatly expanded role for federal regulation and supervision, also matched at the state level, was designed to limit imprudent lending and sustain public confidence in deposit money.

Second, the pre-Great-Depression financial system allowed the overlap of investment banking (underwriting debt and securities) and commercial banking (accepting deposits and making loans). It was widely accepted at the time this led to speculation on the stock market, conflicts of interest between banks and their depositors and outright fraud. A major focus of the reforms was to separate commercial from investment banking to limit risk taking and maintain public confidence in deposit money.

Third, the pre-Great-Depression financial system permitted interest rates in both the direct and indirect financial markets to be market-determined. Market-determined interest rates, especially for deposits, were then regarded as providing incentives to assume imprudent levels of risk taking. As banks competed for deposits with higher interest rates, they were required to make riskier loans as the cost of funds increased. The solution was to place interest rate ceilings on deposits. Demand deposits had a zero ceiling while saving and time deposits were subject to a positive ceiling set by the Federal Reserve, referred to as Regulation Q. Also, to limit usury, many state governments imposed interest rate ceilings on bank credit. Interest rates in direct money and capital markets were permitted to be market-determined, but these markets now came under government regulation and supervision.

17.6 The Great Inflation: A Clash of Federal Reserve Policy Errors and Flawed Financial Regulation

The Great Inflation period was one of intense financial and economic distress in the United States and many countries. The macroeconomic environment of high inflation, high unemployment and low and declining output was accompanied by disruptions in the flow of funds and the ultimate collapse of the S&L industry. The unstable macroeconomic environment and financial disruptions were importantly the result of policy errors on the part of government regulation of the financial system to limit competition; Regulation Q; subsidization of homeownership by protecting the S&L industry as a specialized mortgage lenders; and Federal Reserve easy monetary policy.

Inflation remained low from 1952 to 1965, averaging only 1.5 percent, but four events set the stage for excessively easy monetary policy, the Great Inflation and the loss of any *de facto* independence the Federal Reserve had achieved by the 1951 accord. The easy monetary policy and resulting inflation clashed with a fundamentally unsound financial structure designed to limit competition and support homeownership.

First, the Kennedy administration elevated activist Keynesian demand management policy as part of its "new economic policy", outlined in the *1962 Economic Report of the President* (Kennedy, 1962); second, the Federal Reserve was required to coordinate monetary policy with the administration's fiscal policy; third, the Phillips curve tradeoff between employment and inflation in the context of the Employment Act of 1946 provided incentives to the Federal Reserve to purchase employment with inflation; and, fourth, the Johnson administration after 1963 embarked on an aggressive government spending program, ran large and persistent deficits and was generally unwilling to raise taxes.

Once inflation had become a serious problem the Phillips curve was then used as an argument against anti-inflation policy, because aggressive anti-inflation policy would be "too costly" in terms of lost employment. In hindsight, it is remarkable how influential the 1958 paper by Phillips was on public policy.

The Martin administration was susceptible to inflationary policy because of his particular concept of Federal Reserve independence as independence "within" government and not "from" government. That is, the Martin concept of independence emphasized cooperation with the government and *de facto* dependence irrespective of the *de jure* independence of the Federal Reserve. The concept implied only a one-way relationship. The Federal Reserve accommodated government spending but, as inflation increased, the government was reluctant to take actions to reduce the deficit or permit the Federal Reserve to increase interest rates sufficient to disinflate. This was clearly illustrated in 1968, when the Johnson administration imposed a temporary 10 percent surtax on corporations and individuals; however, its temporary nature ensured a minimal impact on spending, because it was advertised as only temporary. In fact, faith in Keynesian demand management was so entrenched at the time the Federal Reserve was concerned the temporary surtax might lead to "fiscal overkill". As a result, the Federal Reserve continued easy monetary policy.

Martin's administration ended in January 1970, and in February 1970 Burns became chair of the Board of Governors. Burns had established himself as a world-class academic. There was great anticipation that such an academically qualified individual would return Federal Reserve policy to price stability. Instead, Burns continued and accelerated the inflationary policy, such that inflation eventually reached double-digit rates by the late 1970s, accompanied by increasing unemployment. Burns continued the Martin approach to independence and was willing to trade Federal Reserve independence and price stability to work within the government; support administration deficit spending and employment goals; and support the political aspirations of both Richard Nixon and, later, Jimmy Carter. Burns believed the costs of disinflation were politically unacceptable, and, as a result, he and the Federal Reserve became advocates of wage and price controls, which were imposed on the U.S. economy in 1971. They were removed shortly afterwards, causing much distress.

This period saw the collapse of the Bretton Woods fixed exchange rate system in August 1971, when Nixon announced the New Economic Policy, directed at dealing with both internal and domestic issues: ending the convertibility of dollars into gold; imposing a 10 percent surcharge on imports, aimed primarily at Japan and Germany unless they revalued their currencies; and imposing a 90-day wage/price freeze to deal with inflation. The fixed exchange rate system was unsustainable because deficit countries such as the United States were not willing to slow economic growth and surplus countries such as Japan and Germany were unwilling to inflate. The gold standard was never a serious constraint on Federal Reserve policy after WWII; nonetheless, the shift to flexible exchange rates permitted the Federal Reserve to ignore international currency fluctuations to an even greater extent than before. There was a brief period between 1971 and 1973 when efforts were made to maintain the fixed exchange rate system with revalued currencies; however, in 1973 the fixed exchange rate system ended.

The unwillingness of the Federal Reserve to appreciate the relationship between money and inflation is difficult to understand, but the willingness to become advocates of wage and price controls as a solution to inflation is even more difficult to understand. The decision to support controls further eroded the independence of the Federal Reserve and affirmed the public's expectation the Federal Reserve lacked either the power or willingness to bring inflation under control. So, not only did inflation increase but so did expected inflation. The evidence is overwhelming the Federal Reserve under Burns regarded its role as supporting the government. The excerpt from a diary kept by Burns cited in Chapter 11 emphasizes this point. The efforts by Burns to appease the White House and assist Nixon's 1972 reelection are well known. This period is a dark history of the Federal Reserve, and the entire episode of the Great Inflation renders any concept of independence based on the *de jure* perspective irrelevant.

The Federal Reserve not only failed to stabilize the value of the dollar but contributed to intensive disruptions in the financial system as inflation increased the gap between unregulated money and capital market interest rates and the Regulation Q ceilings on deposits at banks and S&Ls. Federal Reserve understanding of the connection between macro-policy and financial regulation was limited. This was especially apparent with any discussion of Regulation Q. Most discussions of Regulation Q were devoid of any awareness of the distorting effects on the financial system of the increasing gap between money market interest rates and the Regulation Q ceilings. Instead, discussion focused on competitive equity between depository institutions and the legality of imposing interest rate ceilings (Meltzer, 2009,

p. 385). This is remarkable considering the adverse impact Regulation Q had on the stability of the financial system in the 1970s. This lack of attention to the resource-distorting effects of Regulation Q was also verified by Mayer (1982) in regard to an action in 1966 by the Federal Reserve to lower Regulation Q as inflation was beginning to increase. This lack of attention to structural flaws in the financial system by the Federal Reserve and failure to consider how easy monetary policy would lead to financial distress was repeated in the first few years of the new century and led to the Great Recession.

Increasing criticism of Federal Reserve policy by a growing number of outside critics was vigorously resisted by the Federal Reserve, which argued that inflation was due to other factors, such as oil price shocks, agricultural price shocks and labor union shocks, and that monetary policy was tight, as evidenced by high interest rates. The critics countered these arguments by pointing out that economic theory and history showed inflation was a monetary phenomenon; that oil price shocks or other discrete events could not explain consistent inflation over time; and that high interest rates indicated easy rather than tight monetary policy because of the Fisher effect.

Congress attempted to rein in the Federal Reserve with the 1978 Full Employment and Balanced Growth Act, which required the Federal Reserve to report to Congress twice yearly; required the Federal Reserve to focus on price stability as well as maximum employment; and required the Federal Reserve to formulate monetary aggregate targeting to better control the inflation rate and economy. The 1978 Act was well intended but only confused the final policy targets by imposing a dual mandate on the Federal Reserve. Nonetheless, the dual mandate was made part of the Federal Reserve Act in 1979 and continues to be the operating framework of the Federal Reserve.

Inflation continued, along with high unemployment. By 1979 the Federal Reserve had lost all credibility for price stability, the public did not anticipate fiscal restraint from the government and, as a result, government spending and deficits were expected to be accommodated by the Federal Reserve. Inflationary expectations continued to increase, shifting the short-run Phillips curve to the right, and thereby increased unemployment at the current inflation rate. Burns wanted to remain chair and, as a result, supported the new Carter administration in 1977 with continued easy policy; however, he was not reappointed. William Miller was appointed chair in March 1978, and was shortly replaced by Paul Volcker in August 1979. Miller's tenure is the shortest and the least successful in Federal Reserve history, because his appointment came at the height of the Great Inflation and Miller did not have the skills necessary to head a central bank.

In 1979 the economy was in economic and political crisis: inflation; high unemployment; high interest rates; increasing gold prices; declining value of the dollar; disintermediation of funds from depository institutions to money markets; insolvency of the S&L industry; financial scandal, involving an effort by two Texas bankers – the Hunt Brothers – to manipulate the silver market; and the need for a large federal loan guarantee to keep Chrysler from bankruptcy. On the political front the Iranian hostage crisis further generated a sense the government was unable to influence its environment. As the 50th anniversary of the Great Depression passed, a large number of policy makers asked whether "it" could happen again.

17.7 Financial Liberalization and the Great Moderation

Three policy tracks were adopted in 1979 and 1980 to deal with the crisis, which set the stage for a two-decade period of economic growth and price stability characterized by financial liberalization with respect to the financial system and the Great Moderation with respect to central bank policy.

The first involved a major regulatory overhaul of the financial system, designed to remove a number of constraints imposed on the financial system during the 1930s; second, the appointment of Volcker as chair of the Board of Governors with a political mandate to return the economy to price stability; and, third, a new set of tactics and strategy for the Federal Reserve that were more rule-based than previously and focused on price stability.

Financial liberalization: The Great Inflation clashed with Regulation Q ceilings and the policy of maintaining S&Ls as specialized mortgage lenders and was the primary cause of the collapse of the S&L industry, over a two-decade period starting in the early 1960s. The S&L industry was regulated to be specialized lenders of mortgage funds to support the social contract to encourage homeownership. The collapse of the S&L industry was officially recognized in 1989 when Congress passed legislation to resolve insolvent institutions, representing the largest collapse of the U.S. financial system since the Great Depression and imposing a taxpayer cost of $124 billion in nominal dollars as of December 31, 1999 (Curry and Shibut, 2000). Assuming an even distribution of this amount over the period from 1990 to 1999, the taxpayer cost was $194 billion in 2013 dollars.

Financial policy designed to support homeownership (Regulation Q interest rate ceilings, specialized mortgage lending status provided to the S&L industry, Fannie Mae, Freddie Mac, etc.) and inflationary monetary policy exposed the S&L industry to interest-rate, liquidity and disintermediation risk in the 1970s that ultimately caused the collapse of the industry in the 1980s. This crisis was caused by the combination of monetary policy failure, a flawed financial system designed to support homeownership and a flawed policy response to the increasing number of troubled S&Ls.

The policy response was anchored in denial and, when denial was no longer credible, in understating the magnitude of the problem, and when a policy response could no longer be avoided the policy response was based on forgiveness and forbearance. Forgiveness involved changing the regulatory parameters to transform insolvent S&Ls into solvent S&Ls. Forbearance involved holding off closing a troubled institution in the hope it would "work its way" out of insolvency. This policy response prolonged the distress and increased the ultimate resolution cost, and had a large moral hazard component. Finally, when significant taxpayer funding was required to bail out the S&L industry, the emphasis shifted to blaming the market and "greedy" financial institutions to cover up the combination of Federal Reserve failure and flawed financial policy to encourage homeownership. This is not to deny there was fraud and gross misrepresentation at the individual S&L level (market failure), but the overwhelming cause of the collapse of the S&L industry resided in its flawed structure and an easy monetary policy that generated inflation in the context of Regulation Q ceilings.

The collapse of the S&L industry and related distress in the financial system forced an attitudinal and policy response that reversed the reforms imposed during the Great Depression. The United States embarked on a financial liberalization process to redesign the financial system by removing interest rate ceilings on deposits and loans; expanding the portfolio diversification powers of financial institutions; ending the separation between investment and commercial banking; and, in general, permitting market forces to play a more important role in allocating credit than previously.

The financial reforms involved major legislation and administrative actions that significantly liberalized the flow of funds in the United States.

Paul Volcker and slaying the inflation dragon: Volcker is the most successful chair of the Federal Reserve in its history in terms of coming into a crisis situation, playing a key role in resolving the crisis and setting the stage for a 15-year period of generally good monetary policy outcomes, referred to as the Great Moderation. Volcker assumed the chairmanship in a crisis with the required reputation; with a correct view of how to bring inflation down via reduced monetary growth; with a correct view of how Keynesian policies had led to the inflation; with a correct view of the importance of the public's inflationary expectations in the process; and, most important, with a realistic view of the costs of reducing the public's inflationary expectations. Volcker saw the Federal Reserve as the primary weapon to "slay the dragon" (Volcker, 2000).

Just as important, however, Volcker had the benefit of a political environment that permitted the Federal Reserve to achieve price stability even though it imposed a rather serious but short recession on the economy. This was needed to reverse inflation expectations, which had been based on over two decades of excessively easy monetary policy by the Federal Reserve, and the complete loss of the Federal Reserve's reputation and credibility for price stability. The Reagan administration assisted the Federal Reserve in reversing inflationary expectations with its general support for price stability and lack of criticism of Volcker, but, most dramatically,

President Reagan's support was demonstrated in the August 1981 showdown with the Professional Air Traffic Controllers Organization, the union representing the nation's airport controllers.

The union declared an illegal strike on August 3, 1981, for higher pay, other benefits and a 32-hour work week. In remarks with reporters on August 3, 1981, Reagan indicated that, if the striking controllers did not return to work within 48 hours, "they forfeited their jobs and will be terminated" (Reagan, 1981). On August 5, 1981, Reagan fired 11,300 air controllers, or about 87 percent of the air traffic controller workforce. The union was decertified a few months later. The importance of this event cannot be understated, and it played a major role in reducing inflationary expectations.

New tactics and strategy for price stability: The formal change in monetary policy came at the October 6, 1979, FOMC meeting accompanied by congressional testimony by Volcker and other public statements. The key elements of the new Federal Reserve policy were: 1), inflation had to be brought under control, to achieve economic growth and end the disruptions in the financial system and in exchange rates: 2), lower inflation would increase employment; 3), control over the money supply (officially redefined as M2, to include a number of financial innovations that had been ongoing for over a decade) was key to reducing inflation; 4), the disinflation process would not be easy and would take time; and, 5), lowering the public's expected inflation rate was essential to the anti-inflation policy.

The Federal Reserve through fall 1982 adopted a "practical" monetarist approach by focusing on monetary control as the policy instrument; however, the monetary control focus was considered difficult, and within a few years the Federal Reserve shifted to targeting the federal funds rate. By fall 1982 the disinflation process was successful and there was growing evidence the public's inflationary expectations were being rapidly reduced. The Federal Reserve abandoned its monetarist approach and returned to interest rate targeting after 1982. By 1986 inflation had been reduced to relatively low and stable rates, the effects of the 1981–1982 sharp recession were in the past and the financial system had stabilized. The disinflation policy of the Federal Reserve from 1979 to 1986 is one of the most significant policy successes in the entire history of the Federal Reserve, in the opinion of many researchers.

17.8 The Great Moderation

Inflation remained under control after 1985. Volcker elevated price stability as the major policy target of the Federal Reserve, which continued for most of the Alan Greenspan (1987–2006) administration. The focus on price stability occurred in the context of macroeconomic thinking that rejected Keynesian demand management policies, especially the Phillips curve tradeoff, and viewed central bank policy as

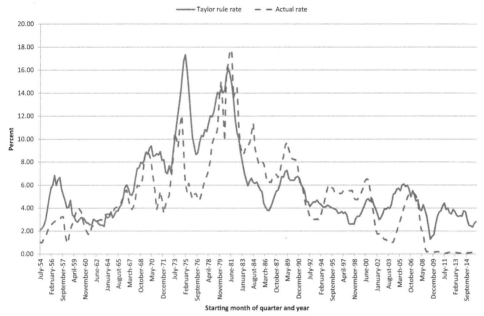

Figure 17.3. Actual and Taylor Rule Federal Funds Rate, 1953:3 to 2016:1. *Sources:* Federal funds rate – FRED, Federal Reserve Bank of St. Louis; Taylor rule, federal funds rate – FRED Blog, Taylor rule, Federal Reserve Bank of St. Louis (https://fredblog.stlouisfed.org/?s= taylor+rule).

neutral in the long run and, thus, price stability should be the central bank's primary objective. Most important, the focus on price stability had political support. Many central banks adopted inflation targets; however, the Federal Reserve did not, and continued to emphasize the dual mandate of price stability and maximum employment. Nonetheless, during the Great Moderation period the Federal Reserve attempted to anchor short-run decisions to the long-run final policy target of price stability and restrain inflationary forces.

In fact, Federal Reserve policy during the Great Moderation, in contrast to the Great Inflation, can be fairly well explained by the Taylor rule, illustrated in Figures 17.3 and 17.4. The Federal Reserve kept the federal funds rate well below what a Taylor rule would indicate from 1965 to 1980. On average, the federal funds rate was 2.66 percentage points lower than the Taylor rule rate from the first quarter of 1965 to the last quarter of 1979. During the Volcker years, from 1980 to 1985, as the Federal Reserve shifted to deflating the economy, the actual federal funds rate was 1.76 percentage points higher than the Taylor rule rate. During the Great Moderation period, from 1986 to 2001, the federal funds rate from 1980 to 2000 was 1.12 percentage points higher than the Taylor rule rate.

The Taylor rule provides a fairly close fit to the actual federal funds rate but, more important, illustrates those periods that were periods of easy monetary policy and those that had tight and restraining monetary policy. The Federal Reserve

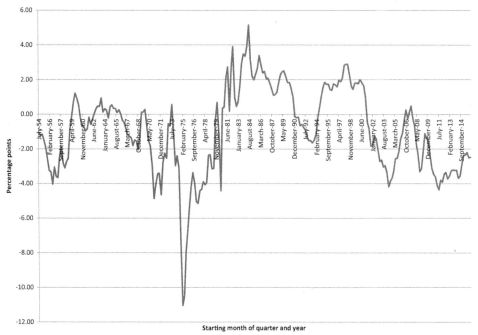

Figure 17.4. Actual − Taylor Rule Federal Funds Rate, in Percentage Points, 1954:3 to 2016:1. *Source:* Based on data in Figure 17.3.

officially states it did not follow a Taylor-type rule, but the consensus is that the Federal Reserve did shift from complete discretion, which characterized monetary policy from the accord of 1951 to the late 1970s, to at least "enlightened discretion", focused on price stability. The Taylor-type rule provides a reasonable representation of monetary policy, despite its limitations.

17.9 End of the Great Moderation and Concern about Financial Liberalization

The Great Moderation approach to central bank policy emerged from the turbulent period of the Great Inflation and the monetarist–Keynesian debate. The turbulent period of the Great Inflation also provided the catalyst for financial liberalization in the United States, because inflation increased market interest rates above regulated interest rates, induced disintermediation of funds from indirect to direct finance, and greatly contributed to the collapse of the S&L industry. Hence, the Great Moderation and financial liberalization are, jointly, major transformations in the nation's financial and monetary framework.

Along with a less activist central bank policy, market forces were permitted to play a much larger role in allocating the transfer of funds from lenders to borrowers than previously. Interest rates were permitted to respond to market forces rather than be regulated by government; financial institutions were permitted to compete directly with each other, rather than be separated by artificial heterogeneity imposed by government; and money and capital markets were expanded and permitted to interact more closely with financial institutions, especially banks. Thus, the Great Moderation and financial liberalization should be seen as complements.

The Great Moderation came to an end in the first few years of the new century, for three reasons. First, the 9/11 terrorist attack on the United States resulted in a significant negative supply shock that monetary policy attempted to mitigate. Second, the United States experienced a stock market bubble from about 1995 to March 2000, when the Federal Reserve raised interest rates. The Federal Reserve then aggressively shifted to easy policy to ensure the collapse of the bubble did not have a serious adverse impact on the economy. Third, more aggressive monetary policy by the Federal Reserve was influenced by the then perceived failures of the Bank of Japan to respond more rapidly to the burst of the real estate and equity bubble in 1990/1991, which is widely viewed as a major cause of Japan's "lost decade" of the 1990s (Cargill and Sakamoto, 2008). The Federal Reserve did not want to make the same mistake. In a sense, the Federal Reserve was and continues to operate in the shadow of the Bank of Japan's experience in the past three decades (Cargill, Hutchison and Ito, 1997, 2000). Fourth, the U.S. economy had had almost 15 years of price stability, but became concerned, in light of Japan's experience, that the low rate of inflation might turn into deflation. Again, the Federal Reserve was in the shadow of the Bank of Japan, as Japan was the only industrialized economy in the world to have experienced deflation in the postwar period. Japan's price level began a downward trend in 1995 that has continued to 2016 with only a few interruptions. Hence, easy monetary policy was rationalized by the fear of repeating Japan's mistake by allowing the economy to drift into deflation.

Financial liberalization had become an ongoing process throughout much of the world by the 1990s but concerns were increasingly being raised about the alleged benefits in light of the stock market bubble in the United States from 1995 to 2000; the bubble and burst of the bubble in real estate and equity prices in Japan from 1985 to 1990/1991; the Asian financial crisis in 1997, which brought the financial systems in a number of Asian economies to the edge of collapse; a large number of banking problems that seemed to be occurring throughout the world on an increasing basis; and fraud and outright criminal behavior, revealed by a series of financial scandals in the first few years of the new century in the United States.

17.10 The Great Recession: Two Views

There are two competing views of the Great Recession.

The first is that the Great Recession is primarily the result of *market failure*. The market failure view is probably the most widely accepted, because it has been advanced by the Federal Reserve, government agencies, many politicians and the news media. The market failure view argues that too much financial liberalization permitted imprudent real estate lending; credit rating agencies overrated low-quality mortgage-backed securities; fraudulent lending practices by financial institutions "talked people" into buying houses they couldn't afford with deceptive mortgage lending contracts; and there was also the role of mortgage brokers, who had no incentive to ensure the quality of a mortgage, since they received a commission on the mortgage, but took no risk in the mortgage, since the mortgage immediately became part of a mortgage-backed security. This view recognizes the historically low interest rates maintained by the Federal Reserve starting in 2001, but argues that the rightward shift in the supply of loanable funds for mortgages came from capital inflows and that low interest rates were not a very important determinant of mortgage lending.

The second view focuses on *government failure*. The government failure view is not as well accepted as market failure, but, in the opinion of this writer, a careful review of the events leading up to the Great Recession suggests government failure is at least as important as market failure. Again, keep in mind that government agencies, including the Federal Reserve, have a vested interest in maintaining and expanding their power and influence and hence are not always objective in assessing potential policy failures that reflect poorly on their performance. It is beyond the scope of this chapter to review all of the issues of this complex period of economic and financial distress in U.S. history. The market failure view is straightforward, has been repeated in many places and, therefore, does not need the same degree of elaboration as the government failure view. The following points help us wade through the events leading up to the Great Recession and provide an alternative perspective to the widely expressed market failure perspective: asset bubbles à la Minsky; the central role of the real estate bubble as the cause of the Great Recession; Federal Reserve policy; financial and regulatory policy to subsidize homeownership; and the collapse of the housing bubble, which directly led to the Great Recession.

17.11 Asset Bubbles *à la* Minsky

Asset bubbles have occurred throughout history. In 1841 Charles Mackey's *Extraordinary Popular Delusions and the Madness of Crowds* was the first to document bubbles and illustrate the ways in which "irrational exuberance" can dominate a market. Asset bubbles possess elements of market failure, because during the bubble asset prices increase far above their economic fundamentals and, as Mackey (1841) indicates, lead to "popular delusions" and the "madness of crowds", who believe, no matter what, that prices tomorrow will be higher than prices today and act on that view. Eventually reality catches up and the bubble bursts. Asset bubbles represent some defect in the market structure that permits prices to increase above their fundamentals, but these defects can be the result of government policy as well as the structure of the private market. In other words, asset bubbles appear to be the outcome of market failure, because asset bubbles are widely viewed as the result of greed and fraud, but, on closer inspection, bubbles can often be the outcome of central bank policy errors in the context of a flawed financial structure established by government regulations; that is, asset bubbles cannot be understood unless the role of government policy is considered. The bubble itself is market failure, but the start of the bubble may be due to government policy and not market failure, or a combination of both.

Hyman Minsky (1982) offers a useful taxonomy of bubbles to understand how they start and how they end. There are four phases to an asset bubble in general: displacement; irrational exuberance; speculative excess; and liquidation.

The *displacement* phase represents a change in the economic performance of the economy that deviates from the past and sets up expectations of a "new era". The displacement can be in the form of a change in economic fundamentals, such as new technology, new markets, new products, foreign direct investment, and so on. The displacement can also be monetary in origin, such as a sudden increase in money and credit; however, even if the displacement is nonmonetary in origin, at some point credit and monetary accommodation needs to occur for asset inflation to reach bubble proportions. In essence, the displacement phase represents the start of the bubble, when asset prices begin to increase above their fundamentals. The displacement phase is a real change in fundamentals and most of the time will not evolve into a full bubble. It's the next phase that turns the displaced increase in asset prices into a bubble.

The *irrational exuberance* phase represents the period when asset prices increasingly depart from economic fundamentals. Prices become dependent on the market's expected price in the future based on the belief that prices will always increase. In blunt terms, this phase is referred to as the "bigger fool" phase of asset pricing. An individual understands that he/she is a fool to purchase a share of Sony stock on the Tokyo stock market or a house in Las Vegas at the current high price, but a bigger fool in six months will pay more for the stock or house simply because prices are expected to continue to increase. This period is probably more understood by psychologists than economists, because it involves complex interactions between individuals' incentives to improve their economic wellbeing and the tendency of individuals to become subject to the "madness" of the crowd and dispense with looking at the fundamentals. The key element of the irrational exuberance phase is that market participants lose perspective, and price expectations are no longer connected to economic fundamentals. Irrational exuberance leads the public to pay higher and higher prices for an asset far beyond what economic fundamentals could rationalize, but irrational exuberance is likewise embraced by economic institutions, politicians and government agencies. Once the bubble psychology comes to dominate price determination of the asset, few are immune. Even those who doubt that prices will continue to increase are caught up in the "madness of the crowds" and are willing to take the risk, purchase the asset, hold it, then sell the asset to the next fool before prices fall.

A characteristic of this phase is the willingness of those who embrace the bubble psychology of price determination to search for explanations as to why this time it's different; that is, why prices will always continue to increase. There is always the "new era" explanation to explain high stock and real estate prices.

The *speculative excess* phase is relatively short and represents a period of intense frenzy by market participants to purchase the asset. This is the stage when people purchase equities or real estate without any understanding of the underlying fundamentals other than a belief that they need to get into the market as soon as possible or else lose out.

The *liquidation* phase is the collapse of the bubble. The collapse may come from the revelation of fraud, the bankruptcy of a major company or sales of the asset on the realization by some that the bubble is nearing its end; but, most usually, the bubble ends when liquidity to continue purchasing the asset dries up. The asset bubbles in Japan ended in 1990/1991 shortly after the Bank of Japan shifted to tight monetary policy and the real estate bubble in the United States ended in late 2005 after the Federal Reserve began to increase the target federal funds rate in June 2004.

17.12 The Central Role of the Real Estate Bubble in the Great Recession

The "bubble" in residential housing prices began around 2000/2001 and ended in late 2005, when house price increases slowed, then in early 2006 began a decline that continued to 2012 (Figure 1.7). The bubble in real estate, however, was not evenly spread throughout the nation, mainly being concentrated in the major metropolitan areas of the country, with California and Nevada being two states that manifested more intense bubbles. Once house prices started to decline, in early 2006, the effects of the falling prices spread throughout the economy. Declining house prices weakened the balance sheets throughout the economy and reduced spending and lending. Housing plays a major economic and policy role in the United States. Housing employment, directly and indirectly, accounts for a large part of total employment. Real estate represents the largest asset on the balance sheet of individuals and is a major asset of financial institutions and the money and capital markets via mortgage lending. The effects of the collapse of the housing market spread through the economy, and by December 2007 the U.S. economy was in recession, according to the NBER.

In late 2008 the decline in the economy turned into a major economic and financial crisis with the collapse of Lehman Brothers and the extraordinary lender of last resort policies of the Federal Reserve. The economic and financial distress in the United States spread to much of the rest of the world. Much of the world recovered from the financial crisis of 2008/2009 within a few years, but the U.S. economy continued to operate below its potential for a much longer period, despite the official start of recovery in June 2009, according to the NBER.

The bubble and then the burst of the bubble in residential housing prices are the most important and immediate causes of the Great Recession; hence, to understand the causes of the Great Recession, one needs to understand the cause of the housing bubble. The fact that economic and financial distress resulted from such a major collapse of housing prices is not remarkable given the role housing plays in the U.S. economy. What needs to be explained is why the bubble started.

17.13 Unprecedented Easy Monetary Policy

The Federal Reserve embarked on an unprecedented easy monetary policy in early 2001 that ended June 2004, and even after the Federal Reserve had shifted to tighter policy the shift was timid and too late, as the damage had already been done. During this period the federal funds rate was lowered from 5.98 percent in January 2001 to 1.00 percent in June 2004. Interest rates in general reached historical lows by June 2004, especially mortgage interest rates. Monetary policy tightened after June 2004; however, the federal funds rate was increased slowly. Inflationary expectations in the first half of the new century were relatively low, in the range of 2 to 3 percent, so that real interest rates were at historical lows and, in some cases, negative. In hindsight, the easy monetary policy from 2001 to 2005 was a policy error. Why did the Federal Reserve pursue such an easy monetary policy and underestimate its effect on the economy?

The Federal Reserve thought it could pursue easy monetary policy for other objectives because the rate of inflation was low and steady. The easy policy can be explained by the Federal Reserve's concern with the effects of the collapse of a stock market bubble in 2000 and the shadow of the Bank of Japan. When stock and real estate prices collapsed in Japan, the Bank of Japan had been slow to inject liquidity into the economy, and it came under much criticism for reacting too slowly and not aggressively enough to prevent a financial and economic crisis. The Federal Reserve did not want to make the same mistake. The 9/11 terrorist attack played a role. Federal Reserve policy was designed to mitigate the negative effects of that event. Irrespective of the reasons, the Federal Reserve pursued an aggressive easy policy after 2001. In terms of Figures 17.3 and 17.4, the federal funds rate was far below the Taylor rule rate. The federal funds rate was 2.46 percentage points below the Taylor rule rate from the first quarter of 2002 to the second quarter of 2006.

There are two important influences on the decision to purchase real estate – the interest rate and loan qualification terms. Federal Reserve policy significantly lowered the cost of purchasing real estate by any standard, and thus contributed to the housing bubble. The Federal Reserve claims its policy played no role in the run-up of housing prices; however, this is difficult to accept, since Federal Reserve policy focused on the interest rate as its policy instrument and interest rates are a major determinant of the ability to purchase a house.

The other condition – loan standards – was not under the influence of the Federal Reserve, but as part of the social contract to support housing loan standards were dramatically lowered and the subprime mortgage became a major financial instrument to support the goal of homeownership.

17.14 Social Contract to Support Homeownership Greatly Expanded

Expanded homeownership has always been a U.S. policy objective; however, it received increased political and financial support starting in the 1990s. There was increasing pressure from politicians and community advocacy groups for private lenders to expand mortgage lending to low- and moderate-income households. The Community Reinvestment Act was revised to put pressure on banks and other lending institutions to expand homeownership to lower-income groups; the U.S. Department of Housing and Urban Development set up targets for Fannie Mae and Freddie Mac (F&F) to support lower-income groups; the subprime mortgage became a standard mortgage instrument offered by lenders and was supported by F&F; key politicians pressured F&F to support mortgages to lower-income groups; and the Taxpayer Relief Act of 1997 exempted from taxation capital gains up to $500,000 for a couple and $250,000 for a single person and thereby doubled the capital gain exclusion. According to the U.S. Bureau of the Census, U.S. homeownership remained fairly constant from 1970 to 1990 (64.2 percent in 1970, 65.6 percent in 1980 and 64.0 percent in 1990); however, homeownership then increased significantly, reaching 68.9 percent in 2005. Ownership increased across all income classes, but especially in the low- to moderate-income groups, as a result of increased subsidization by the government.

The government permitted a dramatic decrease in loan standards to achieve the homeownership goals, ranging from very low to zero down payments to undocumented mortgage applications ("liar" loans) in which there was little effort to verify income-earning claims and past loan history. F&F were more than willing to accept these low-quality mortgages to bundle and sell in the capital markets. F&F had little difficulty raising funds in the capital markets, because their debt was implicitly considered equivalent to government debt because of their role in supporting the social contract to expand homeownership.

Many claim that the problem with low standards was due to the greater role played by mortgage brokers, who earned a fee for each mortgage and had little incentive to impose standards. Mortgage brokers were responsible for a large percentage of subprime or non-standard mortgages; however, without the support of F&F these mortgages would not have been approved. Research now shows that F&F played a far more important role in the subprime mortgage market than claimed by government.

F&F: F&F play a major role in the U.S. market and were established to stimulate mortgage lending by securitizing the mortgage market. In 2005 their liabilities of $3.7 trillion represented 30 percent of GDP and they held or assumed the credit risk of over 50 percent of residential mortgages in the United States. Even though private, they had a "special relationship with the government", in which they received implicit guarantees that meant they could borrow at the government bond rate, they became a "retirement" home for politicians and administration officials and they lobbied politicians for favors and protection, which they were willing to give in exchange for financial support and the support of their clients – low- and moderate-income borrowers. Many economists for years warned that F&F posed a serious systemic risk to the financial system, as they supported expanded mortgage lending under increasingly imprudent terms (low- to zero-down-payment loans and "gimmick" financing, such as interest-only loans and non-documented or "liar" loans).

The implicit government guarantees and close relationship with politicians provided the moral hazard for F&F to support risky mortgage lending. F&F are at the center of the mortgage market, especially the subprime sector, and they played a major role in the run-up of house prices from 2000 to 2006. In 2003 an effort was made to place more oversight on F&F and limit their portfolio as a result of the revelation of accounting scandals at F&F; however, the effort was resisted by Congress. In hearings before the House Financial Services Committee on September 25, 2003, Representative Barney Frank remarked: "I do think I do not want the same focus on safety and soundness that we have in OCC [Office of the Comptroller of the Currency] and OTS [Office of Thrift Supervision]. I want to roll the dice a little bit more in this situation towards subsidized housing . . . " (Wall Street Journal, 2008).

In the aftermath of the collapse many defended F&F, claiming that they had purchased only a few subprime mortgages and that private sector mortgages were more risky than those purchased by F&F and the definition of a subprime mortgage was flexibility. In this debate, too much attention is devoted to the difference between traditional high-quality mortgages and subprime mortgages; however, the more appropriate distinction is between traditional mortgages and nontraditional mortgages with varying degrees of low quality. Also, there is evidence F&F failed to disclose the extent of their nontraditional mortgages. Peter Wallison (2014) has recently presented an exhaustive study of the role of nontraditional mortgages and government policy in the run-up of real estate prices. The argument that government policy and government institutions did not encourage nontraditional mortgages is akin to those who continue to claim the Great Depression was a clear example of market failure. An intellectually balanced view of the run-up in real estate prices must allocate an important role to government policy of at least 50 percent. Even if the private sector issued riskier mortgages than those supported by F&F, F&F became the largest buyers of the AAA tranches of these subprime pools in

2005–2007. Without F&F's support, it is unlikely the pools could have been formed and marketed around the world. "Not only did the GSEs [government-sponsored enterprises] destroy their own financial condition with their excessive purchases of subprime loans in the three-year period 2005 to 2007, but they also played a major role in weakening or destroying the solvency of other financial institutions and investors in the United States and abroad" (Wallison and Calomiris, 2008).

Lax regulatory oversight of banks and S&Ls, mortgage brokers and securities markets: There was widespread knowledge of "liar" loans, "gimmick" loans and other manifestations of imprudent lending, but no one wanted to end the party. Regulatory agencies understood what Congress wanted. It was easier to assume markets would regulate the risk or, in the event of an adverse outcome, plead lack of regulatory authority than publicly point out how U.S. housing policy was exposing the financial system to systemic risk. It is difficult to understand how regulatory authorities could remain silent as mortgages were being approved with little or no equity, as insurance company credit default swaps were being sold with minimal reserves or as credit rating agencies conferred high ratings on mortgage-backed bonds in which the value of the underlying mortgages was based on the expectation that house prices would continue to increase. The lax regulatory oversight was pervasive, because any effort to counter the housing bubble would run into intense political opposition, as indicated by Representative Frank's remarks cited above.

Improper credit ratings by the Big Three: The *Financial Crisis Inquiry Report* made much of the high ratings assigned to mortgage-backed bonds. The degree of inattention to their fiduciary responsibility is difficult to explain, other than the Big Three were susceptible to the "bigger fool" theory of house prices, too preoccupied with the high profits that were being generated in the housing industry or unwilling to disappointment government. The credit rating agencies clearly contributed to the run-up of housing prices, but it is an extreme position to claim their role was necessary and sufficient for the housing bubble. In terms of the factors already discussed, their role is less significant. In addition, the SEC oversees the Big Three and had every opportunity to bring to the attention of government what was being done, and one cannot dismiss the incentives the Big Three had to provide high ratings given the homeownership agenda of the politicians in order to protect their special relationship with the SEC as a nationally certified credit rating agency.

In sum: The above five factors, combined, set the stage for the bubble in housing prices: easy monetary policy; government support of homeownership; F&F; lax regulatory oversight; and unrealistically high ratings assigned to mortgage-backed bonds. These factors explain the displacement and irrational exuberance phases of the housing bubble. The shift in demand for housing supported by easy monetary policy and government-approved lowered lending standards (nontraditional mortgages) started and sustained the real estate bubble. Real estate prices increasingly become disconnected from economic fundamentals. The speculative excess phase occurred in 2005, in which herd-like behavior based on the "bigger fool" theory of asset pricing became widespread. In this situation the purchaser of the asset realizes the price is inflated but believes a bigger fool will soon offer an even more inflated price because that fool also expects prices to increase. All asset bubbles come to an end. The last phase – liquidation – came in late 2005 and early 2006 as tighter credit conditions forced a slowdown in house price increases.

Other factors to deflect attention from government policy: Much blame for the bubble is based on self-interest combined with financial liberalization. Both played a role, but as sustaining elements rather than initiating causes of the bubble. It is a tautology to blame self-interest since self-interest is a driving force in both the market and government at all times. It is the structure of the economy that renders self-interest a problem, and the structure was fundamentally flawed because of government support for the housing sector. Self-interest by itself did not generate the financial crisis, though it clearly played a role in the process as politicians sought to benefit their clients and pursue their value judgments, government officials decided to ignore the housing bubble, financial institutions and markets sought to enhance profits from the bubble in housing and households sought to increase wealth through housing.

Likewise, the financial sector sustained the process by making it easier to finance housing, limiting the transparency of the financial system by introducing increasingly complex derivatives, and increasing the ability to leverage. Some have claimed the 1999 Gramm–Leach–Bliley Financial Services Modernization Act, which eliminated the wall between investment and commercial banking established in the 1930s, is responsible for the financial crisis; however, this view is historically incorrect. The changes introduced in 1999 had little or nothing to do with the run-up in housing prices, imprudent lending and lax regulatory standards.

In Chapter 9 the system of rating securities was discussed, and, while the Big Three grossly exaggerated the quality of mortgage-backed securities, as explained in that chapter, there is a close relationship between the Big Three rating agencies and the government that casts doubt on the claim the government was unaware that high ratings given to mortgage-backed bonds were hidden from the government.

17.15 The Federal Reserve after the Collapse of the Housing Bubble, the Great Recession and Challenges

The Great Recession, even though caused in part by monetary policy errors, has elevated the role and responsibilities of the Federal Reserve. The Federal Reserve received extensive new powers, under the Dodd–Frank Act of 2010, to further its pursuit of macroprudential policy objectives. Federal Reserve policy has entered historically unprecedented territory with its zero-interest-rate policy and QEP. Figure 17.5 illustrates the recent increase in base money in historical context and

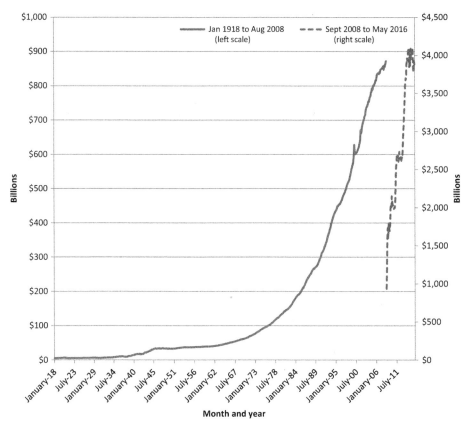

Figure 17.5. Federal Reserve Bank of St. Louis Estimates of the Monetary Base, January 1918 to May 2016. *Source:* FRED, Federal Reserve Bank of St. Louis.

represents a rather remarkable period in Federal Reserve history. The history of the monetary base is divided into two periods: January 1918 to August 2008 and September 2008 to May 2016. Events starting September 2008 are remarkable. In August 2008 the base was $870 billion; it increased to $936 billion in September 2008, and by December 2008 had increased to $1,669 billion. As of May 2016 the base was $3,858 billion. The Federal Reserve has kept the federal funds rate well below the Taylor rule rate (Figures 17.3 and 17.4), and yet the economy continues to operate below its potential. This nontraditional monetary policy has been in place for close to a decade as of 2016 and raises two questions.

Has the nontraditional monetary policy been effective? There is little debate that the initial injection of base money in late 2008 and 2009 was necessary to prevent a liquidity crisis, and, while Monday morning quarterbacking might suggest the Federal Reserve could have handled the situation better, overall the initial Federal Reserve response was appropriate. The real debate is over the continued ZIRP and QEP. The Federal Reserve claims the policies are needed to prevent another Great Depression, but this is an intellectually weak argument because

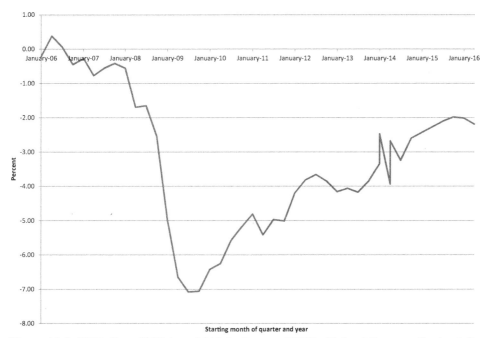

Figure 17.6. GDP Gap, 2000:1 to 2016:1. *Source:* FRED, Federal Reserve Bank of St. Louis.

the real debate is between the actual policy and an alternative policy. Many have suggested the Federal Reserve should have starting shifting to higher interest rates and begun to reduce the size of its asset portfolio (base money) in 2012 or 2013. Setting these issues aside, has the Federal Reserve policy generated significant policy outcomes?

In terms of the performance of the economy, the answer is not positive to the Federal Reserve's position. While the GDP gap has declined since the Great Recession started (Figure 17.6), the output gap remained negative as of early 2016. More important, the economy has continued to grow since 2008, but well below its past long-run trend (Figure 17.7). In Figure 17.7 the solid line is what real GDP would have been starting in 2007 at a 2.5 percent annual growth rate, while the dashed line is actual real GDP. The average annual pre-Great-Recession growth of real GDP since 1990 is 2.8 percent.

Not only have the results been less than promised, but the Federal Reserve's ZIRP has other consequences. The low interest rates have been especially difficult for older Americans who rely on interest earnings for retirement. The low interest rates have encouraged a shift of funds to the stock market and greater risk, especially for pension funds. The low interest rates have exacerbated a serious underfunding problem of state and local government defined benefit plans, which continue to evaluate their long-term liabilities at 7 and 8 percent rates of return. Low interest rates continue to provide incentives to allocate savings and credit to

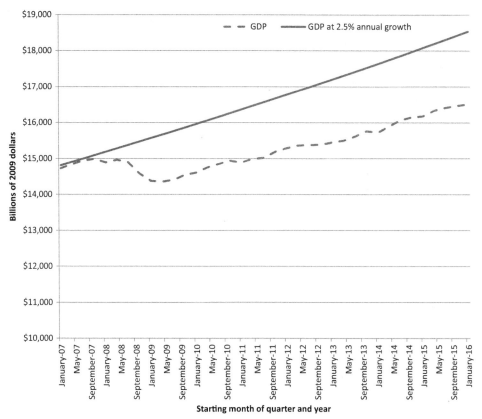

Figure 17.7. Actual GDP and Projected GDP at 2.5 Percent Annual Growth Rate, 2007:1 to 2016:1. *Source:* GDP – FRED, Federal Reserve Bank of St. Louis.

the housing sector. The U.S. economy has paid a high price for supporting the housing sector. The collapse of the S&L industry and the housing bubble and its burst are outcomes of the effort by government to encourage homeownership. This cost might be acceptable if the objective of homeownership had been realized, but, as it turns out, the United States ranks only about 24th among 42 industrial countries in terms of homeownership. Many of the countries do not operate with the same degree of homeownership subsidization as the United States.

In regard to the support of the housing sector, the Federal Reserve's QEPs have turned the Federal Reserve into an instrument of industrial policy. Almost half of the dramatic increase in Federal Reserve assets is represented by mortgage-backed securities. In the past the Federal Reserve confined open market operations to government securities with few exceptions, but the extension of open market operations to include large purchases of privately issued mortgages is a brave new world, which amounts to industrial policy by the central bank.

Why has the increase in base money not generated inflation? The M2 money multiplier framework indicates that an increase in base money will increase the money supply and loanable funds, which in turn will shift AD to the right, increasing inflation and output. The increase in output has been disappointing. The lack of inflation, which many predicted a few years ago, is due to unprecedented holdings of excess reserves by depository institutions (see Figure 13.3, for example); that is, the M2 multiplier has declined because of the increase in the e ratio. These reserves are held for reasons that are not completely understood, but two explanations stand out. The Federal Reserve commenced paying interest on excess reserves October 2008, providing an incentive to hold reserves rather than lend; and depository institutions continue to be risk-averse in light of the past collapse of the housing sector. Most agree that, whatever the reasons, the situation is not sustainable. At some point the economy will expand and ignite inflation with so much potential lending available.

How will the Federal Reserve return to normal monetary policy? By "normal monetary policy", we mean increasing the target federal funds rate in line with what a Taylor-type rule would suggest. The Federal Reserve at the time of this writing has indicated it has no plans to use open market sales to increase the federal funds rate; that is, the Federal Reserve has no plans to reduce its sizable holdings of government securities and mortgages. In fact, the Federal Reserve uses the funds received when these securities mature to purchase replacement funds.

The Federal Reserve has several options, one of which is to increase the interest paid on excess reserves to increase the federal funds rate. By increasing the interest on excess reserves, depository institutions will reduce the supply of federal funds and thus increase the federal funds rate. However, this amounts to fiscal policy, as any increase in interest paid on reserves reduces the amount of revenue transferred to the Treasury. Hence, increasing payments to depository institutions is akin to fiscal policy.

Increased politicization of Federal Reserve policy: Despite claims to the contrary by the Federal Reserve, it is *de facto* dependent on the government, and this dependence has dramatically increased since the Great Recession started. The historically high levels of government securities held by the Federal Reserve reduce its flexibility to restrain prices once they begin to increase. The unprecedented high level of mortgage-backed bonds held by the Federal Reserve renders the Federal Reserve an agent of the government's housing policies. The reliance on the new tool of paying interest on reserves is essentially fiscal policy, further connecting the Federal Reserve to the U.S. Treasury more than previously. The expanded role of the Federal Reserve as a macroprudential regulatory authority raises issues as to whether it is even capable of achieving the objectives of macroprudential policy, especially since it played a contributing role in the house price bubble. It has, however, further politicized Federal Reserve policy.

The end of the story is that the Federal Reserve and central banks in general face many challenges. The basic principles laid out in this book should help the reader understand the evolution of the country's financial and monetary regime, the political economy debates over how it functions and the proper role of government in the regime.

References

Bernanke, Ben S. (2002). "On Milton Friedman's Ninetieth Birthday". Remarks at Chicago University, Chicago, November 8, www.federalreserve.gov/boarddocs/Speeches/2002/20021108/default.htm.

Cargill, Thomas F., Michael M. Hutchison and Takatoshi Ito (1997). *The Political Economy of Japanese Monetary Policy*. Cambridge, MA: MIT Press.

Cargill, Thomas F., Michael M. Hutchison and Takatoshi Ito (2000). *Financial Policy and Central Banking in Japan*. Cambridge, MA: MIT Press.

Cargill, Thomas F., and Thomas Mayer (1998). "The Great Depression and History Textbooks". *The History Teacher*, 31: 441–58.

Cargill, Thomas F., and Thomas Mayer (2006). "The Effect of Changes in Reserve Requirements during the 1930s: The Evidence from Nonmember Banks". *Journal of Economic History*, 66: 417–32.

Cargill, Thomas F., and Takayuki Sakamoto (2008). *Japan since 1980*. New York: Cambridge University Press.

Curry, Timothy, and Lynn Shibut (2000). "The Cost of the Savings and Loan Crisis: Truth and Consequences". *FDIC Banking Review*, 13: 26–35.

Financial Crisis Inquiry Commission (2011). *The Financial Crisis Inquiry Report*. Washington, D.C.: U.S. Government Printing Office.

Friedman, Milton, and Anna Jacobson Schwartz (1963). *A Monetary History of the United States: 1867 to 1960*. Princeton: Princeton University Press.

Henry Morgenthau Diary (1939). Transcript of May 9, 1939, meeting at the U.S. Treasury. Franklin D. Roosevelt Library, Henry Morgenthau Diary, Microfilm Roll no. 50.

Kennedy, John F. (1962). *Economic Report of the President*. Washington, D.C.: U.S. Government Printing Office.

Mackey, Charles (1841). *Extraordinary Popular Delusions and the Madness of Crowds*. New York: Harmony Books.

Mayer, Thomas (1982). "A Case Study of Federal Reserve Policymaking: Regulation Q in 1966". *Journal of Monetary Economics*, 10: 259–71.

Meltzer, Allan H. (2009). *A History of the Federal Reserve*, vol. II, 1951–1986. Chicago: University of Chicago Press.

Minsky, Hyman P. (1982). "The Financial Instability Hypothesis: Capitalistic Processes and the Behavior of the Economy", in Charles P. Kindleberger and Jean-Pierre Laffargue (eds.), *Financial Crises: Theory, History and Policy*: 138–52. Cambridge: Cambridge University Press.

Reagan, Ronald (1981). "Remarks and a Question-and-Answer Session with Reporters on the Air Traffic Controllers Strike". Ronald Reagan Presidential Foundation and Institute, August 3, https://reaganlibrary.archives.gov/archives/speeches/1981/80381a.htm.

Volcker, Paul (2000). "Commanding Heights". Interview with Paul Volcker. Public Broadcasting Service, September 26, www.pbs.org/wgbh/commandingheights/shared/minitext/int_paulvolcker.html.

Wall Street Journal (2008). "What They Said about Fan and Fred". *Wall Street Journal*, October 2, www.wsj.com/articles/SB122290574391296381.

Wallison, Peter J. (2014). *Hidden in Plain Sight: What Really Caused the World's Worst Financial Crisis and Why It Could Happen Again*. New York: Encounter Books.

Wallison, Peter J., and Charles W. Calomiris (2008). "The Last Trillion-Dollar Commitment: The Destruction of Fannie Mae and Freddie Mac", Financial Services Outlook. Washington, D.C.: American Enterprise Institute.

Whaples, Robert (1995). "Where Is There Consensus among American Economic Historians?". *Journal of Economic History*, 55: 139–54.

Index